RESEARCH ON SOCIOCULTURAL INFLUENCES ON MOTIVATION AND LEARNING: VOLUME 2

Edited by

Dennis M. McInerney
and
Shawn Van Etten

INFORMATION AGE
PUBLISHING

80 Mason Street
Greenwich, Connecticut 06830

Library of Congress Cataloging-in-Publication Data

Research in sociocultural influences on motivation and learning / edited
by Dennis McInerney and Shawn Van Etten.
    p. cm.
  ISBN 1-931576-33-5 – ISBN 1-931576-32-7 (pbk.)
  1. Motivation in education–Social aspects–Cross-cultural studies.
2. Multicultural education–Cross-cultural studies. I. McInerney, D.
M. (Dennis M.), 1948- II. Van Etten, Shawn.
  LB1065 .R45 2002
  370.15'4–dc21
                              2002002157

Copyright © 2002 Information Age Publishing

Printed in the United States of America

Research on Sociocultural Influences on Motivation and Learning: Volume 2

CONTENTS

Foreword
Martin L. Maehr   *vii*

Introduction

Bridging the Sociocultural Divide: An Encouragement for
Researchers to Consider a Wheel of Research Perspective
Shawn Van Etten and Dennis M. McInerney   *ix*

Part I.   Focus on Identity

1.   The Self in Cultural Context: Meaning And Valence
     David Yun Dai   *3*

2.   Ethnic Identity and the Sociocultural Playing Field:
     Choices Made by Ethnically Mixed Adolescents in Hawaii
     William L. Greene   *23*

3.   Self-Schema, Motivation and Learning:
     A Cross-Cultural Comparison
     Chi-hung Ng and Peter Renshaw   *55*

4.   Students "At Risk":
     Exploring Identity from a Sociocultural Perspective
     Jennifer A. Vadeboncoeur and Pedro R. Portes   *89*

5.   Person-Environment Fit in Higher Education:
     How Good Is the Fit for Indigenous Students?
     Gerard J. Fogarty and Colin White   *129*

Part II.   Focus on Families and Communities

6.   The Social Construction of Interest in a Learning Community
     Kimberley Pressick-Kilborn and Richard Walker   153

7.   Motivation to Improve Adult Education in Under-Educated
     Adults in Rural Communities
     Eric M. Anderman, Jane Jensen,
     Diana Haleman, and Beth Goldstein   183

8.   Teacher Immediacy and Student Motivation
     Nanette Potee   207

9.   The Social Mediation of Metacognition
     Gregory P. Thomas   225

10. Motivation and African-American Youth: Exploring Assumptions Of
     Some Contemporary Motivation Theories
     Tamera B. Murdock, Megan Brooks Bolch,
     George Dent, & Natalie Hale Wilcox   249

11. Communities Sharing Research: An American Indian Case Study
     Dawn Iwamoto and Henry Radda   273

Part III.   Focus on Methods

12. Cross-Cultural Differences in Affective Meaning of Achievement:
     A Semantic Differential Study
     Farideh Salili and Rumjahn Hoosain   297

13. Motivation and Learning Strategies: A Cross-Cultural Perspective
     David Watkins, Dennis McInerney, Clement Lee,
     Adebowale Akande, and Murari Regmi   329

14. Translation Issues in Cross-Cultural Research: Review and
     Recommendations
     Teresa García Duncan   345

     Author Biographies   367

FOREWORD

There are few topics more interesting and fewer still, more important, than the understanding of 'sociocultural influences on motivation and learning.' We live in an age where cultural borders are regularly and necessarily crossed. The public elementary school down the street from my home once laid claim to uniqueness because 30 language (and doubtless more "cultural") groups were represented among its students. Perhaps that is still a bit unusual, but certainly not unique. One does not have to leave one's country or even one's county to observe at first hand the need for, the importance of, understanding how sociocultural factors influence motivation and learning. Indeed, it is becoming well-nigh indefensible *not* to consider sociocultural influences when conducting educational and psychological research. In such a context, this series has filled a critical need and this volume, like the first, incorporates samples of the best thinking and research on the topic currently available. I am grateful for the privilege to invite readers to partake of and savor the buffet of knowledge, experience, insight and theory spread on the following pages. Those who accept this invitation will not only satisfy their need to know, but be stimulated to learn and know more.

Martin L. Maehr
Professor of Education and Psychology
University of Michigan, Ann Arbor

BRIDGING THE SOCIOCULTURAL DIVIDE
An Encouragement for Researchers to Consider a Wheel of Research Perspective

Shawn Van Etten and Dennis M. McInerney

The aim of this book series is to provide a much needed outlet for research that examines extant and novel motivation and learning foci from a range of sociocultural perspectives. Many chapters in this volume, in particular, attempt to better understand the dynamic sociocultural development of various self processes (e.g., self-concept and self-schema), how those processes affect curricular and pragmatic topics, and how cross-cultural examinations are required to fully appreciate the similarities and differences within and between cultures. Symbolic interactionists (e.g., Herbert Blumer, 1969; George Herbert Mead, 1934) suggest that three axioms drive human understandings:

1. meaning is derived from social interactions;
2. meanings determine how we perceive or react to phenomena; and
3. meanings are modified through experience.

Blumer (1969) further contended that meanings are substantially derived from one's primary reference group; if this view of semantic development is embraced, it is crucial to overcome singular inspections and/or interpretations of phenomena, and to conduct research and examine phenomena from both etic (i.e., an outsider's vantage point) and emic (i.e., an insider's vantage point) perspectives—in order to enhance our understanding of researched phenomena, researchers need to be more cognizant of the entire wheel of research.

EMBRACING A WHEEL OF RESEARCH PERSPECTIVE FOR PROGRAMMATIC EDUCATIONAL RESEARCH

Who is Dick without Jane? Harriet without Ozzy? Instructor without student? Some would say they are much better off. We would say that they are Dorothy without OZ! Historically, theorists and researchers have embraced the 'much better off' position: structuralists supplanted the introspectionists; functionalists supplanted the structuralists; cognitivists supplanted to the behaviorists; and so the cycle continues. In educational research, our story jump starts with: the positivists and the naturalists putting on the philosophical gloves; the quantitative fearful of words and the qualitative shimmering at numbers; and the advocates of unidimensional approaches squaring up those embracing multidimensional approaches; and so the cycle continues. What is wrong with replacing confrontational autonomy with negotiation, compromise, and balance? Contemporary researchers have the knowledge, tools, and skills to achieve much more than mere triangulation, let us start to embrace the entire wheel of research.

The Wheel of Research

The wheel of research metaphor suggests that programmatic research efforts should involve a recursive process of moving back and forth between inductive/exploratory investigations and deductive/confirmatory investigations. In general, inductive/exploratory approaches are used:

1. to map out a broad array of potential variables that can effect a given area of inquiry;
2. to tap participants' understandings from an emic perspective—that is, from an insider's vantage point;
3. to determine if new variables should be permitted into analyses;
4. to discover both central and peripheral information pertinent to the general question(s) under investigation; and
5. to produce potential hypotheses that can be used in future hypothetico-deductive research.

In contrast, deductive/confirmatory approaches are traditionally used to finely detail the etic perspective of relationships between one or a few variables that were a priori determined important by the researcher. How does the researcher determine what variable(s) is/are important to include in these deductive/confirmatory investigations? Well, that answer is often simple: review the extant literature! The only problem in using this approach is that much systematic extant research is based on deductive/confirmatory methods. That is, prior to the behavioral revolution, few systematic inductive/exploratory methods were available, and even when they were available, the actual procedures used in investigations were often haphazard; since the behavioral revolution, only deductive/confirmatory methods have been viewed as robust in nature. What does this all mean?

1. Historically speaking, rarely have investigators used rigorous inductive-exploratory methods to map out important variables; and
2. the bulk of our extant knowledge has been acquired using deductive/confirmatory methods, methods that by nature preclude mapping out a broad array of variables.

Since deductive/confirmatory methods have been consistently used without consideration of inductive/exploratory methods, and since most of us know little about robust inductive/exploratory methods, the remainder of this story will focus on familiarizing you with a particular inductive/exploratory approach, albeit an approach that can incorporate deduction/confirmation: the grounded theory approach.

The Grounded Theory Approach

The grounded theory approach uses ethnographic interviewing to collect data (e.g., refer to Mishler, 1986; Spradley, 1980, 1979) and the method of constant/comparison to analyze and synthesize data (Strauss & Corbin, 1990). It is an exploratory approach allowing researchers to progressively move from induction to deduction and then back to induction. It is primarily a qualitative approach, working with language as the data set; still, it also boasts quantitative components (e.g., researchers using the grounded theory approach sometimes convert participant claims into questionnaire items and administer them to an independent group of participants to further test claims; refer to Van Etten, Pressley, Freebern, & Echevarria, 1998; Van Etten, Freebern, & Pressley, 1997; Van Meter, Yokoi, & Pressley, 1994). Grounded theory is also an approach that can maintain the phenomenology of participants' responses by using various procedures (e.g., member checks).

General Procedures for Creating a Grounded Theory

The first step in the grounded theory approach, similar to confirmatory approaches, is problem formation. Albeit unlike confirmatory approaches, the shape initial questions take are very open-ended and vague, allowing participants to respond with a full-array of potential responses. Hence, grounded theory is a theory that emerges from participant responses, not *a priori* researcher conceptions. As such, aside from stating general research questions, creating preliminary questions, and determining the composition of preliminary interview groups (i.e., the participants and the number of participants that will be interviewed), it is impossible to determine what subsequent questions will need to be asked to what group of participants. This is not to say that chaos abounds, as the general procedures are rather formalized.

Researchers using the grounded theory approach often use ethnographic interviewing to collect data. Ethnographic interviewing typically begins with open-ended questions that are intended to elicit the full array of participant understandings (e.g., the who, what, when, where, why, and how questions are asked; refer to Mishler, 1986; Spradley, 1980, 1979). As interviewers ask questions, they often take notes and/or tape-record responses; tape-recordings allow note clarification and/or serve as an audit trail (e.g., Lincoln & Guba, 1985). In addition, during preliminary interviewing, it is recommended that at least two interviewers be present and take notes. This procedure allows interviewers to assess inter-subjective agreement or inter-rater reliability of preliminary codes; that is, it helps ensure phenomena are perceived at similar levels of detail. It is further recommended that interviewers use variable-sized groups for each phase of interviewing (i.e., with each set of questions). This procedure will avoid social inhibition when using small groups and may also stimulate discussion through social facilitation when using large groups. Interviewers continue to ask participants preliminary questions until codings reveal that no new information is emerging. Codes are then checked for information gaps in the data and/or misconceptions between interviewers (i.e., inter-subjective agreement or inter-rater reliability is assessed).

At the beginning of each phase of interviewing, interviewers should desist from providing participants with response alternatives. Instead, participants should be required to reflect and create their own construal of the question (Van Etten, Freebern, & Pressley, 1997). In other words, interviewers should not lead participant's responses. For example, if an interviewer asked the question what is education(?), and a participant responded what do you mean(?), the interviewer should only respond by reflecting the question back to the participant [i.e., by re-stating the question "what does education mean to you(?)"]. Still, as participants provide responses to questions, it is essential that interviewers attempt to delve deeper into responses. For example, if a participant responds "education is about instructors," the interviewers should ask the participant "what do you mean education is about instructors." This process of response and reflection allows researchers to delve deeply into the meanings attached to responses; gaining a better understanding of the specific semantics that the participant's employ.

During each interview, researchers should record participants' responses by taking notes, tape recording, or both. Researchers who take notes must ensure that they maintain the phenomenology of participants' responses; that is, they must ensure that the full context of the situation is documented. Further, they must ensure that they do not classify participants' responses according to some *a priori* classification variables. Tape recordings allow verbatim transcripts to be written, with this allowing researchers a good reference tool if notes are ambiguous.

How a researcher decides to code notes is variable and the reader is referred to Miles and Huberman (1994) as a good reference. Still, two caveats are offered:

1. if two or more researchers are interviewing participants, they should use the same coding scheme, as this will facilitate the assessment of inter-subjective agreement or inter-rater reliability for codes; and
2. it is probably better to code participants' claims into clausal statements, as these allow the researcher to assess any one-to-one correspondences between variables. Still, these claims must also be coded within the greater context from which they were derived.

Actual coding requires the method of constant-comparison. After researchers code notes or tape-recordings from each interview, they should begin analyzing data. If a researcher chose to code notes into clausal statements, they can begin by picking out a variable and searching through the entire set of codes for the same or related variables. These variables then can be tentatively subsumed in tentative categories of related variables. When coding variables into categories, researchers must be especially cautious to ensure that all potential relationships are identified (refer to Spradley, 1980, 1979 and Lincoln & Guba, 1985 for good references). After all claims are coded into tentative categories, researchers begin contrasting claims within and between categories. Claims are contrasted within categories to assess potential subcategories and the mutual exclusiveness between claims. Once all claims are checked for mutual exclusiveness within tentative categories and subcategories, a between category and subcategory analysis is warranted. If claims are found not to be mutually exclusive between categories, a reanalysis and regrouping of claims is warranted. If more than one researcher is coding claims (and this is well-advised), after each researcher independently codes all claims, they can assess intersubjective agreement or interrater reliability. As additional interviews are completed (using the same questions) and claims coded, these new codes are integrated into the emerging model. Once no new information emerges that warrants code modification (i.e., only functionally equivalent claims are emerging), that set of questions are considered exhausted. At this point, researchers review codes for information gaps and ambiguities (e.g., the researchers may disagree about the prevalence of certain variables), formulating new, more specific, yet still open-ended questions to fill in the blanks. These new questions are then posed to additional participants. This recursive process of data collection and data analysis continue until no new information emerges from analyses (Strauss & Corbin, 1990; Bogdan & Biklen, 1992); to use Strauss and Corbin's (1990) terminology, until theoretical saturation is achieved.

Once theoretical saturation is achieved, some researchers engage in a quantitative exercise to further validate the findings. For example, Van Etten, Freebern, and Pressley (1997) converted participant claims into questions with yes/no, check list, and likert-scale options; each of these items had *a priori* response expectancies. If participants' responses to these questions do not align with expectancies, this would indicate that theoretical saturation was not achieved. Thus, these items should be re-investigated with a new set of questions, allowing adjustment of claims.

There are other criteria that can be used to evaluate the robustness of the grounded theory approach. Lincoln and Guba (1985) detail four main criteria that can be used to evaluate the robustness or trustworthiness of a qualitative investigation: credibility, transferability, dependability, and confirmability. Credibility refers to the extent that the results of a study accurately reflect the reality of the situation under investigation. Thus, credibility is highly dependent on a study's procedures. As for the grounded theory approach, credibility is best assessed through triangulating interviewer's codes and member checking. Member checking is a procedure whereby stakeholders assess the accuracy of codes. Transferability is the extent that the results of an investigation can be adapted to a new situation or new participants. Transferability requires researchers to provide a thick description of contexts, participants, procedures, and results (Geertz, 1973), descriptions that specify necessary information for future implementation. To the extent that a grounded theory provides this information, the potential for transferability increases or decreases. Dependability refers to the extent that results can be replicated and confirmability is the extent that the procedures and data are documented. Dependability and confirmability can both be assessed with an inquiry audit. An inquiry audit often involves an outside consultant who reviews all study records and then re-analyzes data. To the extent that the original investigator has adequately documented records (confirmability), dependability can be assessed (Lincoln & Guba, 1985). The trustworthiness of a grounded theory will be enhanced to the extent that an investigator reflects on these four criteria before, during, and after an investigation.

Embrace the Wheel of Research

How do you, as a researcher, initially identify a topic to investigate? The answer is probably simple, either:

1. the topic is a pragmatic concern that was brought to your attention; or
2. you identified information gaps, misconceptions, or areas requiring further exploration.

In either case, to what extent do you attempt to go beyond the information that is placed in your lap or researched in the journals? In many cases, the responses I hear in discussions with colleagues involved in programmatic research efforts are: "I do not have the time/resources to consider the perspective of all key stakeholders," "I ran a small pilot test to make sure the inventory items correlated and produced strong Cronbach alphas," and "I asked my co-researchers what they thought about the protocol." In each of these senarios, the ecological validity of the studies may be compromised. For example, it is a good idea to solicit feedback from expert colleagues regarding a new protocol, but it also would be ideal to conduct a member check with the relevant participants, as it is this group of stakeholders whose phenomenological ideas you are interested in better understanding. The grounded theory approach and other inductive/exploratory methods can be used to remedy these potential confounds. Bottom line, inductive/ exploratory approaches should be used to map out a broad range of potentially important variables (from a range of alternative perspectives) and then deductive/confirmatory approaches can be used to further validate those findings by testing the relationships between one or a few variables. The wheel of research metaphor advances the idea that programmatic researchers must use a recursive process of induction—deduction—induction—deduction to create the most valid results. The editors and authors of this volume, in various ways, attempt to bridge this methodological/ interpretive gap.

THE AUTHORS AND THEIR CONTRIBUTIONS

The authors in this volume succeed in laying the foundation for a future of inquiry that aims to bridge the socio-cultural gap in the interpretation of identity, families and communities, and methodological research. Each chapter affords fresh perspectives and novel insights, conceptions that will help shape research for many years to come. The chapters are organized into three main sections, research that focuses on:

1. identity;
2. families and communities; and
3. methodology.

Section I. Focus on Identity

David Yun Dai wrote the lead chapter, a review chapter that examines the generalization of self-concept research findings to non-Western cultures, particularly those cultures found in East Asian countries. David demonstrates that research results can be interpreted differently depending on whether or not researchers search for universal self-processes or attempt to find unique meanings and expressions of the self; that is, the same research results can result in grossly alternative interpretations depending on the framework from which one examines outcomes. Based on this finding, David suggests that the self has an inherent cultural component and thus needs to be investigated in specific cultural contexts. He further suggests that the self is a dynamic, constructive process, and therefore any cross-cultural research needs to take an in-depth look at how individuals perceive the valence and construe the meaning of a personal event that has personal consequences and implications for motivation and learning.

The second chapter written by William Greene explores how ethnically mixed adolescents in Hawaii form identities and how their identity choices may influence motivation in school. This chapter is based on research that used an interview methodology to probe and document the self-perceptions, commitments, values, and self-knowledge characteristics associated with the ethnic affiliation of 40 adolescents with mixed ancestries. William speculates on a possible relationship between ethnic self-awareness in a multicultural setting and success-driven motivation for academic tasks. The chapter includes sections on:

1. the contribution of knowledge about how a diverse community influenced the ethnic identification of adolescents;
2. promoting sensitivity to some of the perceptions which shape students' cultural values, relationships, and behaviors; and
3. helping educators better understand how ethnic identity provides insight into school achievement.

The third chapter written by Ng investigates the effects of an academic self-schema on why and how both Chinese and Australian year 10 students learned mathematics. Ng reviews relevant literature and research findings and proposes a hypothesized model stipulating the relationships between an academic self-schema and other important learning variables. Path analyses test the model for the student groups and reveal both similarities

and differences. The results confirm the cross-cultural motivational properties of students' self-schemas. Differences between the two models are
explained in terms of the influences of contrasting cultural models of success that operate in the two different educational systems.

In chapter four Jennifer Vadeboncoeur and Pedro R. Portes present an
approach for the study of identity construction from a sociocultural perspective. Drawing on the work of Vygotsky (1978, 1986) and current sociocultural theorists, the authors trace contributions to this topic from both
Erikson (1963, 1968) and Bakhtin (1986). Organized into four comprehensive sections, the authors review the basic tenets of the sociocultural
approach. Next, they discuss the literature and suggested extensions of
Vygotsky's work through Erikson's psychosocial theory. The third section
explores the complementarity of the work of Vygotsky and Bakhtin. Finally,
the authors conclude the chapter with empirical data that exemplifies a
sociocultural approach to identity with particular regard to the production
of students labeled "at risk."

Jerry Fogarty and Colin White open Chapter five with a brief description
of a young Australian Aboriginal student's first year at University—her
story was typical of the experiences of many Indigenous students attempting to come to grips with life away from home in a competitive higher education environment. The authors use the students' experiences as the basis
for exploring a number of themes that were felt to have an impact on the
academic success of Indigenous students:

1. lack of career knowledge among Indigenous students;
2. the mismatch between what Indigenous students expect to find at
    University and what they actually do find;
3. mismatches between the predominantly collectivist values held by
    Indigenous students and the more individualistic values that pre-
    dominate in Western university settings;
4. external pressures that make study difficult; and
5. the lack of adequate preparation for the cognitive demands of Uni-
    versity study.

Jerry and Colin conclude that the last of these themes has the greatest
immediate impact on performance but that lack of preparation can be
understood only in the context of a wider range of cultural variables.

Section II. Focus on Families and Communities

Kimberly Pressick-Kilborn and Richard Walker author chapter six, 'The
social construction of interest in a learning community.' This chapter
explores the implications for the development of interest as a motivational

construct when co-created in the context of social interaction. Pressick-Kilborn and Walker argue that previous distinctions between individual and situational factors when conceptualizing interest are not as salient when students learn in actual classroom environments. They develop an argument that draws upon Jaan Valsiner's notions of the zone of proximal development and canalization of development, as well as Ann Brown's concept of communities of learners, to support the need to consider interest as created in the dynamic interaction between the individual and the socio-cultural context. An episode from a classroom ethnographic study being conducted by Pressick-Kilborn illustrates the complex development of interest in learning in an actual classroom.

Chapter seven, authored by Eric Anderman, Jane Jensen, and Diana Haleman, summarizes a field-based study of adult learners' motivation toward attending adult education classes in Kentucky. The state of Kentucky has a large high school dropout rate, consequently, the state offers a number of adult education programs, but only a small percentage of the eligible adult population utilizes these classes. Eligible adults are interviewed in order to learn about their motivational beliefs toward adult education. Using both qualitative and quantitative methods, adults' reasons for not participating in these programs are explained using an expectancy X value model of motivation. Several age and gender differences emerge in the analyses. In addition, the economic contexts of these individuals' lives relate in important ways to their motivational beliefs toward adult education programs.

In chapter eight Nanette Potee explores the influence of culture on student and teacher perceptions of teacher immediacy behaviors. The goal is to provide insights into the nature, functions, and implications of instructional communication behaviors in Japanese classrooms. The significance of the findings from this study is that they lend cross-cultural support to basic theories of teacher immediacy. Of additional interest, is the fact that students in this study show preference for behaviors that are not typically found in their cultural context.

Gregory P. Thomas, chapter nine, argues that students' metacognition is strongly influenced by the broad sociocultural milieu that their schooling is located within. Gregory contends that greater consideration of sociocultural factors is necessary if we are to more fully understand the uneven effects of interventions that aim to enhance students' metacognition and learning processes. Case studies drawn from research conducted as part of his doctoral studies illustrate these points. The research occurs in an Australian high school chemistry classroom where he is the teacher. The students in his class exhibit varying levels of resistance and concern regarding becoming more metacognitive and articulate their reasons for such resistance and concern. He uses the concepts of habitus and hegemony drawn from sociology to help explain the variable influence that an intervention centered around the metaphor 'learning is constructing' had on his students.

In chapter ten Tamera B. Murdock, Megan Brooks Bolch, George Dent, and Natalie Hale Wilcox explore possible ways in which motivation theory might expand to better explain the high rates of alienation and school dropout among African-American youth: self-esteem theories and expectancy-value theories. Consistent with Crocker and Major (1989), we suggest that a motivational explanation focusing on personal self-evaluations may be inadequate to explain school behavior among historically discriminated populations, as they discount the relevance of evaluative feedback from formal sources, such as schools and teachers. Murdock et al. also suggest that student's values, rather than their rated-beliefs become a focus of motivation research. Data exploring the relations between values and behaviors, and some possible socializing agents of values are examined in a sample of urban, African-American youth.

Dawn Iwamoto and Henry Radda, chapter eleven, attempt to understand the nature of students' motivation (using samples from an American Indian and a neighboring non-native community) and its influence on retention and completion of high school. The goal of the study is to offer practical and timely recommendations that take into consideration sociocultural issues that can inform policy and practice in the school and tribal community. Eleven hundred students completed the Inventory of School Motivation, the Facilitating Conditions Questionnaire and the Behavioral Intentions Questionnaire. Although the research demonstrates many similarities in terms of motivation and other influential variables across the two groups, there are also clear differences that suggest programming initiatives may assist student motivation and the ultimate successful completion of school for the American Indian students. Recommendations include suggestions for teaching strategies, staff development opportunities, parent and community education, and the facilitation of partnerships between tribal and dominant communities.

Section III. Focus on Methods

Farideh Salili, chapter twelve, explores the similarities and differences in the affective meaning of achievement between British and Hong Kong Chinese high-school students. Participants rate 104 achievement related concepts using the Semantic Differential scales (Osgood, May & Miron, 1975). Cluster analysis of the data show roughly similar clusters of achievement concepts for the two cultures, suggesting that the dimensions of achievement may be the same for both cultures. There were, however, some differences in the composition and in the ratings of the clusters which reflect differences in cultural values of the two groups. The results also show the two cultures hold common stereotypes of sex roles, suggesting that the societal expectations of the gender roles is the same for both cultures.

In chapter thirteen, David Watkins, Dennis McInerney, Clement Lee, Adebowale Akande, and Murari Regmi investigate Western and non-Western secondary school students learning strategies and motivation. Theorists typically propose that the motive(s) with which a student approaches a learning task is likely to influence the strategy they use to tackle that task. However, supporting research on individualistic views of motivation may not be appropriate for non-Western students. This research utilizes the Inventory of School Motivation (ISM; McInerney et al., 2000) which was designed to reflect a wider range of goals relevant for both Western and non-Western students. The participants were 1657 students from typical secondary schools in Hong Kong, Malawi, Nepal, South Africa (separate Black and White samples), and Zambia. The instruments were the ISM and the strategy scales of the Learning Process Questionnaire (LPQ; Biggs, 1987). For all six samples the prediction of the Surface Strategy scale was weak but that of the Deep and Achieving strategy scales was strong. Global Motivation rather than Performance or Mastery Goal scales was the best predictor amongst the general scales while Task Effort was the only consistent good predictor amongst the specific motivation scales. Neither affiliative nor social goals show little association with any learning strategy in any sample.

Teresa Garcia Duncan authors chapter fourteen, a chapter examining one of the greatest challenges to cross-cultural research, designing equivalent instruments. Translating instruments so that items are comparable and meaningful across cultures is no small feat; without well-designed, conceptually equivalent measures, comparisons of learning and achievement across cultures lack validity. The purpose of this chapter is twofold. First, to synthesize the literature from current perspectives on instrument translation and adaptation. The second purpose of this chapter is to offer the reader a concrete set of research-based guidelines to use in adapting instruments. By performing a review of the literature and by offering a concrete set of guidelines to the reader, Garcia Duncan hopes this chapter will be useful to a broad audience of researchers and consumers.

REFERENCES

Bakhtin, M. M. (1986). *Speech genres and other late essays.* Austin, TX: University of Texas Press.

Biggs, J.B. (1987). *Student approaches to learning and studying.* Melbourne, Australia: Australian Council for Educational Research.

Blumer, H. (1969). *Symbolic interaction.* Englewood Cliffs, NJ: Prentice Hall.

Bogdan, R., & Biklen, S. K. (1992). *Qualitative research for education: An introduction to theory and methods* (2nd ed). Boston, MA: Allyn & Bacon.

Crocker, J., & Major, B. (1989). Social stigma and self-esteem: The self-protective properties of stigma. *Psychological Review, 96,* 608-630.

Erikson, E. H. (1963). *Childhood and society.* New York, NY: Norton.

Erikson, E. H. (1968). *Identity: Youth and crisis.* New York, NY: Norton.

Geertz, C. (1973). Thick description: Toward an interpretive theory of culture. In C. Geertz (Ed.), *The interpretation of cultures.* New York, NY: Basic Books.

Lincoln, Y. S., & Guba, E. G. (1985). *Naturalistic inquiry.* Newbury Park, CA: Sage.

McInerney, D.M., Yeung, S.Y., & McInerney, V. (2000). *The meaning of school motivation. Multidimensional and hierarchical perspectives and impacts on schooling.* Paper presented at the annual meeting of the American Educational Research Association, New Orleans, April 24-29.

Mead, G. H. (1934). *Mind, self, and society.* Chicago, IL: University of Chicago Press.

Miles, M. B., & Huberman, A. M. (1994). *Qualitative data analysis: An expanded sourcebook* (2nd ed.). Thousand Oaks, CA: Sage.

Mishler, E. G. (1986). *Research interviewing: Context and narrative.* Cambridge, MA: Harvard University Press.

Osgood, C.E., May, W.H. & Miron, M.S. (1975). Cross-cultural universals of affective meaning. Urbana, IL: University of Illinois Press.

Spradley, J. P. (1979). *The ethnographic interview.* New York, NY: Holt, Rinehart, & Winston.

Spradley, J. P. (1980). *Participant observation.* New York, NY: Holt, Rinehart, & Winston.

Strauss, A., & Corbin, J. (1990). *Basics of qualitative research: Grounded theory procedures and techniques.* Newbury Park, CA: Sage.

Van Etten, S., Freebern, G., & Pressley, M. (1997). College students' beliefs about examination preparation. *Contemporary Educational Psychology, 22,* 1-21.

Van Etten, S., Pressley, M., Freebern, G., & Echevarria, M. (1998). An interview study of college freshmens' beliefs about their academic motivation. *European Journal of Psychology of Education, 13* (1), 105-130.

Van Meter, P., Yokoi, L., & Pressley, M. (1994). College students' theory of note-taking derived from their perceptions of note-taking. *Journal of Educational Psychology, 86,* 323-338.

Vygotsky, L. S. (1978). *Mind in society: The development of higher psychological processes.* Cambridge, MA: Harvard University Press.

Vygotsky, L. S. (1986). *Thought and language.* Cambridge, MA: MIT Press.

PART I

FOCUS ON IDENTITY

CHAPTER 1

THE SELF IN CULTURAL CONTEXT
Meaning and Valence

David Yun Dai

INTRODUCTION

Having anxiously waited for the mid-term exam results, Gao and Chen, two
10th graders in a mainland China high school, finally saw their scores
posted in their classroom. Gao was happy, as his name shines in the top-ten
list, while Chen was disappointed, finding himself in the middle of the
pack. This scenario should not be too strange to students living in Western
cultures, save for the public display of academic performance rankings.
Would Gao and Chen feel and think the same way that their counterparts
in North America, Europe, or Australia do? Would Gao attribute his good
performance to his superior ability or hard work? Would Chen suffer low
self-esteem or desperately try to preserve his positive self-image and self-
worth? Are there basic universal principles that determine how children
and adolescents process social comparison information, social-evaluative
feedback and derive a sense of self from these events they encounter regularly? Or rather, what these events mean to children and adolescents, cog-
nitively and affectively, is strongly influenced by cultural meaning systems?

   In this article, I reflect on the current research on self-concept in an
Eastern cultural context. I particularly focus on how etic (assuming universality of certain psychological regularities) and emic approaches (assuming
uniqueness of cultural experiences) shape the way we come to understand

cultural similarities and differences in the origins and role of self-concept in motivation and learning. I will attempt to show that an understanding of the cultural dimension of the self can not only shed light on related cultural similarities and differences but, more importantly, illuminate the nature of self-concept itself.

DEFINING THE SELF AND CULTURE

Very few today would deny the psychological significance of the self, a topic rejected by mainstream psychology only several decades ago as too mentalistic and not amenable to empirical investigation. William James identified two major dimensions of the self: a) we can experience ourselves as an agent; a statement like "I can do it" or "I made it!" refers to such personal agency. b) we can experience ourselves as an object of our own cognition; a simple self-description "I learn math quickly" indicates this reflective self-image or self-perception (see Harter, 1999 for a review). This distinction is important since the former aspect directly reflects conation or motivation but the latter often indicates self-verification and self-evaluation. Historically, the transactional self (i.e., I-Self) is emphasized by social learning theorists (Mischel, 1973; Bandura, 1977) who view the self as fundamentally situated in specific contexts, who like to use terms self-control, self-reinforcement, and self-efficacy to describe self-engendered influences, and who emphasize the situational determination of self-perceptions. In line with the behaviorist tradition, they tend to avoid trait-like concepts like self-concept and self-esteem. Self-concept researchers, on the other hand, represent a new breed of researchers who believe that self-concepts or self-perceptions, as the outcome of reflective experiences and self-representations (i.e., the Me-Self), have their unique structural properties (Shavelson & Bolus, 1982) and functional significance (Harter, 1999).

Culture is also a concept that is used in different contexts and has different referents. In etic research, culture typically refers to a distinct group of people who live in a certain geographic area, sometimes speak unique languages, and share a common historical tradition in terms of social conventions and belief systems. In this sense, culture represents an unspecified uniqueness that distinguishes itself from other cultures. In a typical etic research, culture serves as a moderator variable so that causal relationships found to be strong in one culture may be weak, or even absent, in another. Thus multiple cultural groups are mainly used to test the generalizability of research findings from one culture to another. Defined as such, culture is purely a descriptive term, and does not hold any explanatory power, for the culture itself needs to be elucidated or "unpackaged" (Leung, 1989). In contrast, in research that has an emic orientation, culture is defined as the way people of a particular cultural origin and affiliation come to understand the world, each other, and themselves (Bruner, 1996), or "as an intersubjective reality through which worlds are known, created, and experienced (Miller, 1997)." One aspect of cultural meaning systems concern reward structure that regulates people's intentions, goals, attributions, and affect. Thus some human activities and attributes are perceived as quintessential in one culture but marginalized in another. Defined as such, culture can refer to any group, small or large, that shares the same ecology of reward system. For example, what Nicholls's (1989) refers to as "competitive ethos" describes school atmosphere or culture as well as the society at large.

THE SELF AS A CULTURE-BOUND PHENOMENON

Can we imagine culture-free self-processes? The answer is no. For the self, whether I-Self or Me-Self, is fundamentally mediated by language, and language as the currency of meanings is culture-bound; that is, it has shared subjective and objective referents based on which mutual understanding and communications are facilitated and cultural norms are established (Bruner, 1990; 1996). The question, then, is where does culture or enculturation start?

To be sure, part of our selves (implicit memory, hidden motives, repressed emotions, etc.) may be highly cryptic, not easily penetrable by our consciousness, as Freud (1953) suggested a long time ago, and demonstrated by the extant literature (Kihlstrom, 1999). What constitutes the phenomenon of the self in question is the human capacity to experience oneself as agent or experiencer of an ongoing or past event (Kihlstrom, 1999). This establishes the principle, first and foremost, that the self is a cognitive developmental event, which is inevitable as long as one, with cognitive maturation and transactions with the environment, becomes aware of the personal significance of certain events and capable of forming mental representations of an event, its context, valence, and meaning to the self. In other words, the self is our subjective experience or reflective consciousness that is made possible by the evolutionary history of the brain and realized in human development. To the extent that it reflects a species-specific trait, it is universal to all cultures, even though specific forms and contents of expressions of the self are different.

However, the construction of the self is mediated by language, as our private or inner speech articulates and organizes most of our reflective consciousness.[1] As illustrated in the research on the interpersonal world of the infant (Stern, 1985), the self as well as interpersonal relationships can be experienced at two levels, one as lived experience, and the other as verbally represented. The human capacity for objectifying the self-experience through verbal representations transcends one's immediate experience (and indeed sometimes distorting it) and leads to our distinct phenomenal self. It is this layer of subjective reality that is penetrable or suggestible by cultural meaning systems. In other words, culture, through its shared meaning system, regulates how we interpret personal, interpersonal, and social events (Miller, 1984), and such regulation constitutes another source of the self and is embedded in social interaction and communication between the child and his/her significant others (Cooley, 1902; Geertz, 1979). The Woolf-Sapir hypothesis (see Worlf, 1956) postulates language as a carrier of cultural meanings that shape and structure individuals' thought processes and subjective experiences. Whether one agrees with this strong version of the argument for linguistic and cultural mediation of the self, one cannot deny the nature of the self as culturally mediated. To the extent that one endorses the functional significance or explanatory power of the self in elucidating the nature of human behavior rather than treating the self as epiphenomenal to more basic psychological processes, one also recognizes the importance of culture.

VIABILITY OF CROSS-CULTURAL INQUIRY: ETIC VS. EMIC

One of the impetuses of cross-cultural research is to find out whether certain psychological principles or theories well established in literature are valid in cultures that belong to distinctly different traditions. Such an approach is not without its critics and skeptics. Messick (1988), for example, raised concerns that the failure to replicate well-documented findings in another culture is difficult to interpret. There could be many causes, not the least of which is the inherent difficulty in ensuring equivalent instruments, measurements, and meanings. Psychological principles may be universal, but specific cultural manifestations may be different (McInerney, 1998), which renders any replication efforts precarious and different findings difficult to interpret. From a more anthropological point of view, Lock (1981) pointed out the inherent difficulty of an etic approach.

> When one proposes some basic universal dimensions from one cultural perspective and finds an apparent fit of other cultural systems to these dimensions, one has not proposed universals at all. Rather, one has constructed a translation and classificatory system which enables one to gain some understanding of an alien culture by locating elements of their systems within the hermeneutic circle of one's own. (Lock, 1981, p. 184)

This statement clearly suggests that even the most fair-minded etic approach to cross-cultural research is culturally biased, for there are always important aspects of a culture that are left out by such an imposed etic approach (Berry, 1969). At worst, by imposing one's own cultural way of thinking, one can completely misread other cultures. However, the statement is much more than a warning against ethnocentrism. Up to date, psychological research has still been carried out in the spirit of positivism. The etic approach fits this mode well because it adheres to the doctrine of determinism, aiming at finding regularities or laws that govern human behavior, not unlike those that govern the behavior of physical objects. The emic approach is phenomenological in nature. That is, instead of deriving a set of propositions that can be subjected to empirical verification or falsification, it is concerned directly with the meanings of human experience in an immediate sociocultural context (Geertz, 1973). Its purpose is not to uncover universal underlying structures and processes but finding appropriate ways to describe and interpret particular cultural experiences (i.e., hermeneutics), and their significance for the human kind. Thus these two distinct approaches to cross-cultural research head in different directions from the very beginning, not unlike the phonetic and phonemic approaches in the linguistics from which the terms etic and emic derive[2].

In addition, the statement reflects a fundamental conundrum of social and behavioral science: what we attempt to uncover is already preempted in our basic assumptions about the nature of human behavior, what Pepper (1942) would call *world hypothesis*. Clearly, etic and emic approaches may reflect fundamentally different "generative metaphors" implicitly or explicitly endorsed by researchers. For instance, etic researchers would agree with Kluchhohn (1954) that "the underlying 'genotype' of all cultures is the same" (p. 955), although the phenotypic manifestations may vary greatly. Cognitive developmentalists, for example, focus on basic cognitive constraints on the construct of self, for example, the ability to infer personal dispositions and attributes through social comparison. In contrast, emic researchers would be more sympathetic to the view of culture as uniquely defining self-experience rather than merely variations of some universal themes or structures (Markus & Kitayama, 1994). They tend to see the construction of the self as diametrically different in the Eastern and Western cultures because of different cultural schemas or frameworks used to interpret personal experiences (Markus & Kitayama, 1991).

In the following sections, I will demonstrate challenges facing cross-cultural researchers in dealing with this etic and emic dilemma. Specifically, I will discuss three issues:

a. How to make our assumptions about self and culture explicit, which may require that we sometimes take a meta-cultural look.
b. How to cast etic research in a rich cultural context and look at alternative perspectives.
c. How to reconcile the two approaches that tend to produce different findings and interpretations.

I will try, in response to skeptics of cross-cultural research, to demonstrate that interpretations are possible if we abandon the positivist creed of objective certainty and cast results in appropriate interpretative frameworks.

Current self-concept research is rooted in two major assumptions:

a. people derive self-knowledge and self-perceptions of competence and personal attributes from performance experiences, social comparison, and social interaction (social feedback); and

b. people's self-knowledge and self-perceptions, particularly of their social and academic competence, has self-evaluative (e.g., self-esteem) and motivational consequences (Harter, 1992; Marsh, 1990; Shavelson & Bolus, 1982).

In the following sections, I will discuss studies that bear on these two issues, alternative interpretations, and inherent challenges.

COGNITIVE AND SOCIOCULTURAL ORIGINS OF SELF-CONCEPT

In one study (Dai, in press, a), I attempted to replicate Marsh's (1990) internal/ external frame of reference model of self-concept development (I/E Model) with a sample of Chinese high school students (N = 266). Marsh's I/E Model assumes that students not only derive their subject-specific self-concept based on their immediate peer group as a frame of reference (external frame) but also infer their academic strengths and weaknesses through comparing their own performance across school subjects, particular with respect to math and verbal competence (internal frame). Thus, not only does the model predict a positive correlation between achievement and self-concept in a matching school subject; it also predicts a negative correlation between achievement in math and verbal self-concept and vice versa; that is, compared to strong performance in one area, one tends to see the other area as relatively weak. My study was based on the previous research findings that the Chinese version of the *Self-Description Questionnaire* (SDQ, Marsh, 1992) has sound psychometric properties such as reliability and internal (factorial) validity (Cheng, Zhu, Ye, & Tang, 1997; Watkins, Dong, & Xia, 1995). In this study, I adhered to a strict back-translation procedure to ensure the equivalency of my translation of the SDQ. A confirmatory factor analysis with the three self-concept measures shows satisfactory data-model fit (Nonnorm Fit Index = .94, Comparative Fit Index = .96). The results are consistent with these predictions (see Figure 1) and seem to suggest that self-concept has more to do with the individual's cognitive disposition and ability to process perfor-

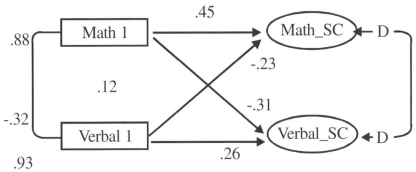

Notes: The measurement component of the model is omitted for presentation clarity. χ^2 (14) = 19.07; χ^2/df ratio = 1.36; Normed FI = .97, Nonnormed FI (Tucker-Lewis) = .98, Comparative FI = .99; RMSEA = .04. (The EQS notation system was used. D = Disturbance.)

FIGURE 1

Structural equation modeling of the I/E effects on adolescent self-concept.

mance and social comparison information rather than with cultural meaning system.

The overall results of my study seem to indicate the cross-cultural validity of the underlying processes under investigation and the validity of the etic approach itself; that is, to test the postulates of universals (Pervin, 1999). However, if Lock (1981) is correct, the similarities found in such an imposed etic approach are cause for concern rather than celebration, as significant cultural differences might be obscured in the seemingly correct claims of universals. Can we tap into more emic phenomenal experiences of Chinese children and adolescents to see whether the meaning of the self-concept is equivalent across cultures?

To answer this question, we can look at several lines of emic-minded research for leads. One of them is on cultural differences in attributions for success and failure. Based on a review of the literature, Holloway (1988) concluded that Japanese children and their parents are more likely to make effort attributions for both success and failure in academic performance. The most telling research about attribution differences come from Hess, Chang and McDevitt (1987), who compared mothers' attributions for their children's math performance. When asked why their children did not do better than they did, Caucasian mothers were mostly likely to make ability attributions (i.e., inferring low ability), followed by Chinese-American mothers, and then their mainland Chinese counterparts. In contrast, mainland Chinese mothers were most likely to attribute under-par academic performance to a lack of effort, followed by Chinese-Americans, and then Caucasian-American mothers. Research also found that Chinese students are more likely to attribute their exam results to effort than to ability

(Hau & Salili, 1991, 1996). It is not surprising that a favorite quote often posted on the walls of many classrooms in China is "Genius is 1 percent inspiration and 99 percent perspiration."

Preferences for effort attribution do not mean that students in some Eastern cultures do not make ability attributions or infer individual differences in that regard. The positive correlations between prior achievement and academic self-concept found in my own and others' research (e.g., Yeung & Lee, 1999) clearly indicates that they do. Rather, the emphasis on effort, as Chen and Uttal (1988) pointed out, is deeply rooted in Chinese cultural beliefs in the malleability and improvability of human abilities (see also Chen & Stevenson, 1995). Such beliefs and their opposite beliefs of ability as fixed and not malleable have been a focus of another line of research. Dweck and her colleagues (Dweck, 1999; Dweck, Chiu, & Hong, 1995) have systematically examined how a person's view of the world and the self influences her goals and reactions in achievement and social settings.

The view of ability as malleable is in sharp contrast to the view of ability as innate capacity. Nicholls and his colleagues (Nicholls, 1989; Nicholls & Miller, 1984) postulated that, with cognitive development and sophistication, children progress from a undifferentiated conception of ability and effort at about 5 years of age to a highly differentiated conception of ability and effort at about 12 years of age. At the lowest level, effort, ability, and performance outcomes are imperfectly differentiated as cause and effect; thus people who try harder are smarter. At Level 2, effort is the cause of outcomes; equal effort produce equal outcomes. At Level 3, effort and ability are partially differentiated; children realize that effort is not the only cause of outcomes and less effort could be compensated for by high ability. At Level 4, ability and effort is clearly differentiated; ability is seen as capacity, which limits or increases the effectiveness of effort on performance. When achievement is equal, low effort implies high ability, and high effort implies low ability. Such an hypothesis of the logical progression of qualitatively different levels or stages of ability conceptions is supported by empirical evidence regarding American children (e.g., Blumenfeld, Pintrich, & Hamilton, 1986; Nicholls & Miller, 1984). However, such logical progression cannot be seen as psychologically inevitable developmental events, but rather primed by the individualistic culture that tends to ascribe personal traits and dispositions to individuals for their behavior (Markus & Kitayama, 1991; Miller, 1984), and further predicated on the Piagetian notion of the development of formal operation (i.e., inference rules based on formal logic), which also has an individualistic bias. Recent research on Chinese folk beliefs and holistic epistemologies (Peng & Nisbett, 1999) suggests that Chinese children may not go through the sequence as Nicholls and Miller (1984) subscribed, since they are less likely than their Western counterparts to exercise their newly emergent analytic ability (e.g., more sophisticated inference rules) to tease apart different components of performance in academic settings. Thus, although Chinese children and adolescents also form self-representations of their abilities based on their performance, social comparison information, and social-evaluative feedback, these self-representations may have qualitative differences that are not captured by the self-concept research.

SELF-EVALUATION AND MOTIVATIONAL CONSEQUENCES

The second key issue of the self-concept research concerns the valence of children and adolescents' self-representations and self-perceptions. Aspects of self-concept tapped by the SDQ and other self-concept measures (e.g., Harter, 1982) are not only self-descriptive but implicitly self-evaluative. A statement "I learn math quickly" clearly has an affective component as well as a cognitive one.

Convergent findings regarding the self-concept research in an Eastern cultural context show that people in these cultures (e.g., China, Japan, Korean) tend to rate themselves lower on the self-concept instruments than their Western counterparts. A study focused on response styles across cultures (Chen, Lee, & Stevenson, 1995) found that Japanese and Chinese students are less likely to endorse extreme values than American students, and more likely to pick midpoint values on a Likert scale. The most dramatic demonstration of this cultural difference is a study by Kwok and Lytton (1996) who compared academic self-concept of Canadian and Hong Kong 4th grade students. Although Hong Kong students outscored their Canadian counterparts on a standard math test, they rate themselves lower on scholastic competence (using the Harter Self-Perception Profile; Harter, 1988). More striking is the finding that the Canadian parents of low achieving students rated their children's math ability higher than the Hong Kong parents of high achieving students; the same is true for children's self-ratings of scholastic competence. The results of my own study comparing American and Chinese adolescents (Dai, 1998) are less dramatic but consistent with the literature. Several hypotheses have been advanced to explain this difference. One is that there is a self-enhancement bias in the response style of American students and a self-effacement bias in that of Chinese students (Bong & Hwang, 1986; Stigler, Smith, & Mao, 1985). According to this interpretation, the self-concept measures may not reveal true self-perceptions since deflating one's self-ratings is socially desirable in Chinese culture just as over-ratings of self-competence is socially desirable in the American culture. Indeed high self-ratings may reveal an air of superiority that would distance others in collective cultures (Kitayama, Markus, & Matsumoto, 1995). An alternative interpretation is that the lower self-concept among Chinese students is real, not merely indicative of a cultural strategy to maintain social harmony but of true differences. One piece of supporting evidence comes from the research on the cultural differences in explanatory style. Lee and Seligman (1997) found that mainland Chinese had the most pessimistic explanatory style, attributing good events to external events and bad events to internal causes (see also Crittenden, 1996).

If the difference is not merely of response style but reflects true self-perceptions, does that mean most Chinese students share a pessimistic view of themselves? To answer this question, one needs to not only look at mean cross-cultural differences but within-culture variations and self-evaluative and motivational correlates of self-concept measures. Even in Kwok and Lytton's (1996) study in which mean differences were quite substantial, correlations between academic self-concept and self-esteem was very comparable between the Canadian and Hong Kong elementary school students. I (Dai, 1998, in press, b) also found a similar pattern of correlations, suggesting that self-concept has the same kind of valence or self-evaluative significance for Chinese students as found in Western cultures. The results seem to confirm the universality of the affective valence of self-concept. This, however, is not the whole story. To understand the importance of self-concept or self-representations, one needs to put them in a broader context of how the self is valued in the Chinese culture.

Back to the distinction between I-Self and Me-Self for the moment. When Walter Mischel (1973) advocated self-regulatory systems such as self-imposed goals and standards and self-produced consequences, he was akin to the Chinese cultural spirit in that they both emphasize the agentic part of the self (what I do) rather than personal trait part of the self (what I am). In Western cultures, particularly the American culture, lack of personal trait such as intelligence is of severe consequence since it indicates a mental deficiency and does not bode well in a meritocratic society. The self-enhancement bias found in the responses of Western samples is probably a self-defense to such a value-system (Covington, 1992). In contrast, the Chinese culture, particularly in the tradition of Confucianism, highlights self-improvement and self-perfection as the most important life task. The whole Analects of Confucius (Confucius, 1989) is replete with teachings of this sort. Banaji and Prentice (1994) identified three primary self-motives: self-verification, self-enhancement, and self-improvement. Self-improvement has a much more salient place in the Chinese culture and maybe other Eastern cultures as well (e.g., Holloway, 1988), thus sampled more frequently in one's memory, to use the term by Triandis (1989), just as self-verification and self-enhancement have a more salient place in Western cultures. This may be why, even with very conspicuous information about relative competence (e.g., public display of academic ranks) that might well heighten ego concerns and the self-enhancement motive, Chinese students still tend to focus on self-improvement (Hau & Salili, 1996). The prevalence of effort attributions by Chinese and Japanese parents should be understood in light of this broad context. Kitayama, Markus, Matsumoto, and Norasakkunkit (1997) further associated this self-improvement motive with the individual's need in a collectivist culture for meeting the standards of excellence shared in a given cultural unit and affirming one's belongingness to that unit.

One cross-cultural difference best illustrates my point. Recall that in Nicholls's (1989) Level 3 and 4 conceptions of ability and effort, given the same performance outcome, high effort implies low ability. This is why effort can be a double-edge sword (Covington & Omelich, 1979; Jagacinski & Nicholls, 1990). Covington's (1992) research focus on how American students manage to preserve their self-worth in achievement settings seems to tap into the psyche of the American culture. More recent research on the use of self-handicapping strategies (Midgley, Arunkumar, & Urdan, 1996; Urdan, Midgley, & Anderman, 1998) further confirms that some students go to great lengths to manage their impression and preserve their positive self-image. Given the lower self-concept scores and absence of self-enhancement bias in Chinese children and adolescents, one may assume that they would more readily admit their less than desirable performance and competence than their American counterparts and less likely to take pains to gloss over their perceived inadequacy. Indeed the very notion of handicapping oneself merely to protect one's self-worth, even at the expense of academic learning and achievement is uncanny in the Chinese culture, for the value of the self is defined more by what one does than what one is. Americans, as Holloway (1988) pointed out, often exert effort primarily to avoid negative consequences, or on the positive side, to bring about desirable outcomes. Thus, effort mainly has instrumental value. In Chinese and Japanese cultures, however, effort itself is deemed virtuous, as White (1987) very nicely put in her book on Japanese culture,

> pushing on, persisting, not giving up, are in themselves important, and show once again the significance of the way something is done as more important than the end accomplishment. (p. 30)

Again the "doing" part of the self is more important than "being" part of the self. There is some evidence suggesting that the positive valence of effort attributions is even stronger than that of ability attribution in cultures like China and Japan. For example, Hayami (1984, cited in Holloway, 1988) examined attribution-affect linkages among Japanese adults, and found that the link between effort and feelings of pride for success (or shame for failure) was stronger than the link between ability and feeling hopeful or hopeless at every age. In sum, self-representations and self-perceptions of ability have different affective valence and self-evaluative consequences between the American and Chinese and other Eastern cultures because different aspects of the self are emphasized in these cultures.

Differences in the salience of self-improvement motives and self-enhancement motives (analogous to learning goal/task involvement, and performance goal/ego involvement; see Dweck, 1999; Nicholls, 1989) naturally lead to the motivational implications of high or low self-concept. One of the impetuses of studying self-concept is the belief that high self-concept contributes to achievement mainly through enhanced motivation. Researchers have associated academic self-concept with various achievement behaviors such as course selection (Marsh & Yeung, 1997), effort expenditure (Helmke, 1987), and interest level (Koller, Schnabel, & Baumert, 1998). My own research (1990) looked at academic self-concept and motivational variables using the model of self-determination theory (Deci & Ryan, 1985). It seems to suggest that for both Chinese and American adolescents, high self-concept is associated with more intrinsic and self-determined forms of motivation, and low self-concept with more introjected forms of motivation (see Table 1).

Although most of the self-concept research is correlational and thus causality cannot be determined, an underlying assumption is that high self-concept and self-esteem instills in the person a sense of agency, control, and optimism, and raises one's aspirations as to what one can potentially achieve, hence having an energizing effect. The association of self-concept and achievement motivation can well be traced back to the notion that human beings have an inherent need for experiencing the self as effective and competent (White, 1959), and tend to gravitate toward those activities in which they have demonstrated a certain degree of promise (Deci & Ryan, 1985). Thus, our motivation is inherently toward self-enhancement. But is this form of motivation culture-free? Kitayama et al. (1997) provided an interesting, and indeed insightful, contrast between self-enhancement in the United States and self-criticism in Japan. According to this study, Americans are more tuned into positive self-relevant information and Japa-

TABLE 1

Intercorrelations of the Measures of Academic Self-Concept, Self-Esteem, and Motivation for the American (N = 153) and Chinese (N = 266) 10th Grade Students

	1	2	3	4	5	6
1. Academic Self-Concept		43**	07	41**	47**	39**
2. Self-Esteem	51**		-26**	20*	18*	06
3. Introjection	-14	-20**		30**	38**	22**
4. Identification	27**	17**	04		67**	39**
5. Intrinsic Motivation	36**	28**	-08	44**		36**
6. Achievement	30**	-01	06	17**	22**	

Notes: Above the diagonal are data for the American adolescents and below the diagonal are data for the Chinese adolescents. All decimal points are omitted. * $p < .05$ ** $p < .01$

nese more sensitive to negative self-relevant information. They explained a Japanese way of motivation probably unknown to individualistic cultures:

> To achieve the task of fitting in, one may need to identify the ideal image of the self expected by others in a relationship, find what may be missing or lacking in the self in reference to this expected, ideal self, and then improve on these deficits and problems. This act of reflecting on one's past behavior in reference to socially shared standards of excellence so as to be able to improve and therefore to be part of the relevant social unit is captured by a frequently used and highly elaborated Japanese concept of hansei, which literally means 'reflection.' (Kiyatama et al., 1997, p. 1254)

Thus, meeting social expectations, and bridging the gap between the real self and the culturally defined ideal self, what Yang and Yu (1988; see also Yu, 1996) called social-oriented achievement motivation, are sources of motivation not well captured by the current self-concept research, which is based on an individualistic assumption of self enhancement or individual-orientated achievement motivation. A recent study conducted by Eaton and Dembo (1997) is quite revealing in this regard. They found that for Asian American students, the best predictor of academic achievement was not self-efficacy, but perceived consequences of academic success and failure. This reminds us that even though self-concept has an important self-evaluative and motivational importance for all students, Asian students included, it may not be the only internal driving force, and indeed, sometimes may not be the most important one.

EPISTEMOLOGICAL AND METHODOLOGICAL ISSUES

The above sections have depicted two pictures, one comfortably confirming the etic assumptions of universality of the construct of self-concept, its cross-cultural validity, the other providing a hidden, emic side of the story. Sometimes I even deliberately challenge the conclusions I drew from my own research in order to venture a new understanding. In so doing, I am trying to respond to Lock's (1981) challenge by making our generative metaphors and methodology explicit.

A typical etic approach to self-concept research uses the principle of operationalism to define and measure self-concept; that is, we try to quantify self-concept and develop a set of variables that represent the construct. At the semantic level, a statement "I learn math quickly" should be quite equivalent whether it is in French or Japanese; thus cross-cultural equivalency or face validity is not difficult to achieve. Even at the structural level, functional equivalency of the self-concept construct (Hui & Triandis, 1985) can also be established, as the data presented has shown. It is at the phenomenological level that uncertainty starts to emerge; that is, how do we know that self-representations are *experienced* the same way across cultures. When self-concept or self-representations are only observed in their most static form (self-report questionnaire) and isolated from the dynamic process of construing and interpreting the significance of ongoing events to the self, the important psychosocial context on which these self-representations are experienced is lost, so is its meaning. That, to me, is a major problem with the current self-concept research, particularly when cross-cultural generality is concerned. A viable generative metaphor for self-concept research is that of a theatre where there are certain events and actors in the spotlight (i.e., in our consciousness), and there is a director or active agent (the transactional and reflective self) that determines how the show will play out. Such a metaphor implies a more contextual model for understanding the self. Several ingredients are hinted at by such a metaphor. First, one needs to consider what is "on stage" and what is "off stage" for a specific individual; namely what is active in one's consciousness. Second, one needs to consider how an individual construes the meaning and significance of an achievement-related event, say, a poor test performance; this will bring developmental levels, personal dispositions, past histories, and cultural beliefs and values to the forefront. Third, one needs to consider how the self is crystallized and shaped from the confluence of all these factors, and how it exerts its directive influence on achievement behaviors. An emic-minded, interpretative science clearly fills the gap left by the etic approach by putting self-concept back in its rich phenomenal context, and revealing its true meaning.

This leads to an ontological (and epistemological) issue, an issue of the self as determined by content vs. process (Pervin, 1999). In short, it is about our "world hypotheses" regarding the self. Do the contents of our reflective thought have their own structural properties and functional significance and explanatory power for behavior regulation, or are they simply manifestations of and epiphenomenal to some basic psychological processes, such as I/E Model (Marsh, 1990), progressive cognitive differentiation (Nicholls, 1989; Piaget, 1971), and basic self-motives (Banaji & Prentice, 1994)? Are basic self-motives and self-processes really basic and culture only regulates them through its belief system, playing down some and playing up some (playing up self-improvement playing down self-enhancement)? Or alternatively, are these basic self-motives actually culture-bound experiences, and our subjective experience fundamentally framed in the cultural meaning systems (Shweder, 1990)? If cultural experiences are consistent, though not uniform, manifestations of the same covert self-processes, an etic perspective is redeemed. If unique cultural experiences are discovered, then, an emic perspective is justified. As is shown in the above discussion, the findings cut both ways. Like the particle vs. wave debate in physics about the nature of light, we can only get half truth whatever method we prefer. It might be that the nature will only reveal its entire truth when multiple, sometimes incompatible, approaches are employed. We will continue to search for causal regularities that are applicable to diverse cultures, as an etic approach has promised. At the same time, we also need to dig deeper into the meaning of human action, to formulate a more viable theory of the mind and the self, of which culture is no small part.

The deeper we are involved in hermeneutics, the realm of subjective experiences, the more there is the need for breaking disciplinary boundaries between natural and social sciences, between sciences and humanities. Although Bruner (1990) argues that disciplinary boundaries are of convenience, not of necessity, are positivist-minded psychologists willing to delve into the realm of interpretive science (see Kagan, 1989)? Although trained mainly in quantitative methodology, I feel that much is to be learned from ethnography and phenomenology. After all, we are all, even radical behaviorists included, making the world (Goodman, 1984). We cannot escape the hermeneutic circle. But we can always develop a more sophisticated analytic framework and methodology so that we can say something more pertinent about the school experiences of Gaos, Chens, and other students living different cultural worlds, and how they make their own worlds.

NOTES

1. In this chapter, the terms "moderator" and "mediator" refer to two distinct types of variables. A mediator variable constitutes a causal link in a chain of events. A moderator variable does not serve such a function between independent and dependent variables but determines the presence and magnitude of a causal relationship. See Baron and Kenny (1986) for a detailed discussion of the conceptual, strategic, and statistical dimensions of the topic.

2. The distinction between etic and emic approaches is a broad one. Sometimes it refers to methodological differences in cross-cultural inquiry, such as ethnographic, naturalistic vs. rational, positivistic approaches. Sometimes it reflects philosophical differences about the nature of the phenomenon under investigation, such as regularities and natural laws vs. meaning and expression of subjective reality. In this article, the distinction is highlighted at both ontological (what is to be studied) and epistemological (how it should be studied) levels.

REFERENCES

Banaji, M. R., & Prentice, D. A. (1994). The self in social contexts.*Annual Review of Psychology, 45*, 297-332.

Bandura, A. (1977). Self-efficacy: Toward a unifying theory of behavioral change. *Psychological Review, 84*, 191-215.

Baron, R. M., & Kenny, D. A. (1986). The moderator-mediator variable distinction in social psychological research: Conceptual, strategic, and statistical considerations. *Journal of Personality and Social Psychology, 51*, 1173-1182.

Berry, J. W. (1969). On cross-cultural comparability. *International Journal of Psychology, 4*, 119-128.

Blumenfeld, P. C., Pintrich, P. R., & Hamilton, V. L. (1986). Children's concepts of ability, effort, and conduct. *American Educational Research Journal, 23*, 95-104.

Bong, M. H., & Hwang, K. K. (1986). The social psychology of Chinese people. In M. H. Bong (Ed.), *The psychology of Chinese people* (pp. 213-266). Hong Kong: Oxford University Press.

Bruner, J. (1990). *Acts of meaning.* Cambridge, MA: Harvard University Press.

Bruner, J. (1996). *The culture of education.* Cambridge, MA: Harvard University Press.

Chen, C., Lee, S.-y., & Stevenson, H. W. (1995). Response style and cross-cultural comparisons of rating scales among East Asian and North American students. *Psychological Science, 6*, 170-175.

Chen, C., & Stevenson, H. W. (1995). Motivation and mathematics achievement: A comparative study of Asian-American, Caucasian-American, and East Asian High School Students. *Child Development, 66*, 1215-1234.

Chen, C. S., & Uttal, D. H. (1988). Cultural values, parents' beliefs, and children's achievement in the United States and China. *Human Development, 31*, 351-358.

Cheng, G., Zhu, X., Ye, L., & Tang, Y. (1997). The revision of the Shanghai norm of the Self-Description Questionnaire. *Psychological Science China, 20*, 499-503.

Confucius. (1989). *The analects of Confucius* (Waley, A., Trans.). New York, NY: Vintage.

Cooley, C. H. (1902). *Human nature and the social order.* New York, NY: Scribner.

Covington, M. V. (1992). *Making the grade: A self-worth perspective on motivation and school reform.* New York, NY: Cambridge University Press.

Covington, M. V., & Omelich, C. L. (1979). Effort: the double-edge sword in school achievement. *Journal of Educational Psychology, 71*, 169-182.

Crittenden, K. S. (1996). Causal attributions among the Chinese. In M. H. Bong (Ed.), *The handbook of Chinese psychology* (pp. 263-279). Oxford, England: Oxford University Press.

Dai, D. Y. (1998). *Relationships among parenting styles, parental expectations and attitudes, and adolescents' school functioning: A cross-cultural study.* Unpublished doctoral dissertation, Purdue University, West Lafayette.

Dai, D. Y. (in press-a). Incorporating parent perceptions: A replication and extension study of the internal/external frame of reference model of self-concept development. *Journal of Adolescent Research.*

Dai, D. Y. (in press-b). A comparison of gender differences in academic self-concept and motivation between high ability and average Chinese adolescents. *Journal of Secondary Gifted Education.*

Deci, E. L., & Ryan, R. M. (1985). *Intrinsic motivation and self-determination in human behavior.* New York, NY: Plenum.

Dweck, C. S. (1999). *Self theories: Their role in motivation, personality, and development.* Philadelphia, PA: Psychology Press.

Dweck, C. S., Chiu, C., & Hong, Y. (1995). Implicit theories and their role in judgments and reactions: A world from two perspectives. *Psychological Inquiry, 6*, 267-285.

Eaton, M. J., & Dembo, M. H. (1997). Differences in the motivational beliefs of Asian American and non-Asian students. *Journal of Educational Psychology, 89*, 433-400.

Freud, S. (1953). The interpretation of dreams. In J. Strachey (Ed.), *The standard edition of the complete psychological works of Sigmund Freud* (Vol. 4-5). London, England: Hogarth Press (Original work published 1900).

Geertz, C. (1973). *The interpretation of cultures: Selected essays*. New York, NY: Basic Books.

Goodman, N. (1984). *Of mind and other matters*. Cambridge, MA: Harvard University Press.

Harter, S. (1982). The perceived competence scale for children. *Child Development, 53*, 87-97.

Harter, S. (1988). *Manual for the self-perception profile for adolescents*. Denver, CO: University of Denver.

Harter, S. (1992). The relationship between perceived competence, affect, and motivational orientation within the classroom: Processes and patterns of change. In A. K. Boggiano & T. S. Pittman (Eds.), *Achievement and motivation: A social-developmental perspective* (pp. 77-114). New York, NY: Cambridge University Press.

Harter, S. (1999). *The construction of the self: A developmental perspective*. New York, NY: The Guilford Press.

Hau, K. T., & Salili, F. (1991). Structural and semantic differential placement of specific causes: Academic causal attributions by Chinese students in Hong Kong. *International Journal of Psychology, 26*, 175-193.

Hau, K. T., & Salili, F. (1996). Prediction of academic performance among Chinese students: Effort can compensate for lack of ability. *Organizational Behavior and Human Decision Processes, 65*, 83-94.

Helmke, A. (1987). *Mediating processes between children's self-concept of ability and mathematical achievement: A longitudinal study*. Munich, Germany: Max Planck Institute for Psychological Research.

Hess, R. D., Chang, C. M., & McDevitt, T. M. (1987). Cultural variations in family beliefs about children's performance in mathematics: Comparisons among People's Republic of China, Chinese-American, and Caucasian-American families. *Journal of Educational Psychology, 79*, 179-188.

Holloway, S. D. (1988). Concepts of ability and effort in Japan and the United States. *Review of Educational Research, 58*, 327-345.

Hui, C. H., & Triandis, H. C. (1985). Measurement in cross-cultural psychology: A review and comparison of strategies. *Journal of Cross-Cultural Psychology, 16*, 131-152.

Jagacinski, C. M., & Nicholls, J. G. (1990). Reducing effort to protect perceived ability: They do it but I don't. *Journal of Educational Psychology, 82*, 15-21.

Kagan, J. (1989). *Unstable ideas: Temperament, cognition, and self*. Cambridge, MA: Harvard University Press.

Kihlstrom, J. F. (1999). The psychological unconscious. In L. A. Pervin & O. P. John (Eds.), *Handbook of personality: Theory and research* (pp. 424-442). New York, NY: The Guilford Press.

Kitayama, S., Markus, H. R., & Matsumoyo, H. (1995). Culture, self, and emotion: A cultural perspective on "self-conscious" emotions. In J. P. Tangney & K. W. Fischer (Eds.), *Self-conscious emotions: The psychology of shame, guilt, embarrassment, and pride* (pp. 439-464). New York, NY: Guilford Press.

Kitayama, S., Markus, H. R., Matsumoto, H., & Norasakkunkit, V. (1997). Individual and collective processes in the construction of the self: Self-enhancement in the United States and Self-Criticism in Japan. *Journal of Personality and Social Psychology, 72*, 1245-1267.

Kluckhohn, C. (1954). Culture and behavior. In G. Lindzey (Ed.), *Handbook of social psychology* (pp. 920-976). Cambridge, MA: Addison-Wesley.

Koller, O., Schnabel, K., & Baumert, J. (1998, April). *The impact of academic self-concepts of ability on the development of interests during adolescence.* Paper presented at the Annual Meeting of the American Educational Research Association, San Diego, CA.

Kwok, D. C., & Lytton, H. (1996). Perceptions of mathematics ability versus actual mathematics performance: Canadian and Hong Kong Chinese children. *British Journal of Educational Psychology, 66*, 209-222.

Lee, Y.-T., & Seligman, M. E. P. (1997). Are American more optimistic than the Chinese? *Personality and Social Psychology Bulletin, 23*, 32-40.

Leung, K. (1989). Cross-cultural differences: Individual-level vs. culture-level analysis. *International Journal of Psychology, 24*, 703-719.

Lock, A. (1981). Indigenous psychology and human nature: A psychological perspective. In P. Heelas & A. Lock (Eds.), *Indigenous psychologies: The anthropology of the self* (pp. 183-201). London: Academic Press.

Markus, H. R., & Kitayama, S. (1991). Culture and the self: Implications for cognition, emotion, and motivation. *Psychological Review, 98*, 224-253.

Markus, H. R., & Kitayama, S. (1994). The cultural construction of self and emotion: Implications for social behavior. In S. Kitayama & H. R. Markus (Eds.), *Emotions and culture: Empirical studies of mutual influences* (pp. 89-130). Washington, DC: American Psychological Association.

Marsh, H. W. (1990). Influences of internal and external frames of reference on the formation of math and English self-concepts: A multiwave, longitudinal panel analysis. *Journal of Educational Psychology, 82*, 107-116.

Marsh, H. W. (1992). *Self-Description Questionnaire-II manual.* Cambelltown, Australia: University of Western Sydney, Macarthur.

Marsh, H. W., & Yeung, A. S. (1997). Coursework selection: Relations to academic self-concept and achievement. *American Educational Research Journal, 34*, 691-720.

McInerney, D. M. (1998, April). *Multidimensinal aspects of motivation in cross-cultural settings and methods for researching.* Paper presented at the annual meeting of the American Educational Research Association, San Diego, CA.

Messick, D. M. (1988). On the limitations of cross-cultural research in social psychology. In M. H. Bond (Ed.), *The cross-cultural challenge to social psychology* (pp. 41-47). Newbury Park, CA: Sage.

Midgely, C., Arunkumar, R., & Urdan, T. C. (1996). "If I don't do well tomorrow, there is a reason": Predictors of adolescents' use of academic self-handicapping strategies. *Journal of Educational Psychology, 88*, 423-434.

Miller, J. G. (1984). Culture and the development of everyday social explanation. *Journal of Personal and Social Psychology, 46*, 961-978.

Miller, J. G. (1997). Theoretical issues in cultural psychology. In J. W. Berry, Y. H. Poortinga, & J. Pandey (Eds.), *Handbook of cross-cultural psychology: Theory and method* (Vol. 1, pp. 171-213). Boston, MA: Allyn & Bacon.

Mischel, W. (1973). Toward a cognitive social learning: Reconceptualization of personality. *Psychological Review, 80*, 252-283.

Nicholls, J. G. (1989). *The competitive ethos and democrative education.* Cambridge, MA: Harvard University Press.

Nicholls, J. G., & Miller, A. T. (1984). Reasoning about the ability of self and others: A developmental study. *Child Development, 55*, 1990-1999.

Peng, K., & Nisbett, R. E. (1999). Culture, dialectics, and reasoning about contradiction. *American Psychologist, 54*, 741-754.

Pepper, S. C. (1942). *World hypotheses.* Berkeley, CA: University of California Press.

Pervin, L. (1999). The cross-cultural challenge to personality. In Y.-T. Lee, C. R. McCauley, & J. G. Draguns (Eds.), *Personality and person perception across cultures.* Mahwah, NJ: Erlbaum.

Piaget, J. (1971). Theory of stages in cognitive development. In D. R. Green, M. P. Ford, & G. B. Flamer (Eds.), *Measurement and Piaget.* New York, NY: McGraw-Hill.

Shavelson, R. J., & Bolus, R. (1982). Self-concept: The interplay of theory and methods. *Journal of Educational Psychology, 74*, 3-17.

Shweder, R. A. (1990). Cultural psychology—what is it? In J. W. Stigler, R. A. Shweder, & G. Herdt (Eds.), *Cultural psychology: Essays on comparative human development* (pp. 1-43). New York, NY: Cambridge University Press.

Stern, D. (1985). *The interpersonal world of the infant.* New York, NY: Basic books.

Stigler, J. W., Smith, S., & Mao, L. (1985). The self-perceptions of competence by Chinese children. *Child Development, 56*, 1259-1270.

Triandis, H. C. (1989). The self and social behavior in differing cultural contexts. *Psychological Review, 96*, 506-520.

Urdan, T., Midgley, C., & Anderman, E. M. (1998). The role of classroom goal structure in students' use of self-handicapping strategies. *American Educational Research Journal, 35*, 101-122.

Watkins, D., Dong, Q., & Xia, Y. (1995). Towards the validation of a Chinese version of the Self-Description Questionnaire-1. *Psychologia: An International Journal of Psychology in the Orient, 38*, 22-30.

White, M. (1987). *The Japanese educational challenge.* New York, NY: The Free Press.

White, R. W. (1959). Motivation reconsidered: The concept of competence. *Psychological Review, 66*, 297-333.

Worlf, B. L. (1956). *Language, thought, and reality: Selected writings.* Cambridge, MA: Technology Press of MIT.

Yang, K. S., & Yu, A. B. (1988). *Social-oriented and individual-oriented achievement motivation: Conceptualization and measurement.* Paper presented at the symposium on Chinese personality and social psychology, 24th International Congress of Psychology, Sydney, Australia.

Yeung, A.-S., & Lee, F. L. (1999). Self-concept of high school students in China: Confirmatory factor analysis of longitudinal data. *Educational and Psychological Measurement, 59*, 431-450.

Yu, A. B. (1996). Ultimate life concerns, self, and Chinese achievement motivation. In M. H. Bong (Ed.), *The handbook of Chinese psychology* (pp. 227-246). Hong Kong: Oxford University Press.

CHAPTER 2

ETHNIC IDENTITY AND THE SOCIOCULTURAL PLAYING FIELD
Choices Made by Ethnically Mixed Adolescents in Hawaii

William L. Greene

I am Japanese by birth but American by upbringing, a combination that is frequently in conflict. Part of me wants to quietly acquiesce, but another wants to stand and scream about injustice. Part of me honors others' accomplishments, but another scrutinizes and questions. It may seem that these separate parts of me provide a behavioral strategy that permits me to fit into any situation. But these same separate parts sometimes cause me to stand apart from the thundering hordes—aloof, distant, and evaluative. (Adult H.S.U.P. Conference Participant, Honolulu, April 26, 1997)

INTRODUCTION: SETTING THE STAGE

Hawaii provided the context of study for this chapter in which I examine how adolescents of mixed ancestry come to understand themselves in relation to others. Just how the interaction of multiple variables such as ethnicity, gender, and residence in a particular community influences ethnic identity development is not fully understood. However, a relationship between perceived ethnic group membership and motivation in school has been suggested by a number of recent studies discussed below. This chapter explores how the sociocultural context—that is, the community in which ways of thinking and behaving are exchanged through interactions and interpersonal relationships—influences the construction of an ethnic identity. The discussion centers on adolescents of mixed ancestry from two different communities in Hawaii and looks at the implications of identity choices on the motivation to succeed in an academic environment. This discussion will:

a.   contribute to our knowledge of how the sociocultural context influences the ethnic identification of adolescents,
b.   promote sensitivity to some of the perceptions which shape students' cultural values, relationships, and behaviors, and
c.   help educators better understand how ethnic identity provides insight into school achievement.

ETHNIC GROUP MEMBERSHIP IN THE CONTEXT OF SCHOOL

A number of studies suggest that the ability of minority group members to achieve a positive and secure self-concept is linked to the way they come to understand their ethnic group membership within the larger society (e.g., Berry, 1993; Phinney, Chavira, & Tate, 1993; Rotheram-Borus, 1989; Whaley, 1993). Recent research on ethnic identification in minority adolescents has raised important issues and concerns regarding its influence on self-perceptions related to school achievement (Davidson, 1996; Ferdman, 1990; Fordham, 1988; Fordham & Ogbu, 1986; Henze & Vanett, 1993; Matute-Bianchi, 1986; Mehan, Hubbard, & Villanueva, 1994; Patthey-Chavez, 1993; Phelan, Davidson, & Cao, 1991; Powell, 1989; Welch & Hodges, 1997). Furthermore, the growing numbers of ethnically mixed individuals raise questions as to the importance and effect ethnic identification will have on their internalization of values and attitudes toward school. This chapter documents the salience of ethnic identity among adolescents of mixed ancestry by exploring their acquired ethnic self-perceptions, commitments, values, and self-knowledge.

Ethnic identity has been defined as the ethnic component of an individual's social identity (Patchen, 1995; Phinney, 1992). One's social identity derives from the knowledge of membership "in a social group (or groups) together with the value and emotional significance attached to that membership" (Tajfel, 1981, p. 255). Extending that definition, ethnic identity is also a "learned aspect of our overall personality development" (Smith, 1991, p. 185) which incorporates cultural knowledge and behavior that defines particular group membership. It is a psychological construct combining self-perceptions along three dimensions defined by Bernal and Knight (1993):

a.   self-identification,
b.   cultural knowledge of an identified ethnic group, and
c.   preferences, feelings, and values people hold about their ethnic group.

The ethnic and cultural features characterizing group identity become the basis for intergroup comparisons and can play a role in the construction of positive and negative self-images. These self-images become incorporated into one's self-concept, a multifaceted construct that combines, among other things, a person's own perceptions of their various experiences with other people's perceptions of that person (Shavelson & Bolus, 1982). School is one of the most influential contexts for acquiring and processing these types of self-evaluations (Ferdman, 1990; Davidson, 1996).

A REVIEW OF RELATED RESEARCH

Ferdman's (1990) description of an ethnic group's cultural identity incorporates aspects of the psychological and perceptual nature of identity construction along with the contribution of sociocultural stimuli:

> Group cultural identity has to do both with the particular features of the ethnic group and with the significance that is attached to these features [by the individual] in a societal context" (p. 190).

Ethnic identity is seen here as a dynamic and multifaceted construct, fluid enough to adapt and change over time and across situations (e.g., Davidson, 1996). New identities may form within distinct subgroups which combine cultural features in unique ways, producing a sense of being "both and neither" (Kich, 1992, p. 317) For instance, the Sansei (third generation) Japanese in Hawaii developed into a distinctly contextualized subculture that facilitated their bicultural behavior as both Japanese and Americans but which provided a unique identity shared among group members (Tamura, 1994).

Thus, ethnic identity is constructed out of the interaction of more universal cognitive and perceptual processes with more situated sociocultural phenomena which define the resources from which perceptions, value systems, and behaviors are derived. Because those resources incorporate the school and classroom, the relative significance of students' perceived ethnicities and associated values affect expectations regarding classroom goals and roles (Yamauchi, 1998). Bandura's (e.g., 1986) social cognitive approach provides another framework for understanding possible links between ethnic identification and aspects of self-perception more explicitly related to academic achievement. Bandura's work highlights the effect of environmental cues on internal mental processes and self-perception.

PERCEPTUAL AND ACADEMIC CONSEQUENCES OF ETHNIC GROUP AFFILIATION

A number of studies have indicated that a positive orientation toward one's racial or ethnic group predicts a higher level of self-esteem (e.g., Goodstein & Ponterotto, 1997; Helms, 1990; Phinney & Alipuria, 1990; Smith, 1991). Higher racial identity attitudes and ethnic identity, measured with different scales, were associated with higher self-esteem among Blacks. Among Whites, racial identity attitudes were not related to self-esteem and ethnic identity was only slightly (Goodstein & Ponterotto, 1997). This may indicate that the contribution of ethnic and racial identity to psychological well-being is stronger for some groups than for others. Smith (1991) asserted that individuals are generally more likely to be psychologically healthy when their identity is "anchored" in a sense of group membership as opposed to a marginal relationship between identity and group (p. 186). For instance, self-esteem among Blacks has been positively associated with community involvement and an appreciation of African-American heritage (Blash & Unger, 1995). In a study of an ethnically diverse group of college students, self-esteem correlated with ethnic identity among Asian American, Black, and Mexican American students (Phinney & Alipuria, 1990). One exception to the studies cited above occurred in research conducted in the Netherlands, where there was no relationship between the perceived importance of ethnic identity and self-esteem of majority and minority adolescent students (Verkuyten, 1995).

The salience of ethnic identity also appears to affect self-concept in the school context. The commitment to values and behaviors of a particular ethnic group may influence judgments related to different aspects of self-concept (e.g., self-esteem or self-efficacy). For instance, in a national study of African American youths, Bowman and Howard (1985) suggested that proactive orientations to perceived ethnic barriers can increase the sense of personal efficacy in an academic environment. Powell (1989) concluded the following from a review of research on African American students:

> Youth whose parents transmitted a consciousness of racial barriers were able to attain better grades than those who were taught nothing about their racial status... [suggesting] academic self-concept is enhanced by pro-social strategies for coping with racism and overcoming the blocked opportunities that youngsters may encounter because of racism. (p. 77-79)

Powell also stressed the importance of having cultural models of self-efficacy among significant and influential individuals in a student's life. Consistent with this, Mehan, Hubbard, & Villanueva (1994) described work with students which affirmed their cultural identity and fostered a recognition of discrimination and prejudice as an ideological barrier to academic success. The program promoted a positive group identity and provided opportunities for friendships with other academically oriented minority students.

These studies suggest a link between performance feedback, modeling, and perception of ability in an academic setting. It seems that the influence of negative academic feedback to groups in school settings affected the performance of students who identified with that group. The stronger students identified with the low scoring group, the more likely that feedback would lower the perception of one's ability within an academic setting. The examples of Powell (1989) and Mehan et al. (1994) have shown that strengthening cultural identity appears to broaden the opportunities and increase self-efficacy in minority students with traditionally fewer academic role models.

Ethnically derived attitudes, values, and affiliations may have a significant impact on the direction and intensity of adolescents' school-oriented behaviors and performance. For instance, research on students managing multiple identities within the sociocultural contexts of home and school has highlighted the relationship between identity construction and academic work (Davidson, 1996; Mehan et al., 1994; Patthey-Chavez, 1993; Phelan et al., 1991).

Other research has extended this issue to exploring the psychological tension created by the interaction of contradicting value systems—particularly with regard to the way identity is established and maintained (Henze & Vanett, 1993). This approach to minority education considers the school as a culture in itself, with its own inherent values, beliefs, and expectations for behavior, most often adopted from the dominant European-American society (Rogoff, 1990; Tharp, 1989).

A growing number of scholars have studied the tension that often exists for students between their ethnic or racial identification and their orientation on school achievement (Cross, 1991; Davidson, 1996; Fordham, 1988; Matute-Bianchi, 1986; Tatum, 1997; Welch & Hodges, 1997). Cross (1991) has argued for a multi-dimensional perspective of Black identity which recognizes there is more than one way to be Black. This is a particularly relevant position given that research on academically successful minority students shows they are often treated as somehow exceptions within their ethnic group who have sacrificed their ethnicity to the process of acculturation. The "path of least resistance" for many of these students may be to mitigate their academic expectations in order to maintain a sense of clarity about their ethnic identification.

Fordham (1988) described the conflict among high-achieving Black students who feel caught between striving for academic success and the subsequent social consequences of what they felt as the more collective nature of their Black American identity. Another example of this conflict occurred in a study of high achieving undergraduate minority students. Discussing how success in a science program affected her ethnic identity, one student remarked, "I knew I wasn't Mexican, but I knew I wasn't American either."

The students grasped science as different and challenging, giving them an identity that separated them from their other Mexican peers. The researcher thought it helped the students succeed that they shared both their ethnicity and their interest in science, a subject traditionally seen as individualistic and competitive (Sessoms, 1997). The presence of academically successful role models and peers who shared an ethnic identity undoubtedly helped these students to integrate perceptions of their ethnic and academic selves.

In a California high school, Matute-Bianchi (1986) found that among students of Mexican descent, those who identified themselves as Mexican or Mexican American did not view their ethnicity as being in conflict with the value of school achievement. However, the students who claimed a Chicano identity had to "choose between doing well in school or being a Chicano" (p.254). The Japanese Americans in the Matute-Bianchi study did not experience a conflict between the values associated with their ethnic identity and the values resulting in school success. As these examples suggest, ethnic identity as it is constructed socioculturally carries with it values, beliefs, and behaviors that contribute to academic outcomes.

Some minority students employ a strategy wherein they accommodate without assimilating (Gibson, 1988), thus enabling them to participate and succeed academically while remaining culturally distinct from mainstream society. However, Erikson (1984) described how Alaskan native youth viewed the acquisition of Western literacy as "a kind of metaphoric adaptation of a new ethnic group identity" and that their resistance to complete assimilation blocked their perception of full membership in either group (p. 539).

While education is generally regarded as a means to improving the future economic and political status of Hawaiian young people (Solomon, 1980; Yamauchi, Greene, Ratliffe, & Ceppi, 1996), the incongruities between the values, expectations, and socialization processes of home and school culture may still be a source of tension and resistance for many students in Hawaii (D'Amato, 1986; Howard, 1974). For example, despite recent increases in college enrollment among Native Hawaiian students, they are still under-represented in higher education and over-represented in special education (Melahn, 1986; Eshima, 1996). Solomon (1980) suggested that the socialization processes in American schooling are not congruent with the "cultural realities of Hawaiian communities" (p. 71), thus placing Hawaiian children at higher academic risk than other groups. Students' perceptions of themselves resulting from these incongruities appear to affect some of the behavioral and motivational constructs often associated with success in school.

In the context of school, students are not passive participants in the activities required of them, but actively engage in defining situations in the classroom (McDermott, 1974). They define situations, moreover, with reference to, and in order to serve, purposes within their ongoing relationships with one another at school (Davidson, 1996). Because schooling is a social activity where norms are defined largely by the dominant culture, the successful students learn to perform social roles, in addition to culturally or ethnically defined roles, which all contribute to their sense of self (Pallas, 1993).

GATHERING DATA

The Context

Life in Hawaii changed dramatically after Western contact around 1778, and so did the ethnic and cultural character of the population. Because an increasingly Western-style economy and the establishment of sugar plantations by foreign-born Caucasians required laborers, a continuous stream of immigrants from around the world, but mostly from Asia, began to establish residences, marry, and raise children in Hawaii (Tamura, 1994). This diversity resulted in high numbers of interethnic marriages and mixed ancestry offspring in Hawaii today (Johnson, 1992; Root, 1992). Today, no single ethnic group constitutes a majority among the student population in Hawaii (Kamehameha Schools, 1993).

Beyond the multiethnic milieu of the State, Hawaii schools provided another important reason to conduct ethnic identity research there; Hawaiians and other Pacific Island groups are underrepresented in the body of literature on ethnic identity formation. A recent study found evidence of systematic variance in ethnic identity salience among 580 adolescents in Hawaii based upon,

  a. their gender,
  b. whether they considered themselves mono- or multiethnic, and,
  c. whether they attended a rural high school on a neighbor island or a more diverse urban high school on Oʻahu (Greene, 1998).

These findings provided evidence of the role specific factors may have in the construction of ethnic identity.

The Participants

This study had both an interview and a survey component. While this chapter reports primarily on findings from the interview component, at times I have referred to comments from the written survey completed by students in their classrooms prior to the interviews. Twenty students from each of two high schools (n = 40) were chosen from a larger pool of students who had earlier completed the survey I conducted. The stratified sample included an equal number of 9th and 12th graders and an equal number of males and females in both grades. Twenty-four reported having more than one ethnicity and 16 reported a single ethnicity when asked which ethnic group or groups they belonged to. This approximated the demographic complexion of single and multiple ethnic identification in the State.

Students and the teachers were asked for their consent to participate in a one hour interview. Then, letters explaining the research accompanied permission slips and were sent home several weeks prior to scheduling any interviews. Each participant and his or her parent(s) were required to provide written consent.

The Interviews

Interviews were conducted on both school campuses during May and June 1997. A semistructured interview protocol was used. Students self-identified the ethnic group or groups in which they felt a membership. Specific topics were adapted from previous qualitative work on adolescent ethnic identity (e.g., Kerwin et al., 1993; Phinney & Chavira, 1995; Thompson, 1995) and from the three aspects of ethnic identity represented in Phinney's (1992) Multigroup Measure of Ethnic Identity (i.e., ethnic behaviors and practices, sense of group belonging, and ethnic identity achievement). Initial questions included: a) Do you spend much time thinking about your ethnic or cultural background? b) Does it make any difference at [name of student's high school] what you look like in terms of your ethnic background? c) Are any ethnic groups considered more desirable than others? and, d) What is it like for a person of mixed ethnicity at this school? Probes were used to encourage elaboration or clarification as comments were offered.

Each of the interview transcripts were initially coded by thematic categories. Those categories were: family, peers, school or community wide generalizations, ethnic self-identity, values, personal changes, intergroup relationships, ethnic group status, perceptions of ethnic groups, mixed ethnicities, differential treatment, and future plans. Initial categories evolved and new categories emerged as the transcripts were read and coded. Using the qualitative data analysis software QSR NUD*IST, the transcripts and coding were entered into the computer software's database. In addition to examining the categorical coding, demographic coding allowed for comparisons across various subgroups of students interviewed.

Demographic variables included: school, grade, gender, birthplace, years of residence, ethnicity (single or mixed), and household make up. Several dichotomous subcategories (e.g., status differences) permitted the use of frequency counts and percentages to establish students' level of agreement in reporting cultural or social knowledge.

WHAT THE STUDENTS SAID

The voices reported herein are those of the students, and a conscious effort has been made to authentically represent their ideas and examples.

Salience of Ethnic Identity

The salience of personal ethnicity and its meaning in the lives of the students varied widely across the interview sample. A summary of their comments is presented in Table 1. As Table 1 shows, comments explaining ethnic identification spanned a range from students referencing genealogical heritages and bloodlines to elaborations of the sociocultural nature of their ethnic identities and personal values. The quantity and depth of the narrative data referencing Hawaiian cultural identification exceeds the data referencing any other single ethnic group; and clearly, this was true at Rural High to a greater extent than it was at Urban High. When students at Rural High spoke about aspects of their ethnicity that were important to them, they more often mentioned individuals—usually family members—from whom values or knowledge were imparted. Urban High students more often spoke about the importance of adapting to "local" culture.

A number of students acknowledged the process of becoming part of the culture that surrounded them and the influence that culture had on their behavior. Although she is not Hawaiian by ancestry, Pamela at Urban High felt she identified more as a Hawaiian than as either of her ancestral ethnicities—Filipino and English. She found herself wanting to know about Hawaiians and how they used to live: "I think it's more a part of me cause it's all around me all the time, everyday. It's kind of hard to avoid, you know" (Text units 110-112).

However, in the same sociocultural community at Urban High, Steven was "kind of confused." His birth certificate read "Hawaiian-Caucasian" and reflected the ethnicities of his adopted parents, but Steven was aware of his Samoan and Black ancestry. He was asked which culture he would feel he most belonged to if he did not know about his blood connections or ancestors: "I would most likely belong to Hawaiian because that's how my family is, yeah." His perception of his affinity with the Hawaiian culture

TABLE 1
Summary of Comments in Personal Plane

Ethnic Identity Salience

	Urban High (14/20 = 60%)*	Rural High (19/20 = 95%)*
Females	I'm more local Japanese	Mixed, though identifies as Haw'n
	I think I'd like to know more	I take it more serious now
	Likes to learn about all cultures	Learning both sides of my ethnic heritage made my vision more great
	Adapts to cultures wherever	
	Hasn't based any decisions on it	Makes you feel special
	Hula helped me feel strong, more in touch with Haw'n ancestry; learned chanting, language	Likes when grandfather discusses culture
		Belongs to Haw'n culture even though Caucasian
		Hula and language important
		Thinks about ethnicity on special occasions
		Important not to lose culture
		Hawaiian history interests me
Males	Feels right to learn Illocano	Wanted to learn more
	Interested in Indonesian culture	Trip to Okinawa heightened interest
	Kind of confused	Need to be in touch with ethnic background
	More local than Filipino background	Important to identify as Haw'n; grandma teaches Haw'n language
	Mixed, though identifies as Japanese culture	Interested in Korean culture
		Important to learn cultural values and culture
		Appreciates Haw'n music, food, fishing
		Strong Haw'n sentiments; Haw'n name keeps with heritage
		Accepts being Filipino and Haw'n
		Learned from songs and teachings of Haw'n elderly

Examples of References to Ethnically-Derived Values

	Urban High	Rural High
Females	Family closeness important	Education and hard work
	Respect for elders	More welcoming, more aloha spirit
	Asking the gods for help	I sometimes think about other gods, even though I believe in one god
		Take care of your family first
		There's more than just one god
Males	Appreciates Polynesian value of sharing	Sharing, family, hard work
	Interested in Buddhism	Important to me to work hard
	Participates in Buddhist ceremonies but doesn't really believe in it	Relationship with environment
Notes:	*Number of students whose comments indicated some interest in their ethnic background.	

has formed, at least in part, through his identification with certain characteristically Hawaiian values which he described this way:

> *Steven:* Like there's a Hawaiian thing that we [should] share. Yeah, that's good. It sticks with me. And, only take what you want and take what you can eat. My other Polynesian friend thinks like I do.
> *Interviewer:* So where do you think you learned those values, those ideas?
> *Steven:* My family.

Stacy identified herself as Hawaiian because "I have more Hawaiian blood in me than any other ethnicity." But she also seemed more conscious of the importance of Hawaiian values to her sense of self than any of the others interviewed at Urban High. Stacy's remarks indicated a level of knowledge and understanding of Hawaiian culture and values that went beyond the cultural knowledge required in order to behave appropriately among peers or to think of oneself as a "local." Her family's chanting to the gods for help, learning the Hawaiian language, and dancing hula have been important to her in connecting to the ethnic part of her identity. Stacy described how hula contributed to her learning process and awareness:

> Like there's many ways, the moves, the ancient ways and then the modernized ways after the missionaries came. What certain plants mean when you're dancing hula. Certain moves, how you feel when you're dancing the song. You have to know what the song is about so you can express that song to everybody else.

Asked how hula affected her sense of being Hawaiian, Stacy replied:

> Hula helped me feel that, that I was strong. I felt more in touch with my Hawaiian ancestry, like learning the chants I could feel like how they would say your ancestor's voice coming out through yourself, and I could understand that.

Stacy's forthright articulation of Hawaiian values was more typical of the Rural High sample where many of the same kinds of references to Hawaiian culture surfaced but with more breadth across the sample and in greater numbers.

It is noteworthy that students appeared conscious, to some degree, of the values they were internalizing and used the comments about their ethnicities to display that awareness. In Wendy's case, she found that identifying with a Hawaiian background helped her "to relate better over here," even though in addition to Hawaiian, her ancestry included Filipino, Irish, Chinese, and Indian. Another aspect of Wendy's Hawaiian identity dealt with the issue of preserving culture, and she felt that she should "try not to lose your culture because it's very important."

Clayton is aware of the influences of both his Samoan and Hawaiian backgrounds. He was able to identify specific values and the way he tried to incorporate them into his life. After mentioning that his grandmother talked to him a lot about Samoan culture and history, he talked about what influence that had on him.

> *Clayton*: It has influenced me a lot because, um, I actually try to find ways to, you know, um, ways to I guess live my life, and with these values, Samoan values, you know such things as keeping families together and working hard in whatever you do. That's what I try to learn. I try to do in my own life as suppose to [in] Samoan culture, the background. And the Hawaiian culture also.

These remarks suggest a deliberate effort on his part to mold his values and behavior in accord with what he has observed and learned about Samoan and Hawaiian culture.

Keawe used his middle name as a primary name because "it keeps me with my [Hawaiian] heritage." In his comments there is evidence that a conscious internalization of selected cultural values is occurring.

> *Interviewer*: Do you spend much time thinking about your ethnic or cultural background?
> *Keawe*: Oh yeah.
> *Interviewer*: What kind of things do you think about?
> *Keawe*: I think about hunting, a lot. I like to sing songs in Hawaiian, play Hawaiian music.
> *Interviewer*: What would be some examples of how your Hawaiian background helps you relate to other people or think about your life?
> *Keawe*: It has taught me to treat others with respect and to not be afraid with anything . . . to take care of plants and animals. And make sure that our land that we live on don't fall into the wrong hands. Cause there are a lot of family burial grounds over there. And it's been in the family for a long time. To always stay strong in Hawaiian [culture].
> *Interviewer*: Where do you think that came from?
> *Keawe*: Songs and teachings from the elderly.
> *Interviewer*: From the elderly?
> *Keawe*: Yeah, from my grandpa when he was alive.

Keawe's comments were another example of how students used Hawaiian cultural activities or resources to explain the relevance of ethnicity in their lives. He not only names the values he has internalized, but also seems aware of the cultural resources from where those values were drawn. The activities he participates in allow Keawe to enact and strengthen his commitment to those values.

Gender Differences

Findings from the present study follow a trend found in other research indicating that women are closer to their ethnic identity than men (Ting-Toomey, 1981; Masuda et al., 1973). More females than males used culturally specific examples to explain their ethnicity, and they referred more often to culturally derived values which they had internalized. For example, nearly half of the females talked about the cultural importance of hula on their intrapersonal development. This appears to illustrate Ferdman's (1990) point that individuals attach significance to particular features of an ethnic group to establish identity in a broader cultural context. Individual choice (e.g., learning hula) derives from the availability of particular sociocultural resources (e.g., Hawaiian hula). Consistent with Bandura's (1986) social cognitive model, the individual's future behavior is shaped, at least in part, by internalizing values, beliefs, and attitudes acquired from activities in which they and their role models are engaged.

I returned to classes at both schools to share information about trends of the ethnic identity data being collected at their school and to elicit students' thoughts about why females tended to talk more about their connection to an ethnic identity than males. Students were encouraged to offer their thoughts about the results and to suggest possible explanations. In four of the classes revisited at Urban High—three 12th-grade and one 9th-grade—hula was given as a reason females may be more aware of their ethnic identity. Many females, it was pointed out, are part of a *halau*, or hula class. Through learning to dance, females also learn Hawaiian culture, tradition, and values. Activities for males tended to be less ethnic or cultural in nature; though some males participate in hula, the consensus among the students indicated that there was less status or peer approval for males who danced hula. Some felt this view might be changing to become more like it was in the hula tradition, more accepted and higher status for males to dance. Many students at Rural High knew males who danced hula, and they suggested the *ku'i* dance as an example of a dance that males do. For the present, males tend to get involved more with sports, surfing, and other outdoor activities than with the study of a traditional cultural practice like hula.

Students at Rural High felt that females compensated for the "activeness" of males, (e.g., sports, staying out later than girls, more freedoms in general), by spending more time in cultural activities, like hula or going to Japanese class. Consistent with this explanation, almost all of the females at Rural High and one at Urban High talked about the cultural connection they achieved through learning hula. Annette's interview highlights the affect of hula on her intrapersonal development:

Interviewer. Do you find yourself learning much about Hawaiian culture through the hula dancing?

Annette. Very much so.

Interviewer. What kinds of things do you learn?

Annette. We learn, like, traditions and, like, the values they had and how they express themselves through dance.

Interviewer. Would you say that's affected you in the way you see life or the way you live your life?

Annette. Oh yeah. It's, like, made my vision more great. It's like I can see everything from everybody's point of view instead of just having tunnel vision.

This example again illustrates how activity (such as hula) and accompanying values in a community becomes integrated into an ethnic identity.

In addition to the availability of hula, most of the 9th-graders in a different class at Urban High agreed that females had a stronger tendency to learn and follow values of the family. Harter's (1990) review of identity literature suggested that identity formation involves different expectations for males and females; males tend to perceive themselves as developing autonomously from others, whereas females tend to perceive themselves in terms of their relationships with others. Building on this idea, where relationships are formed in a context of ethnic or cultural distinctions, it follows that females may become more sensitized to the relational implications of their ethnic identification. Ethnic identity may be more salient for females than males because it affects the establishment of interpersonal and social networks. A male in one of the 9th-grade classes at Urban High speculated that there is a closer social or interpersonal network in Hawaii than on the mainland.

Harter (1990) summarized evidence indicating that females are more concerned with their appearance during adolescence than males; at the same time, females are more dissatisfied with the way they look. Consequently, females' self-esteem and related perceptions of themselves are generally more negative than boys. The opinions of others, particularly peers, may have greater impact on females' self-perceptions than on males'. Students in one 9th-grade class at Urban High came up with a similar explanation of why the opinions of others might be more important to females; in addition to thinking about themselves more, females also ask for self-assurance more often than males and are "scared" of embarrassment and failure (Period 1, personal communication, May 30, 1997).

Whether Harter's discussion of appearance includes ethnic appearance is unclear. But one Urban High female gave an example of her sensitivity to how others reacted to her light skinned complexion. She was part Caucasian, though she reported having "some Chinese" and "about 15% Hawaiian." When she attended a predominantly Hawaiian high school on O'ahu, she recalled that "some Hawaiian students" came up to her one day

TABLE 2
How Ethnically Mixed Individuals Are Viewed by Others

	Urban High	Rural High
Females	Nobody really cares	Being mixed can be an advantage (2)
	People want to know ethnicity if they can't tell	Depends on attitude
		Can be like an identity crisis
	Depends on what you mostly look like	Whatever they are they can fit in
		If they're mixed, they're proud of it
	If mixed and local, then treated same	Mixed is better than Caucasian treated same
Males	No different (2)	Easier if mixed, nobody cares (2)
	Depends on the person	Everybody mixes in
	Easier if mixed, nobody cares	He has no trouble being mixed
	Depends on attitude	Depends on what they are the most

and said something about her being *haole* (Caucasian). The incident bothered her so much that she transferred to another school. Her brother was not as affected by his appearing *haole,* and he stayed at that school. Girls may rely more on support from their ethnic group for identity validation because they may feel they are more attractive or accepted in the eyes of those who share certain physical qualities. Both genders may "turn to the social mirror" for self validation (Harter, 1990, p 368), yet females may develop an earlier need for recognizing their ethnic selves. These examples offer some understanding of why ethnic identity appeared more salient for female adolescents in this study than for males.

Experiences of Ethnically Mixed Individuals

Interview data included responses to questions about the experiences of ethnically mixed students. In the interview, students were asked whether the experiences or treatment of ethnically mixed students was different than the experiences or treatment of single ethnicity students. Transcribed data were coded for the presence of comments addressing this question and examined for similarities and differences among the categories of variables represented in this study.

No patterns of similar or dissimilar statements about the experiences of ethnically mixed individuals were identified on the basis of the categorical variables of interest in this study (i.e., school, grade, gender, and whether or not students were ethnically mixed). Furthermore, no students reported that being ethnically mixed would, by itself, make a peers' experiences more difficult in either context.

As Table 2 indicates, comments tended to support the general senti-
ment expressed across the entire sample that being mixed " doesn't matter" and may actually make it easier for students to fit in. Jay, an ethnically
Japanese senior at Rural High, incorporated an example from the popular
media's portrayal of multiethnic golfing star, Tiger Woods:

> I think it's easier, you know, [being multiethnic] because at least you can say
> "I'm part of this ethnic group" if by some chance right here [at Rural High]
> someone asked, "Oh, are you of this background?" I don't know. It's like
> Tiger Woods in a way, for example, because he's of so many ethnic back-
> grounds that they can't really stereotype him because they say he's Black, but
> he's also White, and he's also has Thailand or some other ethnic back-
> ground.

Several students mentioned that the experiences of multiethnic students may be affected by which of their ethnicities is regarded as the most
prominent, either by the individual or by others. With a heritage of four
ethnicities, Urban High senior, Arleen, thought a person's physical appearance would suggest a lot about a person's perceived ethnicity: "I think it
depends what they look like, actually ... whatever they look like most,
they'll probably end up hanging out with that kind of group of people."

Cody, a Japanese 9th-grader at Rural High, believed that the issue of fitting in ethnically would have something to do with which part of one's ethnic heritage was most prominently expressed:

> *Cody*: If somebody is mixed, it depends like what they really are. Like
>   what is their most, what they look like, like their most ethnicity,
>   their most person that they are. That determines if they're going to
>   fit in or not.
> *Interviewer*: Give me an example, then, of somebody who you think
>   would fit in.
> *Cody*: Like they look Hawaiian.
> *Interviewer*: Even if they're half haole, let's say?
> *Cody*: If they're half haole and half Hawaiian, they would fit in because
>   they have that little look, I guess.
> *Interviewer*: What if they're half Hawaiian and half haole but they look
>   more haole?
> *Cody*: Um, they might, yeah, they probably will, cause if they stayed one
>   half Hawaiian, if they say that, then they might fit in better.

Cody's comment may relate to Annette's suggestion that being perceived as mixed may be an advantage in certain situations over being perceived as "only Caucasian." Although at Urban High, Pamela wrote, "I am
50% of each race [Filipino and Caucasian] and interact with both cultures
just the same" (Excerpt from written classroom survey).

Sometimes multiethnic students seize on one of their backgrounds at the expense of others, according to Tanya whose ethnic heritages include Hawaiian, German, Tongan, and Filipino. A description of her experiences revealed a certain sense of loss when people ignore other ethnicities in their background at the expense of one. Jennie acknowledged that, for some people, having more than one ethnicity may create something like an "identity crisis." Though she knows that her ethnic background is both Hawaiian and Chinese, and though she relates most with her Hawaiian background, she said, "I just go with whatever. I don't really think about, like, 'Oh, who am I with? Am I Chinese or Hawaiian?' I just go."

Robert stated that he did not feel a conflict with recognizing the contribution of his two ethnicities, Filipino and Hawaiian. In fact, he identified with aspects of both and felt they were "moderately" important to his everyday life:

> I've always believed I was of both Filipino and Hawaiian, and I haven't had any trouble dealing with the fact that I was, you know, Filipino and Hawaiian. I just accept it. This is what I am.

Most students seemed to feel that ethnically mixed students adjusted as well or better to social life in the context of their schools than ethnically singular students. A few students, like Robert, thought it might actually be easier for ethnically mixed students to fit in because of their appearance:

> They wouldn't get picked on because of their ethnicity . . . somebody can be Filipino, Hawaiian, Chinese, Portuguese, and Japanese or something and they won't look very much like either one of them.

This example is consistent with other descriptions of Hawaii as an accepting context for ethnically mixed individuals (Johnson, 1992; Mass, 1992). However, several students seemed to feel that, at least on a physical level, some ethnicities (e.g., Hawaiian) might be more easily accepted than others (e.g., Caucasian). At some level then, an individual's physical appearance may trigger perceptions of stigma (if Caucasian) or advantage (if Hawaiian) that influences the initial response of others. One study noted that physical appearance may play a role in how people choose to identify depending on the degree of resemblance to one ethnic group or another; however, experiential and perceptual differences between two groups of people from mixed backgrounds (e.g., Eurasians and Afro Asians) " were largely based on the dominant societies' views and treatments of them" (Williams, 1992, p. 301).

This raises the question of whether one's claim to an ethnic identity will be recognized by others and under what circumstances. If it is acknowledged, for instance, that "cultural depth" (Nagel, 1994, p. 160) is one consideration in ethnic identification, how much consideration does it get compared to phenotype or blood quantum? For the ethnically mixed students in this study, cultural knowledge and appreciation provided a way of securing meaning and fitting in regardless of their blood quantum or ancestry. But do language, social class, adoption, or length of residence serve to further validate a person's claim to an ethnic group affiliation? How large a role will association with a higher or lower status ethnic category play in the identity choices of mixed heritage adolescents? The next section looks at perceived status differences and at examples of how those differences appear in the identity choices of adolescents at the two schools.

Status Differences

A statement was coded for status difference when students singled out one or more ethnic groups as having higher or lower status than other groups. Comparing comments about status differences in each school resulted in seven students (out of 20) at Urban High indicating a belief in the existence of status differences along ethnic lines and five students (out of 20) at Rural High indicating such a difference (Table 3).

Two Urban High students commented that higher status for Hawaiians was reflected in their being chosen more often as Homecoming Queen or for the May Day court, "and always like the runner ups are always Asian or something" (Tina). Shelli thought Hawaiians might have higher status because "it's one of the natural heritages here or something, so they feel they have a right to be here or something, so they feel stronger about it

TABLE 3
Status Differences Reported

	Urban High	Rural High
Highest Status*	Hawaiian (6)	Hawaiian (8)
	Samoan (1)	Filipino (3)
	Japanese (1)	Chinese (2)
		Japanese (1)
		Samoan (1)
Lowest Status*	Caucasian (3)	Caucasian (7)
	African-Americans (1)	Japanese (1)
	Korean (1)	Filipino (1)
	Filipino (1)	Hawaiian (1)
	Foreign Students (1)	

Notes: *Information combined from interview and survey data for each of the 40 interviewees.

and they would, they just band together and form this whole popular group thing." A female with "more Hawaiian blood in me than any other ethnicity" believed Hawaiians were the highest status group. Part of her explanation included that "there are many Hawaiians in the school, but I don't think it makes them popular." But she did feel that it was harder for a person born outside of Hawaii to fit in and be accepted. If that "outsider" happened to be Caucasian or *hapa* (half Caucasian and half other), then people who are "really into being Hawaiian" might treat them more criti cally based on the Hawaiian ancestors' experiences "like what the Hawaiian people went through in the past" (Stacy).

One explanation for the perceptions of status differences at Rural High came from Annette, a ninth grader, who identified her ethnicities as Hawaiian, Filipino, Caucasian, and Guamanian:

> If you're Hawaiian, it's sad to say, but you have to be Hawaiian in order to really, like, fit in with everybody else. Cause, well actually, not only Hawaiian. There's a lot of Filipinos and a lot of like Japanese and stuff that are coming and they have an easier time fitting in. But, it's like, if you're Caucasian, it all depends on how you present yourself to everybody. Cause, I don't know, a lot of my classmates, the boys especially, it's like if you're Caucasian, they tend to dislike you more than other races. You have to sort of like prove yourself to them.

A Japanese twelve grader (Jay) who was born and raised on the island, explained that "Caucasians are treated differently in Hawaii because they are labeled 'the people that stole the land from the Hawaiians'" (Excerpt from written classroom survey). Annette also thought the feelings some had toward Caucasians related to the period of early colonialism in Hawaiian history. According to Annette, a lot of the boys in her classes "blame the Caucasian people for taking away our United Kingdom. . . that's why they sort of take a disliking to Caucasian people." Yet, Annette had stated earlier that "ethnicity in this community really doesn't matter, cause like everybody's family, even though they moved here from someplace else."

The low status sometimes assigned to Caucasians was occasionally reflected in the way students referred to their Caucasian background when multiple ethnicities were indicated. Tanya discussed the dilemma she felt in choosing among her Tongan, Hawaiian, and German backgrounds when asked if she identified any more with one than with another:

> *Tanya*: It, well, depends. It's between Tongan and Hawaiian. I just leave German out.
> *Interviewer*: How come?
> *Tanya*: I no like explain why.
> *Interviewer*: Okay.
> *Tanya*: Um . . .
> *Interviewer*: Not, because it's Caucasian?

Tanya: Yeah.
Interviewer: So you're not interested in that part?
Tanya: Yeah.

By choosing to downplay her Caucasian heritage, Tanya may be responding, at least in part, to the social advantages of emphasizing her Polynesian heritage. While such decisions may also derive from sociocultural values and behaviors outside of school, perceptions of status differences in the testimonials presented above provide some evidence for the kind of identity pressure facing mixed heritage adolescents.

Students at both schools talked about a shared value of ethnic acceptance, though some comments seemed to contradict this ethos with examples of differential treatment. This suggests that racism, at some level, may still be a characteristic of the social fabric in both communities. Hawaiians were mentioned most often as having the highest status and Caucasians most often as having the lowest status. Further evidence of this came from comments explaining that some ethnicities would be more easily accepted than others. At the same time, most students felt that being ethnically mixed was not a detriment to adjusting to the social context of the school. In some cases students reported a social advantage to being ethnically mixed. But the majority thought, as Annette did, that the way an individual behaved would be more important than how they seemed ethnically to others:

> For here it really doesn't matter that much. It's like they no ask you, if like when you come to this school, they no ask you, oh what's your ethnic background? It's like if you...if you get along with everybody, everybody will get along with you.

In spite of this, comments about status differences appeared often enough to suggest that this is a salient aspect of ethnic relationships at both schools, at least in the mind of a sizeable segment of this sample. When juxtaposed to the often mentioned ethos of acceptance, this finding suggests a contradiction between ethnic perceptions at a community-wide level and those at an interactional level. The influence of such a contradiction on the formation of an ethnic identity is unclear, but it becomes more visible when the options of ethnically mixed individuals are verbalized. If perceptions of status differences cause an ethnic identity conflict for students in the "lower" groups, many of them would undoubtedly prefer a more inclusive identity among their peers at school to one relegating them to a group with less status. Liebkind (1992) asserted that children who are ashamed of their ethnic characteristics will avoid identifying with that ethnic group, while children who are proud of their ethnic group will make ethnicity a more salient aspect of their identity. It could also be the case that the threat of outsiders' values, which some may associate with Caucasian or foreign born students, triggers a negative reaction within students whose backgrounds include those ethnicities (Patchen, 1995).

It was clear from this study that establishing an identity link with "Hawaiian-ness" was important for many of the students interviewed. In fact, Hawaiian was repeatedly chosen as the most salient ethnicity in students' lives, even when it was one of several ethnicities from which to choose, as was the case with individuals of mixed backgrounds. In some cases, students talked about ignoring or de-emphasizing their hereditary claim to an ethnic group that was perceived as lower status or less popular. This is consistent with Nagel's (1994) claim that the choices people make about their ethnic identification can only be considered options within localized social and political restrictions, including "varying degrees of stigma or advantage" associated with particular ethnic categories (p. 156). Perceived variations in available (and desirable) options may help explain a pattern of differences observed between the two school communities studied. Urban High students talked more about a multiethnic local identity, where Rural High students talked more about a shared identity that integrated predominantly Hawaiian cultural characteristics. Some reasons for these differences and for variations in the sociocultural resources used in identity formation are offered in the next section.

Sociocultural Dimension of Identity Construction

Despite students' perceptions of ethnic differences at both schools, there was an overwhelming tendency for students to point out characteristics of a shared culture within the school—one that bridged the boundaries of ethnicity. In some respects, the school communities mirrored cultural characteristics present in the larger community. Even though many ethnic groups retain varying degrees of cultural distinctness in Hawaii, a long history of sharing cultural values and island lifestyles has established a pool of sociocultural resources from which individuals choose and construct identities. Individual ethnic awareness is a salient aspect of identity for many, yet in the two contexts studied, the sense of shared values at the community level appears at times to activate another layer of identity which blurs or supercedes individual ethnic identities. Clayton explained it this way:

> The immigrants I guess come here and then they have to take time to, you know, get used to situations here, and they have to learn and grow. But I guess when they're here, they still live their ethnic backgrounds, but they just...they live the traditions that are set here. And they just mix up I guess.

Clayton's insightful comment captures the idea of how one can simultaneously blend cultural features in a seemingly conscious way while remaining cognizant of ethnic differences. Such purposeful blending of identity resources is evidence of how different aspects of one's ethnic or cultural identity can be selectively activated in different situations.

Many of the students' other examples hinted at an intentionality in the selecting and combining of values, attitudes, and behaviors which were available to them as sociocultural resources. The individual agency expressed through the selecting of cultural elements depicts the dynamic interaction between the psychological and the social discussed earlier. Many of the students were even able to talk about how they had internalized values through participation in cultural activities.

One way of constructing an identity that contrasts to others in the same community is by "marking solidarity with a moral community and expressing loyalty to that community" (Shaw, 1994, p 84). In this way, individuals achieve a group identity, though not necessarily an ethnic one. Sometimes, instead of asserting ethnicity, an individual may pursue relationships based on other avenues of social status (Okamura, 1981) or on a plane of community-wide values that de-emphasizes ethnic categories. In the comments of an Urban High 9th-grader who took the survey and later discussed her reaction to the results, there is evidence of her group identity being directed, at some level, consciously: "I'm full Japanese, but I don't know much about it. I *choose* [italics added] to learn more about Hawaiian cultural things because it's like all around me" (personal communication, May 6, 1997). One Urban High female student who was taking the written survey stopped to ask about the item referring to her ethnic group and seemed somewhat confused by the question. "You know," she said with an air of conviction, "here we're all one group. Local." Several days before, the survey had ignited a lively discussion by three students in a 12th grade class at the same school who all agreed with the metaphor describing their community context as a local melting pot culture "because nobody's 100 percent anything."

While ethnicity is clearly not the only distinction these teenagers perceived, their comments about "one group" belie a tacit knowledge of the ethnic heterogeneity represented among them. Author Darrell Lum, whose works depict a "local" lifestyle in Hawaii, remarked that there is a sense of a local identity in Hawaii but that people also have an ethnic identity. Many mistake locals' concern for ethnicity as racism (D. Lum, personal communication, April 23, 1997). Lum's comment implies the coexistence of an ethnic consciousness and local consciousness that function simultaneously in identity construction.

If this observation of a local set of values that may partially transcend or co-exist with ethnic values is accurate about the ethnically diverse context of Urban High, it appeared at least as convincingly in the Rural High context. Other research has characterized Rural High's "somewhat homogenous community" as having an island-wide culture of its own wherein residents share many lifestyle values (Yamauchi et al., 1996, p 19). The Hawaiian cultural revival of the last 30 years has popularized Hawaiian traditions and values in both urban and rural communities (Linnekin, 1983). At the same time, Hawaiian ancestry has become a desirable model of ethnic identity for many young people, a pervasive influence on affiliations, values, and behavior around the state.

With an already high concentration of Hawaiians and part Hawaiians living in the Rural High community, it is not surprising that the island-wide culture referred to earlier includes many of the values important to Native Hawaiians. One might see the other ethnic groups on Rural Island as "marking solidarity" with these values as part of an acculturation process. It could also be the case that the values most compatible with the island have been incorporated into the more general cultural knowledge and identity people have as residents there. This relates to a point made by Knight et al. (1993) that when the agents of socialization, (such as family, peers, and teachers), communicate similar messages about the cultural norms and value system, children's values and behaviors are more predictable. As the messages in the socialization process vary, the values and behaviors of the children become more heterogeneous.

One reason why Hawaiian identity was expressed so consistently at Rural High may have had to do with a stronger implicit sense of Hawaiian cultural knowledge. When Rural High students used the phrase "we're all the same here," it seems to contain a message about their common understanding of Hawaiian culture. Urban High students' sense of being "local" seemed to contain a message about a set of norms and values in their community that included Hawaiian cultural knowledge, but which evoked an identity that existed separately from the borders evoked by ethnic identification. It was almost as though being local involved downplaying one's ethnic identity at Urban High, whereas at Rural High the examples of identifying with the community emphasized values which related specifically to Hawaiian culture. At Urban High, for instance, Howard did not think of himself as Filipino or Hawaiian, his two ethnicities, but as "more local." Bryce used himself as an exception in pointing out that his friends at Urban High "don't take as much pride in their ethnic background as I do." In contrast, at Rural High, Clayton demonstrated an awareness of how the community influenced his values orientation:

> I think it [his values] comes from being around, you know, this type of society. Cause in fact everybody you know, what you learn, is what society around you probably influences me to do. Such as, you know, aloha spirit, people being friendly, and courteous, and um, I guess caring for the land . . . things like that make you want to keep up the tradition and be the same as everybody else. So I try to live up to those expectations and stuff.

To identify with the island community and its values was more important than singling oneself out ethnically. Similarly, students at Urban High discussed themselves in terms of a local identity, though defining local values was, not surprisingly, a more ambiguous task for Urban High students than it was for Rural High students. Both communities have long histories of ethnic group coexistence evolving out of plantation era lifestyles, intermarriages, the "local" and the "outsider" mindset, and the renewal of interest in things Hawaiian. Yet, the students' identities were largely explained with examples of Hawaiian values which seemed to permeate the Rural High community's cultural norms. The examples at Urban High were less indicative of a single, monoethnic culture than they were used to emphasize a kind of consensual group identity in which ethnicity is acknowledged but not as salient as it appeared at Rural High. No doubt the presence of more Hawaiian students at Rural High than at Urban High was an important contextual difference that provides evidence for the situational nature of ethnic identity formation.

Takaki (1998) recognized ethnic identity as a complex and multidimensional construct that surfaces in varying ways depending on the sociocultural context. Ethnic identity is one layer of an individual's identity; there are also class, regional, and national identities. The latter may achieve salience or undergo transformation at different times in a person's life. In Hawaii, Takaki pointed out the shared identity of plantation workers as a class or the shared identification with American ideals co-existed with ethnic group identity. These other layers of identity served to unify diverse cultures. Takaki's explanation implies a dynamic, fluid characterization of identity that is responsive to the overlapping dimensions of interpersonal contexts in which people live and work. In particular situations, certain dimensions of an individual's identity may become more salient than in other situations. If it becomes important for individuals to identify as a laboring class, for instance, the salience of one's ethnic identity may diminish. This notion of identity responsiveness clarifies how adolescents in Hawaii might think of themselves as "local" in the context of a school's ethnic diversity and, in a different context, engage an ethnic sub-identity. In contrast to research based on cultural deficit models, adolescents in the present study who discussed the importance of two or more cultural groups did not indicate a sense of feeling marginalized. This concurred with a previous study in Hawaii which found no evidence for marginalization among mixed-race individuals (Johnson, 1992).

IMPLICATIONS FOR EDUCATORS

Constructing racial/cultural identities in a racist, culture-biased society is a demanding task, one in which democratic schooling must play a key role,

> particularly if we recognize that equality of treatment does not guarantee equality of opportunity. (Cohen, 1993, p. 308)

It has been suggested that a growing recognition for people of mixed heritage has begun among governmental and social groups across the United States (Phinney & Alipuria, 1996). As their numbers swell, multiethnic individuals will increasingly challenge the socially constructed categories of ethnicity and find their way into the critical conversations addressing educational equity and academic opportunities.

The analysis and discussion here have concentrated on the perceptual and sociocultural nature of identity formation among ethnically mixed adolescents. While the general salience of their ethnic identities varied in this study, there seems to be sufficient evidence in the interviews that many of these adolescents are actively, consciously engaged in the process of establishing an ethnic identity. Their comments reflect choices, attitudes, behaviors, and values that carry implications for the context of schooling, including: psychosocial development, academic self-efficacy, curriculum, and instructional practices. The question that emerges is: How do these examples of multiethnic identity formation address motivation, educational achievement, and equity?

One implication that can be derived from this research is that students need to have opportunities to explore personal and societal dimensions of ethnic identification. At a time in their lives when cognitive development allows adolescents to make statements about their personhood, they must also face the consequences of unexamined challenges that might impede or subvert academic opportunity. To this end, Cohen (1993) stated:

> . . . schools [should] go beyond transmitting knowledge about cultural groups to study race, gender, and class as dynamic, interacting social constructs.... Education that invites students to construct cultural knowledge should affirm all of our lived experiences, and engage students in designing their own educations through conscious study and construction of the world we live in. (p. 306-8)

Multiethnic students generally have even fewer cultural guideposts for self-understanding than so-called "monoethnic" students. Where a range of sociocultural options exists, as was the case of the multiethnic adolescents in this study, identity choices undoubtedly reflect a sense of having shared common experiences, values, and cultural practices with the chosen group(s). Those choices might not be obvious to educators who cling to racial and ethnic stereotypes or who rely on school records for cultural information. As students in the present study demonstrated, their identity choices seemed to derive uniquely through a process involving individual agency and sociocultural experiences, some adhering to one, others to several of their ancestral links to group membership.

Without cornering students into a "check all that apply" response, teachers can learn a great deal about issues that are meaningful to their students while providing opportunities for them to validate the multiple facets of their developing ethnic identity. It seems less relevant for the educator to know which ethnic group(s) a multiethnic student presumes they belong to than it is for the educator to understand the beliefs and values a student may attach to group membership. There are at least two reasons for this. First, because these values and beliefs are significant to the students, they are most likely to form self-beliefs that influence social and academic behavior. These values and beliefs become part of the perceptual filter through which individuals measure the importance and success of their work in school. Second, part of engaging students in curriculum is drawing them in through personally meaningful content and examples. As the questions about their multiethnic affinities surface, adolescents need social models and examples to help them validate and legitimize their ethnic feelings and, importantly, to give them a way of understanding how they might move beyond the monoethnic boundaries, real or imagined, imposed by others.

Educators should consider the kinds of activities that are available for students to participate in, including ways to involve positive role models in these activities from the ethnic community of the school. When observers perceive similarities between themselves and a model, they are more likely to conclude that they too might successfully perform the same task (Bandura, 1977). In this way, social comparisons influence what people think they can do. According to Zimmerman (1995):

> This is especially true in educational contexts where academic performances are subjected to a great deal of modeling and comparative evaluation. The successes and failure of others can affect one's own efficacy and motivation through perceived similarity. (p. 206)

Students with mixed ethnic backgrounds need opportunities to hear how ethnically-mixed adults came to understand what was important to them. For instance, a curriculum might include exposure to the thoughts and attitudes of others as students learn more about their own ethnicity. In the course of regular contact, students could explore how ethnicity becomes both an opportunity and an obstacle at the institutional level of society. A number of recent scholars, multiethnic themselves, have written about the excitement and relief expressed by multiethnic college students who, some for the first time in their lives, take a course on multiracial identity that allows them the freedom to explore their multiple heritages, feelings, and experiences (e.g., Williams, Nakashima, Kich, & Daniel, 1996). Clearly, multiracial students do face unique questions about who they are, questions made all the more troubling by a curriculum that ignores or oversimplifies its more traditional and categorical approach to ethnicity.

While several models of ethnic identity formation have been proposed, (e.g. Atkinson et al., 1983; Cross, 1978; Kim, 1981; & Phinney, 1989), little exists on the relationship of this process to the motivation and success of mixed-heritage individuals in the context of school. Further work in this area is needed to better understand the relationship between ethnic identity formation in a variety of sociocultural contexts and its impact on schooling. A theoretical model of this relationship may encourage broader inquiry in this field and may also provide a more concrete framework for educators to consider alternative strategies for meeting the diverse needs of their students.

REFERENCES

Atkinson, D., Morten, G., & Sue, D. W. (1983). *Counseling American minorities.* Dubuque, IA: Wm. C. Brown.

Bandura, A. (1977). Self-efficacy: Toward a unifying theory of behavioral change. *Psychological Review, 84,* 191-215.

Bandura, A. (1986). *Social foundations of thought and action: A social cognitive theory.* Englewood Cliffs, NJ: Prentice-Hall.

Bernal, M. E., & Knight, G. P. (Eds.). (1993). *Ethnic identity: Formation and transmission among Hispanics and other minorities.* Albany, NY: State University of New York Press.

Berry, J. W. (1993). Ethnic identity in plural societies. In M. E. Bernal & G. P. Knight (Eds.), *Ethnic identity: Formation and transmission among Hispanics and other minorities* (pp. 271-296). Albany, NY: State University of New York Press.

Blash, R. R., & Unger, D. G. (1995). Self-concept of African-American male youth: Self-esteem and ethnic identity. *Journal of Child and Family Studies, 4*(3), 359-373.

Bowman, P. J., & Howard, C. (1985). Race-related socialization, motivation, and academic achievement: A study of Black youths in three-generation families. *Journal of American Academy of Child Psychiatry, 24,* 134-141.

Cohen, J. (1993). Constructing race at an urban high school: In their mouths, their minds, their hearts. In L. Weis & M. Fine (Eds.), *Beyond silenced voices: Class, race, and gender in United States schools* (pp. 289-308). Albany, NY: State University of New York Press.

Cross, W. (1978). The Thomas and Cross models of psychological nigrescence: A literature review. *Journal of Black Psychology, 4,* 13-31.

Cross, W. E. (1991). *Shades of black: Diversity in African-American identity.* Philadelphia, PA: Temple University Press.

D'Amato, J. (1986). *"We cool, tha's why": A study of personhood and place in a class of Hawaiian second graders.* Unpublished doctoral dissertation, University of Hawaii at Manoa, Honolulu.

Davidson, A. L. (1996). *Making and molding identity in schools.* Albany, NY: State University of New York Press.

Erikson, F. (1984). School literacy, reasoning, and civility: An anthropologist's perspective. *Review of Educational Research, 54*(4), 525-546.

Eshima, M. (1996). *The native Hawaiian data book.* Honolulu, HI: Office of Hawaiian Affairs.

Ferdman, B. M. (1990). Literacy and cultural identity. *Harvard Educational Review, 60*(2), 181-204.

Fordham, S. (1988). Racelessness as a factor in Black students' school success: Pragmatic strategy or pyrrhic victory? *Harvard Educational Review, 58*(1), 54-84.

Fordham, S., & Ogbu, J. U. (1986). Black students' school success: Coping with the 'burden of acting White.' *Urban Review, 18*(3), 176-206.

Gibson, M. (1988). *Accommodation without assimilation: Sikh immigrants in an American high school.* New York, NY: Cornell University Press.

Goodstein, R., & Ponterotto, J. G. (1997). Racial and ethnic identity: Their relationship and their contribution to self-esteem. *Journal of Black Psychology, 23*(3), 275-292.

Greene, W.L. (1998). *Determinants of ethnic identity among adolescents in Hawaii.* Unpublished doctoral dissertation, University of Hawaii, Honolulu.

Harter, S. (1990). Self and identity development. In S. S. Feldman & G. R. Elliot (Eds.), *At the threshold: The developing adolescent* (pp. 352-387). Cambridge, MA: Harvard University Press.

Helms, J. (1990). *Black and White racial identity: Theory, research, and practice.* New York, NY: Greenwood.

Henze, R., & Vanett, L. (1993). To walk in two worlds—or more? Challenging a common metaphor of native education. *Anthropology and Education Quarterly, 24*(2), 116-134.

Howard, A. (1974). Aspects of self-esteem among Hawaiian-Americans of the parental generation. In W. P. Lebra (Ed.), *Youth, socialization, and mental health* (pp. 87-95). Honolulu, HI: University of Hawaii Press.

Johnson, R. (1992). Offspring of cross-race and cross-ethnic marriages in Hawaii. In M. P. P. Root (Ed.), *Racially mixed people in America.* Newbury Park, CA: Sage.

Kamehameha Schools. (1993). *Native Hawaiian educational assessment: 1993 summary report.* Honolulu, HI: Kamehameha Schools/Bishop Estate.

Kerwin, C., Ponterotto, J. G., Jackson, B. L., & Harris, A. (1993). Racial identity in biracial children: A qualitative investigation. *Journal of Counseling Psychology, 40*(2), 221-231.

Kich, G. K. (1992). The developmental process of asserting a biracial, bicultural identity. In M. P. P. Root (Ed.), *Racially mixed people in America* (pp. 304-317). Newbury Park, CA: Sage.

Kim, J. (1981). *The process of Asian-American identity development: A study of Japanese American women's perceptions of their struggle to achieve positive identities.* Unpublished doctoral dissertation, University of Massachusetts.

Knight, G. P., Bernal, M. E., Garza, C. A., & Cota, M. K. (1993). A social cognitive model of the development of ethnic identity and ethnically based behaviors. In M. E. Bernal & G. P. Knight (Eds.), *Ethnic identity: Formation and transmission among Hispanics and other minorities* (pp. 213-234). Albany, NY: State University of New York Press.

Liebkind, K. (1992). Ethnic identity: Challenging the boundaries of social psychology. In G. M. Breakwekk (Ed.), *Social psychology of identity and the self-concept* (pp. 147-185). London: Surrey University Press.

Linnekin, J. (1983). Defining tradition: Variations on the Hawaiian identity.*American Ethnologist, 10,* 241-252.

Mass, A. I. (1992). Interracial Japanese Americans: The best of both worlds or the end of the Japanese American community? In M. P. Root (Ed.),*Racially mixed people in America* (pp. 265-279). Newbury Park, CA: Sage.

Masuda, M., Hasegawa, R., & Matsumoto, G. (1973). The ethnic identity questionnaire: A comparison of three Japanese age groups in Tachikawa, Japan, Honolulu, and Seattle. *Journal of Cross-Cultural Psychology, 4,* 229-244.

Matute Bianchi, M. E. (1986). Ethnic identities and patterns of school success and failure among Mexican-descent and Japanese-American students in a California high school: An ethnographic analysis. *American Journal of Education, 95,* 233-255.

McDermott, R. (1974). Achieving school failure: An anthropological approach to illiteracy and social stratification. In G. Spindler (Ed.),*Education and cultural process.* New York, NY: Holt, Rinehart and Winston.

Mehan, H., Hubbard, L., & Villanueva, I. (1994). Forming academic identities: Accommodation and assimilation among involuntary minorities.*Anthropology and Education Quarterly, 25*(2), 91-117.

Melahn, C. L. (1986). *An application of an ecological perspective to the study of educational achievement among Native American Hawaiians.* Unpublished doctoral dissertation, University of Hawaii, Honolulu.

Nagel, J. (1994). Constructing ethnicity: Creating and recreating ethnic identity and culture. *Social Problems, 41*(1), 152-176.

Okamura, J. (1981). Situational ethnicity.*Ethnic and racial studies, 4*(4), 452-465.

Pallas, A. (1993). Schooling in the course of human lives: The social context of education and transition to adulthood in industrial society. *Review of Educational Research, 63*(4), 409-447.

Patchen, M. (1995). Ethnic group loyalties and societal strife.*International Journal of Group Tensions, 25*(3), 227-245.

Patthey-Chavez, G. (1993). High school as an arena for cultural conflict and acculturation for Latino Angelinos. *Anthropology and Education Quarterly, 24* (1), 33-60.

Phelan, P., Davidson, A. L., & Cao, H. T. (1991). Students' multiple worlds: Negotiating the boundaries of family, peer, and school cultures.*Anthropology and Education Quarterly, 22,* 224-250.

Phinney, J. (1989). Stages of ethnic identity development in minority group adolescents. *Journal of Early Adolescence, 9,* 34-49.

Phinney, J. (1992). The Multigroup Ethnic Identity Measure: A new scale for use with adolescents and young adults from diverse groups.*Journal of Adolescent Research, 7,* 156-176.

Phinney, J., & Alipuria, L. (1990). Ethnic identity in college students from four ethnic groups. *Journal of Adolescents Research, 13,* 171-183.

Phinney, J., & Alipuria, L. (1996). At the interface of cultures: Multiethnic/multiracial high school students. *The Journal of Social Psychology, 136*(2), 139-158.

Phinney, J., & Chavira, V. (1995). Parental ethnic socialization and adolescent coping with problems related to ethnicity. *Journal of Research on Adolescence, 5*(1), 31-53.

Phinney, J., Chavira, V., & Tate, J. (1993). The effect of ethnic threat on ethnic self-concept and own group ratings.*Journal of Social Psychology, 133*(4), 469-478.

Powell, G. J. (1989). Defining self-concept as a dimension of academic achievement for inner-city youth. In G. L. Berry & J. K. Asamen (Eds.), *Black students: Psychological issues and academic achievement* (pp. 69-82). Newbury Park, CA: Sage.

Rogoff, B. (1990). *Apprenticeship in thinking: Cognitive development in social context.* New York, NY: Oxford University Press.

Root, M. P. P. E. (1992). *Racially mixed people in America.* Newbury Park, CA: Sage.

Rotheram-Borus, M. J. (1989). Ethnic differences in adolescents' identity status and associated behavior problems. *Journal of Adolescence, 12,* 361-374.

Sessoms, D. (1997). *Issues of identity in undergraduate minority students studying science: Are you a sell out if you're academically successful?* Paper presented at the annual meeting of the American Educational Research Association, Chicago, IL.

Shavelson, R., & Bolus, R. (1982). Self-concept: The interplay of theory and methods. *Journal of Educational Psychology, 74,* 3-17.

Shaw, T. (1994). The semiotic mediation of identity. *Ethos, 22*(1), 83-119.

Smith, E. J. (1991). Ethnic identity development: Toward the development of a theory within the context of majority/minority status. *Journal of Counseling & Development, 70,* 181-188.

Solomon, A. L. (1980). *Cross-cultural conflicts between public education and traditional Hawaiian values.* Unpublished doctoral dissertation, Oregon State University.

Takaki, R. (1998, July 16). The national dialogue on race: A view from Hawaii. *Asian Week,* 5.

Tajfel, H. (1981). *Human groups and social categories: Studies in social psychology.* New York, NY: Cambridge University Press.

Tamura, E. H. (1994). *Americanization, acculturation, and ethnic identity: The Nisei generation in Hawaii.* Chicago, IL: University of Illinois Press.

Tatum, B. D. (1997). *"Why are all the Black kids sitting together in the cafeteria?" and other conversations about race.* New York, NY: Basic Books.

Tharp, R. (1989). Psychocultural variables and constants: Effects on teaching and learning in schools. *American Psychologist, 44,* 349-359.

Thompson, V. L. S. (1995). Sociocultural influences on African-American racial identification. *Journal of Applied Social Psychology, 25*(16), 1411-1429.

Ting-Toomey, S. (1981). Ethnic identity and close friendship in Chinese-American college students. *International Journal of Intercultural Relations, 5,* 383-406.

Verkuyten, M. (1995). Self-esteem, self-concept stability, and aspects of ethnic identity among minority and majority youth in the Netherlands. *Journal of Youth and Adolescence, 24*(2), 155-175.

Welch, O. M., & Hodges, C. R. (1997). *Standing outside on the inside: Black adolescents and the construction of academic identity.* Albany, NY: State University of New York Press.

Whaley, A. (1993). Self-esteem, cultural identity, and psychosocial adjustment in African American children. *Journal of Black Psychology, 19*(4), 406-422.

Williams, T. (1992). Prism lives: Identity of binational Amerasians. In M. Root (Ed.), *Racially mixed people in America* (pp. 280-303). Newbury Park, CA: Sage.

Williams, T.K., Nakashima, C.L., Kich, G.K., & Daniel, G. R. (1996). Being different together in the university classroom: Multiracial identity as transgressive education. In M.P.P. Root (Ed.), *The multiracial experience: Racial borders as the new frontier* (pp. 359-379). Thousand Oaks, CA: Sage.

Yamauchi, L. A. (1998). Individualism, collectivism, and cultural compatibility: Implications for counselors and teachers. *Journal of Humanistic Education and Development, 36,* 189-198.

Yamauchi, L., Greene, W., Ratliffe, K., & Ceppi, A. (1996, April). *Rural island culture and education: Native Hawaiians on Moloka'i.* Paper presented at the American Educational Research Association, New York, NY.

Zimmerman, B. J. (1995). Self-efficacy and educational development. In A. Bandura (Ed.), *Self-efficacy in changing societies* (1st ed., pp. 202-231). New York, NY: Cambridge University Press.

CHAPTER 3

SELF-SCHEMA, MOTIVATION AND LEARNING
A Cross-Cultural Comparison

Chi-hung Ng and Peter Renshaw

INTRODUCTION

This chapter examines differences in students' academic self-schemas in two cultural contexts, namely, Australia and Hong Kong. As a child, the first author, Ng, attended school in Hong Kong and eventually taught in the Hong Kong system before moving to Australia to complete doctoral studies. Like many educators and researchers, he puzzled over the dramatic differences in the motivation of students both within and between cultural contexts. This chapter represents one of the outcomes of this process of puzzlement, inquiry and search for understanding. We argue below that a focus on students' self-schemas provides an integrated approach to investigating motivational differences within and between cultural contexts. We suggest that cultural and contextual factors create subtle but important differences in the academic self-schemas of successful and unsuccessful students. Aside from the concern with the consistency of the effects of self-schemas on learning across cultures, cross-cultural comparisons provide insights into how certain salient cultural values influence students' self-schemas, motivational qualities and learning behaviors. These cultural values can be taken collectively as a form of cultural model of success (c.f. D'Andrade & Strauss, 1992). We argue that the different cultural models of success operating in Hong Kong and Australia influence students' self-schemas.

Academic self-schemas consist of students' cognitive generalizations of their selves derived from their past experiences in learning a subject (see Markus, 1977). Similar to self-schemas of personality traits (Singer & Salovey, 1991; Taylor & Crocker, 1981; Thompson, 1985), the generalized knowledge about the self in a subject domain is believed to be highly elaborated, organised and integrated (Lips, 1984). When a student has developed a positive self-schema regarding the learning of a specific school subject from diverse experiences over time, it becomes a central part of his or her desired self-conception (*I am a good mathematics student. Studying mathematics is a vital part of myself*) and can provide great motivational energy to persist at learning tasks. Such self-schemas then can serve as a frame for interpreting incoming stimuli related to this learning endeavor and determine affective, cognitive and behavioral responses. (*My teacher gave me this difficult exercise. I had better spend more time on it; otherwise, I may miss something important*). Over time, a repertoire of subject specific skills, strategies and knowledge develops (*I think I should review these equations and my notes first before I do this difficult exercise*). One of the advantages of conceptualizing motivation in terms of self-schemas, therefore, is the provision of a theoretical frame through which identity, learning and emotion can be integrated.

Although it has been difficult to find a commonly agreed definition of the self, its importance as a source of motivation has generally been accepted (Borkowski, Carr, Rellinger & Pressley, 1990). Many studies have afforded the notion of self a prime position in regulating intentions and behaviors (Cantor, Markus, Niedenthal & Nurius, 1986; Fordham & Ogbu, 1986; Greenwald, 1980; Little, 1993). Recently there has been a call to put the *self* back in the foreground of research on students' motivation (see for example, McCombs, 1991; McCombs & Marzano, 1990; McCombs & Whisler, 1989). We have much to learn from the work of social psychologists who have consistently placed heavy emphasis on the self in understanding motives, intentions and behaviors. In particular, the *self*, conceptualized as a constellation of self-schemas has been studied widely by social psychologists. Following Hazel Markus' (1977) seminal study, social psychologists have established a clear theoretical and empirical basis for research on self-schema. Among educational psychologists, Pintrich (1994) and Murphy and Alexander (2000) have argued that the self-schema concept can advance our understanding of motivation and learning. Our work can be taken as a timely response to these calls and a contribution to the development of this important psychological concept in educational psychology. In the following sections of this chapter, we first review the research on self-schemas, and then report findings from our cross-cultural investigation.

RESEARCH ON SELF-SCHEMA

Self-schemas are cognitive generalizations about the self, derived from past experiences in a specific domain (Markus, 1977). They represent a central store of information related to the self in the long-term memory, either in the form of episodic memories of the self (e.g. I stuttered during my presentation last week) or general abstractions of one's experiences in a specific domain in an organized manner (e.g. I am a poor presenter). These forms of declarative knowledge about the self may include physical characteristics, attitudes and preferences and behavioral regularities (Alexander, 1997). According to Alexander (1997), self-schemas also provide incentives, standards, plans, rules and scripts for behaviors. As such, self-schemas should have important causal effects on students' motivation and learning.

In her original work, Markus (1977) studied 48 female undergraduates in the domain of dependence-independence. According to their self-descriptions and response latency to a list of words related to dependence and independence, Markus classified the sample into three groups: dependent schematics, independent schematics and aschematics. It was found that the schematics differed from the aschematics in their performance on several cognitive tasks related to the processing of self-information in the independence-dependence domain. More specifically, independent schematics endorsed significantly more independence-related adjectives than did aschematics. They also required a shorter processing time to judge whether an adjective related to the dependence-independence dimension was self-descriptive. In addition, they could supply relatively more specific behavioral examples of independence, and they thought they were more likely to engage in future independent behaviors. Furthermore, they were resistant to accepting counter-schematic information about themselves. A parallel pattern of cognitive performance was found with the dependent schematics relative to the aschematics. Markus explained the difference in the performance of schematics and aschematics in terms of the presence or the absence of a well-developed categorization system of the self with regard to the dependence-independence dimension.

Following Markus, subsequent studies focussed on the information processing patterns of schematic and aschematic individuals regarding various personality traits (e.g. Bruch, Kaflowitz & Berger, 1988; and Fong & Markus, 1982), sex roles (e.g. Markus, Crane, Berstein & Siladi, 1982; and Markus, Smith & Moreland, 1985), and physical attributes (e.g. Altabe & Thompson, 1996; Andersen & Cyranowski, 1994). These studies showed that information that is congruent with the self-schemas will be processed faster and deeper, whereas incongruent information is resisted. Self-schemas can facilitate the encoding and recall of self-referent stimuli. In an ambiguous situation where information is not supplied fully, self-schemas function as a reference point to facilitate interpretation and processing.

This is called the "filling in" effect of self-schemas (Markus & Smith, 1981). In addition, these *intra*-individual differences in information processing as a result of the presence of a self-schema were also found during *inter*personal information processing (Fong & Markus, 1982; Lewicki, 1983, 1984; Markus & Smith, 1981; and Markus & et al., 1985).

While there is considerable research on self-schemas in applied fields of psychology (see Ng, 1999 for a review), limited work has been done among educational psychologists. Lips (1984, 1985, and 1995) is among the few who have studied self-schemas in relation to choice of mathematics and science subjects. Using an undergraduate sample of female students, she classified participants into positive and negative schematics in math/science ability according to the results of a self-descriptive judgment task. She found that the relatively low participation rate of female students in mathematics and science was not related to their ability per se but rather to their negative self-schemas in math/science.

Martinot and Monteil (1995) provided empirical evidence for the nature and functions of self-schemas among secondary students. Following Markus' design in their study of 73 Year 8s and 79 Year 9s in France, Martinot and Monteil classified the students into success, average and failure schematics according to their rating on items related to academic success (e.g. *do you think you are academically successful?*), the importance of academic success in general (e.g. *do you think it is important to be a good student?*) and the personal importance attached to academic success (e.g. *do you think it is important for you to be a good student?*). Their findings confirmed that the three groups differed as expected in the speed of processing self-descriptive traits for success and failure. Nonetheless, many students in the failure group still chose positive self-descriptions, suggesting that self-presentation bias may mask negative self-schemas in some students.

Garcia and Pintrich (1993, 1994) have made the most concerted effort in applying the self-schema concept to research on learning and motivation. They proposed a detailed theoretical model for studying the effects of self-schemas on learning. In their model, a self-schema is a composite concept consisting of four complementary dimensions, namely, affect, temporality, importance and efficacy. The affect dimension denotes that people's affective state will be influenced by their current self-understanding. The temporal dimension distinguishes between the past, present and future selves. The value dimension taps into the centrality and importance of a self-schema in defining one's identity or core conception. The efficacy dimension refers to the belief that one has the ability to attain, maintain or avoid a particular self-conception. Garcia and Pintrich (1993) employed this multidimensional model to explore the relationship between the self-schemas of good and poor students, their learning strategies and specific motivational states such as defensive pessimism and self-handicapping strategies. The "good student" schema was composed of a collection of behaviors (understanding everything that teachers explain; finishing class work on time; paying attention when teacher is talking; and following directions while doing class work). Similarly, the "bad student" schema was demonstrated by another set of less desirable behaviors (needing help from classmates; having a hard time finishing homework assignment; not knowing the answer when called on by teacher; being late for class without an excuse; being sent to the principal's office; and talking during class time). The temporal dimension was examined by asking students to respond to the questions "*how much are you like this now?*" and "*how likely will this describe you five years from now?*" Students were also assessed on the value and efficacy dimension of their present and possible "good" or "bad" self-schemas by answering questions like "*how important is being/not being this way in the overall way you think about yourself?*" and "*how sure are you that you can do things to make yourself stay the same/change the way you are?*"

Participants with the present and possible 'good student schema' reported a greater use of volitional strategies. They showed higher levels of control over their attention, encoding and environment during study sessions. The reverse was true for students who saw themselves as bad students now and thought they would be become bad students in the future. In addition, motivational strategies were associated with students' current and future self-schemas. Specifically, students characterized by self-handicapping strategies endorsed a bad student self-schema, however, those who employed defensive pessimistic strategies, characterized by an intense expenditure of effort despite having low expectation and high anxiety, oriented towards a good student self-schema.

In the studies reported below, Garcia and Pintrich's model was adapted to investigate the effects of self-schemas on learning and motivation. Initially, two studies were conducted with year 10 students in Brisbane to explore the predictive power of self-schemas in mathematics on achievement goals (Ng, 1997 & 1998). In these two studies, self-schemas and two environmental variables (teacher's teaching goals and the students' relationship with teacher) were taken as the independent variables, and students' achievement goals as the dependent variables. A self-schema was considered as a hypothetical concept measured through manifested variables including affect, efficacy, temporality and importance. In line with the assumption that the various dimensions of a self-schema form an integrated whole (c.f. Lips, 1984; Singer & Salovey, 1991), we assumed that a student with a positive self-schema in learning mathematics would consider the successful learning of the subject important, would be willing to expend effort to maintain such a self-conception, feel happy about the learning, and have a strong intention to do more mathematical subjects in the future. Therefore, unlike Garcia and Pintrich (1993) who treated these dimensions as separate indicators of a self-schema, we maintained that these schematic dimension were closely related. Therefore, the self-schema concept in the series of studies reported below was considered as a composite variable formed by collapsing the four dimensions into a single higher-order factor called "self-schema in learning mathematics." This theoretical position was supported by factor analyses.

In the first study (Ng, 1997), it was found that a self-schema predicted the pattern of achievement goals held by students and its predictive power outweighed that of the environmental variables (teacher's teaching goals and relationship with teacher). Achievement goals in this study involved the commonly studied mastery and performance goals found in the achievement goal literature (e.g. Ames, 1992; Dweck, 1986; Nolen, 1988; Pintrich & De Groot, 1990). Mastery goals orient students to focus overtly on the task and learning. Students with mastery goals are intrinsically motivated and their aim is to improve comprehension and achieve mastery. In contrast, performance goals are concerned with achievement levels, ability demonstration and comparison. Students with such goals will focus on their ability to perform and comparison with the performance of others. Therefore, performance goals are extrinsic in nature (Ames, 1992; Dweck & Leggett, 1988; Urdan, 1997). In addition, two extra goals were included in this investigation. First, we proposed that students might learn in order to utilize its benefit for fulfilling other important desires like gaining entry to a specific university program. We called this form of achievement orientation "functional goals" because students' focus is on the utility values associated with a specific course of learning. The construction of the functional goals is in line with the concept of extrinsic utility value in the expectancy-value model (Wigfield & Eccles, 1992). Second, we also tested students' prosocial behaviors, which included helping their friends to learn, working with friends in a group and in general trying to be useful to the society. This social form of achievement orientation was labelled "social solidarity goals" in these studies, which is similar to social affiliation goals defined in Dowson and McInerney's qualitative investigation (2001) on social goals. Specifically, our findings showed that a self-schema predicted strongly the endorsement of mastery and functional goals, moderately the endorsement of social solidarity goals and relatively weakly performance goals.

The second study (Ng, 1998), involving 265 Year 10 students from Brisbane, confirmed the predictive power of self-schemas in relation to achievement goals. A self-schema was the most important variable in the equations predicting the endorsement of particular learning goals. The uniqueness index, U, (Hatcher, 1994) demonstrated that the amount of variance in each learning goal accounted for by self-schema was 51 percent ($U = .51$, $p < .001$) for mastery goals, 32 percent ($U = .32$, $p < .001$) for functional goals and 16 percent ($U = .16$, $p < .001$) for social solidarity goals. However, its predictive power was relatively weak with performance goals (7 percent; $U = .07$, $p < .001$).

These two studies together showed the importance of a self-schema in predicting the endorsement of achievement goals that previous research had linked to adaptive and less adaptive learning strategies. Therefore, we decided to expand the study of the effects of self-schemas on other variables related to learning. We proposed that a self-schema in learning mathematics could be taken as an independent variable influencing *why* and *how* students engage in learning the subject, as well as *how well* they perform. Achievement goals, defined as students' perceived purposes for learning could be taken as the indicators for *why* students engage in learning mathematics. Mastery and performance goals were selected as two major constructs for assessing students' purposes in learning mathematics. Approaches to learning (Biggs, 1987) were taken as an indication of *how* students engage in learning mathematics. Past research on secondary students' approaches to learning using Learning Process Questionnaire (LPQ) developed by Biggs (1987) has consistently yielded three different approaches, deep, achieving and surface. Each approach is characterised by a congruent mix of motives and strategies. A deep approach is characterized by an intrinsic interest in the learning materials and the use of deep strategies securing understanding and comprehension. In contrast, a surface approach is instrumental in nature. Students adopting this approach will learn with reproducing strategies to meet learning requirements minimally. An achieving approach is based on the notion of competition and ego enhancement. Students with such an approach will work in an organized and regulated manner in order to attain the highest achievement disregarding whether the learning materials are interesting. The use of approaches to learning for assessing how students learn mathematics in our study is highly relevant, as past research using Hong Kong (e.g. Biggs, 1989; Wong, Lin, & Watkins, 1996) and Australian (e.g. Biggs, 1979 & 1987) samples provided empirical evidence for the validity and reliability of these constructs.

In short, we proposed that a self-schema, achievement goals, approaches to learning and achievement level can be conceptualised in a linear model (Ng, 1999), implying that a self-schema will influence motivational and learning processes, and eventually learning results. This theorization of the effects of a self-schema on motivation and learning is in line with the interpretive functions of a self-schema consistently found in past social psychological studies. In the following sections, we first explain the linkages between various variables in the proposed linear model, and subsequently the results of a cross-cultural study testing the validity of this model are presented and discussed

THE HYPOTHESIZED MODEL

The hypothesized model affords the self-schema concept a central position in explaining students' learning engagement pattern. Two forms of influences originating from a self-schema are proposed in the model, direct and indirect effects. Direct effects stipulate that a self-schema influences achievement goals, approaches to learning and achievement levels separately. Indirect effects mean that the influence of a self-schema is mediated through one or more variables. To accommodate indirect effects, interlinks among mediating variables are assumed in the model. Figure 1 shows the details of the hypothesized model.

Direct Links

Based on the previous findings (Ng, 1997 & 1998), we expected that students' positive self-schemas in learning mathematics would have a strong positive relationship with a mastery goal while a relatively weak link with a performance goal was predicted. In addition, a self-schema was expected to have direct effects on how students learn mathematics and their performance. In particular, the model proposed that a self-schema would be related positively to deep and achieving approaches but negatively to the use of a surface approach. Logically, a positive self-schema would also have a positive relationship with performance level. These assumed relationships are justified because a positive self-schema in learning mathematics

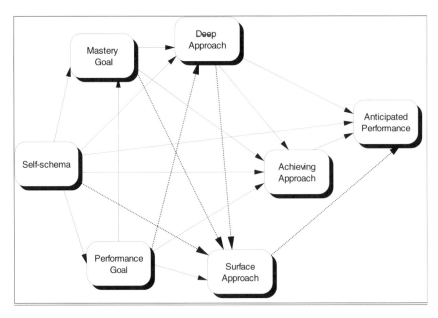

Notes: Dotted arrows representing negative relationships; normal arrows representing positive relationships.

FIGURE 1
The Hypothesized Model

would provide students with not just the motivation but also the means to maintain the desirable self-conception. Learning mathematics with either a deep or an achieving approach will be more likely to guarantee the maintenance of the desirable self-identity for these students. In contrast, a surface approach will usually be avoided, as it will have detrimental effects on learning and hence jeopardize the development of a positive self-conception.

Taken together, these direct links lead to a 'multiple goal multiple approach' hypothesis for explaining the influences of a self-schema on mathematics learning. This hypothesis finds its support from relevant literature which suggests that salient positive self-schemas provide more options and resources that enable students to behave in schema-congruent ways in a variety of different contexts (Day, Borkowski, Dietmeyer, Howsepian & Saenz, 1992).

Indirect Links

We also proposed the following indirect effects of a self-schema in our model. Mastery goals were assumed to be indirectly influenced by a self-schema through performance goals. However, no indirect effect of a self-schema on performance goals was assumed. Both mastery and performance goals would in turn mediate effects of a self-schema onto deep, achieving and surface approaches. Indirect effects of a self-schema on both achieving and surface approach would also be mediated through a deep approach. Finally, a self-schema would also have an indirect effect on the level of performance mediated through various achievement goals and learning approaches. To accommodate indirect effects of a self-schema, interrelationships among achievement goals, among learning approaches, as well as those between these goals and approaches were assumed. Brief discussion of the assumed relationships and their justification are provided below.

Among achievement goals, it was hypothesized that the link from a performance goal to a mastery goal would be significant in the Chinese model but non-significant in the Australian model. The rationale is that given the competitive nature of the Hong Kong education system (Biggs, 1996), Chinese students would perceive that having to strive for a comparatively high performance would enhance their motivation to master the subject matter. In other words, a desire for competitive achievement may drive them towards a mastery orientation. However, Australian students were expected to have a discrete conceptualization of performance and mastery, hence a weak or zero relationship was predicted between these goals. This contention is supported by the past research involving samples from western countries (c.f. Ames, 1992).

Both mastery and performance goals were mediating variables between self-schema and three different learning approaches in our model. Mastery goals with their main focus on understanding and comprehension will strike accord with a deep learning approach, which also places similar emphasis on thorough processing of learning materials. In contrast, mastery goals are at odds with a surface approach as the latter is distinguished by a reproductive learning orientation leading to a minimal understanding. Therefore, mastery goals should relate with a deep approach positively, but negatively with a surface approach. Previous research findings have consistently demonstrated that mastery goals were usually associated with the use of self-regulatory strategies and relatively high achievement levels (e.g. Pintrich, Roeser & De Groot, 1994; Wolters, Yu & Pintrich, 1996). It was assumed here that they would relate with an achieving approach in a positive fashion because an achieving approach is typified by the use of regulating strategies and a focus on high performance in assessment tasks.

The relationships between performance goals and learning are less clear-cut. Early achievement goal researchers (e.g. Ames, 1992; Ames & Archer, 1988; Dweck, 1986) assumed that performance goals are less adaptive and would elicit learning patterns liken those found among students suffered from learn helplessness. More recently, the maladaptive nature of performance goals has been debated and it was proposed that performance goals should be partitioned into two independent orientations, approaching and avoiding performance goals (Elliot, 1997; Elliot & Church, 1997; Elliot & Harackiewicz, 1996; and Harackiewicz, Barron & Elliot, 1998). This revised perspective on performance goals showed that maladaptive effects of performance goals on learning were confined to the avoidance orientation. Approaching performance goals were found to have positive effects on task involvement and intrinsic motivation (Elliot & Church, 1997; Harackiewicz & et al., 1997; Wolters & et al., 1996). However, contradictory findings regarding the effects of approaching performance goals were also reported by Midgley and her colleagues (Kaplan & Midgley 1997; Middleton & Midgley, 1997). They found that approaching performance goals had nonsignificant relationships with self-efficacy, self-regulation, and adaptive strategies but were more positively related to the use of maladptive strategies and test anxiety. To further muddy the water, in a longitudinal study, Pintrich (2000) found that the effects of approaching performance goals were dependent on the interaction with mastery goals. Therefore, the relationships between performance goals and learning are still mixed, albeit of the theoretical refinement Elliot and his colleagues proposed.

When theorizing the relationships between performance goals and learning approaches in the current study, this debate and recent findings concerning performance goals and learning were noted. In keeping with the theoretical refinement Elliot and his colleagues proposed, items assessing performance goals in the Australian survey were approaching in nature. However, because the Chinese survey preceded this theoretical debate, the performance goal construct was a mixture of items assessing approaching (3 items) and avoiding (2 items) goals. Readers should take the hybrid nature of the performance goal construct in the Chinese sample into consideration when interpreting the results related to performance goals. From a theoretical consideration, we expected that performance goals should relate to an achieving approach positively. Performance goals stress high achievement and competitive ability and therefore should have a positive relationship with an achieving approach, which is characterized by a similar concern. The relationship between performance goals and a deep approach was assumed to be nonsignificant or even negative. This assumption is consistent with the accepted extrinsic nature of performance goals. As for the relationship between performance goals and a surface approach, we aligned with achievement goal researchers like Midgley (Kaplan & Midgley 1997; Middleton & Midgley, 1997) to assume that performance goals *on their own* should relate positively with a surface approach. This is because an attention to achievement comparison and ability judgment would cause distraction to learning. In addition, as Pintrich (2000) argued, performance goals would "invoke different types of effort or strategies to attain their goal of being better than others" (p.545); in our case, the use of a surface approach should still be considered viable for attaining the goal of outperforming others. Empirical support for the above assumptions between performance goals and learning approaches can be found in Kong & Hau (1996).

Concerning the links among learning approaches, a deep approach should link negatively with a surface approach as these two approaches are orthogonal in nature (Biggs, 1987, 1989). However, a mixed approach called "deep-achieving" has been described as particularly adaptive with regard to academic tasks (Biggs, 1987 & 1992). In other words, students learning with a deep approach would also work hard to get good grades. As for the relationships among learning approaches and performance, it was expected that the deep and achieving approaches would lead to a high performance, whereas a surface approach would be negatively related to performance (Biggs, 1987).

CROSS-CULTURAL STUDY

In order to test and verify the proposed model, we collected data on the relevant variables from two cohorts of year 10 students in Brisbane and Hong Kong. We selected Year 10 students as they have had extensive experience in learning mathematics and therefore would have well-developed self-schema in this domain. The Australian participants were 704 Year 10 students from four State high schools in Brisbane. At the request of the teachers involved, the students completed the questionnaires in two separate time periods in order to avoid problems of concentration. However, this practice led to a large number of invalid cases, as many students were absent from one of the periods. After data screening, 582 valid cases were recorded, consisting of students from schools situated in various socio-economic suburbs in Brisbane. Among the valid cases, 14.3 percent (N = 83) identified themselves as low achievers in mathematics, 62.7 percent (305) as average achievers and 18.4 percent (N = 107) as high achievers. 4.6 percent (N = 27) did not volunteer any self-assessed information regarding their achievement level. These figures indicate that the sample was composed of students of varying perceived achievement levels. The age of students ranged from 13.0 to 16.5 years with a mean at 14.66 years.

The participants in the Hong Kong sample were nine "Secondary 4" classes (equivalent to year 10 in Australia) from five secondary schools. In total, 329 students completed the questionnaire in one time period. Two cases were judged to be invalid, and were deleted subsequently. The sample of students constituted a mixed-achievement sample. They came from schools of varying achievement bands. Secondary schools in Hong Kong are classified into five different achievement bands according to students' collective performance. Band 1 schools are mainly made up of high achievers while band 5 schools are populated mainly by low achieving students. The participants in this study came from two band 2, one band 3, one band 4 and one band 5 secondary school. The age of the students ranged from 14 to 18 with a mean of 15.36.

Measures

This section describes the questionnaire items of the major constructs of the study. See Table 1 for the details of sample items and the corresponding reliability statistics for each construct. Students rated items measuring the variables on a 5-point Likert scale, ranging from *strongly disagree (1)* to *strongly agree (5)*, or in the case of measuring learning approaches, *very untrue of me (1)* to *very true of me (5)*. It should be noted that the Chinese participants responded to a Chinese version of the questionnaire. Questionnaire items on self-schema and achievement goals from the previous studies (Ng, 1997, 1998) were translated into Chinese by the first author who is a native Chinese speaker. The Chinese version of Biggs' Learning Process Questionnaire (1992) was consulted when the items taken from Liu's Mathematics Learning Process Questionnaire (1997) assessing learning approaches related to mathematics were translated.

TABLE 1
Sample items and Reliability Scores of Major Constructs

Construct	Sample item	(α) Chinese Sample	(α) Australian sample	(α) Ng, 1997 / 1998
Self-schema	N/A	.88	.89	.89 / .89
• affect	I enjoy learning mathematics	.63	.80	.87 / .78
• efficacy	I'm as smart as other in doing mathematics	.76	.69	.79 / .70
• importance	It is important for me to do well in mathematics	.87	.71	.77 / .78
• future self	I'll choose to study mathematics or other related subjects in my future studies	.74	.74	.78 / .74
Mastery goals	I want to master different mathematical skills	.82	.66	.70 / .73
Performance goals	I want to outperform others students	.82	.78	.75 / .63
Deep approach	In studying a new topic in maths, I often recall materials I have learned and see if there is a relationship between them	.73	.82	.73-.80 (Liu, 1997)
Achieving approach	I'll work for top mark in maths whether or not I like the subject	.86	.86	.79-.84 (Liu, 1997)
Surface approach	In maths, I only do enough to get a pass and no more	.70	.55	.77-.69 (Liu, 1997)

Self-schema

Given that the self-schema concept is multidimensional in nature, we designed questions tapping students' responses to the four dimensions (affect, efficacy, importance and temporality) of a self-schema as specified in Garcia and Pintrich's theoretical model (1993, 1994). In the following sections, these schematic dimensions are explained. Readers should consult Table 1 for the corresponding sample items and reliability statistics. The affect dimension concerns the positive or negative affect associated with a particular self-conception. The importance of the affect dimension of self-schema was shown in the Lips (1995) study where subject choice was found to be related mostly to enjoyment of mathematics rather than ability. Likewise, in the current study, the affect dimension of a self-schema for learning mathematics concerns the enjoyment and fun derived from learning mathematical knowledge.

The efficacy dimension is concerned with students' confidence in their ability and effort in maintaining or attaining a desirable self-conception, or avoiding an undesirable one. Day et al. (1992) maintained that students with a developed self-schema in learning should know how to maintain such a self-identity. The efficacy items in the current questionnaire assessed students' self-perceived ability and effort expenditure in doing mathematics.

The importance dimension focuses on the value a student attaches to a particular self-identity. In other words, if success in learning mathematics occupies a paramount position in a student's self-schema, he or she would say definitely that mathematics learning is a valued part of their identity. This construct captures Markus's core concept of self-schemas.

In the current study, the temporal dimension was conceptualised as a future self in learning mathematics. The construct of the future self is tapped by questions related to career plans and future study goals. It is believed that students who think mathematics learning is important, enjoy learning and have a strong efficacy belief in doing mathematics, would normally look forward to maintaining a future self engaging in mathematics in different ways through further studies or career choice. The reverse is held by those who think otherwise.

Consistent with the previous studies (Ng, 1997, 1998), the self-schema concept in the current study was considered as a composite variable formed by collapsing the four dimensions. By treating the four dimensions as integrated parts of a self-schema, the effects of self-schema on other related variables can be assessed more effectively. Previous studies (Ng, 1997 & 1998) provided statistical justification for such theorization and operationalization of the self-schema concept. In the current study, factor analyses extracted one factor from these four dimensions. With an eigenvalue of 3.04 for the Chinese sample and 2.92 for the Australian sample, this extracted factor explained 76 percent and 72.95 percent of the total variance for the Chinese and Australian sample respectively. The high communality values among the four variables forming this factor (ranged between .69 and .81 for the Chinese sample and between .67 and .81 for the Australian sample) indicated that 'affect', 'efficacy', 'importance' and 'future self' were highly related. Given the support of this statistical evidence and our theorization, the scores of these four variables were summed up and the mean score of the sum was taken as a composite variable called "self-schema in mathematics learning". This composite variable had a Cronbach alpha value of 0.89 for both samples. A high score in this composite variable indicated that students in this study held positive self-schemas in learning mathematics.

Achievement Goals

Achievement goals in this study were composed of mastery and performance goals. Mastery goals are characterized by a strong orientation towards understanding and comprehension. Students learning with these goals focus on how well but not on how much they have learnt. Students' performance goals are characterized by a strong orientation towards competition and outcomes. Students learning with these goals focus mainly on how much and how better they have learned comparing with their peers. However, it should be pointed out again that the performance goal construct in the Chinese sample contained a mixture of items assessing both performance approaching (3 items) and avoiding (2 items) orientations. Removing these two negative items resulted in a substantial drop of the internal consistency to an unacceptable level. Therefore, they were retained. However, theoretically, this mixed performance goal construct implies that the Chinese students might not perceive the approaching and avoidance performance goals as two independent orientations as Elliot and his colleagues proposed (Elliot, 1997; Elliot & Church, 1997; Elliot & Harackiewicz, 1996; and Harackiewicz & et al., 1998).

Learning Approaches

Mathematics Learning Process Questionnaire—MLPQ (Liu, 1997) was used to gauge students' approaches to learning mathematics. MLPQ was adapted from Biggs' Learning Process Questionnaire (LPQ). While LPQ measures students' general approaches to learning, MLPQ is a subject specific instrument testing students' approaches in learning mathematics. Burnett and Dart (1997) argued forcefully with empirical support that when analysing the factor structure of an existing scale, one should follow the theoretical model from which the scale is developed. Biggs (1987) proposed a three-factor motive-strategy mix framework of learning approaches. Therefore, a forced factor analysis, specifying a three-factor solution was conducted with MLPQ items. Using a varimax rotation, the result produced a three-factor solution congruent with the Biggs framework in both samples. Factor 1 was labeled as the "Deep Approach." It was formed predominantly by items about students' interest in the subject, their willingness to expend time and effort in learning the subject and their use of strategies that build understanding and mastery. The second factor was labeled "Achieving Approach" as it was concerned mainly with a desire for high achievement, the satisfaction derived for solving difficult problems, an anxiety about poor performance and following teachers' instructions in order to secure a high achievement. The third factor was labeled "Surface Approach." It was characterized by a reluctance to expend effort and time on learning mathematics, and the employment of strategies that lead to a superficial understanding.

Performance

Due to some administrative barriers, students' actual performance was not available from the Chinese sample. Therefore, performance was measured in terms of students' anticipated performance. This of course is a weakness of the current study. However, as self-schemas are considered to have a filling-in effect (Markus & Smith, 1981), it is still advisable to check if students' self-schemas in learning mathematics will direct them to make prediction about their future performance when no information regarding the future examination is given. In addition, there was a close relationship between perceived and actual performance as demonstrated by the strong correlation found for the Australian students ($r = .67$, $p < .001$). Students were asked to rate their possible mark at the end of the academic year using a 6-point scale (A, B, C, D, E and No target grade). As no student chose the 'No Target Grade' response, the scale was transformed to a 5-point scale. (A = 5, E = 1).

RESULTS AND DISCUSSION

After deleting non-randomly and systematic missing values, 327 and 582 cases remained in the Chinese and Australian sample respectively. Path analyses using EQS 5 were conducted with these valid cases. The raw data were transformed into a covariance matrix. The Maximum Likelihood method (ML) was chosen as the estimation procedure as it was shown to perform reasonably well with multivariate normally distributed data and a large sample size (e.g. Chou & Bentler, 1995). The Wald test was consulted to exclude non-significant paths and the Lagrange Multiplier test was used for including paths that contributed significantly to the model.

The Chi-square value (χ^2) was chosen to gauge the overall goodness of fit. However, as χ^2 is based on restrictive assumptions and is sensitive to sample size, it may not be a good estimate of the overall model fit (Tabachnick & Fidell, 1996). Therefore, other fit indices, the Comparative Fit Index (CFI), the Bentler-Bonett Normed Fit Index (NFI), the Lisrel GFI Index and the Root Mean Squared Residual (RMR) were also examined as indicators of the goodness of fit. The CFI, NFI and GFI indices can range

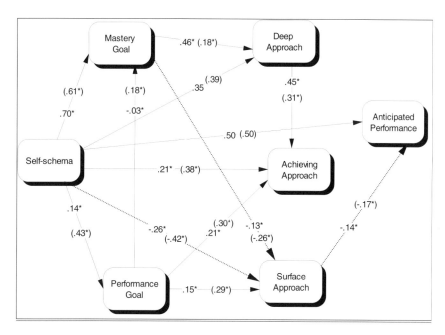

Notes: All paths shown were significant, *p* < .001 (except the path linking performance goal and mastery goal in the Australian model); * indicates path coefficients were significantly different in the two models. Bracketed values represent path coefficients from the Chinese model. Values without a bracket represent path coefficients from the Australian model. Error terms were removed for a clear presentation.

FIGURE 2

A Comparison of Australian and Chinese Models

between 0 and 1. Values of .90 or above in these indices indicate a good model fit to the sample data. A small RMR value (.05 or below) is taken as a corroboration of model fit (Bentler, 1990; Bentler & Bonett, 1980).

Non-significant links were deleted. The resulting Australian model showed an adequate data fit (χ^2 = 16.20; d.f. = 8; *p* = .04; CFI = .99; NFI = .99; GFI = .99; RMR = .02), which was comparable to the final model of the Chinese study (χ^2 = 20.20; d.f. = 8; *p* = .01; CFI = .99; NFI = 98; GFI = .98; RMR = .02). Figure 2 shows the Australian model alongside with the Chinese model.

Significant Direct and Indirect Effects

In general, the two final models corroborated that the hypothesized relationships in model were valid. Table 2 shows the decomposition of the effects of the final models. Concerning the direct effects of a self-schema, as predicted, it had a strong positive link with mastery goals in both samples (ß = .70 for Australian and ß = .61 for the Chinese) while a weaker relationship was found with performance goals (ß = .14 for Australian and ß = .43 for Chinese). A self-schema in learning mathematics also predicted the use of learning approaches. It was positively related to both achieving (ß = .21 for Australian; ß = .38 for Chinese) and deep approaches (ß = .35 for Australian, ß = .39 for Chinese) in both samples while a negative relationship was recorded with a surface approach (ß = -.26 for Australian; ß = -.42 for Chinese). As expected, a self-schema also related to the level of anticipated performance (ß = .50 for both samples). Concerning the indirect effects, as shown in Table 2, a self-schema had significant indirect effects on mastery goals, the three different approaches to learning, and anticipated performance. These results demonstrated the importance of a self-schema in the motivational and learning processes among both Australian and Chinese students in the course of learning mathematics. Taken together, these results lent strong cross-cultural support to our hypothesized model.

However, some of the interrelationships between mediating variables deserve further elaboration. As predicted, the link from a performance goal to a mastery goal was significant (ß = .18) in the Chinese sample, indicating the desire to achieve would provide support for the adoption of a mastery orientation in learning mathematics. The same link, though significant statistically for the Australian sample, explained only a very small amount of variance and therefore no firm conclusion could be drawn.

In addition, it is puzzling why both achieving and deep approaches were not significant in predicting the level of anticipated performance. Concerning the achieving approach, its nonsignificant relationship was caused by the presence of a direct link between a self-schema and anticipated performance. When this link was deleted, achieving approach and anticipated level of performance were significantly related (ß = .31, *p < .001* for Chinese; ß = .18, *p < .001* for Australian). However, we decided to retain the link between a self-schema and anticipated performance but delete the link between achieving approach and anticipated performance. Our decision was informed by both theoretical and statistical consideration. Theoretically, in an ambiguous situation self-schema function to predict schematic related behaviors and cognitions (Markus & Smith, 1981). As our study involved the prediction of future performance without any detailed information regarding the nature of the assessment, the predictive function of a self-schema would be particularly salient. Statistically, if this link were deleted, we would encounter problems in attaining a goodness of fit model. Lagrange Multiplier test in the EQS program suggested that this link should be included.

As for the deep approach in the Australian model, its nonsignificant relationship with anticipated performance was probably caused also by the

TABLE 2

A Comparison of Direct, Indirect and Total Effects of the Australian and Chinese Models

	CHI	*AUS*	*CHI*	*AUS*	*CHI*	*AUS*
	Direct effect	*Direct effect*	*Indirect effect*	*Indirect effect*	*Total effect*	*Total effect*
On mastery goal						
of self-schema	.61*	.70*	.08*	-.004*	.69*	.70*
of performance goal	.18*	-.03	—	—	.18*	-.03
On performance goal						
of self-schema	.43*	.14*	—	—	.43*	.14*
On achieving approach						
of self-schema	.38*	.21*	.29*	.33*	.67*	.50*
of mastery goal	—	—	.05	.20	.06	.21
of performance goal	.30*	.21*	.01*	-.01*	.31*	.20*
of deep approach	.31*	.45*	—	—	.31*	.45*
On deep approach						
of self-schema	.39*	.35*	.13*	.32*	.52*	.67*
of mastery goal	.18*	.46*	—	—	.18*	.46*
of performance goal	—		.03	-.01	.03*	-.01
On surface approach						
of self-schema	-.42*	-.26*	-.05*	-.07*	-.47*	-.32*
of mastery goal	-.26*	-.13*	—	—	-.26*	-.13*
of performance goal	.29*	.15*	.05*	.004*	.24*	.15*
On Anticipated performance						
of self-schema	.50*	.50*	.08*	.04*	.58*	.54*
of mastery goal	—	—	.04	.02	.04	.02
of performance goal	—	—	-.04	-.02	-.04	-.02
of surface approach	-.17*	-.14*	—	—	-.17*	-.14*

Notes: *p < .001. CHI = Chinese; AUS = Australian

presence of the link between a self-schema and anticipated performance. When such a link is deleted, the relationship between a deep approach and anticipated performance remains significant (ß = .11, *p < .001*). However, this was not the case in the Chinese model. The link between a deep approach and anticipated performance remained non-significant when the link between a self-schema and anticipated performance was removed. Nevertheless, it should be noted that the relationship between a deep approach and performance levels is not always clear. Biggs (1988, p.202) warned that 'low correlations between approaches and performance do not necessary signify lack of relationship.' For example, Ramsden, Martin and Bowden (1989) found marginal association between a deep approach and examination performance. They explained that examination pressure might have influenced students to perform less well in the absence of intrinsic interest. In other words, situated factors like assessment requirements may disrupt the relationship between a deep approach and performance. In our case, Ramsden's argument may apply, as the Chinese students would have to face a high stakes public examination in the following year, which determines their academic future. In addition, technically speaking, using a self-report instrument to measure each variable may potentially confound the relationship, which can be another reason explaining the nonsignificant relationship between a deep approach and anticipated performance.

On the whole, the above discussion signifies the important role of a self-schema in predicting the expectation for future performance. Nonetheless, it should be noted that the negative relationship between a surface approach and anticipated performance remained significant despite the presence of the link between a self-schema and anticipated performance. This result suggests that a surface approach will have a unique influence on performance unaffected by a self-schema. In other words, the detrimental effects of a surface approach would contribute uniquely to the low expectation of future performance.

Cross-Cultural Similarities

Overall, these findings lend support to the significance of a self-schema in learning mathematics. Its effects on motivation, learning and expectation for achievement were felt through both direct and indirect links. Cross-cultural validation of these findings corroborates the linear model proposed. In addition, the findings also suggest the following cross-cultural similarities: (1) the importance of self-schema on learning and motivation; (2) contrasting paths to learning; and (3) the filling-in effect of a self-schema on future performance.

1. The Importance of Self-Schema on Learning and Motivation
The final models demonstrated the significant influence of a self-schema on motivation and learning engagement. A self-schema had both strong direct and indirect effects on students' engagement in learning mathematics. The direct effects of a self-schema demonstrated that domain specific self-knowledge predicted students' employment of achievement goals, learning approaches, and more importantly, how students anticipated their achievement levels. A self-schema also had indirect effects on the various learning engagement variables. The significance of a

self-schema was also demonstrated when it took away variance from achieving approach (both models) and deep approach (Australian model only) in explaining the expected levels of future performance, rendering the links between these approaches and anticipated performance nonsignificant. The mediational links among the variables signify an integrative perspective on learning, where the motivation to learn and the processes of learning are causally related. (e.g. Garcia & Pintrich, 1994; Graham & Golan, 1991; Nolen, 1988; Pintrich, 1989). In short, this study showed the important motivational properties of a self-schema. It demonstrated how a self-schema could influence why and how Australian and Chinese students engaged in learning mathematics. In addition, it also revealed that a self-schema is on its own a motivational source providing goals, plans and scripts associated with students' learning in the domain of high school mathematics (c.f. Alexander, 1997).

2. Contrasting Paths to Learning

Day and his colleagues (Day & et al., 1992) maintained that a self-schema provides different options and resources for attaining or maintaining the desirable self-conception. Applied to our final models, it means that a self-schema in learning mathematics would enable students to choose different combinations of goals and approaches congruent with their schematic view for learning. It can be inferred from the path models that a self-schema in both samples opens up two contrasting paths or choices for approaching mathematics learning: An intrinsically engaged path and an extrinsically engaged path. An intrinsically engaged path is characterised by a strong focus on understanding and mastery. This path is represented by the adoption of mastery goals and deep or achieving approach in the models. In contrast, an extrinsically engaged path can also be inferred from the models. This latter path is characterized by a focus on performance. The use of performance goals together with either an achieving approach or a surface approach characterises this path. The strong association between a self-schema and the intrinsically engaged path suggests that a positive self-schema in learning mathematics would be more likely to lead students to learn mathematics with a mastery focus. However, performance goals and other approaches to learning are still within students' options. Further speculation about the relationship between these two contrasting paths and achievement level is not feasible with the current models. Further studies are required to verify these different learning paths and their relationship with students' actual performance.

3. The Filling-In Effect of a Self-Schema on Future Performance

The highly significant link and the strong path coefficient between a self-schema and anticipated performance suggested that students were using their own positive or negative schematic view of learning mathematics to anticipate their year-end grade. This "filling-in" effect of self-schema on future performance has important practical implications, as a low expectation for future success would lead normally to refraining from expending effort and time in an endeavor. In other words, the future self has implications for the current self and the related behaviors within a specific domain, since a low expectation of future success undermines motivation and effort. However, it may be that the self-report nature of these two variables might inflate the relationship.

The similarities between the two models speak to the significance of the self-schema concept and its applicability in investigating motivation and learning in these different cultures. Overall, our findings point to similar patterns of learning engagement across different cultures for both positive and negative schematic students.

Cross-cultural Differences

On the surface, these two models looked exactly the same, with an identical path structure and congruent causal links. However, subtle discrepancies were present in the strength of individual paths. To test if the path coefficients of these two models were different from each other, path coefficients were transformed into Fisher's Z scores, which were then subjected to a test of significant difference, $p < .05$. The result of this set of statistical tests is shown in Figure 2. Path coefficients marked (*) were significantly different from each other.

a. self-schema and deep approach;
b. self-schema and anticipated performance.

These paths, showing no significant difference from each other, can also be taken as the commonality found between the Chinese and the Australian models. In other words, the effect magnitude of a self-schema on anticipated performance and deep approach were similar in both the Chinese and Australian samples.

The path coefficients that were significantly different from each other revealed the subtle differences between the two final models. Notably, the Chinese model against the Australian model manifested stronger path coefficients in the following links:

a. from self-schema to performance goal;
b. from self-schema to achieving approach;
c. from self-schema to surface approach;
d. from performance goal to achieving approach;
e. from performance goal to mastery approach;
f. from performance goal to surface approach; and

  g. from mastery goal to surface approach.

In contrast, the Australian model exhibited relatively stronger paths on the following:

  a. from self-schema to mastery;
  b. from mastery goal to deep approach; and
  c. from deep approach to achieving approach.

The nature of the differences in path strength can be revealed clearly by looking at the direct and indirect effects of the paths.

  Compared to the Australian model ($ß = .14$), the Chinese model ($ß = .43$) revealed a stronger self-schema effect on performance, which in turn, had a stronger bearing on achieving approach ($ß = .30$) than did the Australian model ($ß = .21$). In addition, performance goals in the Chinese model predicted the use of mastery goals in a positive fashion ($ß = .18$), whereas in the Australian models this link was not significant.

  As for learning approaches, the Chinese model showed a stronger total effect of self-schema on an achieving approach ($ß = .67$), which was caused partly by the strong direct effect of self-schema itself ($ß = .38$), and partly by the indirect effect mediated through performance goals and a deep approach ($ß = .29$). Of particular interest is that performance goals in the Chinese model ($ß = .29$) linked more closely with a surface approach than in the Australian model ($ß = .15$).

  Regarding the Australian model, it demonstrated a greater total effect ($ß = .67$) from self-schema to a deep approach, which was due not only to the direct effect of self-schema ($ß = .35$) but also to the mediational effect through mastery goals ($ß = .32$). In addition, the Australian model showed a stronger effect of a deep approach on an achieving approach than did the Chinese model. Although self-schema had an equally strong direct effect on a deep approach ($ß = .39$) in the Chinese model, its indirect effect mediated through mastery goals was relatively weak ($ß = .13$) compared with the Australian model. It is not surprising, then, to find that mastery goals had a far greater effect on a deep approach in the Australian model ($ß = .46$) than in the Chinese model ($ß = .18$).

Cultural Models and Cross-cultural Differences

  These results revealed subtle differences between the Australian and Chinese models. In particular, Australian students were distinguished by their comparatively stronger mastery focus characterized by a combination of mastery goals and a deep learning approach. In contrast, Chinese students held a distinct achievement focus through which they oriented more towards performance goals and an achieving learning approach. In other words, the effect of self-schemas on a performance goal and an achieving approach orientation was more apparent among the Chinese than the Australian high school students. Conversely, the effect of self-schemas was more evident on a mastery goal and a deep approach orientation among the Australian students.

That said, it is important to highlight that in both models self-schemas had a stronger effect on the adoption of mastery goals than performance goals. In other words, students with a positive self-schema from both Hong Kong and Australia would often adopt a mastery goal rather than a performance goal. Nevertheless, the relatively stronger link between self-schemas and performance goals found among the Chinese when compared with the Australians warranted further exploration.

This pattern of differences may be related to the sociocultural values attached to academic success. Differential emphasis on achievement, performance and competition is placed in Hong Kong vis-à-vis Queensland education systems. The Hong Kong education system is well known for its competitive nature. Testing of students in Hong Kong schools is frequent and abundant (e.g. Biggs, 1996; Hamo-Lyons, 1999). It is not uncommon for students to be examined formally for their learning through major tests or examinations three or more times a year. In addition, lengthy assignments are given out frequently. In general, the purpose of these evaluative practices is driven overtly by summative and selective purposes. In other words, assignments, tests and examinations are often designed not for diagnostic checking of students' understanding but for normative comparison. In addition, evaluative pressures come not only from the school, but also through social comparison among peers and family members. Academic achievement is generally considered to be the most important way to future success in life, yet the school banding system and competition between students within bands creates the context where most students can be labeled as failures. Inevitably, these school practices and social mores provide a sociocultural context for the operation of self-schemas where particular salience is given to perceived success at learning.

The education system in Queensland, Australia places less stress on evaluation for selection or summative purposes. Up to year 10, there is no external testing of the curriculum (apart now from testing of literacy and numeracy at years 5 and 7). All assessment is essentially undertaken by the teacher, much of it in the context of the normal activities of the classroom. Teachers are expected to keep records of their students' progress and to provide updated summaries of these for reporting to parents (maybe formally twice a year). As for assessment in the senior forms (year 11 and 12), external examinations were abolished 30 years ago. Assessment is entirely school-based, although there is a system of moderation based on a core skills test, and using expert curriculum panels to ensure comparability of standards in each subject across the state. (G. S. Maxwell, personal communication, August 18, 2000). Students are given an appropriate assignment load for the purpose of mastery, and progressive assessment is very much a characteristic of Queensland education. Students are not required to sit for any high-stakes examination for university entry. More importantly, teachers, peers and parents put more stress on broad personal development in different life aspects, and relatively less stress is placed purely on academic success.

In other words, these two education systems are characterized by a different cultural model of success (c.f. D'Andrade & Strauss, 1992; Kagitcibasi, 1997; Markus & Kitayama, 1991). The Chinese cultural model of success builds on the notions of collectivism, competition and comparison. Academic success is measured in terms of one's relative performance, which brings glory and honor to the family. Academic success is considered the prime key to future success (Ho, 1988; Ho & Chiu, 1994). Alternative routes are not encouraged. In fact, opportunities for exploring alternative routes to success are extremely limited. In a stark contrast, the Queensland system is associated with another form of cultural model of success, building on the notion of individualism, mastery and choice. In the Australian context, success is measured more on the basis of individual mastery. Individual choice and interest are important considerations, and academic attainment is considered one of many paths to future success. Therefore, these cultural models provide a sociocultural context for understanding the cross-cultural differences in self-schemas and the associated effects on achievement goals, learning approaches and anticipated performance.

That said, it is important to reiterate that students with a positive schema in both cultures tended to endorse mastery goals over performance goals and a deep approach over an achieving approach. Our suggestion of the two cultural models of success highlights the importance of the sociocultural influence on students' motivational and learning processes. The relatively stronger orientation for the Chinese schematic students towards performance and achievement than their Australian counterparts suggests the significance of such sociocultural influence on the operation of the self-system. Hong Kong students with a positive schema are tuned to adopt some sort of performance-oriented motivation and strategies. However, this does not suggest that Chinese students are more concerned with ability demonstration than effort expenditure. Neither do we suggest that Australian students are not concerned about competition and achievement.

FUTURE RESEARCH

The significance of this study lies in applying the self-schema concept to the investigation of motivational and learning behaviors. It demonstrated the influence of self-schemas on students' motivation, learning and achievement with cross-cultural evidence. The resulting path models derived from the two culturally different samples provide strong empirical support for the close relationships between self-schemas, motivation and other learning behaviors and outcomes. Nevertheless, self-schemas as a motivational construct still need conceptual and empirical elaboration and verification. There are some important issues future research on self-schemas will need to consider.

Two Levels of Self-schemas

A central issue is related to the possibility of different levels of self-schemas. Our study demonstrated how a subject-based self-schema could affect learning and motivation. However, it does not follow that students will develop a clear self-conception in every school subject. When such a clear subject-based self-conception is not yet developed, students may rely on a more generalized level of self-schema in a related domain to guide their learning and behaviors. Martinot and Monteil's study of academic self-schema, and Garcia and Pintrich's notion of good versus bad student schemas are examples of such generalized self-schema. Complicated issues are involved in differentiating the effects of general versus subject-specific self-schemas. Students may have a general positive academic self-schema while dreading a specific subject. In contrast, students may have developed a well established self in learning a specific subject but nonetheless harbor a very negative general academic self-schema. Future research needs to assess the effects of these two different levels of self-schemas and to differentiate their effects.

Sociocultural Context

Cultural values attached to academic success provide a sociocultural context for the development of self-schemas. While it is maintained that a self-schema in learning mathematics will open up different avenues for academic success, the actual path taken is to a great extent constrained by sociocultural values on academic success prevailing within a specific society. In Chinese societies such as Hong Kong, great emphasis has been given to academic achievement, not just as a personal attainment but also as a social endeavor for bringing honor to the family and to the community (Salili, 1995). This consideration therefore directs schematic students to performance and achievement. In contrast, in Australian society, academic achievement is regarded more as a personal achievement that defines the individual in terms of his or her unique pattern of gifts and abilities. These cultural values create the context within which schematic students focus more on personal understanding and mastery as the path to good performance (c.f. Markus & Kitayama, 1991). In other words, while it can be expected that students with a positive schema in learning mathematics in both Australia and Hong Kong will display similar characteristics like enjoyment in learning mathematics, a strong sense of efficacy, a willingness to expend effort, a sense of importance and a future self related to mathematics, they may choose different paths to maintain such a self-conception.

The discussion above draws us to consider the notion of a contextual understanding of self-schema. Singer and Salovey (1991) posited that schemas have to be understood within the context of activation. The specificity of a situation may make certain schemas more salient. For example, when you are hungry, the schema related to restaurants and food can be activated more readily. Similarly, various contextual factors have to be taken into account to understand the content, structure, and the processing effects as well as the behavioral and emotional outcomes of a self-schema. For example, during the preparation for a major examination, ability considerations are likely to be more readily available for students having a history of failure.

Malleability of Self-Schemas

Related to the sociocultural context of self-schemas' activation is the issue of the malleability of self-schemas. The characteristics and effects of having this or that type of schema can be documented but the process of change and development is less researched and less understood. The cross-cultural study reported in this paper did not include a distinction between or an analysis of positive and negative schemas. We have little knowledge about students' negative schemas and their development. From an educational perspective, however, helping students with a negative schema to change is a crucial issue. Is it possible to change self-schemas once they have developed? What are the conditions of malleability? We have found evidence in an interview study involving a selected group of Australian students that students' negative mathematics self-schemas can be changed (Ng, 1999). Among the interviewees, several reported a change in their self-schemas in learning mathematics. Consider the following excerpts of a year 10 Australian Chinese student named Jack, describing his experiences in learning mathematics before and after the schematic change.

Before schematic change:

I thought maths was really boring. 'Cuz it's always the basic calculation steps, subtraction, addition, multiplication and division. Yeah, it's very boring…And I didn't do my homework. I also didn't do any revision before the exam.

After schematic change:

I no longer thought that maths was boring. I would take the initiative to read extra books in the library about maths…prepare for the coming lesson, like reading over the chapter, and sometimes do some questions…I started to worry about my mark. You would think like, 'I failed this time why was that? What has happened? Ah, it's because of this and that…' Then you would try to do well next time.

I once thought maths was just for calculating the change when you shop in a supermarket. And then I came to realize that maths is required in building a house, like how the light will go and where we should put a lamp. All requires maths. Everything needs maths…I planned to do jobs related to maths after that, yeah…yeah, related to maths. I at one stage wanted to be a maths teacher but later on, I realized that that's not possible. I knew I wouldn't make a good teacher myself.

Effective teaching strategies including designing challenging tasks, making lessons interesting, taking students' needs into consideration, were the reasons Jack quoted to explain his schematic change. Other Australian interviewees quoted reasons such as mastery oriented learning atmosphere, autonomy, achievable targets, teacher's readiness to help, activity based teaching, teaching for understanding, opportunities to participate in classroom activities, constructive and mastery oriented feedback, novel teaching strategies and good student-teacher relationships to account for the change of their self-schema in learning mathematics. These encouraging findings allude to the significant effects of teaching practices and particular teachers—not just on students' learning and motivation, but more significantly on students' own understanding of their self in relation to the learning of the subject. More significantly, the fact that Australian interviewees consistently reported the significance of teacher related factors in contributing to their change of schematic beliefs attest to the impact of teachers and teaching strategies on students' learning and the development of the self.

Nevertheless, while effective teaching strategies can provide students with learning experiences favoring the development of a positive schematic view of learning a specific subject, the issue of malleability involves not just the question of whether students' schematic view can be changed. More fundamental is whether such a change is sustainable. Will students who report a change in their self-schemas in learning a subject hold onto the newly formed understanding of their selves? In other words, is the change temporary or permanent? If the change is temporary, the newly formed schematic view will fade away soon when students are removed from the favorable learning environment.

In conclusion, the current study provided strong cross-cultural evidence regarding the effects of self-schemas on motivation and learning. This can be taken as an initial step unraveling the potentials of the self-schema concept in understanding motivation and learning. Future research needs to address the issues discussed above. In short, considering self-schema as a context-bound concept, evaluating the operation of different levels of self-schemas, investigating students of different characteristics (age, gender, and ethnic backgrounds, educational levels, subject domains) will help to elaborate and verify the validity of this important psychological construct and its effects on motivation and learning.

ACKNOWLEDGMENT

We would like to thank the editors of this research volume for their very helpful comments on the earlier versions of this paper.

REFERENCES

Alexander, P. A. (1997). Knowledge seeking and self-schema: A case for motivational dimensions of exposition. *Educational Psychologist, 32*(2), 83-94.

Allen, L. A., Woolfolk, R. L., Gara, M. A., & Apter, J. T. (1996). Possible selves in major depression. *Journal of Nervous and Mental Disease, 184*(12), 739-745.

Altabe, M., & Thompson, K. J. (1996). Body image: A cognitive self-schema construct? *Cognitive Therapy and Research, 20*(2), 171-193.

Ames, C. (1992). Achievement goals and the classroom motivational climate. In D. H. Schunk & J. L. Meece (Eds.), *Student perceptions in classroom* (pp. 327-348). Hillsdale, NJ: Lawrence Erlbaum.

Ames, C., & Archer, J. (1988). Achievement goals in the classroom: Students' learning strategies and motivational processes. *Journal of Educational Psychology, 80*(3), 260-267.

Andersen, B. L., & Cyranowski, J. M. (1994). Women's sexual self-schema. *Journal of Personality and Social Psychology, 67*(6), 1079-1110.

Bentler, P. M., & Bonett, D. G. (1980). Significance tests and goodness-of-fit in the analysis of covariance structures. *Psychological Bulletin, 88*, 588-606.

Bentler, P. M. (1990). Comparative fit indices in structural models. *Psychological Bulletin, 107*, 238-246.

Biggs, J. (1979). Individual differences in study processes and the quality of learning outcomes. *Higher Education, 8*, 381-384.

Biggs, J. (1987). *Student approaches to learning and studying.* Melbourne, Australia: Australian Council for Educational Research.

Biggs, J. (1988). Assessing student approaches to learning. *Australian Psychologist, 23*(2), 197-206.

Biggs, J. (1989). Approaches to learning in secondary and tertiary students in Hong Kong: Some comparative studies. *Educational Research Journal, 6,* 27-39.

Biggs, J. B. (1992). *Why and how do Hong Kong students learning? Using the Learning and Study Process Questionnaires.* Hong Kong: Faulty of Education, University of Hong Kong.

Biggs, J. (1996). The assessment scene in Hong Kong. In J. Biggs (Ed.), *Testing: To educate or to select? Education in Hong Kong at the crossroads* (pp. 9-12). Hong Kong: Hong Kong Educational Publishing Co.

Borkowski, J. G., Carr, M., Rellinger, E., & Pressley, M. (1990). Self-regulated cognition: Interdependence of metacognition, attributions, and self-esteem. In B. F. Jones & M. Pressley (Eds.), *Dimensions of thinking and cognitive instruction* (pp. 53-92). Hillsdale, NJ: Erlbaum.

Bruch, M. A., Kaflowitz, N. G., & Berger, P. (1988). Self-schema for assertiveness: Extending the validity of the self-schema construct. *Journal of Research in Personality, 22*(4), 424-444.

Burnett, P. C., & Dart, B. C. (1997). Conventional versus confirmatory factor analysis: Methods for validating the structure of existing scales. *Journal of Research and Development in Education, 30,* 126-132.

Cantor, N., Markus, H., Niedenthal, P., & Nurius, P. (1986). On motivation and the self-concept. In R. M. Sorrention & T. E. Higgins (Eds.), *Handbook of motivation and cognition: Foundations of social behavior* (Vol. 1, pp. 96-121). New York, NY: Guildford Press.

Chou, C. P., & Bentler, P. M. (1995). Estimates and tests in structural equation modeling. In R. H. Hoyle (Ed.), *Structural equation modeling: Concepts, issues, and applications* (pp. 37-55). Thousand Oaks, CA: Sage.

Day, J. D., Borkowski, J. G., Dietmeyer, D. L., Howsepian, B. A., & Saenz, D. S. (1992). Possible selves and academic achievement. In L. T. Winegar & J. Valsiner (Eds.), *Children's development within social context* (Vol. 2: Research & methodology, pp. 181-201). Hillsdale, NJ: Erlbaum.

D'Andrade, R. G., & Strauss, C. (Eds.). (1992). *Human motives and cultural models.* New York, NY: Cambridge University Press.

Dowson, M., & McInerney, D. M. (2001). Psychological parameters of students' social and work avoidance goals: A qualitative investigation. *Journal of Educational Psychology, 93*(1), 35-42.

Dweck, C. S. (1986). Motivational processes affecting learning. *American Psychologist, 41*(10), 1040-1048.

Dweck, C. S., & Leggett, E. L. (1988). A social-cognitive approach to motivation and personality. *Psychological Review, 95,* 256-273.

Elliot, A. J. (1997). Integrating the "classic" and "contemporary" approaches to achievement motivation: A hierarchical model of approach and avoidance achievement motivation. In M. L. Maehr & P. R. Pintrich (Eds.), *Advances in motivation and achievement* (Vol. 10, pp. 143-179). Greenwich, CT: JAI Press Inc.

Elliot, A. J., & Church, M. (1997). A hierarchical model of approach and avoidance achievement motivation. *Journal of Personality and Social Psychology, 72,* 218-232.

Elliot, A., & Harackiewicz, J. (1996). Approach and avoidance achievement goals and intrinsic motivation: A mediational analysis. *Journal of Personality and Social Psychology, 70,* 968-980.

Fong, G. T., & Markus, H. (1982). Self-schemas and judgment about others. *Social Cognition, 1*(3), 191-204.

Fordham, S., & Ogbu, J. U. (1986). Black students' school success: Coping with the "burden of 'acting white.'" *The Urban Review, 18*(3), 176-206.

Garcia, T., & Pintrich, P. R. (1993). *Self-schemas, motivational strategies, and self-regulated learning.* Paper presented at the annual meeting of the American Educational research Association, Atlanta, GA.

Garcia, T., & Pintrich, P. R. (1994). Regulating motivation and cognition in the classroom: The role of self-schemas and self-regulatory strategies. In D. H. Schunk & B. H. Zimmerman (Eds.), *Self-regulation of learning and performance: Issues and educational applications* (pp. 127-153). Hillsdale, NJ: Erlbaum.

Graham, S., & Golan, S. (1991). Motivational influences on cognition: Task involvement, ego involvement, and depth of information processing. *Journal of Educational Psychology, 83*(2), 187-194.

Greenwald, A. G. (1980). The totalitarian ego: Fabrication and revision of personal history. *American Psychologist, 35*(7), 603-618.

Hamo-Lyons, L. (1999). Implication of the "examination culture" for (English language) education in Hong Kong. In V. Crew, V. Berry, & J. Hung (Eds.), *Exploring diversity in the language curriculum* (pp. 133-140). Hong Kong: Hong Kong Institute of Education.

Harackiewicz, J. M., Barron, E., Carter, S. M., Lehto, A. T., & Elliot, A. J. (1997). Predictors and consequences of achievement goals in the college classroom: Maintaining interest and making the grade. *Journal of Personality and Social Psychology, 73*, 1284-1295.

Harackiewicz, J. M., Barron, K. E., & Elliot , A. J. (1998). Rethinking achievement goals: When are they adaptive for college students and why? *Educational Psychologist, 33*(1), 1-21.

Hatcher, L. (1994). *A step-by-step approach to using the SAS system for factor analysis and structural equation modeling.* Cary, NC: SAS Institute Inc.

Ho, D. Y. F. (1988). Cognitive socialization in Confucian heritage cultures. In P. M. Greenfield & R. R. Cocking (Eds.), *Cross-cultural roots of minority child development* (pp. 285-313). Hillsdale, NJ: Erlbaum.

Ho, D. Y. F., & Chiu, C. Y. (1994). Component ideas of individualism, collectivism, and social organization: An application in the study of Chinese culture. In U. Kim, H. Triandis, C. Kagitcibasi, S. C. Choi, & G. Yoon (Eds.), *Individualism and collectivism: Theory, method and applications* (pp. 137-156). Thousand Oaks, CA: Sage.

Kagitcibasi, C. (1997). Individualism and Collectivism. In J. W. Berry, M. H. Segall, & C. Kagitcibasi (Eds.), *Handbook of cross-cultural psychology* (Vol. 3, pp. 1-49). Boston, MA: Allyn & Bacon.

Kaplan, A., & Midgley, C. (1997). The effect of achievement goals: Does level of perceived academic competence make a difference? *Contemporary Educational Psychology, 22*, 415-435.

Kong, C. K., & Hau, K. T. (1996). Students' achievement goals and approaches to learning: The relationship between emphasis on self-improvement and thorough understanding. *Research in Education, 55*, 74-85.

Lewicki, P. (1983). Self-image bias in person perception. *Journal of Personality and Social Psychology, 45*(2), 384-393.

Lewicki, P. (1984). Self-schema and social information processing. *Journal of Personality and Social Psychology, 47*(6), 1177-1190.

Lips, H. M. (1984). *Math/science self-schemas and curriculum choices among university women*. Paper presented at the Annual Convention of the American Psychological Association, Toronto, Canada.

Lips, H. M. (1985). *Self-Schema theory and gender-related behaviors: Research on some correlates of university women's participation in mathematics, science and athletic activities*. (ERIC document ED263517).

Lips, H. M. (1995). Through the lens of mathematical/scientific self-schemas: Images of students' current and possible selves. *Journal of Applied Social Psychology, 25*(19), 1671-1699.

Little, B. R. (1993). Personal projects and the distributed self: Aspects of conative psychology. In J. Suls (Ed.), *Psychological perspectives on the self: The self in social perspective* (Vol. 4, pp. 157-185). Hillsdale, NJ: Erlbaum.

Liu, H. K. (1997). *Secondary school students' approaches to learning mathematics*. Unpublished doctoral dissertation, University of Queensland, Brisbane, Australia.

Markus, H. (1977). Self-schemata and processing information about the self. *Journal of Personality and Social Psychology, 35*(2), 63-78.

Markus, H., & Kitayama, S. (1991). Culture and the self: Implications for cognition, emotion, and motivation. *Psychological Review, 98*(2), 224-253.

Markus, H., & Smith, J. (1981). The influence of self-schema on the perception of others. In N. Cantop & J. F. Kihlstrom (Eds.), *Personality, cognition, and social interaction* (pp. 233-262). Hillsdale, NJ: Erlbaum.

Markus, H., Smith, J., & Moreland, R. L. (1985). Role of the self concept in the perception of others. *Journal of Personality and Social Psychology, 49*(6), 1494-1512.

Markus, H., Crane, M., Berstein, S., & Siladi, M. (1982). Self-schemas and gender. *Journal of Personality and Social Psychology, 42*, 38-50.

Martinot, D., & Monteil, J.-M. (1995). The academic self-schema: An experimental illustration. *Learning and Instruction, 5*(1), 63-76.

McCombs, B. L. (1991). Overview: Where have we been and where are we going in understanding human motivation? *Journal of Experimental Education, 60*(1), 5-14.

McCombs, B. L., & Marzano, R. J. (1990). Putting the self in self-regulated learning: The self as agent in integrating will and skill. *Educational Psychologist, 25*, 51-69.

McCombs, B. L., & Whisler, J. S. (1989). The role affective variables in autonomous learning. *Educational Psychologist, 24*, 277-306.

Middleton, M., & Midgley, C. (1997). Avoiding the demonstration of lack of ability: An underexplored aspect of goal theory. *Journal of Educational Psychology, 89*, 710-718.

Murphy, P. K., & Alexander, P. A. (2000). A motivated exploration of motivation terminology. *Contemporary Educational Psychology, 25*, 3-53.

Ng, C. (1997). *Internalisation of teacher's teaching goals: The role of self-schemas and relationship with teacher in affecting students' goal orientations*. Paper presented at the Annual Conference of Australian Association for Research in Education, Brisbane, Australia.

Ng, C. (1998). Subject based self-knowledge, perceived purposes for learning and anticipated future achievement. Unpublished manuscript, The University of Queensland, Brishane, Australia.

Ng, C. (1999). Self-schemas and learning engagement of high school students. Unpublished doctoral dissertation, University of Queensland, Brisbane, Australia.

Nolen, S. B. (1988). Reasons for studying: Motivational orientations and study strategies. *Cognition and Instruction, 5*(4), 269-287.

Pintrich, P. R. (1989). The dynamic interplay of student motivation and cognition in the college classroom. In M. L. Maehr & P. R. Pintrich (Eds.), *Advances in motivation and achievement* (Vol. 6, pp. 117-160). Greenwich CT: JAI press.

Pintrich, P. R. (1994). Continuities and discontinuities: Future development for research in educational psychology. *Educational Psychologist, 29*(3), 137-148.

Pintrich, P. R. (2000). Multiple goals, multiple pathways: The role of goal orientation in learning and achievement. *Journal of Educational Psychology, 92*(3), 544-555.

Pintrich, P. R., & De Groot, V. (1990). Motivational and self-regulated learning components of classroom academic performance. *Journal of Educational Psychology, 82*(1), 33-40.

Pintrich, P. R., Roeser, R. W., & De Groot, E. A. M. (1994). Classroom and individual differences in early adolescents' motivation and self-regulated learning. *Journal of Early Adolescence, 14*(2), 139-161.

Ramsden, P., Martin, E., & Bowden, J. (1989). School environment and sixth form pupils' approaches to learning. *British Journal of Educational Psychology, 59,* 129-142.

Salili, F. (1995). Explaining Chinese students' motivation and achievement: A sociocultural analysis. In M. L. Maehr & P. R. Pintrich (Eds.), *Advances in motivation and achievement* (Vol. 9, pp. 73-118). Greenwich, CT: JAI Press.

Singer, J. L., & Salovey, P. (1991). Organized knowledge structures and personality. In M. J. Horowitz (Ed.), *Person schemas and maladaptive interpersonal patterns* (pp. 33-79). Chicago, IL: The University of Chicago Press.

Tabachnick, B. G., & Fidell, L. S. (1996). *Using multivariate statistics.* New York, NY: Harper Collins.

Taylor, S. W., & Crocker, J. (1981). Schematic bases of social information processing. In E. T. Higgins, C. P. Herman, & M. P. Zanna (Eds.), *Social cognition: The Ontario symposium* (Vol. 1, pp. 89-134). Hillsdale, NJ: Erlbaum.

Thompson, C. P. (1985). Memory for unique personal events: Some implications of the self-schema. *Human Learning, 4*(4), 267-280.

Urdan, T. C. (1997). Achievement goal theory: past results, future directions. In M. L. Maehr & P. R. Pintrich (Eds.), *Advances in motivation and achievement* (Vol. 10, pp. 99-141). Greenwich, CT: JAI Press.

Wigfield, A., & Eccles, J. (1992). The development of achievement task values: A theoretical analysis. *Developmental Review, 12,* 265-310.

Wolters, C. A., Yu, S. L., & Pintrich, P. R. (1996). The relation between goal orientation and students' motivational beliefs and self-regulated learning. *Learning and Individual Differences, 8*(3), 211-238.

Wong, N., Lin, W., & Watkins, D. (1996). Cross-cultural validation of models of approaches to learning: An application of confirmatory factor analysis. *Educational Psychology, 16*(30), 317-327.6

CHAPTER 4

STUDENTS "AT RISK"
Exploring Identity from a
Sociocultural Perspective

Jennifer A. Vadeboncoeur and Pedro R. Portes

INTRODUCTION

Dominant beliefs and social practices established in Western culture have tended to place responsibilities associated with success on individuals. The discourse of individualism—enacted through social practices, language, and speech—presumes that comparable opportunities exist and have existed for some time so that any resulting differences between individuals are assumed to derive from more or less effort, accrued experience, and ability. Our culture assumes success is associated with individual worth, while many of the historical and social constraints that mediate individual agency are largely ignored. The cult of individualism has both immediate everyday consequences, as well as long term effects, in particular when it is embedded in social science disciplines such as psychology. The latter has traditionally assumed both an individualistic and an objectivist stance with respect to various developmental outcomes.

The traditional psychological position has been severely challenged over the last few decades. This challenge is most relevant to our recent work with students who are labeled "at risk." We work with schools where discourses and social practices that highlight individualism and meritocracy, while portrayed as empowering, have serious and deleterious consequences. Meritocracy assumes that students achieve success according to the merit of their work, and that their performance is the result of natural ability or, in some cases, considerable effort. This model views the individual student as largely responsible for school success, school failure, and everything in between. When students do poorly, blame also shifts to individual parents and then to individual teachers, with little if any consideration of the way in which the institutional structure of schools constrains individual and group agency (Portes, 1996).

A meritocracy remains an illusive myth for the simple reason that both the school and the larger social context are far from constant, and far from neutral as well. Historically determined differences in social contexts and opportunities may be seen as barriers for some that serve as bridges for others. The emphasis on individual rights and responsibilities in the United States contributes to a general perception that is uncritical toward the ways in which social structures, and the discourses and practices embedded within them, are centrally implicated in the construction of identity. Maintaining that individuals alone construct their identities, that they choose from among multiple options and settle upon the one that is best for them, is a false and simplistic approach that reflects more our ideological commitment to individualism than the process of identity construction. Instead, we argue for an approach that allows us to explore the co-constitutive relationship between individual agent and social context, enacted through discourses and social practices. Focusing exclusively on individual choice and responsibility in identity construction has devastating results for today's young people and society. In record numbers, children between the ages of 11 and 18 years old are being labeled "at risk" for developing a variety of social identities as they experience school failure, such as those related to drug use, violence, teen pregnancy, and gang membership. School failure, like the "at risk" construct, is a dialectical construct that reflects, in large part, the process of how students from some groups are placed "at risk" by the current organization of schooling.

A comprehensive understanding—and we would add, a sociocultural understanding—of the experiences of students who are at risk for leaving school prior to graduation is needed. As noted by Evans, Cohen, Cicchelli, and Shapiro (1995), over one quarter of the students entering high school as freshmen in 1994 dropped out or were "pushed out of school" by the time their peers marched in the graduation ceremony. The state of Texas has an average rate of 20 percent for drop outs, though some of the larger school districts have averages up to 32 percent (Benton & Appleton, 2001). Nationwide, 50 percent of Native American high school students drop out before graduation (Chavers, 1991). A more conservative view by the National Center for Educational Statistics (NCES) proposes that the drop out rate for students between the ages of 16 and 24 averages 11 percent, though the rates for students who differ in terms of race and ethnicity are quite disparate: in this age group white, non-Hispanic students drop out at a rate of 8 percent, Black students at a rate of 13 percent, and Hispanic students at a rate of 25 percent (NCES, 1998). The drop out rates in this sample underestimate the actual number of students leaving education due to the age range; research shows that this kind of student census fails to consider that students may drop out of school prior to reaching 16 years of age (LeCompte & Dworkin, 1991). Other obstacles plague accurate record keeping, including inconsistency in records, shifting definitions for "drop out," and children who just disappear from state enrollment records without explanation. Even more alarming, perhaps, is that for every drop out, there are probably as many peers who graduate with a level of literacy significantly lower than the level of literacy expected for graduation, by an average of four grade levels (*The Condition of Education*, 1998). Those who drop out may be aware that graduation is not likely to change their future unless a number of other conditions unrelated to graduation change, such as local economic conditions, hiring practices, and dominant attitudes.

In order for us to ask questions about the influence of discourses and social practices on the production of "at risk" student identities, we needed a theory of identity that would allow us to understand the way in which students develop within a particular social surround. For example, a useful theory would need to take into account a specific historical moment, socially constructed values and meanings for "individual characteristics," such as gender, ethnicity, and socioeconomic class, as well as the fundamentally co-constitutive relations between young people, social practices and discourses. In our exploration for a framework that would enable us to approach identity construction this way, we chose to expand a sociocultural perspective, based upon the work of Vygotsky (1978, 1986). Vygotsky's theoretical framework and the ongoing development of the sociocultural approach offers a lens for overcoming the dilemma of Western "cultural blindness" to social structural conditions, specifically by studying how the construction of identity varies for individuals in relation to the history of inter-group relations in a given social context. The main goal of this chapter is to extend and integrate the study of identity within the sociocultural framework, with particular attention paid to how the production of students labeled "at risk" operates in the political economy of schooling.

Recent extensions of the sociocultural framework to include identity construction have focused on the internalization process (Miedema & Wardekker, 1999) and semiotic mediation (Shaw, 1994). In addition, recent work has suggested that certain parallels can be drawn between Erikson's (1963, 1968) psychosocial model and the sociocultural approach as a method for considering identity formation (Penuel & Wertsch, 1995). This chapter provides a review and discussion of the work mentioned, and includes a discussion of our recent shift incorporating Bakhtin's (1986) work. Our chapter is divided into four sections. The first section highlights some of the basic tenets of the sociocultural approach and the work of Miedema and Wardekker (1999) and Shaw (1994). The second section examines the suggested extension of Vygotsky's work with Erikson's (1963,1968) psychosocial model as a means for considering identity development from a sociocultural perspective. The third section presents a discussion of the complementarity of the ideas of Vygotsky and Bakhtin (1986). The fourth section attempts to show how a sociocultural perspective may be employed to frame empirical work exploring the production of students labeled "at risk."

SIGNIFICANT TENETS OF THE SOCIOCULTURAL APPROACH WITH RESPECT TO IDENTITY

Vygotsky's (1978, 1986) ideas have gained popularity over the last four decades due to several factors including: a) the current publication and availability of much of Vygotsky's work with subsequent translations; b) the relevancy of Vygotsky's ideas to issues in education; and c) a growing conviction that traditional theoretical frameworks in psychology are both incomplete and fundamentally flawed (Sarason, 2001; Wertsch & Tulviste, 1996). Current research in psychology pertaining directly to identity formation is based on models that are limited in cultural historical and mediational analyses. Emphasizing the social formation of mind, the sociocultural approach may offer a number of advantages for the study of identity, including the integration of recent research in this field.

The sociocultural approach offers three fundamental differences from traditional approaches to the study of identity.

1. It suggests that many of the characteristics related to learning, such as personality, identity, and other higher mental processes, are dynamic and shift over time and in relation to the activities and contexts in which students participate. Therefore, the notion of identity is fluid rather than static; distributed socially, contradictory rather than unified at times, and open-ended. It can not be reduced to a status except by arbitrary methods.

2. The sociocultural approach emphasizes the mutually constitutive relationship of the individual and the social context. The individual has agency, or the ability to influence the social context, while, in turn, the context influences the individual. This dialectical relationship is what makes the sociocultural approach so important at this juncture in psychology, and in identity formation more specifically.

3. The sociocultural approach focuses on mediated activity, and the discursive practices within particular settings, as both a unit of analysis for understanding consciousness and the process through which identity is mediated by the use of cultural tools.

We will draw on extensions of Vygotsky's work completed by Wertsch (1991), Miedema and Wardekker (1999), and Shaw (1994) in this section to elaborate these ideas.

The sociocultural approach to the study of mind (Wertsch, 1991) emphasizes developmental change over time, or genesis, the dialectical engagement of an individual in relation to social context, and the role of cultural tools as mediational means. By extension then, in order to understand the development of identity—as well as the development of what Vygotsky calls, higher mental processes—one must examine developmental change over time, within and across four genetic domains: microgenesis, the developmental history of mental processes; ontogenesis, the developmental history of a particular individual; sociocultural history, the developmental history of a particular social or cultural group; and phylogenesis, the developmental history of humankind. The relations between and across these domains point to the primacy of the social[1] construction of knowledge and identity. Vygotsky (1978, 1986) argued that human higher level mental functioning exists on an intermental plane initially, and is internalized on an intramental plane secondarily; knowledge construction moves from the social to the individual through dialectical engagement with discourses and social practices. Vygotsky's emphasis on the social origin of higher mental functioning, defined as the general genetic law of cultural development, led to a focus on human action mediated by the use of cultural tools, such as language and number systems, themselves transformed through use. Therefore, and unique to this approach, is the emphasis on language and discourse systems as centrally implicated in both the construction and deconstruction of identity. A discussion of the embedded process of internalization, the dialectical relationship of individual and social context, as well as semiotic mediation, follows.

Internalization and Identity

Miedema and Wardekker (1999) argue that a theory of the development of identity along Vygotskian lines would have two conditions. First of all, internalization would not simply be a transferal of elements of the social context from the "outside" to the "inside" of a developing person. Internalization

> is, rather, the transition from what a child can or wants to do in the context of a social activity ... to what it can or wants to do individually and independently (Miedema & Wardekker, 1999, p. 79).

Accordingly, this theory recognizes the inadequacy of assuming a consistent and "essentialized" individual identity, and instead posits a context sensitive identity that may shift and change given social relations and the

social surround. Indeed, identity becomes a viable construct only in connection with and as representative of particular social relationships and
contexts. For example, a successful academic identity is unlikely to be
internalized where affordances are absent.

Second, the relationship between the individual and the social context
is not one of cultural determinism; identity is not merely a reflection of
social structures and discourses. Miedema and Wardekker (1999) argue
that it is not

> the social structures themselves that are internalized, but the *meaning* the
> individual learns to give to these structures in its interaction with others and
> in relation to what he or she has learned before. Internalization is an activity
> of the giving and incorporation of meaning, not a process of impression in
> which the individual stays passive. (p. 79-80)

Here, it is important to note that the choice of words is crucial to the way
we conceptualize a sociocultural approach to identity construction. We are
not, for example, talking about two separate entities—the individual and
the social context—in a linear, interactive relationship. Rather, we are
defining the contextualized individual as the subject of study, inseparable
from the social context and set of social relations that form the dialectical
whole. In some respects, the difficulties of describing this model reflect the
primacy of individualistic assumptions that have been historically embedded in our academic language, and general psychological concepts (see
for a discussion of the historical shaping of psychological discourse, Graumann & Gergen, 1996).

The Dialectic of Semiotic Mediation

Shaw's (1994) work offers an interpretation that addresses the level of
discourse systems and clarifies the construction of identity for the dialectically contextualized subject through semiotic mediation. For Shaw (1994),
the categories and symbols that comprise and reflect a person's identity
both: 1) "mediate a reflection on self and on the intentions, desires, and
goals that orient the self in a particular behavioral environment" and 2) "at
the same time, identity expressions invoke tacit knowledge of life-chance
difference linked to status domains" (p. 83). Discourse communities provide access to a social conversation, as well as the influence of that conversation. Identity construction occurs in the dialectical relationship between
the two. The self is constructed in relation to a cultural hierarchy of status
domains that mark certain social communities and membership within a
social community as more or less valuable given socially constructed values
and practices. Identifying the self within a particular community allows the

subject a common understanding or conception of what is good or desirable. Here the subject finds reciprocity, loyalty, commitment and shared vision with others "in mind." In turn, the subject finds his or her identity dialectically constituted in the social relations of the community, such that the values and beliefs that locate the community within a particular status domain in the cultural hierarchy are imposed by others on the subject as a result of group membership and inter-group relations (Portes, 1996). Social privileges, oppression, affordances and limitations, are structured and co-produced in this fashion, as well as assigned (i.e., "at risk" group membership).

A sociocultural approach to identity offers researchers a rich paradigm for studying the construction of identity, as well as understanding and explaining the lot of students labeled "at risk" in today's schools on the basis of class, gender, and group membership. Indeed, Vygotsky's contribution turns the traditional psychological approach to knowledge and identity construction—the "objective" study of the individual—on its head. Rather than attempting to identify "essentialized" and universal qualities that are extant in students labeled "at risk" as a method for remediating those students, we may come to understand the complexity surrounding the social construction of knowledge and identity, by taking into consideration the historical development of various groups and the cultural tools and social practices of one community relative to others within a specific historical moment. Understanding the construction of identity as a dialectical process that engages the individual agent within cultural historical contexts provides fertile ground for developmental research.

ADVANCING THEORY: SOCIOCULTURAL AND PSYCHOSOCIAL APPROACHES TO IDENTITY

It is worth noting that current research on identity formation emphasizes two distinct extremes, without much common ground in between. More traditional psychological theorists focus on identifying a single line of identity development in a universal stage like fashion that will hold across contexts (see for example Berzonsky, 1988, 1989; Marcia, 1966; Streitmatter, 1993). These models have been developed mainly with college students and assume that three of Erikson's identity domains—ideology, work, and fidelity—are the central aspects of identity for all persons across cultures. In response to these models, recent work has surfaced in "identity politics" stating that voices from non-dominant groups have been excluded from the research and are therefore, not represented by the models produced. In particular, taking this position are researchers from feminist psychology and science (see for example Gannon, Luchetta, Rhodes, Pardie, & Segrist, 1992; Gilligan, 1982; Harding, 1986), the psychology of different racial and ethnic groups (see for example Fairchild, 1991; Graham, 1992; Malgady, Rogler, & Costantino, 1987), and the psychology of lesbian and gay populations (see for example Herek, Kimmel, Amaro, & Melton, 1991; Morin, 1977, 1978). Others have challenged the traditional psychological model from a sociological perspective (see for example Bourdieu, 1998; Côté, 1996; Côté & Levine, 1988; Giddens, 1991).

Our position is consonant with the latter perspectives in that an articulated sociocultural theory of identity offers an alternative that incorporates the critiques of identity politics and sociology. We feel this can be accomplished for several reasons. First, as mentioned above, Vygotsky's analysis of four developmental domains improves our ability to understand the construction of identity in relation to social and cultural factors, as well as socially constructed cognitive functions and personal traits. Second, Vygotsky's emphasis on the process of internalization, semiotic uptakes, and the dynamic dialectical relationship between individual and social context is crucial for an understanding of the different ways in which individuals are positioned in society and the way in which social identities are co-constructed. Finally, the emphasis on language and discourses as cultural tools provides us with a mechanism for understanding the process of internalization, and also for studying the ways in which identities are constructed dialogically.

The Conversation Between Sociocultural and Psychosocial Models: Commonalities Across Vygotsky and Erikson

The sociocultural approach focuses on the study of change in both individual and societal development (Vygotsky, 1978, 1986). Erikson's (1963, 1968) psychosocial model is also concerned with uncovering explanatory change mechanisms. For our present purposes, only a cursory description of psychosocial development, and extensions of Erikson's work by Marcia (1966), will be provided to identify some of the ideas that overlap or contrast, as well as some of the implications for a sociocultural framework.

Erikson's experiences during and after the Second World War forced him to confront cultural factors in developing a psychosocial theory capable of explaining, in part, the horrors of World War II. His account of how the Jews became "at risk" for extermination was based largely on a psychosocial analysis of the development of a pseudo-identity for the dominant German group. The latter could be extended to other conflicts in history, including parallels with the domination and oppression of cultural groups based upon religious or ethnic differences. Erikson's concern in this area is reflected across his writings, which included Native American youth in two tribes and African Americans in the United States. He wrote of the post-Versailles German youth who developed an oppositional identity, whose identity formation (Kultur), and their ideology rested on a pseudologic perversion of history, totalism and radical exclusion of foreigners/ness.

Erikson (1968) was most concerned about the development of identity in contexts where a person's "revolution of awareness" might be related to crises, not only normative ones, but also those stemming from inter-group relations. He wrote of man's creation of conceptions "necessary to heal himself of what most deeply divides and threatens him, namely, his division into what we have called pseudospecies" (Erikson, 1968, p. 298). In the above statement, Erikson reveals his awareness of the interplay of cultural historical factors with identity formation from two opposing perspectives. First, from the perspective of those whose deep-seated belief in the inherent superiority of their group (pseudospecies), leads to the construction of an identity that is interdependent with the second one. The second perspective is that of the "others" who occupy the degraded, inferior positions in a given social context. The dialogic relationship here, the objective and subjective, are in line with a unit of analysis in the sociocultural approach, namely the activity setting. It is in the post World War II context that Erikson considered the issues of culture, caste, and race in the development of identity in a general sense. He became painfully aware of the negative impact that discrimination and prejudice can have on identity formation and mental health in general, in his own life. The individual's ego and personality becomes defined through relationships with family members, peer groups, significant others, and interactions with the larger society. Hence, the formation of identities positioned "at risk" in the social context and other groups, becomes relevant from his pychosocial expansion of psychoanalysis.

Unfortunately, the psychosocial theory reflected in most human development texts today does not address the complexity of identity formation processes outside the mainstream context. Nor does it attend to the positive as well as the negative aspects of this process, particularly with regard to pathogenesis at the individual and collective levels. Both Erikson and Vygotsky would consider schools, among other contexts, as linked instrumentally to the identity development of students labeled "at risk." The post-Eriksonian literature seems to have taken a turn away from the original concerns expressed by him to the elaboration of stages and operationalization of identity achievement, which introduces major problems in terms of cultural validity (Portes, Dunham, & Del Castillo, 2000). First, Erikson addressed the topic as a problem for all of us who need to transcend the ethnocentric (or "pseudo") tendencies for what is really at stake, a wider global transcultural identity, the creation of a new order, and the outgrowth of prejudice. For example, he believed that gender differences in identity development are largely a function of the respective cultural expectations of men and women. We can extrapolate from that with regard to ethnic identity formation, as well as the identity formation of students "at risk."

The Identity Status Paradigm

Post-Eriksonian research has followed Marcia's (1966) extension paradigm during adolescence with four identity statuses ranging from diffusion and foreclosure to moratorium and achievement. Briefly, two dimensions of comparison—exploration and commitment—are operationalized in assigning an identity status to a subject. A diffused identity reflects low exploration and low commitment; best described, perhaps, as a denial of the developmental task of identity construction from the outset. A foreclosed identity reflects low exploration and high commitment, as in the case of a young adult adopting the beliefs of significant adults without question and without personal exploration. An identity in moratorium reflects high exploration and low commitment, which is theoretically representative of adolescents and, in this society at least, associated with a healthy identity. The achieved identity reflects exploration before commitment. Cultural, ethnic, gender, and social class comparisons have been the focus of this narrow version of identity research.

Marcia's (1966) extension of Erikson's work, though widely used and the sole basis for several different quantitative measures, has produced a conflict that goes beyond political and into scientific correctness. Most ethnic, and/or "third world," samples turn out to be less achieved and more foreclosed than mainstream, Western college samples belonging to the culture upon which the model was founded. The "deficit" implied in the literature today turns out to be a problem because healthy psychological development is defined by "achieving" an identity only after crisis, "sturm und drang," and periods of exploration. The achievement of a healthy identity is predicated upon a Western post-industrialized society that promotes individualism and, at the same time, produces the bulk of the models constructed in the field. "Less achieved" groups tend to value collectivism (Triandis, Bontempo, Villareal, Asai, & Luca, 1988) and may perhaps be goal oriented in other domains. Theories regarding identity formation may be biased toward values and cultural practices prevailing in a particular societal context. A strong belief endures in the United States that material success depends, for the most part, on individual effort and entrepreneurship. It is not surprising then, that personal growth and health are also believed to be optimal when predicated by individualism as a value and a social practice that is culturally situated.

In sum, such findings illustrate some of the ethnocentric assumptions found in post-Eriksonian models, as well as reveal how different value orientations influence theory development, and the paradigms that produce research findings. The latter research has been fertile in producing numerous studies comparing cultures in terms of identity achievement that indirectly helps to apply or elucidate a sociocultural interpretation. The above also illustrates the process through which a social identity such as "at risk" is co-constructed and structured continually. Labeling practices serve an instrumental function for society. Fortunately, a more sensitive discourse has emerged in the recent literature with regard to students *placed* "at risk" that implies the agency of others, as well as the social context, in the process of co-construction.

The Mediated Action Approach

Penuel and Wertsch (1995) highlighted a discussion of fidelity, ideology and work, three domains emphasized as central for identity formation in Erikson's model. Unfortunately, they did not address Marcia's (1966) paradigm which has guided the literature on identity, or Erikson's epigenetic principle, which is derived from prenatal growth. Penuel and Wertsch (1995) purposed a "mediated action approach" for the study of identity formation, that is in line with the development of other higher psychological processes. They presented an excellent summary of sociocultural theory's main tenets and elaborated on the ways in which Vygotsky's ideas, as noted above, could help extend Erikson's work on identity formation. Identity, as such, may be viewed as a concept of self that evolves gradually, between a maturing mind and society.

Using a mediated action approach to address the ideological domain might suggest that identity for students labeled "at risk" is subject to similar principles of cultural identity formation. For example, a mediated action approach considers the function labeling serves for the dominant, as well as the labeled groups. Identity development in general appears to be comprised of biological and social elements, as well as an ontological or agentic component. Identity development is fundamentally tied to the formation of an ideology about self, in relation to others, which consists of various facets (i.e., physical, sexual, social, vocational, and other components). Some are more salient than others in the self, something that is reflective of, though not determined by, what is salient in the social plane. In sum, the co-construction of higher psychological traits includes the area of identity. As noted in relation to Shaw's (1994) work earlier, individual and group agency need to be considered in terms of how persons negotiate and convert identity options offered in the social plane. For example, a young person may reject certain aspects or markers of her ethnicity and construct a mainstream identity while another may do the opposite. One may have a wider set of options than another. The person's context and "spirit of the times" may also play a role in determining whether one's ethnicity is fashionable to celebrate or something to be downplayed.

Considering Identity Construction Generally

An extension of both models may seem to argue that there are strong parallels in the processes of identity formation between the group and individual level, through a dialectical, mutually constitutive relationship. For example, let's take a relatively new cultural identity in the making, such as the technologically sophisticated adolescent, or Bar-Code Swiper (Luke

& Luke, 2001), and Gee's (2001) Millennials, denoting children born in 1982 or later and contextualized by rampant consumerism. Generally, there is the initial process of individuation from a larger social host that leads to independence of the new group. At this stage, the group's identity is somewhat diffused and based largely on its opposition to the host or dominant group. After a period of exploration, testing the fidelity of its constituents, and usually after within or inter-group conflicts, a point of stability is reached and maintained which reflects the maturity, or perhaps the achievement, of a positive, functional identity. According to Erikson, it is at this point that a group may turn to others to establish cooperative or antagonistic relations, but generally not before having established a solid intra-group identity or ideology among constituent members.

Some cultural groups attempt to forge an independent identity, but are censured by others, while other groups "get away with" more agency by virtue of differences in developed potential or tools that underlie mediated action, such as navigating school rules and responsibilities successfully or camouflaging school success. Similarly, a young person attempts to "come together" by defining what is part of the self and what is not, as suggested by classic psychosocial theory. What is missing from the latter is the role of mediated action in forging an identity and the role of context in defining the status of different aspects of identity, such as ethnicity or, more specifically, "at riskness."

Considering Ethnic Identity

Ethnic identity is conditional, and latent in everyone. It remains dormant unless certain context-person conditions are present, which then are included in the individual's consciousness. Once awakened, particular aspects of identity of the self may be subject to different courses of development, some of which have been described in the literature, in particular for ethnic identity development (Helms, 1990; Matute-Bianchi, 1986; Phinney & Chavira, 1992). These courses or paths may be regarded as variations around classic psychosocial themes, variations between conformity and foreclosure on one hand and moratorium and exploration on the other. In the case of students labeled "at risk," it is unclear how these young people form a common identity, or indeed, if they do. The extent to which they learn to assume this ascribed characteristic is open to question.

At a more specific level, the physical and sexual components of identity may weigh more heavily on the basis of what Vygotsky refers to as the "natural line of development." It is here that a discussion of Erikson's epigenetic principle becomes important. According to Erikson (1968),

> this principle states that anything that grows has a ground plan, and that out of this ground plan the parts arise, each part having its time of special ascendency, until all parts have arisen to form a functioning whole. (p. 92)

While he notes that there will be variation from culture to culture, Erikson argues that healthy development remains within the proper rate and sequence. Ultimately, he notes that personality develops according to "steps predetermined in the human organism's readiness to be driven toward, to be aware of, and to interact with a widening radius of significant individuals and institutions" (Erikson, 1968, p. 93). Vygotsky's work qualifies the epigenetic principle by arguing that the natural line, and its basic functions should be distinguished from the "cultural line" of development, which corresponds to higher psychological functions. Hence, in approaching the study of identity development, the phylogenetic domain becomes part of the analysis, but mainly with respect to inter-group relations. The cultural historical level is one where cultural capital, social policies and changes in economy, attitudes and activities might be considered in predicting the emergence, type or strength of different kinds of social identities. Some components of identity become relevant, but always in a fashion that is relative to social "others."

For example, a useful way to understand the complex influence of ethnicity in identity formation is that it is a domain that stems only partly from the natural line. For the most part, an ethnic identity is one that depends most on the cultural line of development, which depends on language, values, artifacts and social interaction. In many situations, ethnic identity is correlated with phenotypic traits that, in part, help define one's concept of self. The latter, however, is not essential nor a criterial attribute. Ethnic identity may be defined as a particular type of cultural identity, which involves an interaction between at least two parties. Exploring and then, committing to an ideology, vocation or set of moral beliefs to which one is faithful may be regarded as the essence of identity achievement in general, and for some cases, may include components of ethnic identity formation, in particular. However, other paths exist which account for the formation of the latter. These components are situated in a context that depends on certain forms of social organization and cultural practices. For example, a vocational identity is a component that is also subject to market conditions, and the positioning of individuals in a late modern, economically global society.

One must often search and make commitments within a cultural menu of options that is generally offered, unless one happens upon a moment of cultural transformation, as exemplified by the Bar-Code Swipers above (Luke & Luke, 2001), and is therefore able to enact a historically new social identity. One general observation is that the tension generally found in adolescent identity formation for students "at risk," initially described as storm and stress by Hall (1904), may be reflective of tensions found at the societal level. Sociocultural tensions at the group level may become played out in the person's individual experience under some circumstances. For example, during the turbulence of the 1960's surrounding the Civil Rights Movement, a secular effect may have been established that influenced the

identity formation, collectively, of a whole generation or cohort. Historically, ethnic identity has been even more situated or contingent upon
social conditions, namely those that involve intergroup contact and individual development in bicultural or multicultural contexts. Contrary to
what is suggested by much of the current literature, the identity formation
process is not necessarily tied to adolescence in a neat, stage-like sequence.
Rather, because of its social nature and dependence on intergroup relations, it is a process that interacts with and may continue long after adolescence, influencing relationships across contexts.

Any theory of identity formation, must be able to explain the regenera-
tion of adolescent academic, professional, age, gender, and ethnic forms of
identity. For example, some adolescents actively explore their cultural
identity options, which may include an ethnic component. Others have no
choice but to deal with their ethnicity. Still others do not explore and thus
accept or conform to some form of cultural identity without experiencing
stress and tension on this dimension. In Erikson's terms, they may remain
diffused, not having de-individuated or searched actively. Under some historical periods, identities may be constrained more by ascription than
under others. Finally, the achievement of identity is not an actual state or
point in development. A person may reach "achievement," or a stable
period of identity in selecting one ideology over another. However, ideologies and people change with time.

The question of commitments to ideology, work and fidelity in Erikson's
model imply a certain amount of cultural situatedness, along with the consequences of membership in social communities as articulated earlier by
Shaw (1994). Ideology and work are two of over half a dozen identity components, some which stem from the natural and/or the cultural lines of
development. Fidelity, on the other hand, refers to staying on course with
previously made commitments, which may weigh more heavily on the
agentic, individual side. Hence, a sociocultural approach would require
qualification of any existing identity formation paradigm and include
one's agency inside a network of social, intergroup relations. The inclusion
of agency would lead us to consider change reciprocally from both directions, societal and individual.

In sum, we would argue that Vygotsky would distinguish between the
two lines of development in sorting the various identity components. While
he did not address our topic, we think he would agree that the identity
domains noted by Erikson reflect some of the main types of sociocultural
identities that may emerge on the basis of the natural line of development
(i.e. physical, sexual), in relation with the cultural line (e.g., ideological or
vocational identity components). In the case of identity, it is worth reem-
phasizing the first tenet of sociocultural theory mentioned earlier: that of
the genetic analysis of developmental change over time and across microgenesis, ontogenesis, sociocultural history, and phylogenesis. Therefore,
when discussing both the natural and cultural lines of development, inter-

cultural-phylogenetic interactions are to be included as well. That is, a person's group of origin, and its status may serve to mediate the process of adaptation between individuals and other groups in society. The cultural history of identities, as in the historical production of certain groups as "at risk," would surface here in turn.

Cautious Eclecticism: Recognizing Deeper Differences Between Erikson and Vygotsky

After the first glance by Penuel and Wertsch (1995), pursuing a more in depth examination of the connections between Erikson's psychosocial theory and Vygotsky's sociocultural approach becomes consequential for the field. We have found ourselves concerned about several theoretical issues that reflect important limitations. In this section, we consider Vygotsky's work, not as a singular body of research, but dialogically. With an interpretation of his exchange with the written work of both Piaget and Freud, his own critiques of aspects of their theoretical frameworks, and Erikson's reliance on their work, we find reason enough to pause prior to attempting to integrate components of Erikson's model of psychosocial development with a sociocultural approach.

From the outset, it should be noted that although comparisons between Erikson and Vygotsky seem appealing in this area, it is important to keep in mind that:

1. Erikson's psychosocial theory is primarily a "social" extension of psychoanalysis that has been situated in psychology. Identity formation during adolescence represents a shift of the self or ego-identity from a mostly other-constructed individual towards one that permits the individual more affordances than before in terms of advances in cognition and socio-biological factors.

2. The questions Erikson sought to answer in the work that produced his stage theory of psychosocial development and the identity dynamics and themes such as fidelity and others were considerably different from those of Vygotsky. Erikson's great insight was that cultural forces or voices that extend beyond the family of origin influence the identities of youth considerably. Adolescence is a critical period for the acquisition of ideological stances and social identities in terms of vocation, politics and morality.

3. Vygotsky did not extend psychoanalysis as a paradigm for the study of mind. On the contrary, after an initial interest in this approach, he rejected it totally and began to build what he believed to be a broader, more valid and scientific paradigm for the study of human consciousness and higher psychological functions (see van der Veer & Valsiner, 1991). Specifically, Vygotsky rejected the monism inherent in psychoanalysis, and long before Erikson, recognized the role

      of social processes as inseparable from the (social) formation of
      mind.

4. Vygotsky and the other founders of sociocultural theory developed
      a paradigm that addresses identity implicitly as a higher level func-
      tion, at least as higher level concepts (of self), but like so many
      other areas of psychology, the development of this approach was
      truncated ironically by cultural historical events. In reviewing his
      writings, one does not find discussions about identity, ego or self,
      but rather consciousness. Identity may be defined perhaps then as a
      type of consciousness or awareness of enduring and changing
      aspects of an internalized and projected, social concept of self.

Several more specific points will be elaborated further in this section.

As noted by van der Veer and Valsiner (1991), Vygotsky studied and
worked with Freud's psychoanalytical model of the psyche in *Pedagogical
Psychology*, though by the time he wrote *The Psychology of Art*, he had taken
on a critical perspective. Later, in his critical analysis of *Thought and Language* (edited by Kozulin, 1986), Vygotsky's critique of Freud's ideas, and
Piaget's as well, becomes central to the articulation of his own theoretical
position. Vygotsky (1986) attempted to differentiate his ideas from Freud
and Piaget along several dimensions, only a few of which are discussed
here. In so doing, he intended to address the crisis which split psychology
into two irreconcilable halves: "a 'natural' science branch that could
explain elementary sensory and reflex processes, and a 'mental' science
half that could describe emergent properties of higher psychological processes" (Cole & Scribner, 1978, p. 5). The gap between explanation and
description was a result of the "prevailing duality" between materialism
and idealism, and was reflected in the creation of multiple incompatible
systems of psychology by theorists such as Freud, Levy-Bruhl, and Blondel
(Vygotsky, 1986). Evidence of the crisis was "reflected in the incongruity
between these theoretical systems, with their metaphysical, idealistic over-
tones, and the empirical bases on which they are erected" (Vygotsky, 1986,
p. 13-14). While Piaget attempted to sidestep this duality, ultimately
Vygotsky believed he was caught up in it nonetheless, arguing that Piaget's
effort to focus on the facts of cognitive development as constitutive of theory, was supplanted by the very hypotheses and choice of experiments that
Piaget used as tools for obtaining the facts to begin with (see for discussion, Vygotsky, 1986).

A point of concern for Vygotsky that linked both Freud and Piaget was
their emphasis on the development of the personality from the biological
line. For example, as noted by van der Veer and Valsiner (1991), Freud
claimed "that the social behavior of man could be understood by reference
to biological drives and instincts" (p. 89). And Vygotsky (1986) argued that
even if Piaget had not mentioned Freud in his work, "it would be clear nevertheless that what we have here is the biological concept attempting to

derive the specificity of the child's psyche from his biological nature" (p. 45-46). An issue here is more than a simple biological-environmental or individual-social dichotomy. Instead, the shift that Vygotsky attends to is a shift away from the simplistic dichotomization of the individual-social interaction, to an understanding of the central role of cultural mediation: the role of cultural tools, such as language, in the co-construction of knowledge and identity.

Two Interpretations of Egocentric Speech

Perhaps the most clearly delineated area of difference between Vygotsky and Piaget is Vygotsky's critique of Piaget's interpretation of egocentrism and, in particular, egocentric speech and language learning, which again employs aspects of Freud's model of the psyche. For Piaget, autistic thought, or unconscious and undirected thought has its origins in the pleasure principle which precedes the reality principle in development (Vygotsky, 1986). As the precursor to all mental development, according to Freud and Piaget, autistic thought is based on a form of hallucinatory imagination directed toward the fulfillment of pleasure, for Freud specifically sexual pleasure (see discussions of Freud's (1988) theory of infantile sexuality). Egocentric speech then, is a marker for the bridge between autistic thought and directed thought, which develops over time as the reality principle begins to gain prominence. This process is elaborated by Piaget in his stage theory of cognitive development that moves from mental thought defined by sensorimotor exploration through to the development of reason and formal operations highly connected with viable constructions of "objective" reality.

Rather than an externalized expression of the limitations placed on thought by the pleasure principle, Vygotsky argued that egocentric speech marked the developmental process of initial internalization: the very moment when social language begins to move inward, external speech becomes inner speech, and thinking takes on a verbal and fundamentally social form. From this moment onward, the "child begins to perceive the world not only through his eyes but also through his speech" (Vygotsky, 1978, p. 32). Speech plays a fundamental mediating role in cognitive development as a complex cultural tool that aids in the self-regulation of behavior.

The Emphasis on Structuralism for Erikson

Erikson critiqued Freud's emphasis on sexuality, and argued for a central role for the "social" in his shift from Freud's psychosexual development to psychosocial development. Ultimately, Erikson argued for the unity of biological, psychological, and social factors in development and differentiated his structural conception of the ego from Freud's classic psychodynamic model, which identified the ego as an organizer, through balancing and regulating multiple functions, such as impulse control. Erikson's move to a structural model redefines the ego "as an intrapsychic organization—an internal structure that develops over time through a hierarchical sequence of qualitatively different stages, which in turn, give meaning and coherence to both internal and external experience" (Kroger, 1992). Kroger (1992) highlights the way in which Erikson noted structural features in adolescent intrapsychic organization in his discussion outlining the stages of ego growth. For example, Erikson (1968) argued that the "schedule" for ego growth begins with introjection, based on the incorporation of the image of the "mothering adult(s)" which establishes initial mutuality, to childhood identification through satisfactory interaction with "trustworthy representatives of a meaningful hierarchy of roles as provided by the generations living together in some form of family," to identity formation (Erikson, 1968, p. 159). Identity formation

> arises from the selective repudiation and mutual assimilation of childhood identifications and their absorption in a new configuration, which in turn, is dependent on the process by which a society (often through subsocieties) identifies the young individual, recognizing him as somebody who had to become the way he is and who, being the way he is, is taken for granted. (Erikson, 1968, p. 159)

Therefore, the movement from childhood identifications toward a new configuration, which is capable of filtering, selecting, and reflecting new ways of participating in the world, represents two "distinct forms of structural organization," according to Kroger (1992). In turn, Marcia's (1980) extension paradigm is articulated in structural terms.

While some of Erikson's and Vygotsky's ideas are complementary, in particular in terms of the words used if not necessarily the meanings, as noted by Berzonsky (1988), Erikson's conceptualization of ego identity in structural terms parallels the unified organization of the notion of *structure d'ensemble* emphasized by Piaget. And certainly, Erikson's (1968) reference to the work of Piaget, along with the noted importance of formal operational thought for identity development, firmly locates Erikson's ideas within a structural paradigm that shares Piaget's central role for the biological, the individual, and the internal, in spite of a different emphasis for social influences (and different definition for the word "social," see footnote 1).

Two Perspectives on Development

Other issues that require caution include the problems inherent with stage theories of development in general, exemplified by the work of Rousseau, Piaget, and Erikson, and in particular with concerns regarding "developmental readiness," as noted by Rousseau and Piaget. Perspectives regarding the process of development as ordered, sequential, and cumulative, along with the assumption of continuous forward and linear progression, differentiate stage theorists from Vygotsky (1978), who argued for uneven developmental processes and open-ended progressions:

> Our concept of development implies a rejection of the frequently held view that cognitive development results from the gradual accumulation of separate changes. We believe that child development is a complex dialectical process, characterized by periodicity, unevenness in the development of different functions, metamorphosis or qualitative transformation of one form into another, intertwining of external and internal factors, and adaptive processes which overcome impediments that the child encounters. (p. 73)

Taking the zone of proximal development as a model for the relationship between learning and development, the notion of development as recursive, and potentially regressive, surfaces.[2] Defined as the developmental area between actual development—the tasks and capacities the child has mastered—and those tasks at which the child is successful with adult assistance or the guidance of a more experienced peer, the zone of proximal development identifies potential, and the developmental abilities on the verge of mastery (Vygotsky, 1978). When engaged in a social activity, utilizing the zone of proximal development offers teachers, peers, and individual students themselves, positions as active and socially situated constructors of knowledge and identity, as an alternative to roles described for teachers as assessors of "developmental readiness" who conform to "developmentally appropriate practice."

Each of the issues raised in this section—from Erikson's use of Freud's model to his reliance on Piaget's stage theory for cognitive development and, in particular, the relationship between the development of formal operational thought as unfettered rationality, marked by the ability to take different perspectives on topics including alternative forms of identity—give us reason to pause. While it is worthwhile to compare the conceptualizations of both Erikson and Vygotsky, and we have highlighted just a few points of comparison here, the similarities nonetheless remain limited in scope. While Erikson was a social thinker and pushed the boundaries of psychodynamic theory, he was ultimately unable to transcend it. These theoretical limitations, along with perhaps more powerful insights on knowledge and identity construction, lead us toward the extension of sociocultural theory through the work of Bakhtin.

BAKHTIN'S CRITIQUE OF STRUCTURALISM AND THE AUTHORSHIP OF THE SELF IN UTTERANCE, GENRE, AND DIALOGUE

Bakhtin's theory of "communication" (Holquist, 1986) is suggestive of the work of Miedema and Wardekker (1999), in particular the discussion of internalization and meaning making, and Shaw's (1994) description of the mediation of identity through speech that links us to social communities, and ultimately life pathways in status domains. Bakhtin's contribution provides a complementary framework for sociocultural theory and for examining the way in which utterances, speech genres, and dialogue itself, both position people as they are utilized and internalized and are, in turn, transformed through being re-voiced, or re-spoken, by speaking subjects. The compatibility of aspects of Bakhtin's ideas with Vygotsky's and the sociocultural approach were alluded to a decade ago by Kozulin (1990) and Wertsch (1991), and even earlier by Emerson (1986). Bakhtin's work has followed a path in some sense similar to Vygotsky's, from publication dates long after the completion of the work to belated translations. In addition, Bakhtin published under several names, was exiled in the early 1930's (Clark & Holquist, 1984), and some of his work was narrowly rescued from a damp basement, partially unrecoverable (Hicks, 2000).[3] We highlight just a few ideas from Bakhtin here—his critique of structuralism, and his concepts of utterance, genre, and dialogue as constitutive of identity. The dialogical aspects are inherently embedded in sociocultural theory as cultural tools through which psychological phenomena are constructed.

A Critique of Structuralism in Linguistics

As suggested by Morson (1986a), Bakhtin's most important contribution may lie in his challenge to and reconsideration of traditional oppositions or binaries: "of the individual to society, of self to other, of the specific utterance to the totality of language, and of particular actions to the world of norms and conventions" (p. xi). In arguments with the ideas of Freud and Marx, Bakhtin questions the assumptions upon which structuralism rests and, in doing so, anticipates post-structuralism with a critique of structuralist assumptions. In the simplest terms, along with his critique of binary categories, Bakhtin saw language as inherently asystematic, as a constant struggle of systematic and unsystematic factors, and he disputed the view of structuralists who argued that language was systematic, coherent, and governed by set rules and definitions.

In particular, Saussure, a structuralist, distinguished between language as a system (*langue*), characterized by abstract and timeless qualities, and as performance (*parole*), characterized by the particular and socially situated (Holquist, 1986). Saussure worked mainly in the sphere of *langue*, and implied that the systematic categories developed there would apply to the level of *parole* as well. According to Bakhtin (in Voloshinov, 1973/1986), Saussure argued that *langue* stands in opposition to *parole* "in the same way as does that which is social to that which is individual" (p. 6). But for Bakhtin, these two levels are completely distinct, though they always operate together, reflecting the contextuality of the social / individual relationship so central to Vygotsky's (1978, 1986) work. The place "where they inter-mingle, the force that binds them and the arena where the strength of each is tested, is the utterance" (Holquist, 1986, p. 62).[4] This relation is rel-evant to the understanding of how identities are formed and performed in different contexts.

Utterance: A Speech Act

Utterance, the fundamental unit of analysis for Bakhtin, is a unit of speech communication and, as noted by Wertsch (1991), it is embedded in situated action rather than a representation of an analytical category abstracted from language. Quoting Bakhtin (1986),

> speech can exist in reality only in the form of concrete utterances of individ-ual speaking people, speech subjects. Speech is always cast in the form of an utterance belonging to a particular speaking subject, and outside this form it cannot exist" (p. 71).

An utterance is bounded by the change of speaking subjects, rather than a grammatically structured sentence or complete thought. For Bakhtin (1986), words, themselves, have semantic content, for example, what is found in a dictionary. However, once a word is spoken, once a phase or sentence is uttered, it takes on a meaning that is dialogic and social.

This distinction between the abstracted qualities of language, in terms of syntax and grammar, and utterance, in terms of social communication, is compatible with Vygotsky's (1986) notion that words have meaning, but speech has sense:

> A word acquires its sense from the context in which it appears; in different contexts, it changes its sense. Meaning remains stable throughout the changes of sense. The dictionary meaning of a word is no more than a stone in the edifice of sense, no more than a potentiality that finds diversified real-ization in speech. (p. 245)

For both Bakhtin and Vygotsky, oral and written language becomes meaningful only through social communication and dialogue. The social relationships formed, the way the speakers are positioned, and the tone and content of the speech shape the construction of identity for the partic-ipants in that social space. For example, in a dialogue in which a speaker challenges the listener's cherished beliefs unexpectedly, the speaker may be re-positioned in light of his or her new comments. If, however, the speaker's words are anticipated, or alternately, in line with the listener's feelings, his or her position may remain unchanged, or become one reflective of the shared feelings.

Speech Genres

Each sphere of social communication and activity develops "relatively stable types" of utterances, which Bakhtin calls, speech genres. Military commands, presidential addresses, and story book fictions are examples of speech genres. In education, classrooms and classroom activities, reflect speech genres as well, from "show and tell" for primary school students to oral and written presentations of science labs for secondary students. These social activities follow certain discourse patterns, such as, for a science lab, introducing the research question, stating a hypothesis, discussing the method, describing, analyzing and interpreting the results, and finally, concluding with a statement that addresses the research hypothesis. Speech genres provide frameworks for understanding classroom communication, learning, and the co-construction of identities. In addition, they also reveal social relations, expectations for behavior, and social values, including those that are privileged and those that resist, positions that are contested and often contradictory. An utterance is individual, for Bakhtin, though it utilizes and builds upon the ideas and voices of other people, termed "heteroglossia." Heterogeneity surfaces through genre, as well, in the constant struggle of discourses which work to stratify, diversify, and at the same time maintain aspects of randomness.

Speech genres, the conventions by which utterances are organized, then, develop and shift and change historically, and can be said to reflect a particular activity within a social context at a particular historical time. This presents another parallel between Bakhtin and Vygotsky, the contextualization provided by the activity, social context, and historical moment. Although neither focused explicitly on identity formation, one may easily see the relevance and influence of socially constructed speech genres, and their communities of practice, in the construction of identity. This is because identity construction is dialogical in nature. So is ethnicity and "at riskness," and thus the study of the way young people construct identity becomes didactic and strategic for this field.

Identity as a Dialogical Process

Each utterance assumes a response, whether the context of the dialogue is between several people, two people, or an individual conversation occurring through inner speech. And through the activity of dialogue, people—

alone, with another, or in groups—engage in acts of creation, which both constitute and are constituted by the speaker's identity. For Bakhtin, each act of speaking is an act of creation; "we are all creators: a speaker is to his utterance what an author is to his text" (Holquist, 1986, p. 67). Formal acts of creation, such as literary works, stand alongside of our everyday dialogic creations, as another type of text, rather than as privileged texts. And, according to Bakhtin, "our ultimate act of authorship results in the text which we call our self (Holquist, 1986, p. 67). Identity is produced by speech, "particularly through the contradictions of narrative" (Stewart, 1986, p. 51). In turn, rather than start with the concept of the "real" person" as the beginning point of ideology, "Bakhtin would say that it is precisely within narrative, and within ideological structures, that the concept of the individual subject," is born (Stewart, 1986, p. 52). We would add that stability in identity may thus be reflected by the ideological structures that constitute and are expressed over the course of social, and more precisely, dialogical narratives.

Morson (1986b) highlights the complimentarity of both Bakhtin and Vygotsky with regard to the overlay of social and ideological values embedded in utterance, genre, dialogue and identity:

> We describe Bakhtin and Vygotsky as, at their most basic level, maintaining the social as primary in the sense that selves are constituted and composed of 'the social.' Selfhood, they argued, derives from an internalization of the voices a person has heard, and each of these voices is saturated with social and ideological values. Thought itself is but 'inner speech,' and inner speech is outer speech that we have learned to 'speak' in our heads while retaining the full register of conflicting social values. (Morson, 1986b, p. 85)

Working with ideas from Bakhtin and Vygotsky, we have in common an emphasis on the social construction of both knowledge and identity, with the primary cultural tool, spoken language, exemplified by particular utterances, speech genres, and discourses at the center of the process. And, we would again emphasize the active role of the individual, his or her will in transforming speech and voice dialogically. For example, the consistent patterns of response to the real or imagined utterances of others may be related to strong and positive or vulnerable and damaged identities.

From our view, there may be little difference between an expanded view of self-concept and the sociocultural perspective of identity. Mediated action, through others' voices and perspectives are constitutive of self (see also, Cooley, 1925 from the perspective of symbolic interactionism). One other point merits mention in this respect. Within the structural camp of Piaget and Erikson, we note Elkind's (1978) expansion of theory and recognition of the other with the term "imaginary audience." Adolescent behavior and thinking is mediated by others when acting "as if" one can be observed anticipating responses to physical, sexual, social, and other components of identity. This shift in awareness is considered to account for much of the stress of adolescence, and where the foundations of identity are to be found. The imaginary audience, along with the "personal fable" and similar behavior and thinking patterns are viewed as the effects of formal operational thinking. This stage, interestingly, is recognized, but remains largely unexplained by these theorists.

Indeed, logical thinking emerges from and depends totally upon culture. We would argue that increased awareness of others begins to play a major role in identity construction long before adolescence and long after it. Second, while the structure of concrete and formal thought has served a useful purpose for decades in describing "individual" mental development, it has been reified and become a good example of a concept that is made real through social construction. Third, it is clear that Piaget's inability to account for the development of formal operations lies in contrast with Vygotsky's account. Vygotsky easily explains this and other higher order psychological processes through the general genetic law of cultural development.

Finally, and of importance, utterances are shaped by the power and position of the person speaking. What is said is important, but to capture what is said we must also concern ourselves with *who is talking* (Holquist, 1986). For Bakhtin, position is defined through a visual metaphor that takes into account both space and time: as I view an event, I view it from a specific place, with a particular visual perspective, and at a specific moment in time. By necessity, because my partner can not be in exactly the same space, at exactly the same time, his or her visual perspective must be different. Therefore, the *law of placement*, entails the noncoincidence of perspectives; my perspective and my partner's will always be different. Clark and Holquist (1984) elaborate this idea as follows:

> From the unique place I occupy in existence there are things only I can see; the distinctive slice of the world that only I perceive is a 'surplus of seeing,' where excess is defined relative to the lack all others have of that world shaped exclusively by me. (p. 71)

Bakhtin's notion of noncoincidence applies not only to the noncoincidence of my self and another, but also to my self and signs which signify me, and to my self and my perception of self.

The activity of achieving a self, for Bakhtin, remains an incomplete, open, timeless process, though when I perceive my partner, I perceive a complete human other. This sense of *completeness* that we bestow on others, in turn, others provide for us. I gain categories for ordering my self from other selves. Clark and Holquist (1984) clarify this idea when they note,

> I cannot see the self that is my own, so I must try to perceive it in others' eyes. This process of conceptually seeing myself by refracting the world through

values of the other begins very early, when children first begin to see themselves through the eyes [of their significant care givers]. (p. 73)

For Bakhtin, we get our self from the other, and we give the other the gift of a self; the gift exchanged is the gift of a self that is perceivable, or visible, to one's self. This exchange is not a simple reflection, we do not reflect passively the other. Rather we actively *refract* the other to him or her self, and receive the active *refraction* of our self through the other's perspective, or in Bakhtin's words, their optic. Through this exchange the social construction of identity takes place. In this sense, identity is that self that is constructed again and again, dialectically with others over time, and situated within social relations. Other voices and perspectives are offered by people with whom we are active, including adult and peer voices, voices from the media, and traditional and popular culture.

In the last section our endeavor is to explore and understand the way secondary students, many ethnically, linguistically, economically, or sexually different from the dominant group, come to be labeled "at risk." We share some of our research in the following section as an example of some of the ways these ideas may buttress a sociocultural approach to identity.

SOCIOCULTURAL RESEARCH: A LOOK AT DIALOGUE AND POSITIONING IN HIGH SCHOOL

Over the last three years the first author has been involved with a writing class for students in an alternative high school program for 92 students, grades nine through twelve. Each of these students has been labeled "at risk" for leaving school prior to graduation; some by virtue of failing in their coursework in the main high school, and others, merely because they have chosen to attend this program. They are an extremely diverse group of students including single mothers, young people who are homeless, students from both the working and middle classes, and European and Native American students. Many have supportive and caring parents, and others have legal guardians. The common ground between them seems to be that none of them feel comfortable in the main high school, which serves 2,000 students in a sprawling building, in a Northwestern university town of 32,000 people.

Methods and Analysis

The research described and examined in this chapter is excerpted from a large body of data which includes oral texts gathered from interviews with students and teachers, written and oral class requirements and classroom dialogue, the language of district documents and local newspaper reports, and the conversation of students outside of school. Data collection for this long term study has utilized ethnographic methods such as participant observation and longitudinal interviews. Students have contributed their informal journal entries, and their polished stories and poems as examples of written work. Informal conversations within the classroom and outside of school have been recorded along with member checks which allow the students and teachers to reflect on what has been observed about them and recorded from them, so that they may confirm or challenge the data. Informal conversations and formal interviews have been held with teachers at both the main and alternative high school.

Finally, a *constant comparative analysis* (Glaser & Strauss, 1967), coupled with a more specific *critical discourse analysis* (Luke, 1995), has been ongoing across the data collected with students and teachers, and includes an analysis of district and local documents, and the local newspaper. Examining the beliefs and attitudes of community members with regard to the alternative program, allows us to inquire into the range of "social identities" made available to the students in the local context.

Dialogue About and Between Young People

Several selections of text are presented here, reflecting informal conversations between inservice and preservice teachers and between students, to illustrate the way in which possible student identities are constructed and positioned through dialogue. Each text is paired with another, to juxtapose two perspectives on a common theme. In Text 1 and Text 2 below, an experienced teacher sits with a preservice teacher involved in a practicum experience, and shares some advice about students in the class. According to the experienced teachers involved, both texts are examples of what "caring about your students" looks like. Text 1 occurred in the main high school, while Text 2 is taken from the alternative program. All names in the following texts are pseudonyms.

Text 1: Experienced Teacher Advising Preservice Teacher in Main High School

Teacher: I always start my week with the, the Police Blotter ... you know, that section where the incidents involving the police are reported, in the paper ...

Preservice Teacher: Uh-huh, yeah ...

Teacher: ... that list that runs down the side of the page ...

Preservice Teacher: Right. Sure. I know the one.

Teacher: Just to see what's going on ... see who's doing what ...

Preservice Teacher: Uh-huh, see who's there …
Teacher: Right. Just a way to, to keep track of their lives …
Preservice Teacher: Yeah.
Teacher: … see what's going on for them …

In an interview following this interaction, this experienced teacher described her actions as evidence of her feelings for her students; she cares about her students, wants "to keep track of their lives," wants to "see what's going on for them." Reviewing the Police Blotter each week allowed her to see if any of her students had gotten into trouble with the police over the weekend. If they had been arrested, for example, this might explain why they may not be in class. Or if they arrived to school in a "bad mood," getting into trouble over the weekend may have been the reason. Later, when asked how frequently she recognized the names in the Police Blotter as being one of her student's, she replied, "Oh, just a few times a year. Very infrequently really." In a follow up interview with the preservice teacher, he was asked how frequently he thought the experienced teacher recognized names in the Police Blotter. His response was, "Well, she does it every week, so she must find kids in there frequently."

Text 2: Experienced Teacher Advising Preservice Teacher in Alternative Program

Teacher: Joe's having a rough day today; he looks tired. Do you think you could work with him … so he can finish, but check on the boys too?
Preservice Teacher: Okay, I'll just work with Joe, Ryan, and Tyler … for that assignment that was due Friday?
Teacher: [Nodding] … that would be great.
Preservice Teacher: Okay, I'll …
Teacher: Oh, and remember …
Preservice Teacher: … Yeah …
Teacher: … remember, don't take stuff personally, don't let him, don't take on his being tired, or feeling cranky, as your fault. Keep encouraging him. I know he can do this.
Preservice Teacher: … Yeah … okay, I know he can too.

Text 2 also reflects the way in which an experienced teacher "cares about" her students. For Joe, caring about him included not taking his "tired" behavior or his "cranky" feelings personally. Doing so might have discouraged the preservice teacher and might have made her feel that he was simply choosing not to do the work, rather than responding, perhaps, to a difficult situation in his personal life. Instead, the experienced teacher emphasized the importance of encouraging him and believing in his ability to finish the work. In a follow up interview with the teacher, she argued that,

> Sometimes the kids are just waiting for you to confirm that they can't do it. Somehow they get switched around, and instead of looking for confirmation that they *can* do something, they just wait for you to agree that they *can't* do it. Then when it happens, everything comes to a halt. Maybe they began to doubt themselves earlier, and your doubt tells them that they were right.

Later, the experienced teacher's view was re-voiced in the language of the preservice teacher, who noted, "The kids may doubt themselves, but I will never doubt them."

Discussion of Texts 1 and 2

From a sociocultural perspective, both Texts 1 and 2 are snapshots of preservice teachers constructing knowledge on microgenetic level about their future students, while, at the same time, the experienced teachers are expressing both their own knowledge about students and assumptions about students which have been constructed over sociocultural history. Their knowledge is situated within the context of a teacher education program that requires practicum experiences with experienced teachers and it is mediated by the cultural tool of speech.

The utterances captured above form a dialogue that follows a pattern that we might call a genre of "giving advice." In both Texts 1 and 2 the experienced teacher takes the position of the expert, while the preservice teacher takes the position of the novice. The topic of the dialogue makes "students" the subject of the exchange, and in doing so, positions secondary students as "others" with certain identities. According to Bakhtin, we could say that the experienced teacher in Text 1 *refracts* her students, through her own "optic," as possible juvenile offenders, as likely to appear in the Police Blotter. It is unclear whether or not the inservice teacher may begin looking in the Police Blotter himself for a few students to have repeated offenses or several students, overall, to be arrested. Text 2 positions a particular student named Joe, as "a doubter," as someone who lacks confidence in his abilities as a student. The experienced teacher in Text 2 *refracts* her student, through her own "optic," as a doubter. The process of *refraction* is a constructive act that offers a completed and singular identity for the secondary students or for Joe to the preservice teachers in Texts 1 and 2.

Luke (1995) notes that through critical discourse analysis we can explore "how teachers' and students' spoken and written texts shape and construct ... 'versions' of successful and failing students" (p. 11). As these two texts illustrate, it is easy to see not only how students are afforded particular identities, but also how expectations for certain identities are reproduced. The two experienced teachers in the texts above, have positioned themselves similarly, as adults who "care about" their students. As role models for the preservice teachers, the privileged status of their words is inherent in their position as experienced teachers. Their influence can be seen in the responses of the preservice teachers, or what Bakhtin calls "heteroglossia," the multivocality of the preservice teachers words incorporating the voices of the experienced teachers. The preservice teacher's expectations for finding students in the Police Blotter, in Text 1, is increased as a result of this exchange.[5] And in Text 2, the preservice teacher verbalizes her role as someone who encourages the students, and provides the confidence they lack.

It is important to emphasize that we are not claiming that the experienced teachers' perspectives are absorbed completely by the preservice teachers, as a "transmission of information" about students. Nor are we suggesting that the identities afforded by the two experienced teachers determine the only identities available to their students. Rather, what we are suggesting is that secondary students construct their identities based, in part, on a dialectical negotiation enacted through relationships with their teachers and other cultural voices, including adults, peers, and how they are portrayed in film, television, and media. Teachers create possible identities for students dialogically, and these possible identities may be reproduced through conversations with other teachers or teacher education students following the genre of giving advice within practicum experiences.

The next series of texts surfaced in informal hallway conversations in the alternative program; Text 3 reports the dialogue of two teachers and Text 4 reports a dialogue between two students. Both texts capture the response of teachers and students to a newspaper article that had appeared the previous weekend, after the graduation ceremony for seniors. The article was a celebration of the accomplishments of the students and had a positive tone as perceived by the teachers. For the students, however, the article mentioned only two of the thirteen scholarships awarded, and in doing so, the journalist stereotyped and homogenized all of the other students in the program on the basis of the type of scholarship.

Text 3: Hallway Conversation About Newspaper Article Regarding Graduation Ceremony Between Two Teachers

Teacher 1: Nice work on the ceremony, Jeanne …

Teacher 2: … well thanks, it did work out nicely.

Teacher 1: … the article in the paper was really good this year too!

Teacher 2: I was pleasantly surprised, they really seemed to focus on the students' accomplishments and … their future …

Teacher 1: I noticed that too. The picture was even good … now that's [shared laughter]

Teacher 2: Yes, that's saying a lot! If the picture's even good!

Both teachers in Text 3 felt the newspaper article was quite positive; the journalist emphasized the accomplishments of the students and discussed their future plans. The positive tone in the text was further enhanced by a picture that captured the celebratory nature of the event, with some students tossing their caps, others hugging, and all of them smiling. In an interview with one of the teachers several days later, the article and picture were raised as a topic of conversation with regard to both the journalist's perceptions and the perceptions of community members toward the students in the alternative program. She said,

> You know, last year, the article seemed to have a 'these kids,' or 'those kids' kind of tone. Like, this is the ceremony for 'those kids.' The picture was on Sally … remember, she had a virus when she was real young, and all her hair fell out. Well, there she was, looking cute as ever, big smile on her face, bald head, no eyebrows, and I know that people that … don't know her, think, she's one of 'those kids.' This year, all the kids looked good, normal. It was a relief.

The concern for the teacher here was that last year's picture, with Sally's image, was used to stereotype the students in the program—as punks with shaved heads and eyebrows—even though her hair loss was due to medical reasons and was permanent.

Text 4: Locker Conversation About Newspaper Article Regarding Graduation Ceremony Between Two Students

Becca: Did you see it?
Darcy: Yeah … paper's in the library …
Becca: Same ol' thing …
Darcy: Yeah, we're always gonna be those AA kids, junkies "who overcome family crisis and alcoholism to do great things" [said in deep journalistic voice]… that guy was full of shit …
Becca: We're all the same, even when we're not …

With regard to the same article, the response of two students, both juniors, was quite different from the teachers noted above. They noticed that only two out of thirteen of the scholarships had been reported, and the two that were mentioned were awarded by the local Alcohol and Drug Services organization, to students who had overcome alcohol and drug related problems. Along with the brief mention of the organization, the award amount, and the students' names, the journalist quoted the official awarding the scholarship as saying it was an award for students who "overcame adversity in their lives stemming from alcohol or drugs." For Darcy and Becca, the silence surrounding the other scholarships, stereotyped and homogenized all of the students in the program. They felt that all the students were being stereotyped as alcoholics or drug users, as a result of the article.

Discussion of Texts 3 and 4

Texts 3 and 4 illustrate a general principle and the dependence of individual identities on categories provided to us through others' perspectives. Those perspectives of the other serve to crystallize one's own or one's group identity. The general principle here is that reality depends on perceptions that the world is as one sees it mediated by the "surplus of seeing" granted to us by others (Clark & Holquist, 1984, p. 71). Both texts represent casual conversations from two different perspectives on a common text, a newspaper article. Recalling Vygotsky's discussion of genetic domains, the newspaper article operates significantly in the sociocultural domain. Clearly present in both the newspaper article this year, as well as the choice of last year's accompanying picture, are the assumptions of the dominant discourse which tend to represent social relations that are the products of power, "history, social formation, and culture … as if they were the product of organic, biological, and essential necessity" (Luke, 1995, p. 12). This occurs by virtue of both what is said and what is left unsaid about the students, and in this case, about which scholarships were awarded.

For the teachers conversing in Text 3, their response to the article and picture, in general, is one of relief. They appreciate the journalist's positive tone, his emphasis on the students' futures, and the picture which represents the typical graduation scene. Remembering the picture that was used after the graduation ceremony the year before, and their concerns about it stereotyping the students, the teachers do not, however, seem to recognize the image that is embedded in the words used to describe the students in the article. The teachers do not see something that the two younger students see, and the two younger students do not realize that what they see has a history. That history continues to maintain the stereotyping of the students in their program. The two students recognize how their group is *refracted* by the journalist, as well as the power of the journalist to position them in the community. Only two of the thirteen scholarships are mentioned in the newspaper article, and the two that are described were awarded on the basis of "overcoming" alcohol and drug use, an accomplishment that is necessarily preceded by alcohol and drug abuse. The scholarship requirements that are *not* mentioned were based on "grade point average," "artistic or creative aptitude," "academic promise," "actions of exceptional worth within the school and community," and "leadership," or a combination of these qualities. For whatever reason, mention of these more typical scholarships is excluded. The two students in Text 4, recognize not only the silence surrounding the other eleven scholarships, but also the effect that the mention of the two Alcohol and Drug Services scholarships will have on the community's perception of students in the program. Here, as highlighted by Luke (1995) above, the dominant discourse naturalizes the exclusion of "these kids" from the main high school:

the students who are in the alternative high school program become identified, homogenized as alcohol and drug abusers.

Two important points should be emphasized here. First, the newspaper article positions the students in the program for the general public. The journalist *refracts* the students through his "optic," not as they are—a heterogeneous bunch of young people who have multiple reasons for attending the alternative program—but as a homogeneous group of alcohol and drug abusers. Students arrive at this program for many different reasons, such as pregnancy, single parenthood, family dysfunction, and / or failure in the main high school, and for the less obvious reasons of "not fitting in," "the high school's too big," and "all my friends go here." The latter statements can be seen as part of the wide spread failure of schools to educate students placed "at risk." Indeed, for the students in this program, the teachers are most concerned about issues other than alcohol and drug use, such as nutrition, cigarette smoking, lack of sleep, caffeine consumption, and transportation.

The second point follows from the first and from the shift required by the sociocultural approach to highlight the social construction of identity, mediated through cultural tools. The words that are used to initially *describe* the students in the alternative program, actually become an *explanation* for their participation in the program. Therefore, in this particular situation, the newspaper article further reifies the individual "type" or identity of a student that attends the alternative program, however invalid, and masks the more troubling social structural reasons for attendance, such as poverty, teen pregnancy, and school failure. When adults locate the source of the problems of "those students" inside "those students," or the groups to which they belong (Portes, 1996), then we exempt ourselves from taking responsibility for the problems or the students, or for asking questions about why "those problems" exist in the first place. And even more troublesome, while the traditional individualistic perspective hides the dialectical relationship between individual and social context, it also affords its users a stance that blames individual students while ignoring school and social structures that may have produced an artificially limited range of possible identities for students to begin with. Restating Bakhtin's (1986) position, we must understand the power of others, in this case teachers and adults, to tell young people who they are and to give them categories for identifying themselves.

A Sociocultural Perspective on Identity

The basic tenets of the sociocultural approach require that we emphasize three principles when exploring identity:

1. identity is dynamic and develops over time and across genetic domains;
2. identity is negotiated in the dialectical relationship between person and social context; and
3. the negotiation of identity takes place in particular social and historical activity settings mediated by discursive practices.

The third principle, in particular, is elaborated through Bakhtin's work. More specifically, elaboration occurs with respect to the way in which discursive practices mediate the construction of identity through utterance, speech genre, and dialogue, and by the identity positions made available through self-other relationships. Employing ideas from both Vygotsky and Bakhtin we can say that identity construction is a higher mental process, that begins as a function of *inter*psychological relationships, becoming *intra*psychological through the on-going process of internalization. The construction of identity is continuously mediated by the images, ideas, and identities offered to us in our social activities and social relations. Rather than a socially deterministic process, identity construction is a process that is dialectical and transformative; reflecting the tension between individual agency and social context and meaning.

Each text and coupling of texts provides the reader with dialogue that constructs the identities of high school students along with a brief analysis of the way this occurs. The coupling of texts offers a juxtaposition that allows us to highlight facets that are most pertinent to our discussion here. Texts 1 and 2 reflect examples of professional knowledge that is constructed within teacher education and the professional life of teachers that follows a genre of advice giving. Through the exchange of utterances, experienced teachers shared with preservice teachers possible identities for high school students *refracted* through their own optic. Their position as experienced teachers and as supervisors of preservice teachers is quite powerful. Evidence for this power surfaces as the preservice teachers re-voice their words.

Texts 3 and 4 emphasize two competing perspectives of a newspaper article and picture regarding the graduation ceremony for the alternative program. These texts allow us to see the way in which social identities are made available for high school students, and communicated between the community, school, and classroom contexts. The dialogue between two teachers in Text 3 supports the representation of the high school students in the newspaper article and picture uncritically. The dialogue between two students, represented in Text 4, contests and resists the homogenized representation of the students. The topic of these texts engages the social construction of identity at the sociocultural level, incorporating the lives of the particular students in this program, in this town, at this time, in a larger social conversation. This conversation attends to the need for alternative programs, the identities of the students who are participants, along with the role that social institutions, such as schools and the media, play in *the creation of* the need for alternative programs and the students who become engaged within them.

CONCLUDING THOUGHTS

We have attempted to address four distinct, but overlapping, topics in this chapter in extending a method for exploring identity from a sociocultural perspective. In the first section we briefly noted the main tenets of Vygotsky's sociocultural approach, reflecting on current extensions of his work by Wertsch (1991), Miedema and Wardekker (1999), and Shaw (1994). The second section examined an extension of Vygotsky's work through ideas offered by Erikson's psychosocial model, including complementary conceptions and the limitations of Erikson's theory. Important differences were noted between the social emphasis in psychoanalytic theory that remains grounded in the individual ego and that of a general theory of mind that, in turn, is inseparable from society. In the third section, we offered a brief discussion of the compatibility of several of Vygotsky's ideas with Bakhtin's, with an eye toward utilizing Bakhtin's concepts of utterance, genre, and dialogue as moments of identity construction. Finally, in the fourth section we exemplified how a sociocultural perspective might be employed to frame and analyze research exploring the production of students labeled "at risk."

While young people in schools across the United States—positioned by family and group of origin—are often assumed to be individually responsible for creating their own success, as well as identity, they are in fact negotiating identity from a limited number of socially available options. The latter have less to do with their "choices" and more to do with the perceptions and possibilities afforded by adults. Textual examples in the last section of this chapter offer a small glimpse of the issue at hand, focusing only on general dialogical constructions in conversations between experienced and preservice teachers, and between teachers and between students with regard to a third text from a newspaper. Layers that have not been discussed include informal student discussions about possible identities and identity construction, along with the possible identities negotiated through relationships with parents and significant adults. In addition, our data here are themselves bounded by sociocultural theory; our research takes place in the United States, in the late 1990's and first years of the 21st century. Our culture is becoming increasingly market oriented through the commodification of everything from time, sold as advertising time, to space, including advertisements on billboards and web page text boards. Young people are targeted, sold to, and shut out when they cease to conform, and instead, resist or abandon school structures and social institutions that are alienating. A larger social analysis is crucial to explore these issues, but we will save this for another time.

We believe that the shift that we are describing in identity research will have a large impact on the way that psychologists and educators think about young people. In addition, we hope that we will be able to encourage a move away from "fixing children" which has historically been, and continues to be, the most common approach to working with students labeled "at risk" in educational settings. Instead, we propose a sociocultural view which suggests that the new unit of analysis for research is the student in relation to a particular context, mediated through activity in discourse communities. More simply, we argue that the "at riskness" of students labeled this way is not necessarily an individual psychological phenomenon or a characteristic of the particular child, but a product of a jointly constructed relationship between the child and the social context.

Finally, this chapter's main thrust lies in showing how a sociocultural theory may be extended in the area of identity. Sociocultural thinking is inherent in the work of several major figures during and after the founding of the theory itself. For reasons discussed elsewhere (Cole, 1996; van der Veer & Valsiner, 1994), the theory remained hidden, underdeveloped and applied to a limited number of domains. In this chapter, we test the fruitfulness and explanatory power of the theory and some of its closest allies. In so doing, important differences may be noted relative to how mainstream psychology has approached, and continues to approach, the identity construction of young people. Our main conclusions can be restated briefly as follows.

1. While we recognize Erikson's indebtedness to Freudian theory, along with the inability of psychosocial theory to transcend its roots in psychoanalytical theory, we find his analysis of identity development far more sociocultural than the individual orientations and expansions that prevail today in North American psychology.

2. Sociocultural theory can not be reconstituted from the writing of its founder. It must be extended and integrated with compatible work in various fields, such as linguistics, that are now current in developmental psychology with respect to the development of language and consciousness. Applications to identity construction are well founded and add a dimension that has not surfaced in the traditional psychological literature.

3. The rationale for advancing the sociocultural approach in identity construction, as well as in other areas ranging from literacy and policy regarding groups placed "at risk" to counseling and psychotherapy, is noteworthy. As with knowledge, higher level psychological functions are involved, which implies studying identity dialogically in a reciprocal relationship with the social context, and through cultural tools as mediational means.

In conclusion, identity is viewed here as a central aspect of human consciousness. Consciousness about the self is relational to others and constructed dialogically, by the interplay of social voices, and through utterance and the organizing pattern of speech genre. Identity is a dynamic category that may shift and change, from one context to the next, from one social activity to the next, from one set of relationships to the next. In some respects, identity also situates the development of consciousness. It does so over the history of individual development, which may vary depending on levels of mental development, group membership, and positioning within a social and historical context.

NOTES

1. It is important to note here Vygotsky's unique meaning of the word "social." While the natural line of development is emphasized in infancy and early toddlerhood, by the time children are about two and a half years old, the social line of development merges with and supplants the natural line. At this time young children express themselves with gestures and speech, which ultimately moves from external speech that directs activity to inner speech that aids self-regulation. After this time, even solitary activities are social in nature given the use of internalized verbal speech as inner speech, and finally thought.

2. See Chapter 6 in Vygotsky (1978) for a discussion of the relationship between learning and development, including the positions of several theorists and Vygotsky's alternative.

3. There is still considerable debate surrounding the authorship of several pieces. For example, *Marxism and the Philosophy of Language* was published under the name of V. N. Voloshinov, though some attribute the work to Bakhtin. At this point, we will take the position, as do Clark and Holquist (1984) and Emerson (1986), that this book was written largely if not completely by Bakhtin.

4. Holquist's (1986) chapter is quite helpful in clarifying the ideas of Saussure and Bakhtin and, in particular, noting the common ways in which comparisons between the two are oversimplified, due in no small part to the fact that they use several concepts in common, though with quite different meanings associated.

5. As mentioned earlier, member checks were used as interview tapes were transcribed, allowing the first author to discuss the discrepancy between the perspectives of the inservice and preservice teacher with them separately. Shortly thereafter, the inconsistency was cleared up.

REFERENCES

Bakhtin, M. M. (1986). *Speech Genres and Other Late Essays.* Austin, TX: University of Texas Press.

Benton, J. & Appleton, R. (2001). Through the cracks: Texans who drop out face bleak futures defined by limitations. The Dallas Morning News, May 20, 2001. http://www.dallasnews.com/dropouts...stories/372252_dropreck_20met.html

Berzonsky, M. D. (1988, March). *The structure of identity.* Paper presented at the biennial meeting of the Society for Research on Adolescence, Alexandria, VA.

Berzonsky, M. D. (1989). Identity style: Conceptualization and measurement. *Journal of Adolescent Research, 4,* 268-282.

Bourdieu, P. (1998). *Practical reason.* Cambridge, UK: Polity Press.

Chavers, D. (1991). *The Indian dropout: An annotated bibliography.* Albuquerque, NM: Coalition for Indian Education.

Clark, K. & Holquist, M. (1984). *Mikhail Bakhtin.* Cambridge, MA: Harvard University Press.

Cole, M. (1996). *Cultural psychology: A once and future discipline.* Cambridge, MA: The Belknap Press of Harvard University Press.

Cole, M. & Scribner, S. (1978). Introduction. In Vygotsky, L. S. (1978). *Mind in society: The development of higher psychological processes.* Cambridge, MA: Harvard University Press.

Cooley, C. H. (1925). *Social organization: A study of the larger mind.* New York, NY: Scribner.

Côté, J. E. (1996). Sociological perspectives on identity formation: The culture-identity link and identity capital. *Journal of Adolescence, 19,* 419-430.

Côté, J. E. & Levine, C. (1988). A critical examination of ego identity status paradigm. *Developmental Review, 8,* 147-188.

Elkind, D. (1978). *The child's reality: Three developmental themes.* Hillsdale, NJ: Erlbaum.

Emerson, C. (1986). The outer word and inner speech: Bakhtin, Vygotsky, and the internalization of language. G. S. Morson (Ed.), *Bakhtin: Essays and dialogues on his work.* Chicago, IL: University of Chicago Press.

Erikson, E. H. (1963). *Childhood and Society.* New York, NY: W. W. Norton.

Erikson, E. H. (1968). *Identity: Youth and Crisis.* New York, NY: W. W. Norton.

Evans, I. M., Cohen, M., Cicchelli, T. & Shapiro, N. P. (1995). *Staying in school: Partnerships for educational change.* Baltimore, MD: Brookes Publishing.

Fairchild, H. H. (1991). Scientific racism: The cloak of objectivity. *Journal of Social Issues, 47,* 101-115.

Freud, S. (1988). *Three essays on the theory of sexuality.* New York, NY: Basic Books.

Gannon, L., Luchetta, T., Rhodes, K., Pardie, L., & Segrist, D. (1992). Sex bias in psychological research: Progress or complacency? *American Psychologist, 47,* 389-396.

Gee, J. P. (2001). *Millenials and bobos, Blue's Clues and Sesame Street: A story for our times.* Paper presented at the conference, "New Literacies and Digital Technologies: A Focus on Adolescent Learners." University of Georgia, Athens, Georgia.

Giddens, A. (1991). *Modernity and self-identity: Self and society in the late modern age.* Stanford, CA: Stanford University Press.

Gilligan, C. (1982). *In a different voice: Psychological theory and women's development.* Cambridge, MA: Harvard University Press.

Glaser, B. G. & Strauss, A. L. (1967). *The discovery of grounded theory.* Chicago, IL: Aldine.

Graham, S. (1992). "Most of the subjects were White and middle class": Trends in published research on African Americans in selected APA journals, 1970-1989. *American Psychologist, 47*, 629-639.

Graumann, C. F. & Gergen, K. J. (1996). *Historical dimensions of psychological discourse.* New York, NY: Cambridge University Press.

Hall, G. S. (1904). *Adolescence: Its psychology and its relations to psychology, anthropology, sociology, sex, crime, religion, and education.* New York, NY: Appleton-Century-Crofts.

Harding, S. (1986). *The science question in feminism.* Ithaca, NY: Cornell University Press.

Helms, J. E. (1990). Toward a model of white racial identity development. In J. E. Helms (Ed.), *Black and White racial identity: Theory, research and practice.* Westport, CT: Greenwood Press.

Herek, G. M., Kimmel, D. C., Amaro, H., & Melton, G. B. (1991). Avoiding heterosexist bias in psychological research. *American Psychologist, 46*, 957-963.

Hicks, D. (2000). Self and other in Bakhtin's early philosophical essays: Prelude to a theory of prose consciousness. *Mind, Culture, and Activity, 7*(3), 227-242.

Holquist, M. (1986). Answering as authoring: Mikhail Bakhtin's trans-linguistics. G. S. Morson (Ed.), *Bakhtin: Essays and dialogues on his work.* Chicago, IL: The University of Chicago Press.

Kozulin, A. (1990). *Vygotsky's psychology: A biography of ideas.* Cambridge, MA: Harvard University Press.

Kroger, J. (1992). Intrapsychic dimensions of identity during late adolescence. G. R. Adams, T. P. Gullotta, & R. Montemayor (Eds.), *Adolescent identity formation.* Newbury Park, CA: Sage.

LeCompte, M. D. & Dworkin, A. G. (1991). *Giving up on school: Student dropouts and teacher burnouts.* Newbury Park, CA: Corwin Press.

Luke, A. (1995). Text and discourse in education: An introduction to critical discourse analysis. In M. W. Apple (Ed.), *Review of Research in Education 21.* Washington, DC: AERA.

Luke, A. & Luke, C. (2001). Adolescence lost/childhood regained: On early intervention and the emergence of the techno-subject. *Journal of Early Childhood Literacy, 1*(1), 93-122.

Malgady, R. G., Rogler, L. H., & Costantino, G. (1987). Ethnocultural and linguistic bias in mental health evaluation of Hispanics. *American Psychologist, 42*, 228-234.

Marcia, J. E. (1966). Development and validation of ego-identity status. *Journal of Personality and Social Psychology, 3*(5), 551-558.

Marcia, J. E. (1980). Identity in adolescence. In J. Adelson (Ed.), *Handbook of adolescent psychology.* New York, NY: John Wiley.

Matute-Bianchi, M. E. (1986). Ethnic identities and patterns of school success and failure among Mexican-descent and Japanese-American students in a California high school: An ethnographic analysis. *American Journal of Education, 95*, 233-255.

Miedema, S. & Wardekker, W. L. (1999). Emergent identity versus consistent identity: Possibilities for a postmodern repoliticization of critical pedagogy. In T. S. Popkewitz & L. Fendler (Eds.), *Critical theories in education: Changing terrains of knowledge and politics.* New York, NY: Routledge.

Morin, S. F. (1977). Heterosexual bias in psychological research on lesbianism and male homosexuality. *American Psychologist, 32,* 629-637.

Morin, S. F. (1978). Psychology and the gay community: An overview. *Journal of Social Issues, 34,* 1-6.

Morson, G. S. (1986a). Preface: Perhaps Bakhtin. G. S. Morson (Ed.), *Bakhtin: Essays and dialogues on his work.* Chicago, IL: University of Chicago Press.

Morson, G. S. (1986b). Dialogue, monologue, and the social: A reply to Ken Hirschkop. G. S. Morson (Ed.), *Bakhtin: Essays and dialogues on his work.* Chicago, IL: University of Chicago Press.

National Center for Education Statistics. (1998). *Digest of education statistics.* Washington, DC: U. S. Department of Education.

Penuel, W. R. & Wertsch, J. V. (1995). Vygotsky and identity formation: A sociocultural approach. *Educational Psychologist, 30*(2), 83-92.

Phinney, J. S. & Chavira, V. (1992). Ethnic identity and self-esteem: An exploratory longitudinal study. *Journal of Adolescence, 15,* 271-281.

Portes, P. R. (1996). Culture and ethnicity in education and psychology. In D. Berliner & R. Calfee (Eds.), *The handbook of educational psychology.* New York, NY: McMillan Publishing.

Portes, P. R., Dunham, R. M., & Del Castillo, K. (2000). Identity formation and status across cultures: Exploring the cultural validity of Eriksonian theory. In U. P. Geilen & A. Communian (Eds.), *Human development and cross-cultural perspective.* Padua, Italy: CEDAM.

Sarason, S. B. (2001). *American psychology and schools: A critique.* New York, NY: Teachers College Press.

Shaw, T. A. (1994). The semiotic mediation of identity. *Ethos, 22*(1), 83-119.

Stewart, S. (1986). Shouts on the street: Bakhtin's anti-linguistics. G. S. Morson (Ed.), *Bakhtin: Essays and dialogues on his work.* Chicago, IL: University of Chicago Press.

Streitmatter, J. (1993). Identity status and identity style: A replication study. *Journal of Adolescence, 16,* 211-215.

The Condition of Education. (1998). Washington, DC: United States Government Printing Office.

Triandis, H. C., Bontempo, R., Villareal, M., Asai, M., & Luca, N. (1988). Individualism-collectivism: Perspectives on self-in-group relationships. *Journal of Personality and Social Psychology, 54,* 323-338.

van der Veer, R. & Valsiner, J. (1994). *The Vygotsky reader.* Cambridge, MA: Blackwell.

van der Veer, R. & Valsiner, J. (1991). *Understanding Vygotsky: A quest for synthesis.* Cambridge, MA: Blackwell.

Voloshinov, V. N. (1973/1986). *Marxism and the philosophy of language.* Cambridge, MA: Harvard University Press.

Vygotsky, L. S. (1978). *Mind in society: The development of higher psychological processes.* Cambridge, MA: Harvard University Press.

Vygotsky, L. S. (1986). *Thought and language.* Cambridge, MA: The MIT Press.

Wertsch, J. V. (1991). *Voices of the mind: A sociocultural approach to mediated action.* Cambridge, MA: Harvard University Press.

Wertsch, J. V. & Tulviste, P. (1996). L. S. Vygotsky and contemporary developmental psychology. In H. Daniels (Ed.), *An introduction to Vygotsky.* New York, NY: Routledge.

CHAPTER 5

PERSON-ENVIRONMENT FIT IN HIGHER EDUCATION
How Good Is the Fit for Indigenous Students?

Gerard J. Fogarty and Colin White

INTRODUCTION

Born and raised in an Aboriginal community on the outskirts of Cairns, Vanessa was undertaking an Associate Diploma in Community Welfare at the college of Technical and Further Education when she attended a University careers presentation. Expressing her interest in working with and helping people, Vanessa decided to enrol in a psychology course at the University of Southern Queensland.

Vanessa's initial challenge was to uproot herself from her family and community and move to a city 1800 kilometers away from her social support network. After negotiating a number of obstacles including some family resistance and dealing with the Aboriginal Education Branch of the then Department of Employment, Education and Training (DEET), Vanessa arrived in Toowoomba in February 1993 to commence her studies. Due to unfamiliarity with her new environment, Vanessa initially chose to stay in University college accommodation. Fees charged left very little available for personal expenses and the purchase of required course materials. These difficulties were exacerbated by delays in the processing of her study allowance application. As these difficulties were overcome, Vanessa settled into her studies and with tutorial assistance performed very well in her first semester passing all three of her enrolled units. However, as the semester progressed, financial difficulties remained and she moved into share accommodation with several other indigenous students. Although accepted by the local Aboriginal community, she was still seen as an outsider and as the weather became colder in this Southern part of the state, she began to pine for her family and home community and attendance at lectures and tutorials began to become less frequent.

Vanessa went home to her community at the mid-semester break but returned to the University two weeks late. Attempting to catch up, Vanessa had some difficulties in understanding the relevance of subjects such as Statistics and Biological Bases of Behavior to her goal of working with and helping people. Motivation/persistence began to wane and this combined with continued financial pressures again led to less than ideal attendance patterns at lectures and tutorials. Falling behind in her assignments, Vanessa sat for exams in only two of the four units in which she was enrolled. She returned home prior to the other two exams and expressed surprise that she could be failed for the two subjects for which she did not sit. Her results for the semester were one unit passed and three failed.

Returning with renewed enthusiasm in her second year, Vanessa progressed well until the eighth week of semester when a family situation arose which necessitated her return home. A switch to external mode of study was negotiated but assignment returns became irregular and Vanessa again did not sit for her exams. Semester results were 0 out of 4 units. Vanessa was asked to show cause why her enrollment should not be discontinued. Successfully negotiating her 'show cause' notice due to family circumstances, Vanessa returned in second semester to continue her studies on campus. Loss of library privileges and fines due to the loss of several books loaned to another student, combined with continuing financial pressures and crowded accommodation, appeared to lead to diminished motivation and a fatalistic approach to studies. Vanessa's attendance at lectures and tutorials became sporadic and she expressed bewilderment/disillusionment at the theoretical and apparent non-practical aspects of her course. Falling behind in her assignments, Vanessa sat for her end-of-semester exams but passed only 1 of the 4 units. Again she was asked to 'show cause' as to why her enrolment should not be discontinued. Vanessa chose not to respond and withdrew from her studies.

Vanessa was a very capable student with the academic skills necessary to successfully negotiate a degree course. However, isolation from her community and family, continued financial difficulties, and a less than adequate appreciation of rules, regulations and requirements of a tertiary environment combined to produce diminished motivation and persistence and led to her ultimate decision to withdraw. Her academic record will show that she passed five out of fifteen units attempted. The reality is that she passed five out of nine attempted and with adequate family support, understanding of the tertiary environment, and lack of financial pressures, should have been able to pass all units attempted.

THE EDUCATIONAL CONTEXT

The story as related above is familiar to those working with Indigenous students. It is only since the late 1980's that Aboriginal students in Australia have been enrolled in tertiary institutions in large numbers and Vanessa belongs to what might be called the first generation of Indigenous higher education students. Among these students, the parameters of mainstream tertiary educational institutions are not yet fully understood. Vanessa's story raises a number of themes that we seek to explore in this chapter: a) lack of career knowledge among Indigenous students; b) the mismatch between what Indigenous students expect to find at University and what they actually do find; c) mismatches between the predominantly collectivist values held by Indigenous students and the more individualistic values that predominate in Western university settings; d) external pressures that make study difficult; and e) the lack of adequate preparation for the cognitive demands of University study. Before exploring these themes in more detail, however, we will set the scene by providing some background information on the involvement of Indigenous students in Higher Education in this country and at this University.

The involvement of Australian Indigenous people in higher education has increased significantly over the past 10 to 20 years. From an estimated 854 Indigenous students enrolled in Higher Education in 1982 (DEET, 1990), the number enrolled in Australian tertiary institutions increased to 6,956 in 1996 (Stanley & Hansen, 1998) and to 8,001 in 1999. This represents 1.3 percent of the total non-overseas student enrollments in Australian tertiary institutions (Encel, 2000). Despite this growth, Indigenous people remain significantly disadvantaged in comparison to non-Indigenous students in a number of areas. The main ones are as follows:

- comparatively lower levels of educational achievement at primary school level reflected in lower participation and attendance rates compared with non indigenous students;
- declining participation in secondary schooling where, in recent years, apparent retention rates have fallen by three times that of all Australians at Year 10 level;
- much lower levels of attainment in terms of course completions in the Technical and Further Education (TAFE) sector; and
- substantial under-representation in higher education graduates, a situation that is getting worse proportionally as the Indigenous population grows at a faster rate than the Australian population (Stanley &

Hansen, 1998, p. 43). For example, after examining academic outcomes in 1998 for students commencing undergraduate award
courses at the same institution in 1992, Encel (2000) reported that
32.9 percent of Indigenous students had completed an award course,
4.6 percent were still enrolled but had not completed a course, and
62.5 percent were no longer enrolled and had not completed an
award course. Comparative percentages for non-Indigenous students
were 62.7 percent, 9.5 percent, and 33.8 percent respectively.

The report 'Equity in Higher Education' (DETYA, 1999) noted
that the access rate of Indigenous people to higher education (1.5
percent of commencing students) is now only slightly less than their
share of the Australian population (1.7 percent). However, the report
also notes that their academic success and retention rates in higher
education remain very low. High attrition means that participation by
Indigenous people in higher education overall hovers around 65 percent of what would be expected from their share of the general population. Similarly, the success rate (proportion of units passed) for
Indigenous students for the whole of Australia is 79 percent of the
success rate of non-Indigenous students (DETYA, 1999).

Since the early 1970's there have been many national reports, reviews,
and policy documents focussing directly on Indigenous education
(Schwab, 1995). The intention of the initiatives described in these various
reports has been to improve the access of Indigenous people to education
with the intention of improving educational success and retention rates.
Despite these initiatives, Indigenous people continue to perform poorly
within the school system and have the lowest retention rate of any group in
Australia (Stanley & Hansen, 1998).

These disturbing progression and attrition rates can, in part, be attributed to the lower education level of Indigenous students entering university compared with non-Indigenous students. Encel (2000) reported that
Indigenous students are less likely to have prior qualifications and that
they are more likely than non-Indigenous students (47 percent versus 10
percent) to be admitted to higher education on the basis of special entry
schemes, rather than higher education or school education. Other contributors to performance include the fact that Indigenous students like
Vanessa are more likely to come from isolated rural areas and to have
moved away from their home towns in order to enrol in higher education
(Encel, 2000).

Statistics compiled over a seven-year period (1992-1998) at the University of Southern Queensland (USQ) indicate that the annual attrition rate
for Indigenous students fluctuated between 38 and 57 percent, with a
median close to 43 percent. The figures for non-Indigenous students were
much higher. For example, in 1999, the year following our own data collection, Encel (2000) reported that the retention rate for Indigenous students

at USQ was 42 percent compared with 70 percent for non-Indigenous students. During this same period, academic progression (defined as number of units passed as a percentage of units enrolled) ranged between 40.27 and 52.74 percent. Encel (2000) reported a 41 percent progression rate for Indigenous students in 1998 compared with 75 percent for non-Indigenous students. These figures vary according to whether students were studying on-campus or studying via distance education, but the variations in study mode do not overshadow the differences between Indigenous and non-Indigenous students.

Concern over these retention and progression problems led the authors of this chapter to conduct a series of studies that focussed on possible psychological reasons for the poor performance of Indigenous students. These studies will be summarized and discussed in the present chapter after first explaining the broad research paradigm we employed.

SEARCHING FOR PERSON-ENVIRONMENT FIT

The term "congruence" is often used to describe the match between an individual and the environment, otherwise known as person-environment fit and usually abbreviated to P-E fit. From its early rather narrow usage as a term denoting the match between a person and a job, the definition of congruence has broadened to include more generally the relation between desires and supplies (Tinsley, 2000) or "the correspondence between one's needs, wishes, and preferences on the one hand and situation, rewards, and gratification on the other hand" (Spokane, Meir, & Catalano, 2000, p. 139). A whole research paradigm has been built around the notion of P-E fit or congruence (we shall use these terms interchangeably), based on the premise that where congruence is high, outcomes are favorable and where it is low, outcomes are more likely to be unfavorable.

P-E fit is a particularly useful paradigm for examining the situation of Indigenous students. Vanessa's story can be easily recast as a case of someone who did not "fit" into life at university. The course did not appear to be relevant to her needs, the university environment was unfamiliar, the rules and regulations were stumbling blocks, and she missed her family and community. Such scenarios are familiar to those who work in higher education. For example, in their study of attrition in Australian higher education, McInnes, Hartley, and Teese (2000) highlighted factors such as: a) wrong choice of program; b) dissatisfaction with aspects of institutional provision; c) inability to cope with the demands of the course; d) matters relating to financial need; and e) poor quality of the student experience. All of these themes appear in Vanessa's story.

In the studies to be discussed in the remainder of this chapter, we went beyond the anecdotal level and searched for empirical evidence that factors such as those outlined by McInnis et al. (2000) are associated with academic performance among Indigenous students. Specifically, we looked at congruence between the interests of the students and the content of their chosen course, congruence between the expectations of the students and the expectations of the University, congruence between value systems held by Indigenous students and the values that characterize higher education settings and, finally, congruence between the cognitive skills of Indigenous students entering university and skills demanded by the courses they choose. All studies, along with the relevant literature, are summarized in the sections that follow.

STUDY 1: CAREER INTEREST AND COURSE CONGRUENCE

Background Literature on Course Congruence

Holland's (1985) theory of vocational personalities and work environments is based on the assumption that people will achieve vocational satisfaction if their personality is congruent with their work environment. At the heart of his theory is the notion that people can be described in terms of six basic types and that work environments can be similarly described. The six types are Realistic (R), Investigative (I), Artistic (A), Social (S), Enterprising (E), and Conventional (C). The relations among the types are captured by Holland's now well-known hexagonal configuration, where each type is situated on a different point of the hexagon (see Figure 1).

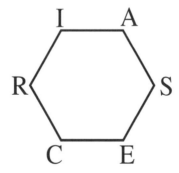

FIGURE 1
Holland's Hexagonal Model Representing Different Vocational Types
(Holland, 1985, p. 29)

Types that have much in common (e.g., Realistic and Conventional) occupy adjacent points whereas types that are opposed to each other (for example, Realistic and Social) are at opposite locations on the hexagon. Holland's (1988a) Self-Directed Search (SDS) can be used to obtain scores on each of these types. Typically, the three highest scores are used to represent a person's type. For example, someone classified as IAS would have obtained his or her highest scores on Investigative, Artistic, and Social, in that order. Similarly, Holland's (1985) Environmental Assessment Technique (EAS) has been used to classify almost every known job in terms of the type of person best suited to that job. Thus, a job classified as IAS would suit the person described above very well. Congruence exists when there is a fit between the person and the environment, that is, when the personality type and the environment are the same. Incongruence exists when the person and environment are located at opposite points of the hexagon.

Holland argued that where congruence was high, satisfaction, stability, and achievement should follow (Holland, 1985). A person with a realistic personality working in a realistic environment, other things being equal, should have an advantage over an individual with a social personality working in that same environment. This principle also applies to study environments. The EAS has been used to classify college majors and there are studies of congruence in this environment. Khan et al. (1990), for example, found reasonably high levels of congruence among the Fine Arts, Social Work, Medicine, and Engineering students in their study. They also found a relationship between congruence scores and career readiness. Other studies (e.g., Camp & Chartrand, 1992) have been less conclusive, suggesting that the link between course congruence and academic performance needs further investigation. We are not aware of any research that has looked at relations between course congruence and academic achievement among Indigenous students. Encel (2000) reported that Indigenous students tend to enrol mostly in a) arts, humanities, and social sciences (35 percent) or b) education (30 percent). These proportions are much higher than for non-Indigenous students, raising the possibility that some of these students may have too narrow a view of career options and could be aligning themselves with courses that do not match their interests. Study 1 was designed to explore this possibility.

Description of Study on Course Congruence

We administered Holland's (1988a) SDS to all 71 Indigenous students enrolling for the first time at USQ in 1998 and 1999. Survey forms were administered to the students by one of the researchers who had extensive contact with the students during the first weeks at University. Sixty-six (29 males and 37 females) returned the survey forms. Two-letter codes were derived to describe each student's main areas of interest. For example, the code IS would indicate that the student was predominantly Investigative with some Social interests as well. Holland's (1988b) Jobs Finder was used to obtain a two-letter code classifying the various majors offered at USQ. Congruence was assessed by using an adaptation of the Zener-Schnuelle (1976) index of agreement: if the two-letter codes for the student and the course were identical, the course congruence score was 5; if the two letters were the same but in reverse order, the score was 4; if the first letter was the same, the score was 3; if the first letter of one code was the same as the second letter of the other, the score was 2; otherwise the score was 0. The measure of academic achievement was progression rate, the proportion of units of study undertaken which have been successfully completed in a year. This measure was collected after the first semester of study.

Approximately 25 percent of the students were aged between 17 and 21 years, a further 35 percent were aged between 22 and 30 years. The predominance of mature age students was characteristic of the University. Students were enrolled in Business (21 percent), Arts (20 percent), and Social Science (30 percent) courses, with very minor enrolments in other disciplines. Surprisingly, there were few students enrolled in Education, a discipline identified by Encel (2000) as one of the most popular for Indigenous students. Over half (n = 34) this sample of Indigenous students scored highest on the Social type, 12 scored highest on Conventional, 7 on Investigative, 6 on Artistic, 4 on Enterprising, whilst only 3 students achieved their highest score on the Realistic type. The high social and low enterprising scores support claims by Fogarty and White (1994) that Indigenous students tend to have collective, as opposed to individualistic values. We shall explore this theme in more detail in Study 3.

Because no data yet have been published concerning the use of Holland's SDS with this population, reliability and validity checks were conducted as part of the preliminary analyses. SPSS was used for this purpose. Most of the Cronbach alpha reliability estimates were above .90 with the estimates ranging from .80 for the Social scale to .92 for the Investigative scale. Principal components analysis, admittedly conducted on a very small sample, supported the factor structure of the SDS with the Investigative, Realistic, Artistic, and Conventional factors emerging clearly. Social and Enterprising factors were also identifiable, although not as clear as the first four.

Having established the suitability of the SDS for use with Indigenous students, we proceeded to examine the course congruence and performance statistics. Progression rates were low overall, with an average progression rate of 19 percent. This figure is more easily understood if one rounds it upwards to 25 percent. The maximum number of units possible in a semester is four, and a mean progression rate of 25 percent would indicate that, on average, students were passing one out of four units. The mean progression rate of 19 percent was based on all 66 students who completed the SDS at the start of the semester. Included in these analyses were 25 students who dropped out before attempting any assessment. The mean progression figure is higher (30 percent) and closer to the figure cited by Encel (2000) if these students are excluded from the analysis. The difference between our own figure and that reported by Encel is almost certainly due to the fact that we collected data during the students' first semester at university when attrition was highest and when adjustment problems were at their peak.

When examining the relationship between course congruence and performance, we based our analysis on the full sample. That is, we included withdrawals and scored them as having zero progression even though, as Vanessa's story makes clear, official progression rates tend to underestimate actual levels of achievement (her official rate was 33 percent but careful scrutiny of her record shows that it should have read above 50 percent). We had no way of making such adjustments for all students in this sample and therefore used the official rates. The relationship between congruence and progression is shown in Table 1.

It can be seen that congruence scores formed a flat distribution with roughly equal numbers in each category except for "Very High", with only 8 students falling into this category. Univariate analysis of variance indicated that there were no significant differences between groups, $F(4, 61) = .96$, $p > .05$. That is, those with more congruent career choices did not perform better academically. The average level of congruence of Indigenous students was just below Moderate (3). Whilst this may seem low, it actually compares favorably with a sample of non-Indigenous students from the same university whose mean congruence level was closer to Low (Sutherland, Fogarty, & Pithers, 1995). Comparison of congruence levels across different types indicated that there were significant differences overall, F

TABLE 1

Relationship Between Interest Congruence and Academic Progression

	Progression Rate		
Degree of Congruence	*N*	*M*	*SD*
Incongruent (1)	14	.13	.30
Low (2)	15	.21	.39
Moderate (3)	19	.16	.28
High (4)	10	.12	.29
Very High (5)	8	.38	.43

(6, 56) = 1.97, $p < .05$, with post hoc invariance tests showing that Social and Artistic types had higher levels of course congruence.

We conclude that whilst low power may have reduced our chances of detecting a reliable relationship, there is little doubt that even if a significant effect were to emerge in future studies, it is unlikely to be a large one. Course incongruence, measured in the way we have measured it here, does not account for much of the variance in progression rates for Indigenous students.

The lack of a direct relationship between congruence and performance, however, does not rule out the possibility that course incongruence may be an important background factor. Its influence could well be mediated by variables like motivation. In the scenario we presented at the outset of this chapter, Vanessa suffered some lack of motivation when she found herself studying Statistics and Biology as part of a Psychology course that she hoped would lead to a career in helping. Data that we review in the next study suggests that students are very much aware of course incongruence and rather than dismissing it as irrelevant, it is better to say that, at this stage, we are not sure of the pathways by which it influences performance.

STUDY 2: CONGRUENCE BETWEEN EXPECTATIONS AND DEMANDS, SOME INTERVIEW DATA

A second aspect of congruence concerns the correspondence between what a student expects to find at university and the demands actually encountered. A feature of the admission criteria at the University where these studies were conducted was that Indigenous students were exempt from qualifying standards. As noted by Encel (2000), this is common practice in Australia. Whilst the policy is motivated by equity considerations, it has some obvious drawbacks, foremost among which is the fact that some students will not be prepared for university study. The link between admission criteria and academic performance amongst all students has been documented at this University. It is known that the average progression rate for all students across all faculties is between 70 and 80 percent. However, this figure drops below 60 percent when the analysis is confined to bands of students who only just met the selection criteria. These figures are stable across an 8-year period. It is reasonable to assume that unless remedial steps are taken the progression rate will be lower still for groups, such as the Indigenous students, who do not have to meet any selection criteria.

The University was aware of the possible consequences of not employing selection criteria and introduced a preparatory studies program tailored to the needs of the Indigenous students. White and Brown (1994) interviewed a sample of 66 students (these were not the same students that participated in Study 1) who had completed this course to determine their reasons for coming to university and their perceptions of the preparatory studies program and the university environment. Wherever possible, students who discontinued were contacted and an attempt was made to determine why these students had dropped out. The findings of this study are reported below.

Regarding reasons for enrolment, all but one of the 66 students thought that it was important for Indigenous students to attend university. Students mainly came to this decision by themselves, or in conjunction with family members, and enrolled with a sense of the importance of education to their people. Regarding the match between expectations and reality, the majority (57.5 percent) found university to be different from their expectations. What was different varied widely. Most of the reasons related to course experiences, rather than the university environment itself. The course not being relevant for career plans was the most cited difference (42.4 percent), raising once again the issue of course congruence. Other commonly cited problems included the course having too much theory, not being practical enough, too difficult, or a combination of these factors (24.2 percent). Insufficient time to complete work requirements was the next most cited factor (16.7 percent). When asked what they found least satisfying about university, lack of support and lack of opportunity for engaging in personal relations were the most cited reasons, again emphasizing the need that these students have for personal contact.

Students who discontinued were difficult to track down and we have little reliable data on reasons for discontinuation. Twelve students who were contacted listed multiple causes, prominent among which were relationship problems, lack of relevance, and family commitments back home.

STUDY 3: VALUES CONGRUENCE

Background Literature

The comments of the Indigenous students in the preceding study suggest that there is a substantial mismatch between what many of them expect from a university course and what is demanded in a contemporary tertiary environment. The sources of these expectations are found in deep-seated psychological factors and cultural traditions. Guider (1991) suggested that many of the reasons given to explain the general failure of education for Indigenous people relate to anthropological theories that highlight differences between traditional Indigenous and non-Indigenous values and practices. He further argued that the classroom behavior of Indigenous students, their motivation to learn, styles of learning, and pattern of school attendance can be linked to traditional cultural influences. Other researchers in both Australian and Native American education settings cite the conflict and stress of either assimilating into the dominant culture through school, or rejecting assimilation and therefore rejecting school, as being potent negative factors in academic persistence (Dehyle, 1992; Hampton, 1993; Peacock, 1993). These views suggest that some of the barriers experienced by Indigenous students may be rooted in cultural incongruence between the educational system and the worldview and learning styles of minority students (Bourke, Burden & Moore, 1996).

Other researchers have argued that the situation goes beyond lack of congruence to actual conflict between worldviews and/or value systems of Indigenous students and those fostered in our education systems, and that the conflict is an underlying reason for lowered educational attainment and persistence of Indigenous students (e.g., Christie, 1985; Guider, 1991; Harris, 1988; Hughes, 1984). These arguments, together with the substantial literature which posits differences in cultural outlooks, values and worldviews as contributing to lowered achievement outcomes for minority and indigenous groups, prompted the present investigators to examine the extent to which values of Indigenous students differed from those of non-Indigenous students and the extent to which values predict academic achievement

In searching for a vehicle to use in our investigation of the role of values in education, the authors chose Schwartz's (1992, 1994) model of universal values. This model postulates that there is a basic set of values shared by all societies. These values can be measured by the Schwartz Values Survey (SVS: Schwartz, 1992). Findings obtained from 97 samples using the SVS in 44 countries between 1988 and 1993 provided substantial support for the universality of the 56 values used in the survey and, through the use of Smallest Space Analysis, their composition into ten major value types which tended to form two bipolar dimensions (Schwartz, 1994). The motivational types and associated values of the revised theory are as follows:

1. Self-Direction (creativity, freedom, choosing own goals, curiosity, independence);
2. Stimulation (variety, excitement);
3. Hedonism (pleasure, enjoyment of life);
4. Achievement (ambition, success, capability, influence intelligent);
5. Power (authority, wealth, social power, public image, social recognition);
6. Security (social order, family security, national security, reciprocation of favors, cleanliness, sense of belonging, healthy);
7. Conformity (obedience, self-discipline, politeness, honoring parents and elders);
8. Tradition (respect for tradition, humility, devoutness, acceptance of one's portion in life, moderation);

9. Benevolence (helpfulness, loyalty, forgiveness, honesty, responsibility, truth, friendship, mature love);
10. Universalism (broadmindedness, social justice, equality, world at peace, unity with nature, wisdom, protection of the environment).

Schwartz concluded that the values demonstrated sufficient equivalence of motivational meaning across cultures to justify their use to form indexes of the importance of the value types in different cultures. Schwartz (1994) further postulated that actions taken in the pursuit of each type of value have psychological, practical and social consequences that may conflict, or may be compatible with the pursuit of other types. This pattern of conflict and compatibility among value types resulted in the theoretical structure of value systems as shown in Figure 2.

In this portrayal, competing value types emanate in opposing directions from the center, complementary types are in close proximity going around the circle (Schwartz, 1994, 1996).

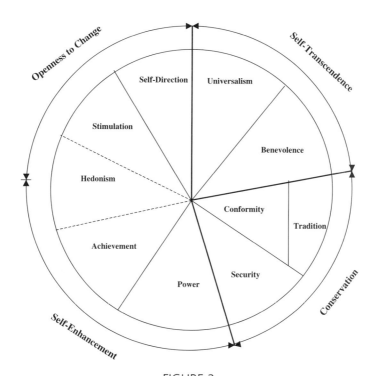

FIGURE 2
Relations Among Motivation Types Of Values, Higher Order Value
Types, and Bipolar Value Dimensions (Adapted from Schwartz, 1994).

Description of Study on Values Congruence

In order to explore the notion that differing value priorities impact on the educational attainment of Indigenous people, White and Fogarty (2001) administered the SVS to a total of 202 Indigenous and 194 non-Indigenous students over a period of six years. This study is described in detail elsewhere, so a brief overview will suffice. Initial analysis of the sub-scale scores indicated that the Indigenous and non-Indigenous groups differed significantly on value types associated with Tradition, Conformity, Security, and Power, with Indigenous students according higher priority to these value types. The first three of these are normally associated with Collective values or, in Schwartz's 1994 revised terminology, Conservation values. These findings parallel those of Fogarty & White (1994) and are in accord with much of the literature regarding Australian Indigenous culture which asserts that Australian Aborigines are orientated collectively (Elkin, 1954) and are a conservative people (Berndt & Berndt (1992). The type of behavior exhibited by Vanessa is typical of a person coming from a collectivist society: the importance of community, the priority accorded to family matters, and the sense of isolation in a new environment.

The utility of the value types in predicting academic progression was investigated using standard regression techniques. Regression analysis suggested that the value types were only marginally related to the prediction of academic progression, accounting for 9 percent (R^2) of the explained variance for the Indigenous group and 10 percent (R^2) for the non-Indigenous group. Whilst these relationships were statistically significant, they left much of the variance in academic performance unexplained.

A possible reason for the low correlations between academic progression and value types is that no real choice or conflict between values was involved when students were actually filling out the questionnaire. Schwartz (1996) suggested that values may play little role in behavior except when there is value conflict. The activation of values as guiding principles may require an active choice between competing demands. The SVS as used in this study asked respondents to rate the importance of values as guiding principles in their lives and did not involve elements of choice. For example, it is possible that a person might rate ambition as being very important yet chose not to seek promotion for family or security reasons. Similarly, it is possible for respondents to attach high importance to values such as independence, success, and capability yet make no deliberate choice to implement these values in a study environment. As Blamey and Braithwaite (1997) suggested, values may be useful, not necessarily because of their closeness to behavior, but because they inform us about the ways in which individuals frame the decisions that lead to behavior.

STUDY 4: CONGRUENCE BETWEEN ACADEMIC SKILLS AND COURSE DEMANDS

Perhaps the most obvious way in which to think about the congruence between students and academic settings is in the match between cognitive skills and the skills demanded by the courses. After all, the development of cognitive skills lies at the center of the educational enterprise. White and Fogarty (2001) were able to collect data on the reasoning skills of a subset (n = 160) of the Indigenous students who participated in their study on the role of values in educational achievement. The reasoning tests were the Higher Tests ML-MQ (2nd edition) published by the Australian Council for Educational Research (ACER). These tests are similar to the more widely know Scholastic Aptitude Test in the US. The tests are primarily intended as a measure of general scholastic ability in the prediction of achievement in school. They are also used for counselling in relation to training and other situations where the ability to think clearly with words and numbers is involved (ACER, 1981). Glietman (1981) indicated that validity coefficients, that is, the correlation between test scores and academic success, are generally in the neighborhood of .50 or .60. Normative data provided by the Queensland Department of Education (Byrne, Glen & Phillips, 1983) supports these validity estimates.

Indigenous students normally completed the tests during interviews prior to their commencement of tertiary studies or in the first few weeks after commencing studies. Because the main interest was in assessing the level of verbal and numerical ability rather than speed, the tests were administered without any time restrictions. For both the verbal (ML) and numerical (MQ) tests, possible scores ranged from a minimum of zero to a maximum of 34.

Two aspects of this study are of interest here: the performance of the Indigenous students on the ML and MQ tests and the relationship between test scores and academic performance. White (1996) addressed the first of these questions. To summarize his findings in relation to the ML test, White found that for the verbal reasoning test, two-thirds of the students scored at or below the 49th percentile when compared to the normative sample of 15-yr old school leavers. In other words, the Indigenous students, on average, obtained scores on a verbal reasoning test that would place them in the bottom half of a group of 15-yr olds who did the same test. When one considers that the test was not timed and that the average age of the Indigenous students was 27.34 years, the scores obtained were probably somewhat inflated compared with what would be achieved under normal, timed conditions. Further analysis by White confirmed that the deficit in verbal reasoning scores was not confined to a single area but was spread across Verbal Analogies, Verbal Reasoning, Verbal Classification, and Same or Opposite type questions. "This is indicative of general rather than specific, verbal abilities" (White, 1996, p.31).

The implications of this low average score need to be spelled out. Verbal reasoning skills are essential in the courses undertaken by the Indigenous students participating in this study. As Schonell, Roe, and Meddleton (1962) argued: "Abilities to reason and to appreciate fine discriminations are necessary in all university courses and verbal abilities generally play a predominant part." (p.57). One of the assumptions underlying tests such as the ML is that students who have trouble with the test will probably have trouble with course content as well. White and Fogarty (2001) examined the relationship between ML and MQ scores and found that there was indeed a strong relationship. The correlation between ML scores and progression rate was .54 ($R^2 = .29$, $p < .05$), a figure that is very similar to the reported validity coefficient in the test manual.

White (1996) concluded that differences in the form of English used by Indigenous Australians including phonetics, phonemics, grammar, and vocabulary—leaves them under-prepared for the complex verbal requirements of higher education, with consequent dramatic effects on performance in their chosen courses, all of which place a heavy demand on verbal skills. Christie (1985) made similar claims when he argued that in traditional Aboriginal learning, the role of language is reduced because of the reliance on participation in group activities. The relative lack of a written tradition further encourages Aboriginal people to think and perceive in ways not constrained by the serial and sequential nature of verbal thinking.

CONCLUSIONS

Over the years, many factors have been proposed to account for differences in achievement and participation rates for Indigenous students when compared with non-Indigenous students. Some of these include lowered self-esteem, traditional learning styles which differ from those used in Australian schools and society, negative early school experiences, home environments detrimental to academic learning, inability of parents to provide necessary assistance and support, and western prejudices and stereotypes (Honeyman, 1986). Other factors that have been proposed include deficient language skills, poor discipline and academic motivation, socialization practices at variance to mainstream culture, and cultural conflict (McInerney, 1991). We have tapped only a section of this literature in our own research program.

In this chapter, we have attempted to bring a different perspective to the debate by introducing P-E fit theory and reviewing some of own work with Indigenous students that falls within this paradigm. We have shown that wherever you look, there is evidence of incongruence between the person and the environment.

- The fit between career interests and course choice is only moderate. As Sutherland et al. (1995) demonstrated, it is no better for non-Indigenous students but this should not be allowed to overshadow the fact that there is a need for better career counselling before students commence study. Vanessa's initial disappointment at the failure of her psychology course to match her expectations is echoed by students in other courses and other institutions (McInnis et al., 2000). To some extent, it is always going to be difficult to overcome this problem, especially with the move towards more content-oriented education at the undergraduate level and more career-oriented skills training now occurring at postgraduate level. Career counselling will have to prepare students for what can be a long, theory-based introduction to various professions.

- there is also incongruence in the fit between what Indigenous students expect to find at university and what they actually do find. Better information is the solution to this problem and a wider range of options at university to cater for the needs of this population. As we mentioned when telling Vanessa's story, she is among the first generation of Indigenous students attending higher education in this country, and there is still much to be learned about the support mechanisms required for students like her. Simple things that other students take for granted, such as rules and regulations, are not always understood by minority cultures.

- Values incongruence exists but we are not sure just how important this dimension is in the wider scheme of things. Values are fundamental aspects of cultures and individuals and we found evidence that they related to academic outcomes but did not explain a major part of the variance (8 percent). Our suggestion is that this failure could be due to the way in which we have measured values, allowing participants to endorse all values if they wished. If the true character of values emerges in situations of conflict and choice (as argued by Schwartz, 1996), we have not yet captured this in our measurement processes.

- Incongruence at the cognitive skills level undoubtedly exists for a significant proportion of the Indigenous students involved in our studies. Given that university success is determined by highly structured examination processes, it is not surprising that of all the facets we examined, we found it easiest to demonstrate the limitations imposed by deficits in this area. Vanessa was quite capable of handling the work required but White's (1996) analysis of commencing Indigenous students indicated that many of her fellow students fell short of what would be regarded as required levels of competency in verbal and numerical skills for university study. There is little point in allowing students to enrol in university courses if they are not adequately prepared for those courses. The solution is twofold: a) more careful screening processes so that those who are seriously deficient in these areas are encouraged to consider other career options; and b) extended bridging courses so that students can develop their verbal and numerical skills to the required level before commencing university study.

In concluding, it is important to point out that although cognitive incongruence stands out among the variables that we examined as a contributor to low progression rates of Indigenous students, we do not claim that it is the most important variable. ML scores, although significantly related to academic progression, accounted for just over 25 percent of the variance in progression. A further 7 percent is explained when MQ scores are added to the equation and another 8 percent when values were added, still leaving 60 percent or more (depending on variable overlap) of the variance unexplained. For some of the facets of incongruence we examined, we were not able to estimate their impact on progression.

The majority of Indigenous students who participated in this study tend to take pride in their Aboriginality and cultural difference. In general, Aboriginal students tend to be more oriented to their family and their in-group and more traditional and conforming in the values they endorse. The ways in which these differences may impact on attitudes and behaviors in a school or tertiary environment has not been ascertained in our studies. Ogbu (1987, 1990) argued that in addition to the role of the larger society and the school, minorities also contribute to their own school success or school failure because of the nature of their cultural model. These cultural models certainly incorporate values, attitudes and beliefs, which can impact on the students decision to resist or accommodate the mainstream school culture and adopt behaviors either detrimental or conducive to school success. It is perhaps concepts such as "Aboriginality as resistance," as suggested by Keeffe (1992) that need to be further explored in order to provide a more complete understanding of the relationships among values, attitudes and educational outcomes for Indigenous students. A not uncommon coping mechanism for many Indigenous students in this study when faced with a difficult or challenging academic situation was to respond That "whitefella" way—we do it "blackfella" way. While there is certainly more than one way to "skin a cat," divergent, innovative, creative or differing cultural viewpoints are often not readily accepted in academic environments structured for throughput, output, and maintenance of dominant societal values.

FUTURE DIRECTIONS

What we have presented here is a collection of studies, conducted at different times, the one common link being that they were all concerned with problems of attrition among Australian Indigenous students. The focal points of each of the studies were separate factors that have been identified in the literature as being implicated in student attrition, including course incongruence, values incongruence, inadequate cognitive preparation, and unrealistic expectations of the university environment. The P-E fit approach, however, demands that we explore these factors, not in one-off studies as we have done here, but in large multivariate studies that allow for inspection of the influence of individual variables and also the interactions among these variables. White and Fogarty (2001) made some progress in this direction with their study of the combined effects of values and abilities, explaining close to 40 percent of the variance in academic progression rates.

Future studies of this kind could expand the range of variables still further. An excellent example of this kind of research can be found in the field of intelligence where the modern paradigm of intelligence differentiates the notion of intelligence-as-typical performance from the notion of intelligence-as-optimal performance (Ackerman & Heggestad, 1997). This new perspective has encouraged and enabled researchers such as Ackerman and his colleagues to investigate the overlap between intelligence and personality, and intelligence and interests. Through their research, they have identified four trait-complexes:

a. Social, which consists of Enterprising and Social interests, Extraversion, Social Potency, and Well-Being;
b. Clerical/Conventional, comprising Perceptual Speed, Conventional interests, Control, Conscientiousness, and Traditionalism;
c. Science/Math, which consists of Mathematical Reasoning, Visual Perception, and Realistic and Investigative interests; and
d. Intellectual/Cultural, made up of Investigative and Artistic interests, Crystallized Intelligence, Ideational Fluency, Absorption, Typical Intellectual Engagement, and Openness.

Although at this stage the framework does not include values, it could be expanded to include other individual differences variables.

We believe that broad, integrative approaches such as those used by Ackerman, although extremely difficult from a data collection point of view, hold much promise for explaining variance in academic achievement. The variables included in his grouping are already known to be important in this field, and the notion of typical as opposed to maximal performance is surely worth exploring among Indigenous peoples. In those brief periods when Vanessa applied herself, we saw examples of her maximal performance. What Vanessa left behind was more a record of her typical performance. The two should not be confused. If we can reduce the gap between the person and the environment, the typical should move closer to the maximal.

REFERENCES

ACER. (1981). *ACER Higher Tests ML-MQ and PL-PQ manual* (2nd ed.). Victoria, Australia: Australian Council for Educational Research.

Ackerman, P. L., & Heggestad, E. D. (1997). Intelligence, personality, and interests: Evidence for overlapping traits. *Psychological Bulletin, 121*, 219-245.

Berndt, R. M., & Berndt, C. H. (1992). *The world of the first Australians: Aboriginal traditional life. Past and present.* Canberra, Australia. Aboriginal Studies Press.

Blamey, R., & Braithwaite, V. (1997). The validity of security-harmony social values model in the general population. *Australian Journal of Psychology, 49* (2), 59-63.

Bourke, C. J., Burden, J. K., & Moore, S. (1996). *Factors affecting performance of Aboriginal and Torres Strait Islander student at Australian universities: A case study.* Canberra, Australia: AGPS.

Camp, C.C., & Chartrand, J.M. (1992). A comparison and evaluation of interest congruence indices. *Journal of Vocational Behavior, 41*, 162-182.

Christie, M. (1985). *Aboriginal perspectives on experience and learning: The role of language in Aboriginal education.* Victoria, Australia: Deakin University Press.

DEET. (1990). *Aboriginal and Torres Strait Islander students: Higher education series report no.3.* Canberra, Australia: Department of Employment, Education and Training.

Dehyle, D. (1992). Constructing failure and maintaining cultural identity: Navajo and Ute school leavers. *Journal of American Indian Education, 31*, 24-47.

DETYA. (1999). *Equity in higher education* (Occasional Paper Series 99-A). Canberra, Australia: Department of Education, Training and Youth Affairs.

Elkin, A. P. (1954). *The Australian Aboriginies: How to understand them.* Sydney, Australia: Angus & Robertson.

Encel, J. D. (2000). *Indigenous participation in higher education* (Occasional Paper Series 00/C). Canberra, Australia: DETYA.

Fogarty, G. J., & White, C. D. (1994). Differences between values of Australian Aboriginal and non-Aboriginal students. *Journal of Cross-Cultural Psychology, 25*(3), 394-408.

Glietman, H. (1981). *Psychology.* New York, NY: Norton.

Guider, J. (1991). Why are so many Aboriginal children not achieving at school? *Aboriginal Child at School, 19*(2), 42-53.

Hampton, E. (1993). Toward a redefinition of American Indian/Alaskan native education. *Canadian Journal of Native Education, 20*, 261-309.

Harris, S. (1988). 'Coming up level' without 'losing themselves': The dilemma of formal tertiary training for Aboriginies. In B. Harvey & S. McGinty (Eds.), *'Learning my way'. Papers from the national conference on adult Aboriginal learning.* Perth, Australia: Western Australian College of Advanced Education.

Holland, J.L. (1985). *Making vocational choices: A theory of vocational personalities and work environment* (2nd ed.). Englewood Cliffs, NJ: Prentice Hall.

Holland, J. L. (1988a). *The self-directed search Australian edition.* Victoria, Australia: The Australian Council for Educational Research Ltd.

Holland, J.L. (1988b). *The occupations finder. For use with the self-directed search.* Victoria, Australia: The Australian Council for Educational Research Ltd.

Honeyman, K. (1986). Learning difficulties of Aborigines in education. *Aboriginal Child at School, 14*(3), 17-36.

Hughes, P. (1984). Towards a new pedagogy. *Education News, 18*(11), 46-48.

Keeffe, K. (1992). *From the centre to the city: Aboriginal education culture and power.* Canberra, Australia: Aboriginal Studies Press.

Khan, S.B., Alvi, S.A., Shaukat, N., Hussain, M.A., & Baig, T. (1990). A study of the validity of Holland's theory in a non-Western culture. *Journal of Vocational Behavior, 36*, 132-146.

McInerney, D. M. (1991). Key-determinants of motivation of non-traditional Aboriginal students in school settings: Recommendations for educational change. *Australian Journal of Education, 35*(2), 154-174.

McInnis, C., Hartley, R, & Teese, R. (2000). *Non-completion in vocational education and training in higher education.* DETYA.

Ogbu, J. U. (1987). Variability in Minority School Performance: A problem in search of an explanation. *Anthropology and Education Quarterly, 18*, 313-334.

Ogbu, J. U. (1990). Cultural model, identity, and literacy. In J. W. Stigler & R. A. Shweder & G. Herdt (Eds.), *Cultural Psychology* (pp. 521-541). Cambridge, UK: Cambridge University Press.

Peacock, L. (1993). Absenteeism and the Aboriginal child. *Aboriginal Child at School, 21*, 3-11.

Schonell, F.J., Roe, E., & Meddleton, R. (1962). *Promise and performance.* Brisbane, Australia: University of Queensland Press.

Schwab, R. G. (1995). *Twenty years of policy recommendations for indigenous education: overview and research implications.* Canberra, Australia: Centre for Aboriginal Economic Policy Research, ANU.

Schwartz, S. (1992). Universals in the content and structure of values: Theoretical advances and empirical tests in 20 countries, *Advances in Experimental Social Psychology, Volume 25*: Academic Press.

Schwartz, S. (1996). Value priorities and behavior: Applying a theory of integrated value systems. In C. Seligban & J. M. Olson & M. Zanna (Eds.), *The psychology of values: The Ontario symposium, volume 8* (pp. 1-24). Mahwah, NJ: Erlbaum.

Spokane, A.R., Meir, E.I., & Catalano, M. (2000). Person-environment congruence and Holland's theory: A review and reconsideration. *Journal of Vocational Behavior, 57*, 137-187.

Stanley, O., & Hansen, G. (1998). *Abstudy: An investment for tomorrow's employment.* Canberra, Australia: ATSIC.

Sutherland, L., Fogarty, G., & Pithers, R. (1995). Congruence as a predictor of occupational stress. *Journal of Vocational Behavior. 46 (3)*, 292-309.

Tinsley, H.E. A. (2000). The congruence myth: An analysis of the efficacy of the person-environment fit model. *Journal of Vocational Behavior, 56*, 147-179.

White, C. (1996). Verbal reasoning abilities of Aboriginal and Torres Strait Islander tertiary applicants. *Australian Journal of Indigenous Education, 24*(2), 27-32.

White, C., & Brown, L. (1994). Kumbari/Ngurpai Lag students, past and present. In L. Brown & D. Bull (Eds.), *Papers from the Jilalan project seminar.* Toowoomba, Australia: University of Southern Queensland.

Zener, T.B., Schnuelle, L. (1976). Effects of the Self-Directed Search on high school students. *Journal of Counselling Psychology, 23*, 353-359.

PART II

FOCUS ON FAMILIES AND COMMUNITIES

THE SOCIAL CONSTRUCTION OF INTEREST IN A LEARNING COMMUNITY

Kimberley Pressick-Kilborn and Richard Walker

About half-way through a science unit in which her class was learning about egg-laying animals, Cara brought a shoe box to school. What Cara, a grade 5 student, had carefully placed inside the box was a gift for her friend, Belinda. Belinda opened the box excitedly to find some cocoons placed amongst bark, sticks and leaves. "Wow! Where did you find these?" Belinda asked.

"I found some caterpillars in the garden at home and I made an enclosure for them in an old fish tank. I've been watching them spin cocoons. I wanted to share some of these cocoons with you," Cara replied, smiling at her friend's obvious delight.

During the morning, moths emerged from a few of the cocoons and at recess Belinda took her box into the playground and carefully took one moth out. While she was cradling it in her hand, it laid some eggs! News spread quickly around the playground and when Miss Wheeldon, the grade 5 teacher, met her class at the end of the morning break, the students were waiting excitedly beside the classroom door to tell her about this amazing occurrence. In the science lesson the next day Miss Wheeldon referred to this shared experience. She introduced the focus activity of the lesson by linking it with the moths, which by now had been safely returned to Belinda's box.

INTRODUCTION

The creation and development of interest in learning is something that many educators would undoubtedly seek to support in their classrooms. Yet educational research has provided limited insight into the ways in which interest is created and develops in authentic learning environments over time. Although a focus on authentic contexts for learning is emerging within motivational research (Ainley, 1998; Dowson & McInerney, 2001; MacCallum, 2001), for the most part, interest research has consisted of experimental and correlational studies which have been relatively short-lived and in contexts designed specifically for the purposes of the research (Harp & Mayer, 1997; Isaac, Sansone & Smith, 1999). Experimental studies, for instance, have examined such issues as the benefits of cognitive interest over emotional interest in learning scientific explanations (Harp & Mayer, 1997) and ways in which problem-solving with other people contributes to interest and future task engagement (Isaac, Sansone & Smith, 1999). Correlational studies have investigated relationships between interest and other aspects of learning such as prior knowledge and depth of learning (Tobias, 1994; Schiefele & Krapp, 1996). While both types of studies have produced significant findings, they have usually involved tasks and learning conditions considerably removed from those of actual classrooms. Both types of studies have also been guided by the conceptualization of interest as situational or individual and have tended to focus on either situational interest (for example, Mitchell, 1993) or individual interest (for example, Schiefele & Krapp, 1996). More recently, however, Ainley and her colleagues (Ainley, Hidi & Berndorff, 1999; Ainley & Hillman, 1999) have considered situational and individual interest within the same experimental studies. While clearly advancing the understanding of interest as a motivational construct these, and other studies so far undertaken, have yet to capture the complexity of interest creation and development over time in an actual classroom environment.

In this chapter, we argue that the exploration of this complexity may best be achieved by the development of a sociocultural approach, deriving from the work of Vygotsky, to the conceptualization of interest. A sociocultural approach to interest developed from this perspective differs from previous conceptualizations in several ways:

1. It focuses upon the creation of interest, its maintenance, and subsequent developmental trajectory.
2. It emphasizes the dynamic nature of the transactions between the individual and the environment, which give rise to interest. Consideration is given to ways in which both the physical and social environment constrain and offer possibilities for the creation and maintenance of interest (Valsiner, 1997).

3.   It gives priority to understanding how key sociocultural notions such as communities of practice, zones of proximal development, and cultural tools and artifacts impact on interest formation and development.
4.   It opens up a broad range of methodological research possibilities with complex, qualitative designs considered as important as the experimental and correlational designs common in current interest research.

The development of a sociocultural perspective on interest in this chapter draws upon two established sociocultural approaches: firstly Jaan Valsiner's (1987, 1997) sociocultural writing concerning the canalization of development and his work on the zone of proximal development and other related zones of development, and secondly on investigations of one type of community of practice, classroom learning communities (for example, Brown, Ash, Rutherford, Nakagawa, Gordon & Campione, 1993; Brown & Campione, 1994; Brown, 1997). It is argued that Valsiner's notions of canalization and self-canalization and his development and extension of the zone of proximal development provide important insights and can aid an understanding of the creation and subsequent development of interest. It is also argued that learning communities, and other communities of practice, play important roles in assisting or constraining the development of interest.

We suggest in this chapter that some early and contemporary interest research and theorizing, as well as some current directions in motivational research more generally, are consistent with a sociocultural approach. Furthermore, we suggest that while there is value in distinguishing between situational and individual interest, from a sociocultural perspective this distinction is less salient than in the current interest literature. We also outline an ethnographic study of the development of interest, undertaken by the first author, in a naturally occurring classroom and consider its relevance for a sociocultural theory of interest. Finally we consider implications and applications of this research, and of a sociocultural theory of interest more generally, for learning in classrooms and other settings.

THE ORIGINS OF INDIVIDUAL DEVELOPMENT AND LEARNING IN SOCIOCULTURAL ACTIVITY

Sociocultural approaches to learning and development, which have their origins in the work of Vygotsky and his colleagues, are based on

> the concept that human activities take place in cultural contexts, are mediated by language and other symbol systems, and can be best understood when investigated in their historical development. (John-Steiner & Mahn, 1996, p. 191)

Accordingly, sociocultural theorists consider that individual development and learning have their origins in social activity, with processes of individual development and learning constituted by activities and practices that are interpersonal and cultural-historical (Rogoff & Chavajay, 1995; Wells, 1999). Sociocultural theory, therefore, adopts an integrated perspective on development and learning which emphasizes a dynamic interdependence between social and individual processes (Rogoff & Chavajay, 1995; John-Steiner & Mahn, 1996).

The Vygotskian concept of the zone of proximal development (ZPD) is an important aspect of the sociocultural explanation of the interdependence of the social and the individual. The most commonly cited definition of the ZPD is

> that difference between a learner's actual development level as determined by independent problem-solving and the level of potential development as determined through problem-solving under adult guidance or in collaboration with more capable peers (Vygotsky, 1978, p. 86).

It is through the creation of zones of proximal development that children, and other learners, are able to internalize or appropriate (Rogoff, 1998) the understandings, skills and roles of their communities. Through the process of guided interaction, mutual understanding or intersubjectivity is initiated and allows the negotiation of shared purpose, focus and values. Therefore, in sociocultural theory, it is through the creation of intersubjectivity that development and learning become possible (Rogoff, 1998).

The interdependence of social and individual processes in sociocultural theory is further explained through the notion of communities of practice (Lave & Wenger, 1991; Rogoff & Chavajay, 1995; Rogoff, 1998). The term 'community of practice' refers to a sociocultural group that collaborates to achieve shared goals through particular practices and activities. Members of the sociocultural group or community vary in their mastery and competence of these practices and activities and consequently some, with high levels of competence, are considered legitimate members (Lave & Wenger, 1991) while others, with little competence, are peripheral members. New members of the community, children or novices, are enculturated into the practices of the group and may, over time, move from peripheral participation to legitimate (Lave & Wenger, 1991) or established participation. These practices are highly valued by community members (Miller & Goodnow, 1995) and they provide the context in which human development and learning occur. Children working as a community of learners in a classroom, a type of community of practice, for instance learn that their academic activities are valued within the learning community and they learn strategies for mastering the activities (Brown & Campione, 1994). As individuals are enculturated into the practices of a community their identity undergoes change (Rogoff, 1998) and they may likewise contribute to change in the practices of the community. A dynamic relationship therefore exists between the individual and the community of which they are becoming a member.

SOCIOCULTURAL PERSPECTIVES ON MOTIVATION

While sociocultural theories of cognitive development originating from the work of Vygotsky have been prevalent for some years, only recently has consideration been given to motivational constructs from a sociocultural perspective. Although limited literature addresses motivation from a sociocultural perspective, there is an increasing interest amongst motivational researchers in the impact of social and contextual factors on motivation. Consequently, there are currents in contemporary motivational research which are compatible with a sociocultural approach to motivation.

Sociocultural perspectives on motivation (Sivan, 1986; Hickey, 1997; Paris & Turner 1994; Brophy, 1999) have considered the impact of tools and artifacts, intersubjectivity, the zone of proximal development, and the social and physical context for learning, on motivation in academic contexts. Along with these analyses, classroom-based research (Forman & McPhail, 1993; Oldfather & Dahl, 1994) has also considered motivation from a sociocultural perspective. As part of a broader study of children's collaborative problem solving from a Vygotskian perspective, Forman and McPhail (1993) examined the processes of social interaction effective in fostering motivation to both solve and understand complex problems. They suggest that the mutual and equal nature of the relationship between two students working together is a possible explanation for their interest in engaging in the task. Similarly, in an investigation of literacy learning conducted through two classroom ethnographic studies, Oldfather and Dahl (1994) concluded that sociocognitive and affective processes experienced by learners as they engaged meaningfully in tasks are the origins of motivation. As is typical of much sociocultural research, each of these empirical studies makes use of qualitative methodology to support their sociocultural analyses.

While there has been limited theoretical and empirical analysis of motivation from a Vygotskian sociocultural perspective, there are current motivational perspectives which have much in common with a sociocultural perspective. The well established theory of Csikszentmihalyi (1990, 1993, 1997), for instance, recognises the impact of culture and social systems on motivation and focuses upon interrelationships amongst the person and the social and cultural context. The notion of 'flow' on which Csikszentmihalyi's research is based contributes to a theory of 'emergent' motivation and enables consideration of the positive experience of people engaged in specific tasks where challenges are optimally balanced with skills. Unlike other theories of motivation that emphasize intraindividual aspects of motivation, Csikszentmihalyi's flow construct focuses upon interaction and negotiation between an individual and the social world in which they participate. In his empirical studies, Csikszentmihalyi captures the dynamic nature of motivation through the Experience Sampling Measure (ESM), a technique used by participants to record their responses to the context that they are experiencing when they are electronically 'paged' as part of the research. In this way information is gathered about participants' thoughts and feelings as they engage in activities and insights into their subjective states in particular sociocultural contexts are made possible.

A concern with social and contextual issues is also evident in the current work of other motivational researchers (Turner et al, 1998; Turner & Meyer, 2000; Pintrich 2000; MacCallum, 2001). Pintrich (2000) has called for greater consideration of context in studies of motivation, drawing attention to the need for sociocultural research to "conceptualize and understand how the individual and context work together to facilitate and constrain learning" (p. 223). Similarly, Turner and her colleagues (Turner et al, 1998; Turner & Meyer, 2000) argue strongly for the need to consider motivation as situated in classroom activities. Further, they emphasize the importance of qualitative and multimethod approaches to research design and analysis for exploring the 'how and why' of learning, motivation and social processes in classroom interaction. Lastly, the classroom is one of the six sociocultural contexts for individual motivational change considered by MacCallum (2001) in her study of students' goals and theories of success. MacCallum (2001) focuses on the contexts of the self, peers, teacher, subject area, school organization and family to discuss students' perceptions of change as they move from primary school to high school. Consideration of sociocultural contexts in this study is central to understanding motivational change.

These writings, considered together, clearly recognize the social nature of much academic motivation and provide the foundations for the development of a sociocultural approach to motivation. They also recognize the importance of context for motivation and provide examples of the ways in which the social and contextual nature of motivation can be explored using qualitative and multimethod research approaches. Recognition of the social nature of one form of motivation, that of interest, is also evident in the research literature.

CONCEPTUALIZATIONS OF INTEREST AND THEIR COMPATIBILITY WITH A SOCIOCULTURAL APPROACH

The theoretical construct, interest, is one that has been considered and examined in educational psychology since the late 19th century. Both William James (1890/1950, cited in Schiefele, 1991, and Rathunde, 1993) and John Dewey regarded interest as central to educational theory and practice. The theory of interest developed by Dewey (1913) distinguished between two different elements of interest, identification and absorption. In emphasizing the importance of identification, Dewey (1913) asserted that, "The genuine principle of interest is the principle of the recognized identity of the fact to be learned or the action proposed with the growing self" (p. 7). He regarded interest as a form of self-expression that was developmental in nature and which, therefore, varied with age, prior experiences, social opportunities and "individual native endowments" (p. 67). Dewey regarded children as more likely to be 'social' in their interest than adults. He considered children's activities to be so embedded in the social that the boundary between the individual and social activity is rarely considered by children, as is evident from their play. Dewey argued that the distance between the person, materials and the results of action are 'annihilated' with interest as a sign of 'organic union' (Dewey, 1913, p. 17). 'Genuine interest' is therefore defined as "the accompaniment of the identification, through action, of the self with some object or idea, because of the necessity of that object or idea for the maintenance of a self-initiated activity" (Dewey, 1913, p. 14). Through this definition, Dewey recognized interest as a dynamic, active state based on real objects and the pleasure associated with them. He emphasized the place of interest in the maintenance of an enduring activity that develops over time, and also acknowledged the interactive relationship between the individual and aspects of the environment in the creation of interest.

Dewey's social conceptualization of interest and his emphasis on the dynamic transaction between person and environment which leads to the development and maintenance of interest is compatible with a sociocultural perspective. While some attempts have been made in recent interest research to emphasize the dynamic interplay of personal and situational factors, this emphasis is currently underdeveloped in the literature. Although some theories of situational interest (Mitchell, 1993; Hidi & Harackiewicz, 2000) have elaborated Dewey's emphasis upon the dynamic nature of interest, interest researchers in general, as Hidi and Harackiewicz (2000) note, differ considerably in the extent to which they emphasize the personal and situational origins of interest. The literature on situational and individual interest, therefore, varies in the extent to which the dynamic interplay of personal and environmental factors is recognized.

Situational and Individual Interest

The distinction between two conceptions of interest, situational and individual interest, has been made by Schiefele (1991). The basis of situational interest is an external locus, defined as "an emotional state brought about by situational stimuli" (Schiefele, 1991, p. 302). This form of interest is also referred to as 'interestingness' and is the basis of approaches to studying interest that aim to identify features of a specific context that arouse and capture interest. It tends to be more short-lived and superficial than individual interest (Alexander & Jetton, 1996) and is generally aroused by specific features of an activity or task (Schiefele, 1998). Two aspects of situational interest, 'catch' factors (which trigger interest) and 'hold' factors (which maintain interest), have been studied by Mitchell (1993), while Harp and Mayer (1997) distinguish between cognitive and emotional interest, the latter aroused by 'seductive details' in text. Renninger (2000) indicates that an assumption about a high level of content knowledge cannot be made when considering situational interest, as knowledge can either be high or low for a person with a situational interest.

Individual interest is defined as "a relatively stable evaluative orientation towards certain domains" (Schiefele, 1998, p. 93) or towards particular classes of objects, events or ideas (Krapp, Renninger & Hoffman, 1998). Individual interests have personal significance and are usually associated with high levels of knowledge and value, positive emotions and increased reference value (Krapp, Hidi & Renninger, 1992; Renninger, 2000). In this framework, individual interest develops and remains a stable and enduring factor in one's learning over an extended period of time. It may be considered dispositional and internally oriented (Krapp et al., 1992; Alexander & Jetton, 1996; Bergin, 1999). Renninger (2000) incorporates stored knowledge and stored value as components of individual interest, which emphasizes a cognitively-oriented approach. Schiefele (1991, 1998) considers individual interest as both a latent and an actualized characteristic, with the latent characteristic further divided into feeling-related valences (i.e. feelings associated with a topic or object) and value-related valences (i.e. the attribution of personal significance to an object). Although differing slightly in emphasis, both Renninger's and Schiefele's conceptualizations of individual interest consider the value or personal meaning of a subject or object as a defining feature of such interest. Individual interests appear to be more, rather than less, stable in children, although children are also always in the process of consolidating, merging and developing new interests (Fink, 1995; Renninger, 1998, 2000).

Considering Relationships Between Situational and Individual Interest

This conceptualization of interest, described above as comprising both situational and individual components, is the basis for the majority of recent empirical studies of interest, both explicitly (for example, Mitchell, 1993; Schiefele & Krapp, 1996; Hoffman, Krapp, Renninger & Baumert, 1998) and more implicitly (for example, Anderson, Shirey, Wilson & Fielding, 1987; Wade, Schraw, Buxton & Hayes, 1993). It is evident, however, that the relationship between situational and individual interest is an issue that has not been thoroughly explored (Hidi & Berndorff, 1998).

Researchers have generally focused upon one of these conceptions of interest at the expense of the other in their empirical studies, with the notable exception of the recent work of Ainley and her colleagues (Ainley, Hidi & Berndorff, 1999; Ainley & Hillman, 1999), which has incorporated measures of both situational and individual interest within the same study. Through considering actualized interest, Ainley (1998) qualitatively analyzes the way in which an individual student participates in two classroom science lessons. The focus upon both the behaviors of the student during the lessons and the personal meanings articulated by this student in interviews following the lessons brings together situational and individual aspects of interest.

In considering possible relationships between situational and individual interest, some contemporary interest researchers with a focus upon the development of interest have suggested that individual interest arises and develops through experiencing an activity that holds special personal significance (Hidi et al., 1992). These researchers suggest that this development probably takes place over time, with repeated exposure to and experience of related topics or activities. As knowledge and value of an initially situational interest increases, it shifts to hold a personal value, or individual interest (Hidi & Anderson, 1992; Alexander & Jetton, 1996; Alexander, 1997). The suggestion of this process of development, however, has not been explored empirically beyond Alexander's research into text-based interest. Alexander has developed the three-stage Model of Domain Learning (MDL), in which situational and individual interests have distinctly separate trajectories (Alexander, 1997). In the MDL, Alexander acknowledges the critical role of motivational forces, particularly interest, in the process of individuals achieving expertise within a domain of learning. Individual interest, or 'personal investment' as Alexander sometimes refers to it, is the motivational source leading to competence and expertise. While situational interest is considered vital during the first stage and does remain a force across all three MDL stages to some extent, Alexander (1997) claims that these two aspects of interest may at times operate in opposition to one another to the detriment of development within a domain. In this process, situational interest thus sometimes acts as a distracter from the motivating force of individual interest.

Focusing on Transactions Between the Individual and the Environment: A Potential Key to Understanding Interest Development

The ongoing and dynamic relationship between the individual and the environment has recently been further developed by Renninger (2000) in her conceptualization of individual interest. While apparently maintaining a clear distinction between situational and individual interest, there are indications that Renninger is beginning to incorporate notions from sociocultural theory into her understanding of interest through her consideration of interactions between the individual and the social context, and possibilities for apprenticeship. Renninger (2000) emphasizes that "well-developed individual interest cannot develop without the continued challenges that stem from modeling, opportunities to apprentice, and interaction with others and text" (p. 396). Ongoing person-environment transactions are thus identified as being crucial for the development of individual interest, with individual interest apparently associated with a person's activity. Renninger (2000) argues strongly for individual interest as the "intersection of cognitive and affective functioning" (p. 378), with this construct being characterized by stored knowledge and value. However, while the 'conditions' for individual interest to develop are discussed at length, the possibilities for the relationship between situational and individual interest receive limited discussion by Renninger (2000). The developmental sequence implied by her analysis begins with an attraction toward subject content that may develop into situational interest, which may in turn develop into a less well-developed individual interest and subsequently into a well-developed individual interest (Renninger, 2000).

The need for theoretical integration of situational and individual interest has also been recognized by Rathunde (1993), who argues that this becomes possible through focusing upon the *experience* of interest. Where analysis of individual interest considers a person's long-term orientation toward the object or content of interest, analysis of situational interest considers the properties or qualities of that object or the content. Rathunde claims that both levels of analysis can be united through considering the experience of interest and develops this notion by drawing upon Csikszentmihalyi's (1990) theory of flow, in which there is a negotiated balance between a person's skills and challenges. Rathunde acknowledges flow as a more intense experience than interest, because of the extreme concentration and sense of transcendence often associated with the former. However, he maintains that the negotiation of interest is similar to that of flow, because of the balance between spontaneity and goal direction needed to experience the mode of 'serious play' that is interest (Rathunde, 1993). If this relationship is not balanced, 'fooling' (spontaneity without goal direction) or 'drudgery' (working towards goals without immediate involvement) may result. According to Rathunde (1993), 'disinterest' arises if a person perceives a task as neither goal-related nor involving. Through considering the experience of interest, it becomes possible to conceptualize interest in a way that moves beyond the distinction between situational and individual factors.

In the literature discussed above, it is evident that situational and individual interest interact with, and are influenced by, each other (Krapp et al., 1992; Mitchell, 1993; Hidi & Harackiewicz, 2000; Renninger, 2000); however, it is equally evident that questions surrounding this interaction have not been included in recent research (Hidi & Berndorff, 1998) beyond the work of Rathunde (1993). Returning to Dewey's (1913) definition of 'genuine interest', which incorporates notions of activity and identification with activity, enables consideration of the interrelationships between the individual and the social and physical environment. These interrelationships are important in sociocultural theories. It is, therefore, suggested that approaching the study of interest from a sociocultural perspective would suit the task of exploring the relationship between situational and individual interest.

CONCEPTUALIZING INTEREST WITHIN A SOCIOCULTURAL FRAMEWORK: ZONES OF DEVELOPMENT AND COMMUNITIES OF LEARNERS

The separation of the individual and the situational in contemporary studies of interest, as discussed in the previous section, weakens the emphasis on the dynamic and interdependent relationship between the self and the environment which was a feature of Dewey's (1913) theory of interest. This dynamic interdependence of the individual and the social is also a concern of sociocultural theory. Consideration of interest from the point of view of sociocultural theory and research, specifically from the perspectives of Valsiner's (1987, 1997) theoretical development and extension of the notion of the zone of proximal development and empirical investigations into classroom learning communities (for example, Brown, 1997), provides the beginnings of a framework for the development of a sociocultural approach to motivation and interest.

Co-creating Possibilities for the Development of Interest Within Zones

Although Valsiner's writings on the zone of proximal development and other zones do not give any consideration to the development or maintenance of motivation or interest he has, in other work (Valsiner, 1992), considered the way in which the social world influences the development of interest. He has also highlighted the problems posed by attempts to empirically examine its emergence and development. Valsiner (1992) suggests that in empirical studies, an important issue concerns the use of common-sense, everyday language to refer to the psychological construct, interest. The personal sense with which the term 'interest' is used by a participant in a research study may not be the same as the more 'general shared meaning' in which the psychologist is using the term. This is problematic in terms of the operationalization of interest in empirical investigations, in which the assumption is often made that self-reports of 'interest' directly represent the psychological concept. Valsiner (1992) therefore claims that "in order to study interest one cannot study 'interest', but something else from which recognizable 'interest' emerges" (p. 33). Interest is conceptualized as being "not in the object, nor in the mind of the child, but it emerges as a result of processes that link the two in irreversible time" (Valsiner, 1992, p. 33). The study of interest, therefore, becomes the study of developmental processes that give rise to what is labelled as 'interest' in every day terms.

> A move to a process-oriented theoretical view of 'interest' is based on the recognition of the process of constant irreversible person <-> environment transaction. Once an emphasis is placed upon the process aspects of transactions, the question of 'interest' is no longer limited to an ontological issue ("what is interest?"), but acquires a developmental focus as well ("how does whatever is interest emerge from whatever interest is not?"). (Valsiner, 1992, p. 33)

Thus, rather than placing emphasis preferentially on either the individual or the situation when conceptualizing interest, as has been the underlying approach in most previous studies, interest is conceived as a dynamic, developmental process of interaction between the individual and the situation.

From a sociocultural perspective, social processes that expand or limit the activities of an individual may also assist or constrain the emergence and development of interest (Valsiner, 1992). Through the notions of canalization and self-canalization, Valsiner explains how the social world and the opportunities available to individuals create the context in which interest may emerge. Canalization by the social world refers to the ways in which other people, consistent with their values and goals, channel a learner's activities in certain ways. Self-canalization refers to the developing person's construction of "his or her own psychological functions in the process of social experiencing" (Valsiner, 1992, p. 34), a process which Valsiner terms internalization. According to Valsiner, interests 'emerge' when an individual translates internalized information and functioning into externally observable actions. "'Interest' can be described as emerging from the structure of my 'personal senses' in my personal culture at a given time" (Valsiner, 1992, p. 35), a description which recognises the changing and self-constraining nature of interest. Self-canalization is likely to take place simultaneously with canalization through interaction with others within the communities of practice in which an individual participates.

The notion of canalization has been employed in a sociocultural investigation of the creation of intersubjectivity and interest conducted by Lightfoot (1988). In this study Lightfoot investigated the interaction between a mother and her infant in the negotiation and canalization of interest as the infant gained competence in climbing up and down a step in the home. The relationship between the child and the environment was highlighted by Lightfoot (1988) as a "co-constructed totality" (p. 63). The mother responded to cues provided by the child's affective and sensorimotor actions in order to ascertain how she could transform and structure the child's environment. These responses were directed so as to create interest and foster the development of competence. Lightfoot's (1988) study provides an example of the way a mother's values and goals, presumably consistent with those of her communities of practice, encourage negotiation with the infant and channelling of activities and interest as intersubjectivity is created.

Although Valsiner has not brought together the concept of canalization of interest and the zone of proximal development, we consider that this is a theoretically useful development. By consideration of these two aspects of his sociocultural theory, an explanation of interest development becomes possible. We consider interest to be canalized within a 'zones system', part of Valsiner's reconstructed notion of the zone of proximal development (Valsiner, 1987, 1997). Zones are described by Valsiner (1997) as transient, abstract organizational devices that provide the framework for constraints and affordances to development in the present, and possible directions of nearest future development. Within these zones, paths of action and development are constrained or limited (*Zone of Free Movement—ZFM*), as well as promoted (*Zone of Promoted Action—ZPA*), and possibilities for action within the ZFM/ZPA system become actualized (*Zone of Proximal Development—ZPD*). Valsiner (1997) proposes that the zones are useful in explaining regulation of the ongoing developmental process, through the restructuring of the zones and the relationships between them.

The Zone of Free Movement (ZFM)

The ZFM is a means to describe the structuring of a child's access to different aspects of his or her environment. It includes the objects that are available to the child within this accessible area and the ways in which the child acts with those available objects within the accessible area (Valsiner, 1997). The zone is socially constructed, in that it is based on the cultural meaning systems of the child's caregivers, who lead the organization of the ZFM for the developing child, and is formed in interaction with them. When a new setting is entered by the child and caregiver, the ZFM is reconstructed through the caregiver's analysis of the possible actions afforded by the new environment and a knowledge of the previous action of the child. Thus, the organization of the dynamic relationship between the child and the environment is on the basis of the cultural meanings of the communities of practice in which the child participates, as well as the caregiver's knowledge of the specific child's actions and development. Valsiner (1997) argues that as the child develops, the ZFM becomes internalized, providing a structure for personal thinking and feeling through semiotic regulation.

The main implication of the ZFM for interest is that it promotes canalization through the constraints created on the possible child-environment interactions. The child's access to areas of the environment, which includes the social environment, and the objects within it, along with the possible actions with those objects, will guide the interest of the child that is co-constructed within the setting. The relationship between the child and the caregiver, including perceptions of interest and participation, and the caregiver's knowledge of the child's skill development, will also be crucial factors in the co-construction of this zone.

The Zone of Promoted Action (ZPA)

The ZPA is conceptualized by Valsiner (1997) as mutually intermapped with the ZFM to constitute a functioning system: the ZPA is focused upon the promotion of new skills and the ZFM on constructed constraints. The ZPA is conceptualized as those actions of the child with a set of activities, objects or areas in the environment that are encouraged by the caregiver (Valsiner, 1997). As a zone, it can include areas currently outside the ZFM to focus upon development across boundaries, but has a non-binding nature. As a consequence of the latter, the child may reject the promotional efforts of the caregiver and choose to act in other ways within the ZFM. However, in common with the ZFM, the ZPA provides canalization of the process of development and an internalized or semiotic level of the ZPA emerges, "constructing a new personal relationship with the action—ZFM/ZPA domain" (Valsiner, 1997, p. 194) within the cultural meaning system. The ZPA may be co-constructed in order to promote interest in an activity, object or aspect of the environment, with actions encouraged that are within and contribute to the cultural and personal meaning systems.

The Zone of Proximal Development (ZPD)

While Valsiner (1997) uses the notion of the Zone of Proximal Development, it is reconstructed with the aim of fitting it with his other two zone concepts, ZFM/ZPA. Thus, the

ZPD becomes a zone that denotes the range of possible nearest-future trans-formations of present psychological processes, conditional on the present organization of the ZFM/ZPA structure. It is obvious that the ZPD in that sys-tem becomes subservient to the present-state field-theoretic explanation and is oriented toward explaining the social roots of individuals' experiences. (Valsiner & van der Veer, 1993, pp. 56-7)

While the ZFM/ZPA structure describes the present constraints and promoted actions in the child's development, the ZPD is the zone that con-tains all of the possibilities for development, given the present, and as such the ZPD is "empirically unaccessible" (Valsiner & van der Veer, 1993, p. 57). If field observations are the basis of a study, then it will only be an actu-alized subset of the possibilities within the ZPD which are studied.

Stephanie's Story: Integrating the Concept of Interest Canalization and Valsiner's Zones

The experiences of Stephanie, a grade 6 child who we would recognize as being interested in soccer, illustrates our integration of the concept of canalization of interest and the zones system. Stephanie, who earlier this year began to enjoy watching televised soccer matches with her granddad, is given a soccer ball by her grandparents for her birthday. Stephanie takes her ball to school and organizes soccer games with friends in the play-ground at lunch time. In time, and with her parents' encouragement, she joins her local soccer club with some of her friends and plays in a competi-tive team on weekends. The soccer club organizes an outing to watch a live state soccer match and Stephanie buys a cap and has it signed by some of the players. The soccer club holds a holiday camp for skill development and she is awarded new soccer boots for being the most improved player. At the end of the year, Stephanie asks her parents to seek a high school that includes girls in its soccer teams for inter-school sports competitions. Participation in the soccer club and the support of her family and peers serve to constrain and promote the development of Stephanie's interests and involve her in the activities of that specific community, structuring sup-port for her motivation and skill development in culturally valued ways. Within the environment for learning that is created, canalization of Stephanie's interest by her social world and self-canalization are processes occurring concurrently.

In the example of Stephanie, the ways in which the zones system is being negotiated to foster her interest becomes apparent. In the ZFM/ZPA system, where interest is being constrained and promoted, it is evident that access to various aspects of playing soccer is being fostered by Stephanie's family and pursued by Stephanie herself. Following Stephanie's display of initial interest, recognized by her granddad, her family and peers respond to create further opportunities for this interest to develop. Stephanie receives encouragement to participate in socioculturally appropriate novice activities within the soccer community, joining a club, playing in more formal games as part of a team and attending the outings of the group. She is given access to the soccer community through the encouragement of other people around her who value and promote soccer as a valid interest for an eleven-year-old girl. Further self-canalization of this interest is apparent and opportunities for future development within the ZPD is made possible through Stephanie's desire to attend a high school that offers participation in interschool soccer matches to girls, and her parents' ongoing support of her developing interest.

In studying the emergence of interest through children's participation in authentic activities, such as playing soccer in community-based clubs and daily learning in classrooms, we suggest that an emphasis upon the social origins of development and learning through the negotiation of zones that promote and constrain actions, provides important insights for theory development. An enriched understanding of the processes by which interest develops in and through every day activities may be gained by considering the interrelationships between the individual and the environment, rather than primarily focusing upon one (individual interest) or the other (situational interest) as in previous contemporary conceptualizations of interest.

In considering the dynamic interrelationships between the individual and the sociocultural context, it follows that the motivational implications of learning in the system of the ZFM/ZPA and ZPD cannot be made without acknowledgment of the broader purpose for learning. As suggested earlier in this chapter, this purpose for learning is created within the broader context of participation in communities of practice, specifically communities of learners when considering the context of school-based education. Thus, it becomes important to consider the argument that the

> ZPD needs to be theorized simultaneously …as a process of knowledge co-construction and as a process of becoming a member of a community… the ZPD is more than a social space within which skills, strategies and knowledge are acquired. The ZPD is the space that enables communities to be established and identities to be transformed. (Renshaw, 1998, p 88)

While the ZPD as part of Valsiner's zones system canalizes the development and learning of the individual, the constraints and promoted actions contribute to the practices of the community and result from community membership. It is through the ZPD that learners become a part of a community of practice and, through the same process, the practices of the community are transformed.

Learning Communities/Communities of Practice

Sociocultural perspectives on learning have led researchers with dual interests in learning and the design of innovative classroom environments to conduct empirical investigations of classroom learning communities. Well known investigations of learning communities have been conducted by Ann Brown and her colleagues (Brown, 1997; Brown, Ellery & Campione, 1998; Brown & Campione, 1994; Brown, Ash, Rutherford, Nakagawa, Gordon & Campione, 1993), Bereiter and Scardamalia (1993; Scardamalia, Bereiter & Lamon, 1994), and the Cognition and Technology Group at Vanderbilt University (1994; 1997; Vye, Schwartz, Bransford, Barron, Zech & The Cognition & Technology Group at Vanderbilt, 1997). Other investigations of learning communities have been conducted by Riel (1998), Renshaw and Brown (1997), Roth (1996; 1998), and Walker and Lambert (1995). These investigations have in common an underlying sociocultural theory of learning, an emphasis on collaborative student learning, and student classroom engagement in various inquiry oriented learning and thinking practices for the purpose of knowledge building.

Although the term 'communities of learners' has been used to describe these investigations, they can also be considered, in recognition of the academic practices engaged in by the students, as communities of practice. These academic practices, as with all other cultural practices (Miller & Goodnow, 1995), carry with them normative expectations about how things will be done and what knowledge areas are appropriate objects of interest. In turn, these expectations reflect value commitments held by members of the community. From the perspective of one sociocultural theory (Rogoff, 1998), learning is conceptualised as the transformation of participation in such communities of practice. In these communities, learning is scaffolded by the activities of students, the teacher, and the tools and artefacts used by students in the classroom. They thus involve, as Brown (1997) notes, the creation of multiple zones of proximal development, while from the perspective of Valsiner's (1987, 1997) sociocultural theory, they involve processes of canalisation, including self-canalisation.

In relation to the Fostering Communities of Learners project, perhaps the best known of the learning community investigations, Brown (1997) has identified four key ideas—*agency, reflection, collaboration* and *culture*— which contribute to the development of a 'culture of learning' within the classroom. These four ideas are also central, as Renshaw (1998) has indicated, to the notion of the ZPD in which the context of learning is that of participant in a community of practice. Through participation in a community of practice, learners are enculturated into activities in which certain objects of interest and ways in which interest is demonstrated are valued more highly than others. However, this is not a one-way process. The novice learner, or peripheral participant, collaborates with other community members (or caregivers, in Valsiner's terms) in order to actively learn, reflect upon and appropriate the cultural meanings and practices within that community. Through this process, the learning culture (or cultural meaning systems) of that community develops, responding to the perceived needs and interests of the novice learners. The culture of the community, which encompasses the values and purpose negotiated and upheld within that community, canalizes the development of the novice learners as part of the process of enculturation. The development of interest in learning is part of this process of enculturation, as activities within specific communities are structured so as to support the social, cognitive and affective development of learners. Communities of practice thus also provide contexts and support for the social construction of motivation.

The social construction of interest, likewise, develops through social interaction in communities of practice. As learners participate in culturally valued activities, their participation is canalized by the community of which they are a member, such as in the soccer example presented earlier in this chapter. Participation in communities of practice and the active internalization of their cultural meaning and value systems also leads to self-canalization which further contributes to interest development through focus upon certain types of activities, processes and objects across the communities of practice in which the individual participates. The child who demonstrates interest in soccer within the social context of her family also demonstrates her interest across other communities, such as her school and classroom communities and soccer club community.

When considering the social construction of motivation in a community of practice, it is important to recognize that all members of a community participate in multiple communities of practice both within and outside the school learning context. In these different communities of practice, individuals interact with other groups of people working towards the goals of their community and engage in practices relevant to the achievement of those goals. Often, the goals and practices of these communities will overlap in ways that reinforce and strengthen the individual's developing motivation and interest. When students in a class group participate in an excursion to a museum, for example, they become part of a transient community of museum visitors interacting with museum staff and the museum exhibits (Matusov & Rogoff, 1995). The engagement of these students in valued activities related to their ongoing classroom endeavors is likely to further develop students' interest in aspects of their school activities (Brophy, 1999; Renninger, 2000). Where the goals and practices of different communities are in opposition, however, the development of motivation and interest may be impeded as learners place greater value on one set of goals and practices at the expense of another set of goals and practices. In academic contexts, this may result in student resistance (Renshaw, 1998), and consequent low motivation, towards the practices of the community. Participation in multiple communities of practice, therefore, provides possibilities and constraints for the social construction and canalization of motivation and interest.

STUDENTS' INTEREST AS PARTICIPANTS IN A LEARNING COMMUNITY: FURTHER DEVELOPING A SOCIOCULTURAL THEORY THROUGH AN ETHNOGRAPHIC STUDY

Considered from a sociocultural perspective, the co-construction of interest, the creation of intersubjectivity and active internalization within the ZFM, ZPA and ZPD can assist in the explanation of the process of interest development. The development of interest, as indicated in the preceding section, also needs to be explained in the context of participation in a community of practice that values community activities and supports interest in the process of learning. Personal value and the construction of meaning have social origins and these canalize or channel the development of interest. This is an important notion for future empirical studies considering developmental processes, with the situated nature of learning and motivation essential in consideration of the constraints on interest. Social and physical contexts in which children interact, such as classrooms, the playground and field study venues, each provide sites for learning that create possibilities and constraints for interest development. A challenge thus exists in capturing this process in empirical studies, to enable further conceptualization and understanding of how the individual and context interact (Valsiner, 1992; Pintrich, 2000).

An empirical study is currently in progress in an attempt to further understand the process of interaction between individuals and context which foster the development of interest in learning. In attempting to develop a sociocultural theory of interest, Kimberley Pressick-Kilborn, the first author of this paper, is conducting a classroom-based ethnographic study; this study is important in the process of theory development as it provides an empirical context for examining issues discussed earlier in the chapter. The present study's focus is upon the classroom as a research site over time, with the aim of gaining insight into the interactions amongst students and teachers within specific activity contexts. As a result, qualitative methodological approaches, such as participant observation, audio-recordings of small group conversations and interviews, have been utilized. These approaches endeavor to capture the richness, complexity and constantly changing system of the classroom as a process of becoming, not as a static phenomenon (Hammersley, 1990; Brown, 1992; Skeggs, 1999). The methodology of the study is therefore consistent with other research conducted from a sociocultural perspective (Lightfoot, 1988; Jacob, 1992; Rogoff, Mistry, Goncu & Mosier, 1993).

The present study is exploring interest development by considering one specific grade 5 classroom context over a six month period, as students learn together in science and technology lessons. This enables a focus upon the personal cultures that develop and contribute significantly to the interpsychological and intrapsychological canalization processes of students' interest and, more broadly, to their motivations for learning. Detailed field notes are being kept as part of the process of participant observation and both the class teacher and students are also regularly writing reflections on the teaching/learning process. An aspect of students' reflections includes the charting of a personal interest 'trajectory', which involves students indicating their perceived level of interest in completing an activity in relation to other activities within the unit. Trajectories have been recorded both at the level of an individual lesson and at the level of the term-unit and these enable insight into changing patterns of interest at both an individual and class level. In making close observations of classroom interaction, small group activities are frequently audio-recorded and some interaction has also been video-recorded so that visual cues can also be captured and included in subsequent detailed analyses. Brief, informal interviews with the teacher and students occur in the course of lessons, as well as semi-structured interviews with six focus students following lessons at three points throughout each term. This enables further information to be gathered about the developing meanings being created by different participants.

From these varying sources, themes are being inductively generated and data is being categorized to make sense of the classroom activities and the participation of the students and teacher within this learning community. Audio-recordings of small-group conversations are also being closely considered to analyze at a more micro-level the ways in which peer interaction is creating and canalizing interest within an activity. The final stage of analysis involves a consideration of the ways in which the themes and categories emerging from the data contribute to the development of a sociocultural theory of interest, using Valsiner's theoretical lens and the concept of canalization within communities of learners.

Revealing Complex Relationships Between Contexts and Individuals: Michaela's Early Experiences When Learning About Electricity

Investigating interest within a classroom ethnographic study is revealing the complex relationships between students' perceptions of interest and observable behaviors which could be described as externalized interest.

Michaela, one of the students in grade 5, was adamant in an interview at the outset of term 1 that she really did not enjoy science and technology lessons compared with other subjects. "You enjoy learning when you are interested", she wrote to me in a reflective postcard a week or so later, and maintained throughout these early weeks of small group investigations that she wasn't interested in either the topic of electricity or science more broadly. This was especially the case when compared with social studies, in which she had chosen to do research about Ned Kelly, an infamous Australian bush ranger whose last stand took place near where she used to live.

It was evident that Michaela was able to make a personal connection to her social studies lessons which was absent from her science and technology lessons—"Everyone knows about electricity and it's boring" summed up her value of the topic. Her own categorization of herself as not being interested in science and technology was self-canalizing possibilities for interest development as she often participated in tasks in restricted ways. In week 2 when the students were completing exploratory activities about electricity in rotating groups, Michaela did only as required by the teacher at a station involving consideration of transformation of energy in a range of household appliances. She then sat looking around her at other groups completing activities at different stations, whereas other groups used any extra time to further explore the materials at the station, beyond the tasks stated by the teacher. She approached the teacher and commented that she was bored and wanted to move on. Michaela's self-reported claims of disinterest in science were channelling her participation in ways that constrained her own interest development. She was choosing to participate in very limited ways within the ZFM/ZPA structure that was being created in science and technology lessons, being quite strongly directed by her self-perception of disinterest in both science and the topic of electricity. This was despite involvement in science lessons being obviously promoted and encouraged by Miss Wheeldon, the class teacher, through her offering choices amongst tasks to complete to students and opportunities for collaboration in small group investigation tasks.

Participation in Multiple Communities of Practice Provides Meaning to Classroom Activities for Michaela

However, classroom observations over the term indicated a change in Michaela's participation. About half-way through this electricity learning unit, Michaela became visibly excited when a design, make and appraise task was introduced in a lesson. It was as though she'd forgotten this was science! The class were seated on the floor, listening to Miss Wheeldon's explanation of the possible choices within the task, with occasional exclamations of "Cool!" audible from the group. Noticeably, Michaela raised herself onto her knees and started bobbing up and down and smiling. She became even more excited when she found out they would be creating individual products, rather than producing one per group. Michaela chose to make a torch and actively engaged with her small group in planning her design, playing a central role in fostering the focus of her small group on the design task at hand. When asked later why she had appeared so excited at the prospect of this task, Michaela said that she was going to use it on the school's 'Dads and Daughters' camp in a few weeks' time. While she maintained that she wasn't really interested in science during a subsequent interview, it appeared as though Michaela had 'connected' with this activity through the real-life purpose she had identified. She also stated that she found hands-on tasks interesting.

Michaela's Own Interest Canalises the Interest of Her Peers

During the design, make and appraise task, Michaela also played an important part in creating interest in and focus on the task within the small group with whom she was designing her torch. In discussing ways that the electrical circuit inside the torch could be designed to include a switch, the teacher suggested they might like to experiment with the circuitry equipment that was on the benches at the side of the classroom, left there from the station activities week. The teacher was extending the ZFM/ZPA structure for this group through her reaction, encouraging interaction with tools for learning that had not been included in the original directions for the design activity. Michaela was the dominant group member in initiating the exploration of the circuits to include a switch, bringing other peer group members back to focus on the issue of circuit design when conversation deviated. Through her efforts to engage her peers in experimenting with the circuit, Michaela was actively canalizing the interest of the students with whom she was working, drawing their attention purposefully to the task that she wanted them to undertake.

Michaela's Valuing of the Task of Designing and Making a Torch is Revealed

Despite her maintenance of disinterest in science during conversations and interviews away from the classroom, Michaela's valuing of the task was most evident during the lesson in which the students were actually making their products. Michaela had been obviously engaged in this task throughout the 50 minute lesson, constructing her circuit within the torch, complete with switch, and then encasing her circuit with electrical tape. She took great care winding the tape in a spiral around her circuit, which she was fixing to a block of timber. Once the taping was complete, Michaela attempted to switch on her torch. There was no light. She tried again. Still no light. She then burst into loud sobs of disappointment and frustration, storming over to her desk and putting her head on the table. She muttered that she knew that the circuit was correctly wired, because it had worked when she and her dad had tried it at home. The devastation apparent in Michaela's reaction could only have been possible through her valuing and caring about this task, which had been promoted not only at school, but also through 'rehearsing' the task with her dad at home.

Any claims after this lesson made by Michaela that she had not been interested in completing this task could not be considered seriously. It was as though her 'cover' of disinterest in the unit had been blown to those peers and teachers present and no longer could she feign total disinterest, despite her continuing resistance in science lessons. However, from her perspective, her initial lack of success in making her torch could also be confirmatory of her disinterest in science; why would this negative experience promote interest in the specific topic or the subject more generally? In the concluding interview for the term, Michaela said that while there had been some activities during the term that she did enjoy because they involved hands-on work, such as making her torch, she had not changed her mind about disliking science or the topic of electricity.

Within the ZFM/ZPA structure made available to her through the science and technology activities of the classroom, Michaela is also creating constraints and possibilities for her own development of interest in learning. At times, it appears to be almost to spite her teacher, Miss Wheeldon, who is striving to develop lessons that enable the students to collaborate, negotiate and have choices in their learning, that Michaela resists the creation of intersubjectivity between her and Miss Wheeldon. This one brief example provides an indication of the rich, complex picture of individuals interacting within a specific classroom context that is made possible through longitudinal, ethnographic studies of motivation. However, it also raises issues regarding the extent to which behavioral indicators of interest observable in the classroom can be used to infer the experience of interest of individual students who are resistant to participation in activities in ways that could lead to the development of interest and personal identity with a subject's content. A sociocultural approach to conceptualizing interest and a qualitative study that focuses on processes and meanings does seek to explore such complexities, in that it makes possible a consideration of the individual and situational factors that transact to canalize the development of interest in learning.

FUTURE DIRECTIONS FOR RESEARCH: IMPLICATIONS AND APPLICATIONS

The qualitative study discussed in this chapter is reflective of the emergence of a broader range of research approaches in motivational research.

Qualitative studies of motivation in classroom environments are increasingly being designed to focus on contexts for learning (Ainley, 1998; Dowson & McInerney, 2001; MacCallum, 2001). As such research focuses upon the ways in which social dimensions of learning contribute to the development of value-aspects of motivation (Brophy, 1999), these studies echo concerns within sociocultural theories, as outlined in this chapter. Focusing on value aspects of motivation enables consideration of both the development of interest in learning, as well as resistance towards learning (Renshaw, 1998), in classroom learning contexts. The ethnographic study described in this chapter has both strengths and limitations in its focus on one specific grade 5 classroom, and the interactions within it, as the students learn science and technology. Strengths lie in the richness of data collected and the insight being gained into various events contributing to processes of interest development of individual students over a six month period. There are limitations, however, in conducting the study in one independent girls' school where the students' families generally value school education highly and where there is the expectation that girls, families and teachers will be actively involved in the school's community. Future research, therefore, needs to consider different school contexts, such as co-educational schools and schools in lower socioeconomic areas, as well as primary and secondary schools. Numerous studies of children's motivation suggest that as children grow older, there is a tendency for deterioration in their interests and attitudes towards school generally and specific subject areas, including science (Hidi & Harackiewicz, 2000). The design of classroom-based studies over longer time periods and incorporating a number of subjects across the curriculum would further enable insight into the changes that take place in the development of interest as students learn with different teachers in different classroom environments. Philosophies of teaching and learning and opportunities for peer interaction in other classrooms may also be quite different from those in the study described in this chapter.

School students, along with their teachers, participate in multiple, overlapping communities of practice. As highlighted in this chapter, this participation serves to canalize students' interest, as the values of their family, classroom, school and other contexts support and foster motivation for certain activities. The sociocultural theory of interest proposed in the chapter, therefore, has implications for children's learning in out-of-school contexts; that is, in physical, social and cultural sites for learning such as the family and other learning organizations such as sports clubs, religious groups and museums. Constraints and possibilities for development, opportunities for making meaning, and the co-learners available to children within these contexts will often differ from classrooms (Matusov & Rogoff, 1995). The implications are that children need opportunities to engage with people, cultural tools and artifacts within these settings, so that processes of developing interest are modelled, negotiated and supported. The sociocultural value of the object/idea about which interest may develop also needs to be socially accessible to the child. Thus, the creation of intersubjectivity is also important to consider as interest is studied in out-of-school settings.

CONCLUSION

In this chapter, we have attempted to create a framework for the development of a sociocultural approach to interest through the integration of sociocultural notions of canalization, the ZPD and related zones, and communities of practice. We have argued that such an approach to interest will emphasize the social processes involved in the emergence and development of interest, and the way in which these processes afford or constrain this emergence and development. In developing a sociocultural approach, the chapter attempts to show the extent of compatibility of current motivational and interest research with sociocultural theory. In particular, we believe that current attempts to integrate individual and situational interest share much in common with a sociocultural approach. To assist in the process of theory development, in this chapter we have presented classroom-based ethnographic findings, interpreting them in the context of the sociocultural notions of canalization and the zones system. As Valsiner (1992) has identified, capturing the process of interest creation and development in empirical studies is a challenge. This ethnographic study in progress is an attempt to meet that challenge and contribute to the development of a sociocultural theory of interest.

REFERENCES

Ainley, M. (1998). *Some perspectives on interest in learning and classroom interaction.* Paper presented at the Annual Conference of the Australian Association for Research in Education, Adelaide, Australia.

Ainley, M., Hidi, S. & Berndorff, D. (1999). *The role of situational and individual interest in the cognitive and affective aspects of learning.* Poster presentation session: Motivation, goals and self-regulation at the Conference of the American Educational Research Association, Montreal, Canada.

Ainley, M. & Hillman, K. (1999). *Individual and situational interest: Gender and interest in prescribed English texts.* Symposium Paper presented at the Eighth European Conference for Research on Learning and Instruction, Goteborg, Sweden.

Alexander, P.A. (1997). Mapping the multidimensional nature of domain learning: The interplay of cognitive, motivational and strategic forces. In M.L. Maehr and P.R. Pintrich (Eds.), *Advances in motivation and achievement Vol. 10* (pp. 213—250). Greenwich, CT: JAI Press.

Alexander, P.A. & Jetton, T.L. (1996). The role of importance and interest in the processing of text. *Educational Psychology Review, 8,* 89-121.

Anderson, R.C., Shirey, L.L., Wilson, P.T. & Fielding, L.G. (1987). Interestingness of children's reading materials. In R.E. Snow & M.J. Farr (Eds.), *Aptitudes, learning and instruction, Vol 3: Conative and affective process analyses* (pp. 287-299). Hillsdale, NJ: Erlbaum.

Barron, B. J. S., Schwartz, D. L., Vye, N. J., Moore, A., Petrosino, A., Zech, L., Bransford, J. D., & The Cognition and Technology Group at Vanderbilt. (1998). Doing with understanding: Lessons from research on problem-and project-based learning. *The Journal of The Learning Sciences, 7,* 271-311.

Bereiter, C. & Scardamalia, M. (1993). *Surpassing ourselves: An inquiry into the nature and implications of expertise.* Chicago, IL: Open Court.

Bergin, D. A. (1999). Influences on classroom interest. *Educational Psychologist, 34,* 87-98.

Brophy, J. (1999). Toward a model of the value aspects of motivation in education: Developing appreciation for particular learning domains and activities. *Educational Psychologist, 34,* 75-85.

Brown, A.L. (1992). Design experiments: Theoretical and methodological challenges in creating complex interventions in classroom settings. *The Journal of the Learning Sciences, 2,* 141-178.

Brown, A.L. (1994). The advancement of learning. *Educational Researcher, 23,* 4-12.

Brown, A. L. (1997). Transforming schools into communities of thinking and learning about serious matters. *American Psychologist, 52,* 399-413.

Brown, A.L., Ash, D., Rutherford, M., Nakagawa, K., Gordon, A. and Campione, J.C. (1993). Distributed expertise in the classroom. In G. Salomon (Ed.*), Distributed cognitions: Psychological and educational considerations* (pp. 188-228). New York, NY: Cambridge University Press.

Brown, A.L. & Campione, J.C. (1994). Guided discovery in a community of learners. In K. McGilly (Ed.), *Classroom lessons: Integrating cognitive theory and classroom practice* (pp. 229-272). Cambridge, MA: MIT Press.

Brown, A. L., Ellery, S., & Campione, J. C. (1998). Creating zones of proximal development electronically. In J. G. Greeno & S. V. Goldman (Eds.*), Thinking practices in mathematics and science learning* (pp. 341-368). Mahwah, NJ: Erlbaum.

Brown, R.A.J. & Renshaw, P.D. (1997). *Journeys from participating on the periphery to peripheral participation in a collaborative primary classroom.* Paper presented at the Annual Conference of the Australian Association for Research in Education, Brisbane, Australia.

Cognition and Technology Group at Vanderbilt. (1994). From visual word problems to learning communities: Changing conceptions of cognitive research. In K. McGilly (Ed.), *Classroom lessons: Integrating cognitive theory and classroom practice* (pp. 157-200). Cambridge, MA: MIT Press.

Cognition and Technology Group at Vanderbilt. (1997). *The Jasper project: Lessons in curriculum, instruction, assessment, and professional development.* Mahwah, NJ: Erlbaum.

Csikszentmihalyi, M. (1990). *Flow: The psychology of optimal experience.* New York, NY: Harper & Row.

Csikszentmihalyi, M. (1993). *The evolving self: A psychology for the third millenium.* New York, NY: Harper Collins.

Csikszentmihalyi, M. (1997). *Living well: The psychology of everyday life.* London: Weidenfeld & Nicolson.

de Sousa, I. & Oakhill, J. (1996). Do levels of interest have an effect on children's comprehension monitoring performance? *British Journal of Educational Psychology, 66,* 471-482.

Dewey, J. (1913). *Interest and effort in education.* Cambridge, MA: Riverside Press.

Dowson, M. & McInerney, D. M. (2001). Psychological parameters of students' social and work avoidance goals: A qualitative investigation *Journal of Educational Psychology, 93,* 35-42.

Fink, R.P. (1995). Successful dyslexics: A constructivist study of passionate interest in reading. *Journal of Adolescent and Adult Literacy, 39,* 268-280.

Forman, E.A. & McPhail, J. (1993). Vygotskian perspective on children's collaborative problem-solving activities. In E.A. Forman, N. Minick & C.A. Stone (Eds.), *Contexts for learning: Sociocultural dynamics in children's development* (pp. 213-229). New York, NY: Oxford University Press.

Hammersley, M. (1990*). Classroom ethnography: Empirical and methodological essays.* Milton Keynes, UK: Open University Press.

Harp, S.F. & Mayer, R.E. (1997). The role of interest in learning from scientific text and illustrations: On the distinction between emotional interest and cognitive interest. *Journal of Educational Psychology, 89,* 92-102.

Herrenkohl, L.R., Palincsar, A.S., DeWater, L.S. & Kawasaki, K. (1999). Developing scientific communities in classrooms: A sociocognitive approach *The Journal of the Learning Sciences, 8,* 451-493.

Hickey, D.T. (1997). Motivation and contemporary socio-constructivist instructional perspectives. *Educational Psychologist, 32,* 175-193.

Hidi, S. & Anderson, V. (1992). Situational interest & its impact on reading and expository writing. In K.A. Renninger, S. Hidi & A. Krapp (Eds.), *The role of interest in learning and development* (pp. 215-238). Hillsdale, NJ: Erlbaum.

Hidi, S. & Berndorff, D. (1998). Situational interest and learning. In L. Hoffman, A. Krapp, K.A. Renninger & J. Baumert (Eds.), *Interest and learning: Proceedings of the Seeon Conference on interest and gender* (pp. 74-90). Kiel, Germany: IPN.

Hidi, S. & Harackiewicz, J.M (2000). Motivating the academically unmotivated: A critical issue for the 21st Century. *Review of Educational Research, 70,* 151-179.

Hoffman, L., Krapp, A., Renninger, K.A. & Baumert, J. (Eds.) (1998).*Interest and learning: Proceedings of the Seeon Conference on interest and gender.* Kiel, Germany: IPN.

Isaac, J.D., Sansone, C. & Smith, J.L. (1999). Other people as a source of interest in an activity. *Journal of Experimental Social Psychology, 35,* 239-265.

Jacob, E. (1992). Culture, context and cognition. In M.D. LeCompte, W.L. Millroy & J. Preissle (Eds.), *The handbook of qualitative research in education* (pp. 294-335). San Diego, CA: Academic Press.

John-Steiner, V. & Mahn, H. (1996). Sociocultural approaches to learning and development: A Vygotskian framework.*Educational Psychologist, 31,* 191-206.

Krapp, A., Hidi, S. & Renninger, K.A. (1992). Interest, Learning and Development. In K.A. Renninger,, S. Hidi & A. Krapp (Eds.), *The role of interest in learning and development* (pp. 3-26). Hillsdale, NJ: Erlbaum.

Krapp, A. Renninger, K.A. & Hoffman, L. (1998). Some thoughts about the development of a unifying framework for the study of individual interest. In L. Hoffman, A. Krapp, K.A. Renninger & J. Baumert (Eds.), *Interest and learning:*

Proceedings of the Seeon Conference on interest and gender (pp. 455-468). Kiel, Germany: IPN.

Lave, J. (1991) Situating learning in communities of practice. In L.B. Resnick, J.M. Levine & S.D. Teasley (Eds.), *Perspectives on socially shared cognition* (pp. 63-82). Washington, DC: APA.

Lave, J. & Wenger, E. (1991). *Situated Learning: Legitimate peripheral participation.* New York, NY: Cambridge University Press.

Lightfoot, C. (1988). The social construction of cognitive conflict: A place for affect. In J. Valsiner (Ed.), *Child development within culturally structured environments: Social co-construction and environmental guidance in development,* (Vol. 2, pp. 28-65). Norwood, NJ: Ablex.

MacCallum, J. (2001). The contexts of individual motivational change. In D.M. McInerney & S. Van Etten (Eds.*) Research on sociocultural influences on motivation and learning* (Vol. 1 pp. 61-98). Greenwich, CT: Information Age Publishing.

Matusov, E. & Rogoff, B. (1995). Evidence of development from people's participation in communities of learners. In J. Falk & L. Dierking (Eds.), *Public institutions for personal learning: Establishing a research agenda* (pp. 97-104). Washington, DC: American Association of Museums.

Miller, P.J., & Goodnow, J.J. (1995). Cultural practices: Toward an integration of culture and development. In J.J. Goodnow, P.J.Miller & F. Kessel (Eds.), *Cultural practices as contexts for development* (pp. 5-16). San Francisco, CA: Jossey-Bass.

Mitchell, M. (1993). Situational interest: Its multifaceted structure in the secondary school mathematics classroom. *Journal of Educational Psychology, 85*, 426-436.

Paris, S. G. & Turner, J.C. (1994). Situated motivation. In P.R. Pintrich, D.R. Brown & C.E. Weinstein (Eds.), *Student motivation: Cognition and learning* (pp. 213-237). Hillsdale, NJ: Erlbaum.

Pintrich, P. (2000). Educational psychology at the millenium: A look back and a look forward. *Educational Psychologist, 35,* 221-226.

Rathunde, K. (1993). The experience of interest: A theoretical and empirical look at its role in adolescent talent development In M. Maehr & P.R. Pintrich (Eds.), *Advances in motivation and achievement* (Vol. 8, pp. 59-98). Greenwich, CT: JAI Press.

Renninger, K.A. (1998). The roles of individual interest(s) and gender in learning: An overview of research on pre-school and elementary school-aged children/ students. In L. Hoffman, A. Krapp, K.A. Renninger & J. Baumert (Eds.), *Interest and learning: Proceedings of the Seeon Conference on interest and gender* (pp. 165-174). Kiel, Germany: IPN.

Renninger, K.A. (2000) Individual interest and its implications for understanding intrinsic motivation. In Sansone, C. & Harackiewicz, J.M. (Eds.), *Intrinsic and extrinsic motivation: The search for optimal motivation and performance* (pp. 373-404). San Diego, CA: Academic Press.

Renshaw, P. (1998) Sociocultural pedagogy for new times: Reframing key concepts. *Australian Educational Researcher, 25,* 83-100.

Renshaw, P., & Brown R. A. J. (1997). Learning partnerships: The role of teachers in a community of learners. In L. Logan & J. Sachs (Eds.*), Meeting the challenges of primary schooling* (pp. 200-211). London: Routledge.

Riel, M. (1998). Learning communities through computer networking. In J. G. Greeno & S. V. Goldman (Eds.), *Thinking practices in mathematics and science learning* (pp. 369-398). Mahwah, NJ: Erlbaum.

Rogoff, B. (1998) Cognition as a collaborative process. In W. Damon (Ed-in-chief), D. Kuhn & R. Siegler (Eds.), *Handbook of child psychology vol 2* (5th ed. pp. 679-744). New York, NY: Wiley.

Rogoff, B., Mistry, J., Goncu, A. & Mosier, C. (1993). Guided participation in cultural activity by toddlers and caregivers. *Monographs of the Society for Research in Child Development, 58* (8).

Rogoff, B. & Chavajay, P. (1995) 'What's become of research on the cultural basis of cognitive development?', *American Psychologist, 50*, 859-877.

Roth, W.M. (1996). Knowledge diffusion in a grade 4-5 classroom during a unit on civil engineering: An analysis of a classroom community in terms of its changing resources and practices. *Cognition & Instruction, 14*, 179-220.

Roth, W.M. (1998). *Designing communities.* Durdrecht, Netherlands: Kluwer Academic Publishers.

Scardamalia, M., Bereiter, C., & Lamon, M. (1994). The CSILE Project: Trying to bring the classroom into world 3. In K. McGilly (Ed.), *Classroom lessons: Integrating cognitive theory and classroom practice* (pp. 201-228). Cambridge, MA: MIT Press.

Schiefele, U. (1991). Interest, learning and motivation. *Educational Psychologist, 26*, 299-323.

Schiefele, U. (1998). Individual interest and learning—what we know and what we don't know. In L. Hoffman, A. Krapp, K.A. Renninger & J. Baumert (Eds.), *Interest and learning: Proceedings of the Seeon Conference on interest and gender* (pp. 91-104). Kiel, Germany: IPN.

Schiefele, U. & Krapp, A. (1996). Topic interest and free recall of expository text. *Learning and Individual Differences, 8*, 141-160.

Schraw, G. (1997). Situational interest in literary text. *Contemporary Educational Psychology, 22*, 436-456.

Sivan. E. (1986). Motivation in social constructivist theory. *Educational Psychologist, 21*, 209-233.

Skeggs, B. (1999). Seeing differently: Ethnography and explanatory power. *Australian Educational Researcher, 26*, 33-53.

Tobias, S. (1994). Interest, prior knowledge and learning. *Review of Educational Research, 64*, 37-54.

Turner, J. C., Meyer, D.K., Cox, K.E., Logan, C., DiCintio, M. & Thomas, C.T. (1998). Creating contexts for involvement in mathematics. *Journal of Educational Psychology, 90*, 730-745.

Turner, J.C. & Meyer, D.K. (2000). Studying and understanding the instructional contexts of classrooms. *Educational Psychologist, 35*, 69-85.

Valsiner, J. (1987). *Culture and the development of children's action.* Chichester, UK: John Wiley & Sons.

Valsiner, J. (1992). Interest: A metatheoretical perspective. In K.A. Renninger,, S. Hidi & A. Krapp (Eds.), *The role of interest in learning and development* (pp. 27-41). Hillsdale, NJ: Erlbaum.

Valsiner, J. (1997). *Culture and the development of children's action: A theory of human development* (2nd edition). New York, NY: John Wiley & Sons.

Valsiner, J. & van der Veer, R. (1993). The encoding of distance: The concept of the Zone of Proximal Development and its interpretations. In R.R. Cocking & K.A. Renninger (Eds.), *The development and meaning of psychological distance* (pp. 35-62). Hillsdale, NJ: Erlbaum.

Varelas, M., Luster, B. & Wenzel, S. (1999). Making meaning in a community of learners: Struggles and possibilities in an urban science class. *Research in Science Education, 29,* 227-245.

Vygotsky, L. S. (1978). *Mind in society.* Cambridge, MA: Harvard University Press.

Wade, S.E., Schraw, G., Buxton, W. & Hayes, M.J. (1993). Seduction of the strategic reader: Effects of interest on strategies and recall. *Reading Research Quarterly, 28,* 93-114.

Walker, R. A. & Lambert P. E. (1995). *Designing electronic learning environments to support communities of learners: A tertiary application.* Paper presented at the Annual Conference of the Australian Association for Research in Education, Hobart, Australia.

Wells, G. (1999). *Dialogic inquiry: Towards a sociocultural practice and theory of education.* New York, NY: Cambridge University Press.

CHAPTER 7

MOTIVATION TO IMPROVE ADULT EDUCATION IN UNDER-EDUCATED ADULTS IN RURAL COMMUNITIES

**Eric M. Anderman, Jane Jensen,
Diana Haleman, and Beth Goldstein**

INTRODUCTION

LeAnn Jacobs[1] is twenty-six years old. She and her husband have been married ten years and do not have children. Although an excellent student, LeAnn dropped out of school at the age of sixteen while in the tenth grade.

> I was married at the time and I said, "Well, I'm married, I don't have to go." So, I got the big head and quit. I liked school for awhile, then when you're a teenager you don't like it no more and my mom had a hard time keepin' me in school. I said, "Well, my mommy don't have to tell me what to do," so I got married and just quit.

In LeAnn's case, neither of her parents finished high school, nor did her sister who also married young and dropped out. LeAnn's mother tried unsuccessfully to keep her daughters in school.

> 'Cause she wanted different [for us] than what she had. She was growin' up hard and she wanted her kids to have better than what she had. I mean, my

> Mom's smart. She helped me on my high school work, and she just went to the eighth grade. She helped me on my history and she's good in history.

Even though her mother obviously encouraged LeAnn and helped her with schoolwork, she was unable to prevent both LeAnn and her sister from dropping out of school.

LeAnn stayed home briefly after her marriage but started working at age seventeen and has been employed in the hotel where she currently works since that time.

> I used to clean and mop at the lounge and then I was a maid and now I'm in the office. I'm a desk clerk now. That's easier on the body, but when you're dealin' with the public, it's hard. 'Cause some of 'em's hateful and some of 'em's nice. And you have to say, "Yes, sir," and "No, sir," no matter what.

In addition to her full-time work at the hotel, LeAnn also does lawn work with her husband in the evenings and on weekends. Rather than being "extra" income, this additional work is necessary for their financial survival and demonstrates the work ethic necessary to individuals living in poverty.

> I work six days a week. And I don't get home to sometimes 7:00 or 8:00 [o'clock]. I cut grass for extra money on the side. I get more money cuttin' grass than I do here. Sometimes it takes me and my husband about an hour, sometimes it takes us two hours. We double up. Sometimes we do two yards and sometimes we do one. It's accordin' to how much time we have to do it. If we're behind, we double up and do two yards a day.

Even with both of them working full-time, it is difficult for LeAnn and her husband to survive financially. She related, "When you're makin' minimum wage—$5.15 [an hour]—you have to get a lot [of hours]. Even though I don't have kids, it's still hard to make a living."

Whereas LeAnn values education and indicated she would like to complete her GED (equivalency diploma), she does not see it as an essential requirement for intelligent behavior and job competence. From her perspective, hard work and a positive attitude are far more important characteristics.

> I mean, it's good goin' to school and everything, but you really don't have to have a high school education to be smart. You really don't. You have to want to work. You have to have pride in your work. You know, I had pride when I did my rooms when I was a maid. I made sure the beds was clean, put new sheets on it and stuff like that. If you don't have pride then you're not goin' to do a good job. You have to have a attitude in wantin' to do it. If you don't want to do it then you might as well stay home and let somebody else that wants a job do it.

As her comments clearly indicate, LeAnn has a strong work ethic. LeAnn's positive school experiences and above average high school grades also indicate that she would most likely succeed in a GED program within a reasonable time frame. Her decision not to pursue further schooling, therefore, represents her assessment of formal education relative to her financial needs, allocation of time, and personal goals rather than shame at previous educational failures or a lack of motivation.

Why is LeAnn's Story Important?

Studies of motivational variables in under-educated adult populations are distinctly absent from the motivation literature. The purpose of the present study is to gain an understanding of the motivations and obstacles that influence educational decision-making among adults without high school diplomas or the equivalent. The study incorporates multiple methodologies, and uses a sample of adults from rural regions in the state of Kentucky.

This project began in response to a request by the Kentucky Department for Adult Education and Literacy (DAEL) to investigate why under-educated adults choose not to participate in adult education programs. At the time, the adult education and literacy programs sponsored by the state served only 5 percent of the potential pool of learners. In 1999, approximately 36 percent of adults in Kentucky had not completed high school or the GED and these numbers were even higher in counties experiencing economic distress. While the department was aware that there were a number of factors such as transportation and childcare that deterred adults from attending programs, they were interested in learning more about the underlying reasons individuals chose not to pursue further formal education.

The following research questions were included in the research design presented to the state:

- What kinds of internal and external motivational variables affect the educational decision-making of adults who choose not to pursue adult education or literacy training?
- How do individuals' past experiences with schooling affect their current levels of motivation toward adult education? How does dropping out of school influence later perceptions of adult education and literacy programs? What are the implications of both school experiences and later work experiences for conceptualizing alternatives to the GED?
- In areas where unemployment is high, how does the lack of economic opportunity affect motivation to attend adult education/GED

classes? Conversely, where employment is high, how does the availability of work affect participation in adult education programs? How do local economic conditions and attitudes toward education influence the perceived value of adult education programs? (Jensen, Haleman, Goldstein, & Anderman, 2000, p. 13)

Theoretical Background

Although a variety of motivational perspectives have been used to study motivation in adults, many of these studies have focused on motivation in college students (e.g., Harackiewicz, Barron, & Elliot, 1998; Pintrich, 1989). Populations such as under-educated adults from rural areas for the most part have not been included in studies of adult motivation.

Nevertheless, there is ample reason to study such groups. Although the educational attainment of 25 to 29 year olds in the United States has increased over the past 25 years (National Center for Education Statistics, 2000) many adults who have not completed the twelfth grade do not utilize educational services that are available (Kentucky Department for Adult Education and Literacy, 1999). In our minds, motivation is clearly a factor in the decision not to participate. Whereas ample services are available, many adults seem not to be motivated to use those services.

An Expectancy X Value Approach to Understanding Motivation.

One of the fundamental questions that needs to be answered when trying to understand why some adults are unmotivated to attend adult education classes is the question of whether or not adults

a.   expect to be successful in such a course, and
b.   value the course. In the present study, we focus in particular on the *value* component of the expectancy X value model.

Eccles and her colleagues (e.g., Eccles, 1983; Eccles & Wigfield, 1985; Wigfeld & Eccles, 1992) have identified four dimensions of achievement values. For a specific task, an individual's *attainment value* refers to how important the individual perceives the task to be; *interest value* refers to how intrinsically appealing the task is perceived; *utility value* refers to perceived usefulness of the task; and *cost* refers to negative aspects of engaging in a particular task. Extending this model to adult education/GED programs, one could argue that an individual who perceives adult education/GED programs as important would have high attainment value; perceptions of adult education as interesting would yield high interest value; perceptions of adult education as useful would be related to high utility value. The "cost" component is somewhat different. An individual might choose not to participate in an adult education program because the cost (e.g., the amount of time spent in the program) might not be worth the time that would have to be given up on other activities (e.g., time spent with family, time at work, etc.).

Research with children and adolescents conducted by Eccles and her colleagues indicates that expectancy beliefs predict actual achievement, whereas values are better predictors of actual behaviors (e.g. course enrollment) than are expectancies (e.g., Eccles, 1983). Consequently, it is possible that adults who highly value the activities and outcomes of adult education/GED programs may be more likely to enroll in such programs. Therefore, the value component served as a guide for many of the questions asked of participants in this study.

Motivation Toward Literacy

One of the fundamental aspects of GED programs is the acquisition of literacy skills. Whereas much research has examined influences on children's motivation to engage in literacy activities (e.g., Baker, Scher, & Mackler, 1997), less research has focused on motivation toward literacy in adult populations. In particular, studies of literacy motivation in under-educated adults have been scarce. In general, research indicates that having positive experiences with reading and literacy during childhood is related to more frequent reading later in life (Baker et al., 1997). However, studies have not examined how these early experiences interact with other negative school experiences, including dropping out of school.

Although studies of literacy motivation in adults have been scarce, there has been some research on adult reading practices. For example, Smith (1996) analyzed data from the National Adult Literacy Survey (NALS). In that study, various types of literacy activities were examined. One of the more intriguing findings related to motivation for reading: young adults tend to spend time reading brief documents for work, whereas older adults tend to spend more time reading newspapers. Nevertheless, the study did not directly examine non-readers' interest or literacy-related behaviors.

METHODOLOGY

This study presented a number of intriguing methodological challenges. Survey research investigating adult education participation has been tried in Kentucky but with limited effectiveness (Freeman, Milkman, McCoy, Armon, & Gill 1997). First, the use of written instruments is unadvisable when many of the target population are functionally illiterate. Second, the target population is defined by their lack of participation in formal programs, therefore contacting respondents and attaining an appropriate return rate for a pen and paper or phone survey design is difficult to do. Finally, many of the reasons or excuses individuals give for not participating such as a lack of child care or transportation are known and testable through a positivistic design, but the underlying reasons an individual chooses not to continue his or her formal education are not. Therefore, qualitative field methods and theoretically guided analysis were used. Specifically, our research is based on in depth interviews that allow respondents to describe their experiences in their own words. Although the primary analyses of those interviews were qualitative in nature, we also employed several descriptive quantitative analyses in order to verify and triangulate our findings.

Sample

Seven rural counties in Kentucky were selected for the study with diverse economic profiles as defined by the United States Department of Agriculture (USDA). The funding agency also requested the inclusion of a county adjacent to a metropolitan area but it was later dropped from the study due to difficulties in obtaining access to interview subjects. The final sample included three mining, two manufacturing, and two non-specialized counties. (Non-specialized refers to an economic base that includes a variety of influences or, in the case of economically distressed counties, a lack of a strong economic influence.) The sites were geographically dispersed across the state including three counties west of Louisville, two counties in central Kentucky, and three counties in eastern Kentucky.

Data Collection

We conducted a pilot study in the fall of 1998 to test the research design and assumptions. Nine interviews were conducted that revealed the importance of work-related variables and community context to educational decision-making. As a result, we revised the interview protocol and instructions for field researchers to emphasize the exploration of economic and employment conditions as well as attitudes about available work and attitudes toward education in general. We designed the interview protocol to include a series of common questions asked of all interview respondents in addition to instructions on probing and soliciting narrative material. A demographic data sheet with questions to be completed at the beginning and end of the interview was created.

Field research and interviews were conducted by a team of researchers beginning in September of 1998 through August of 1999. Prior to visiting each site, we contacted the adult education provider(s) and reviewed available documentation regarding the educational structure and economic history of the area. During site visits we talked with educators, social service administrators, and employment services. We purchased subscriptions to local newspapers and contacted non-profit organizations, churches and civic organizations. Because of time limitations we focused on the local economic environment but also spent time in places of public talk such as little league games and social service waiting rooms. Through this field-work and conversations with local leaders, counselors, and administrators we gathered leads on potential interview participants, we asked about the economy and how local residents felt about future including attitudes about education. The information gained from these site visits informed our interviews, allowing us to understand references to local people, places, and organizations and providing a framework for probing cursory answers. We also conducted informal phone interviews with adult education providers in 193 sites across the state (1999 DAEL grant recipients) and focus group interviews with current students in three of the research sites to provide background for our interviews.

Our goal for each site was to locate a purposeful sample of 10-12 individuals who had not finished high school or the GED and were *not* participating in adult education at the time of the study. We attempted to include both men and women of diverse ages, occupations, and educational experiences and consulted with each other throughout the fieldwork process to assess the development of our pool of participants. Previous welfare and workforce investment programs in Kentucky required educational testing of clients; thus many of the individuals we contacted had participated in an adult education program in the past although often going no further than the intake process. Others reported having visited an adult education program voluntarily once or twice but had not reached their goals. Consequently, almost two-thirds of our interview participants had some personal experience with adult education and finding individuals who had never crossed the threshold of an adult education program was rare. Eighty-four interviews were conducted, with approximately 10-13 in each county.

The interview protocol[1] was designed to lead the respondent through a narrative describing what they had accomplished and decisions they had made since leaving school. After asking a series of demographic questions, we asked respondents where they went to school and why they had decided to leave. We then asked what they did next. For each major life change, such as getting married, having a child, getting a new job, and/or losing a job, we would ask whether or not they had considered returning to school.

In this way, we generated a life history narrative that focused on choices rather than failures.

Our interview protocol also included questions about respondents' impressions of adult education: whether they knew where services were located, whether different locations or times of classes would encourage them to attend, what would make them uncomfortable, and similar questions. At the end of the interview, we tried to isolate, as much as possible, the specific barriers to participation that might still exist. For example, if a respondent mentioned the lack of childcare as a barrier we would offer a hypothetical solution such as: "If you could take your children with you and have free childcare, would you go?" In this way, we tried to probe logistical reasons for not pursuing further education to determine if there might be underlying barriers to participation.

At the end of the interview we returned to the data sheet to collect further information from each respondent regarding demographics, homeownership, access to transportation, library and computer use, and to confirm whether or not they were receiving or had received government assistance. We also asked all respondents, one final time, what the primary motivator to continuing their education would be and what the biggest deterrent would be. These final questions were intended to help the interviewer confirm or revise his or her understanding of the respondents' position regarding pursuing further education.

Analysis of Data

When conducting research using qualitative techniques, analysis is ongoing. While we followed the same research protocol in each site, the sequence of activities—where each researcher went and to whom he or she talked was decided as each case study unfolded, following leads and pursuing opportunities. These decisions were recorded in the field notes kept for each field site and are an example of what is called emergent design. Further analysis took place during the reading and coding of the interview transcripts and field notes.

A three-member qualitative research team including one member who had not participated in the data collection process analyzed the field notes, transcripts, and documents related to each site. This process began by reading and re-reading the interview transcripts using open coding techniques (Emerson, Fretz, & Shaw, 1995). The transcripts were sorted for the first round of reading based on the site selection criteria of geographic location and economic type. The team then discussed the key themes to emerge and created a new set of categories with which to sort the transcripts. The transcripts were re-read by the analysis team resulting in the creation of a set of categories that were organized into a coding scheme. A third reading of the transcripts using a focused coding technique allowed patterns and variations in relationships between categories to emerge. This last set of readings specifically focused on gender differences, age or generational differences, the influence of learning difficulties, and work-related issues. During each phase of this analysis, the team met regularly to discuss the emergent themes.

Quantitative Analysis

Whereas the qualitative analysis was ongoing, a quantitative analysis team conducted a separate coding and analyses of the interviews. These analyses were undertaken for several reasons. First, we wanted to examine demographic characteristics of the sample. Second, we wanted to examine motivational variables using a prior coding system, in order to examine demographic trends in motivation toward attending adult education classes.

Two doctoral level graduate students (one of which had participated in the data collection process) were hired to code the surveys (for a detailed discussion of the coding scheme, see Jensen et al., 2000). After the coding was completed and checked for reliability, descriptive analyses were performed, using the SPSS computer package. Most of those analyses included chi square tests, t-tests, and simple ANOVAs. These analyses were conducted in order to examine demographic differences (e.g., gender differences, age differences, county differences, etc.). A description of the full sample is presented in Table 1. The results of this analysis were then reviewed by the entire research team and are reported here to enrich the description of the emergent themes.

Emergent Themes

Through the process of reading and re-reading the interview transcripts several themes emerged clearly as important to understanding the educational decision-making of the participants in the study. These themes became the organizing ideas for writing up the research—an analytic process in itself. In this section, we focus on the major motivation-related themes to emerge from the study illustrated by excerpts of narrative compiled from interview transcripts (for a more detailed report, see Jensen et al., 2000).

Generational Differences

We quickly realized that the length of time since leaving school made a significant difference in how an individual thought of himself or herself

TABLE 1
Description of Sample

Variable	Categories	N	Percentage
County	1	12	14.3%
	2	12	14.3%
	3	17	20.2%
	4	9	10.7%
	5	12	14.3%
	6	13	15.5%
	7	9	10.7%
Gender	Female	39	46.4%
	Male	44	52.4%
Number of Children	0	29	36.3%
	1	18	22.5%
	2	17	21.3%
	3	7	8.8%
	4	5	6.3%
	5	3	3.8%
	6	1	1.3%
Home Ownership	Does not own home	41	52.6%
	Owns home	37	47.4%
Marital Status	Unmarried	33	41.3%
	Married	47	58.8%
Public Assistance	No Assistance	56	70.0%
	Receives Assistance	24	30.0%

relative to being a student. Younger respondents for whom school life was relatively recent talked about adult education in very different terms than individuals who had left school twenty or thirty years before. These differences have important implications for motivation to attend or not attend adult education programs. Life-stage is an important variable regarding educational decision-making.

Gender Differences

Men and women have very different priorities relative to adult education needs and goals. The life experiences of men and women differ dramatically (e.g., Goldstein, 1996; Gowen, 1992; Winkelman, 1998). The experiences of the individuals in our study reflect this in that the under-educated men tend to structure their lives around work. Women—even those who work outside the home—are far more likely to structure their lives and important life decisions around family responsibilities.

Local Economic Context

Under-educated adults tend to receive lower wages than high school graduates do. In some of the areas we studied, however, jobs are scarce even for those with educational credentials. In some cases acquiring a GED would not change an individuals' chances of increasing their wage-earning potential. In other areas, work is plentiful and employers desire educational credentials, but the actual work available to individuals with low level educational credentials does not require the mandated academic skills. These contradictions negatively affect attitudes toward education despite mostly positive comments made by respondents regarding the efficacy of education in general.

Commonalities Across Themes

These three themes overlap in complicating ways. For example, older men may be concerned about their ability to continue in labor intensive work because of health issues and would talk about retirement while older women may be taking on new responsibilities as care-takers of their extended families. Respondents' decisions were also affected by relationships, logistics of childcare and transportation, and, for many, learning problems that would likely impede efficient progress toward the credentials needed for improving wage-earning potential.

The Value Component of the Expectancy X Value Model and Adult Education

Throughout the interviews, there was ample evidence of the various components of Eccles et al.'s model of achievement values. Nevertheless, some of the components of the model were more evident than were others. In the next section, we present findings related to the four parts of the value-component of the expectancy X value model.

Cost

The cost component of the expectancy X value model becomes particularly important in trying to explain the lack of motivation of many adults to attend adult education classes. As discussed by Eccles and her colleagues (e.g., Wigfield & Eccles, 1992), cost refers to "the perceived negative aspects of engaging in the task" (Pintrich & Schunk, 1996, p. 295). For many adults, the cost of enrolling in and participating in adult education programs is simply not worth the sacrifices that they will have to make. Specifically, because conditions of poverty severely stress monetary and time resources, many respondents felt they had to choose between adult education programs and paid employment and unpaid work needed for daily survival. Of necessity, the choice typically favored work obligations and the often meager income they provided over education programs. Most respondents didn't have the luxury of postponing—even temporarily— paid employment to devote themselves exclusively to educational goals. In summary, interviewees often indicated that they had many family and work-related responsibilities, and that it just wasn't worth it to them to attend adult education programs, because of the amount of time that it would take from their jobs and their families.

This was particularly true of the interviewees who were between the ages of 25-45. Within this group, many (59.5 percent) were married, and 63.3 percent had children at home. When faced with a choice between self-improvement through education and family responsibilities, this group clearly indicated that their families must come first. What we called "mid-career" respondents (we used this label because these respondents identi-fied themselves more closely with their work or family responsibilities than the independence of youth or the transitional period of retirement) strug-gled to balance family and work demands and were understandably con-cerned with time constraints and economic considerations. For example, one interviewee stated:

> A lot of times I work overtime, especially here lately. We've been real busy and we're getting busier and we're leaving our shop and we're gettin' a big-ger shop. . . [And] my wife works late sometimes. I gotta take care of the kids then, you know, and by the time I get them took care of, washing and teeth brushed and them in bed, I'm wore out.

Full-time workers found it difficult to imagine finding time for adult education classes after work. Many had additional non-wage work responsi-bilities that further consumed their time and energy. For most of our respondents, the wages to be earned by working or the obligations they faced for non-wage work were essential and non-negotiable. Any free time was already allocated to family and community activities. Using an expect-ancy X value framework, the payoff for attending such classes was not worth the cost.

> I'd like to get my diploma. Sometimes it's a little hectic to have to work and try and get it, you know, if you have other things planned . . . it cuts back on some of the things that I would rather be doing.

Another interviewee stated:

> I can't go during the day because of my workin' hours and I need the money more than I need the education at this point. I know that sounds dumb, but that's the way it is.

Female interviewees in particular indicated that family responsibilities were paramount, and that the cost of participating in adult education programs was not worth any potential payoffs. Some women, including those who worked outside the home, reported they had dropped out of adult education programs that interfered with family responsibilities.

> I was cleanin' 'til about 5:00 pm and they started their program at 6:00 pm. Well, my kids needed to be fed and taken care of and I had no one to do it but my older son. The children needed me, and to me that was more important at the time.

Extrinsic Utility Value

For the older interviewees (older than 45 years of age), it became rather clear that the perceived utility of adult education specifically, and of education in general, was different than for the younger respondents. For these older individuals, leaving school when they were younger did not carry as much of a social stigma as it does for students today. For many of these individuals, leaving school prior to graduation was the norm. Many of these interviewees left school because they had to work, but they did not feel stigmatized or socially isolated because of this. Significantly, many rural respondents withdrew from school at an early age to help with farm responsibilities.

> We had to work. I was raised on a farm and we had dairy cows. Some had the opportunity [to finish school] and some didn't. Back in them times, people raised crops and they depended on crops and they kept us home a whole lot, you know, working in crops. That's one reason we didn't get our school finished, 'cause when we come of age, well, then we stayed home and worked. They needed us.

Thus for many of these individuals, school simply was not perceived as a useful part of life. These individuals had to leave school at an early age, and those missed years of schooling didn't seem to influence these interviewees' lives. Consequently, schooling in general wasn't perceived as useful by many of these older respondents.

For these older respondents, the lack of a high school degree did not equate with the lack of skills or ability. Many respondents pointed out that life experiences provided the best education. These individuals learned what was useful *on the job*, as the following comments by a Department of Transportation employee indicate:

> I think it's what you learn while you're workin'. I've learned a lot since I've been here. I had to get my CDL (Commercial Driver's License) and stuff like that and I didn't, never had drove a truck. I had to take a class over here and get my permit.

Another respondent indicated that he and his wife had learned how to build houses, not through formal training in construction, but simply by doing it:

I've built five houses by myself. Me and my wife done it practically all ourselves, you see. I first started out when I was about twelve years old, puttin'
down hardwood floors and finishing 'em. So, to see somebody do a little
something, you know you can do it too. That's how come me to build my
houses myself. I said, "Well, they can do it. Why can't I?" So I just went ahead
and built 'em."

Respondents also indicated that the type of material learned in adult
education/GED classes would not be useful to them. Specifically, there was
a perception that the type of material learned in "school" was not useful on
the job:

You can't sit and read the book and go out and weld. You have to do it, you
know. You have to learn it. . . I can sit and read a book about anything and fifteen minutes later I couldn't tell you what it was about. I just never was a big
reader and never did like to read. Now if I was doing it, I would learn it and
pick it up. But if I was reading, I wouldn't comprehend.

Thus local economic conditions and the availability of jobs clearly
affected respondents' assessment of the value of further education. Nevertheless, some adults clearly indicated that they perceived that the material
taught in adult education classes might actually be useful:

You got to know something about everything, no matter what job you're on.
You got to know math in everything. You got to know how to spell 'cause if
you don't write that down right, how they going to know what you're saying?
Especially if you're writin' down what you need. If you don't know how to tell
'em then they don't know. You got to know how to read and write and all
that.

Attainment Value

The attainment (importance) value component was evident in a number of interviews. Specifically, there were some examples in the interviews
of respondents indicating that adult education/GED programs were really
not important in helping an individual to do his or her job. These types of
comments were particularly evident in the older respondents.

One catalyst for these comments is the increasing trend toward creden-
tialing. Many employers now encourage their employees to seek credentials such as the GED. For example, at the time of our study, the Kentucky
Department of Transportation had recently made an agreement with the
DAEL to require the GED of new workers and for salary increases. For
many older workers in Kentucky, there is some resentment against this
trend. Indeed, there is a feeling that if one successfully has been working at
a job for many years, why should the individual have to go back and earn
some type of credential later in life?

The only job I've had is when I got on here. Seems like it was, I'll be honest with you, seems like it was easier to come to work for the state than when I would try to get other jobs. It seems like it wasn't that big of a deal here. . . I have been going on fourteen years now. I was hired, you know, without a high school education and they didn't bring all this up then. You still work your same job.

Similarly, another respondent related:

I'm a special equipment operator. And when I come here I started at the bottom and climbed my way up. I mean, I think if a man can do his job and do it right, they ought to give him the money. Whether they have a high school education, or four years of college, or eight years of college.

These older workers felt that the requirement that they complete the GED was unimportant and inappropriate, in that it penalized them even though they demonstrated daily that they were able to do the work they originally had been hired to do. To these individuals, there was no perceived attainment value (importance) attached to earning a GED. They had been successful all their lives without such a credential, so there was no perceived need to get one now.

However, for some female participants, the perceived importance of attending adult education classes motivated them to actually attend. In particular, some female participants who had children that lived at home felt that attending these classes would allow them to help their children with homework, and would provide a good example for their children.

When I read my oldest a story and I did not know the words, I would just make up words. And when they got into school, time they got into kindergarten, I realized that wasn't going to work. So I started makin' myself learn. When my oldest one brought homework home, we would sit down and figure it out. If I did not know the word, he knew it.

Many female respondents were adamant about the importance of education for their children and pushed their children to finish school. They were especially proud of their children's educational success.

My son's in college now. He's in computers. My grouchin' has paid off. I pushed him to go to school. He does pretty good for hisself. I don't know how.

Conversely, another woman whose children dropped out of school reported:

If I had've got mine, my kids might would have gone on and got theirs. They look at me and say, "Well, Mom quit, I'll quit." So I feel like I let them down."

Local economic contexts were related strongly to adults' perceived importance of adult education/GED programs. Many of the interviewees made adult education decisions based on a rational assessment of the relative value of further education, given their local economic context. In areas where few jobs were available, the incentive to attend adult education classes was diminished. In such areas, there was little perceived importance for attending adult education classes. One respondent argued:

> There's never no work around here. What are you goin' to do if you had your GED? Where are you going to work? Flip hamburgers?

Intrinsic Value

The intrinsic (interest) component of the expectancy X value model was the component of the model that was the least evident in these interviews. However, there was some evidence of this component of the model.

In particular, some participants perceived adult education/GED programs as being "boring", based on information from past experiences. In some cases, this was a general assessment of the program as indicated by an adult education student who reported, *"The center itself, you know, it's just dull."* Other students referred specifically to instructional materials and methods.

> I went one time up in Indiana. And they was this older woman, she come in there and, I don't know, she just sort of bored me out. She was talkin' about "dog" and "cat" and all that stuff. I mean, I already know all that stuff. . . She had me writin' letters, and I told her, "I know all of this." I thought, "Well, we'll start here today and keep goin'," but it just stayed there and stayed and stayed.

Importantly, we asked *all* of our interview respondents if they thought adult education classes would be interesting. When presented in such a way, most responded that they thought it would be. Experiences such as that of the student above, however, are more likely to be passed along and are part of the common knowledge on which individuals base their decisions whether or not to attend. Former students who found the work to be too hard or too easy and who did not see adequate improvement were frequently discouraged and were thus more likely to drop out of adult education programs.

QUANTITATIVE ANALYSES OF RESPONSES TO INTERVIEWS

Quantitative analyses were performed in order to examine the demographic characteristics of the sample, as well as to elucidate some of the qualitative findings.

Sample Characteristics by Gender

   Several demographic characteristics were examined by gender of participant. These data are presented in Table 2. More females than males
reported receiving public assistance (χ^2 (1) = 12.04, $p<.001$). Specifically,
of all of the public assistance recipients in the sample, 25 percent were
male, whereas 75 percent were female; in contrast, of the participants who
did not receive assistance, 67.3 percent were male, whereas only 32.7 percent were female. Of the respondents who owned their own home, significantly more participants were male (70.3 percent) than were female (29.7
percent), χ^2 (1) = 6.01, $p<.01$. Female participants reported having more
school-aged children living at home than did males (M_{Female} = 1.87, M_{Male}
= 1.02, t (77) = -2.56, $p<.01$). This may be related to female interviewees'
emphasis on the well being and education of children. Females were more
likely than were males to report being unemployed, whereas males were
more likely than females to report being employed full-time, χ^2 (2) =

TABLE 2
Sample Characteristics By Gender

Variable	Categories	Male	Female
Receipt of Public Assistance** *	Does not receive Assistance	37 (67.3 %)	18 (32.7 %)
	Receives Assistance	6 (25%)	18 (75%)
Home Ownership**	Does not own home	17 (42.5 %)	23 (57.5 %)
	Does own home	26 (70.3 %)	11 (29.7 %)
Previous Experience with Adult Education	Has not had friend or relative in adult education	16 (59.3 %)	11 (40.7 %)
	Has had a friend or relative in adult education	24 (49.0 %)	25 (51.0 %)
Library Usage	Never used a library	18 (69.2 %)	8 (30.8 %)
	Has used a library	23 (47.9 %)	25 (52.1 %)
Number of children**	Mean number of children	1.02	1.87
Current Employment ***	Part-time/self-employed/ placement	4 (36.4 %)	7 (63.6 %)
	Unemployed	9 (32.1 %)	19 (67.9 %)
	Employed Full-time	30 (75%)	10 (25%)
Motivation for Adult Education*	For money or job-related reasons	22 (61.1 %)	14 (38.9 %)
	For the sake of learning	15 (75%)	5 (20%)
	For family-related reasons	4 (9.3%)	11 (73.3 %)
	No motivation	2 (40%)	3 (60%)

Notes: p < .05 ** p < .01 *** p < .001

13.88, $p<.001$. These data shed some light on the male interviewees' tendencies to focus on employment and economic issues, as opposed to home and family issues.

Sample Characteristics by Age

Participants in the study were broken down into three age categories: ages 18-24 (21.8 percent), ages 25-45 (55.1 percent), and ages 46 and older (23.1 percent). Descriptive data were examined separately for each age group. These data are presented in Table 3. Several variables differed across age groups. Older participants were more likely than younger participants to report that they owned their own home (χ^2 (2) = 14.29, $p<.001$). Library usage also varied by age. Of those participants who reported having never used a library, a smaller percentage were in the youngest group (7.7 percent) than in the oldest group (38.5 percent), χ^2 (2) = 9.35, p<.01. In contrast, only 12.5 percent of those who reported having the used a library were in the oldest group. Older participants reported having had significantly fewer children living at home than did both the youngest and the middle-aged group, F (2, 75) = 7.30, $p<.001$. This may be related to some of the older participants' negative attitudes about adult education.

Differences Between Counties

In order to assess adequacy of our sample, we examined demographic differences across the participating counties in the study. Distributions were equivalent across counties for gender (χ^2 (6) = 9.69, NS), marital status (χ^2 (6) = 6.11, NS), home ownership (χ^2 (6) = 5.25, NS), library usage (χ^2 (6) = 8.96, NS), and years of schooling (F (6, 75) = 0.74, NS).

There were some noteworthy differences in sample characteristics across counties. Receipt of public assistance was higher in two of the counties than in the other five counties in the study (χ^2 (6) = 27.58, $p<.001$). There was a difference between counties in terms of number of children, F (6, 73) = 3.44, $p<.01$, although post hoc Tukey comparisons did not indicate significance between county differences. These economically based differences are related directly to the focus that some interviewees had on jobs and on the economic contexts of their communities, and the availability of jobs.

Motivation to Attend Adult Education

Participants' were probed regarding their motivation to attend adult education programs. Responses were coded into four categories: (1)

TABLE 3
Sample Characteristics By Age

Variable	Categories	Ages 18-24	Ages2 5-45	Ages 46+
Receipt of Public Assistance	Does not receive Assistance	12 (22.2 %)	27 (50%)	15 (27.8 %)
	Receives Assistance	5 (20.8 %)	16 (66.7 %)	3 (12.5 %)
Home Ownership** *	Does not own home	14 (35.9 %)	22 (56.4 %)	3 (7.7%)
	Does own home	3 (8.1%)	20 (54.1 %)	14 (37.8 %)
Previous Experience with Adult Educa-tion	Has not had friend or relative in adult education	6 (22.2 %)	12 (44.4 %)	9 (33.3 %)
	Has had a friend or relative in adult education	10 (20.8 %)	29 (60.4 %)	9 (18.8 %)
Library Usage**	Never used a library	2 (7.7%)	14 (53.8 %)	10 (38.5 %)
	Has used a library	15 (31.3 %)	27 (56.3 %)	6 (12.5 %)
Number of chil-dren***	Mean number of chil-dren	1.71	1.79	0.33
Current Employment	Part-time/self-employed/place-ment	1 (10%)	7 (70%)	2 (20%)
	Unemployed	7 (25%)	17 (60.7 %)	4 (14.3 %)
	Employed Full-time	9 (23.1 %)	18 (46.2 %)	12 (30.8 %)
Motivation for Adult Education	For money or job-related reasons	10 (28.6 %)	18 (51.4 %)	7 (20%)
	For the sake of learn-ing	2 (10%)	11 (55%)	7 (35%)
	For family-related rea-sons	4 (28.6 %)	9 (64.3 %)	1 (7.1%)
	No motivation	1 (20%)	3 (60%)	1 (20%)

Notes: p<.05 ** p<.01 *** p<.001

attending for financial or job-related reasons, (2) attending purely for the sake of learning, (3) attending for family-related reasons, and (4) no indi-cation of any motivation to attend. One participant indicated that it would be socially desirable to attend adult education classes; however, that partic-ipant was not included in this set of analyses.

Based on those categorizations, there were no differences in motivation to attend adult education by county (χ^2 (18) = 21.87, NS), age (F (3, 70) = 2.42, NS), years of schooling (F (3, 71) = 0.30, NS), number of children (F (3, 72) = 0.22, NS), marital status (χ^2 (3) = 5.76, NS), home ownership (χ^2 (3) = 2.65, NS), whether or not respondents received public financial assistance (χ^2 (3) = 2.27, NS), whether or not friends or family members had attended adult education programs (χ^2 (3) = 0.51, NS), and whether or not the county was a low or high-unemployment county (χ^2 (3) = 0.93, NS).

Current employment status was broken down into three categories: employed full-time, unemployed, or other (part-time employment, job placement, self-employed, etc.). Current employment status was unrelated to motivation (χ^2 (6) = 4.57, NS), and was unrelated to having had friends or relatives who attended adult education programs (χ^2 (2) = 1.37, NS).

There were gender differences in motivation to attend adult education programs, (χ^2 (3) = 9.6,3 p<.05). Females (73.3 percent) were more likely than males (26.7 percent) to indicate that they were motivated to attend for family-related reasons, whereas males (76.2 percent) were more likely than females (23.8 percent) to indicate that they were motivated to attend merely for the sake of learning. In addition, males (61.1 percent) were somewhat more likely than females (38.9 percent) to report being motivated to attend for job-related purposes. These findings exactly mirror the comments that participants made during the interviews—males seemed to think about adult education in terms of their jobs, whereas females were more likely to think about adult education in terms of their families.

Participants also were asked about motivational *deterrents* to participation. Responses were coded into six categories:

1. job-related time constraints,
2. child-related time constraints,
3. other types of time constraints,
4. cost or transportation issues,
5. confidence in one's abilities, and
6. no or other reasons.

Deterrents were unrelated to county (χ^2 (30) = 26.07, NS), marital status (χ^2 (5) = 5.95, NS), home ownership (χ^2 (5) = 6.29, NS), number of children (F (5, 71) = 1.67, NS), age (F (5, 69) = 1.08, NS), years of schooling, (F (5, 70) = 0.72, NS), and whether or not the county was a low or high-unemployment county (χ^2 (5) = 2.40, NS).

Deterrents were related to gender, (χ^2 (5) = 14.87, p<.01). Job-related time constraints were more typical for males (78.9 percent) than for females (21.1 percent), whereas child-related constraints were more typical for females (90 percent) than for males (10 percent). Concerns about confidence were more typical for males (66.7 percent) than for females (33.3 percent). Again, the gender-related findings in the quantitative analyses mirror the themes that emerged in the interviews.

Motivational deterrents also were related to whether or not participants received public assistance (χ^2 (5) = 15.47, p<.01). Cost and transportation were greater deterrents for assistance recipients (75 percent) than for non-recipients (25 percent), whereas job-related time constraints were greater concerns for non-recipients (84.2 percent) than for recipients (15.8 percent).

METHODOLOGICAL ISSUES

Some important methodological issues emerged during the course of this study. First, we discovered that some of the motivational constructs that we asked about always seemed to elicit socially desirable responses. For example, all respondents were asked if adult education programs were important. When asked this way, all respondents indicated that it in fact was important. Nevertheless, additional probing helped us to realize that much of the actual information covered in these programs actually is not perceived as important to these individuals.

Second, results of the present study suggest that survey methodologies, while extremely useful, often may not be able to tap into some of the more delicate and detailed facets of individuals' motivation. Narrative analysis of a transcript, taking into account the whole story rather than a single response to a single question, allows for a more complete analysis of the respondents' intentions.

For example, one of our respondents told his interviewer repeatedly that he was unlikely to attend an adult education class. In response to all prompts in the interview protocol, he stated that he did not plan to continue his education. When coded for quantitative analysis, the researchers would most likely record this respondent as unmotivated to pursue further education. Narrative analysis of this same interview, however, revealed that the man was interested in improving his math and reading skills. He spoke extensively about his children. He regretted not "being there" for his older son because of his heavy work schedule as a coal miner and, now unemployed, he was grateful for the opportunity to spend time with his five-year-old son. In the course of the interview he mentioned his desire to "do for" his younger son, including reading to him regularly and wanting to help him with his schoolwork when the time came. Although this man responded negatively to direct questions regarding *his* educational aspirations, he was hopeful if not positive about the possibilities of improving his knowledge for the sake of his child.

We hope that other individuals will continue this line of research in the future. There are many additional questions that need to be addressed. For example, in the present study we focused on the value component of the expectancy X value model. Whereas we did ask questions using goal orientation theory constructs, those did not emerge as important themes in the interviews. Specifically, when probed about performance goals, individuals often felt that the questions were inapplicable—they simply did not think much about how they compared to others; they were much more concerned with the value of attending adult education classes (e.g., what would they get out of it?). In terms of mastery goals, most of the respondents were not really focused on mastering the material—if they decided to pursue adult education, it would be for extrinsic reasons.

DISCUSSION

The present study was an investigation of adults' motivation to either attend or not attend adult education classes. Whereas there are many adult education centers and programs available in the state of Kentucky, few adults who are eligible to participate in these programs actually utilize them.

We used both quantitative and qualitative methods to examine the interview data. In terms of motivation and the expectancy X value approach, the qualitative analysis yielded the most compelling information. We found evidence of all four components of Eccles et al.'s model: intrinsic value, attainment value, utility value, and cost. However, the results of the quantitative analyses clearly supported some of the main themes that emerged from the qualitative analyses (particularly with regard to gender differences).

Whereas it may appear reasonable *on the surface* to assume that undereducated adults do not value education, this assumption is strongly contradicted by the data collected through this study. Time and again study participants stated that they do in fact value education highly. Most regret not finishing school. Many stated that they liked to read, indicating that they may continue to learn, albeit through non-formal means. Virtually all who are parents vow to do everything within their power to help their children finish high school. In most cases, their work experiences and economic situations have made it amply clear to them that education is important. Having struggled to find jobs that allow them to support their families, most study participants clearly value education, both for themselves and for their children.

> It's held me back. I mean, I could have got a better job if I had of finished high school and had a diploma. If you don't have a high school diploma or GED they won't hire you, there's a whole bunch of factories that just won't do it . . . I want my kids to finish school, number one. And they will if I have anything to do with it. That's what I want for them.

Nevertheless, the majority of these adults do not choose to enroll in adult education programs. Although all four components of the expectancy X value model yield insights into this phenomenon, the *cost* component was particularly useful with these data. Most of the adults interviewed felt that for various reasons, it was not worth the time and effort to enroll in and complete one of these programs. Participation in these programs would interfere with job and family responsibilities. Whereas job-related issues were more salient for men and family-related issues were more salient for women, the overall theme of the perceived cost of attending these programs prevailed throughout many of the interviews.

Is it possible to nurture a sense of appreciation for the skills and techniques taught in adult education classes? Many researchers (e.g., Ames & Archer, 1988; Anderman & Maehr, 1994; Covington, 1999; Maehr & Midgley, 1996) argue that the promotion of mastery goals will lead to increased motivation in learners. Indeed, much research supports these recommendations. Covington (1999) argues that in general, subject-matter appreciation can be encouraged in most learning environments. Specifically, Covington argues that learners will value the material that they are studying when they are meeting their grade goals, when they are studying material that is interesting to them, and when learning is task/mastery-oriented, as opposed to "self aggrandizing or failure avoidant" (Covington, 1999, p. 127).

Such recommendations might help to motivate adults to attend adult education classes. However, we asked all of our participants to talk about goals (e.g., mastery, performance, etc.). These did not seem to be issues for most of our participants. Results of the present study do suggest that to really motivate this population to attend these classes, these individuals must become convinced that the amount of time and effort that they would have to devote to these programs would be worth the effort.

ENDNOTES

1. This is a pseudonym.
2. The full interview protocol is available from the first or second authors.

REFERENCES

Anderman, E.M., & Maehr, M.L. (1994). Motivation and schooling in the middle grades. *Review of Educational Research, 6,* 287-309.

Baker, L., Scher, D., & Mackler, K. (1997). Home and family influences on motivations for reading. *Educational Psychologist, 32,* 69-82.

Covington, M.V. (1999). Caring about learning: The nature and nurturing of subject-matter appreciation. *Educational Psychologist, 34,* 127-136.

Eccles, J.S. (1983). Expectancies, values and academic behaviors. In J.T. Spence (ed.), *Achievement and achievement motives* (pp. 75-146). San Francisco, CA: Freeman.

Eccles, J.S., & Wigfield, A. (1985). Teacher expectancies and student motivation. In J. B. Dusek (Ed.), *Teacher expectancies* (pp. 185-226). Hillsdale, NJ: Erlbaum.

Emerson, R.M., Fretz, R.I., & Shaw, L. (1995). *Writing ethnographic fieldnotes.* Chicago, IL: University of Chicago Press.

Freeman, S.H., Milman, M.I., McCoy, J.P., Armon, P.J., & Gill, J.L. (1997).*Identifying barriers to enrollment and completion.* Report prepared for the Kentucky Department for Adult Education and Literacy.

Goldstein, B. L. (1996, June) *Rereading self and family in the rural U.S.: Mothers' tales of family literacy programs.* Paper presented at the National Women's Studies Association Annual Meeting, Saratoga Springs, New York, NY.

Gowen, S.G. (1992). *The politics of workplace literacy: A case study.* New York, NY: Teachers College Press.

Harackiewicz, J.M., Barron, K.E., & Elliot, A.J. (1998). Rethinking achievement goals: When are they adaptive for college students and why?*Educational Psychologist, 33,* 1-21.

Jensen, J., Haleman, D., Goldstein, B., & Anderman, E.M. (2000).*Reasonable choices: Understanding why under-educated individuals choose not to participate in adult education.* Report prepared for the Kentucky Department of Adult Education and Literacy.

Maehr, M.L., & Midgley, C. (1996). *Transforming school cultures.* Boulder, CO: Westview Press.

National Center for Education Statistics (2000). *Fast facts.* Available at http://nces.ed.gov/fastfacts/display.asp?id=27.

Pintrich, P.R. (1989). The dynamic interplay of student motivation and cognition in the college classroom. In M.L. Maehr & C. Ames (Eds.),*Advances in motivation and achievement: Motivation enhancing environments* (pp. 117-160). Greenwich, CT: JAI Press.

Pintrich, P.R., & Schunk, D.H. (1996). *Motivation in education: Theory, research, and applications.* Englewood Cliffs, NJ: Prentice Hall.

Smith, M.C. (1996). Differences in adults' reading practices and literacy proficiencies. *Reading Research Quarterly, 31,* 196-219.

Wigfield, A., & Eccles, J.S. (1992). The development of achievement task values: A theoretical analysis. *Developmental Review, 12,* 265-310.

Winkelmann, C. L. (1998). Unsheltered lives: Battered women talk about school. In C. Fleischer and D. Schaafsma (Eds.), *Literacy and democracy: Teacher research and composition studies in pursuit of habitable spaces* (pp. 104-134). Urbana, IL: National Council of Teachers of English.

CHAPTER 8

TEACHER IMMEDIACY AND STUDENT MOTIVATION

Nanette Potee

INTRODUCTION

As I stepped into the classroom, I felt excited and slightly nervous, but confident. I had taught this introduction to communication course several times before and was looking forward to the new class I was about to encounter. All thirty students were sitting quietly in their seats, facing forward. I introduced myself, explained a bit about the course, and asked for questions or comments. I waited, and waited, and then prompted again. "Would anyone like to ask a question about me or the course?" No one raised a hand or a question, so I chalked it up to first day jitters and moved on. I attempted to get a class discussion started about communication. I wanted them to tell me what they thought communication was, what it wasn't, how we do it, what does it do for us...anything! What I got was blank, slightly embarrassed stares (eyes averted or down) and silence. Finally, I called on a student who seemed to have been watching me and asked if he would like to contribute something to the discussion. He mumbled something I couldn't quite understand and lowered his head. After several more failed attempts at getting students motivated to start a discussion, I gave up. I was at a loss. I wasn't quite sure how to continue so I dismissed the class early and tried to re-group. My confidence was shaken and I suddenly felt very discouraged. What was I doing wrong? Why weren't they talking? This type of activity had always worked in my classes at home. At home.

The problem was, I was not at home. In fact, I was 7,500 miles away from home. I was in Japan; a country that I had long been fascinated with, but at the moment seemed more foreign than ever. I have spent five years teaching various communication courses to Japanese students at an American university in Japan. As a teacher, one of the greatest challenges I faced was that the communication concepts I was trying to introduce were as foreign to the students as I was. Therefore, a great deal of my first year in Japan was spent learning *how* to teach Japanese students. Although I was familiar with basic Japanese customs and philosophies I was not prepared for what I experienced in the classroom. I was accustomed to students who engaged openly in class discussion, asked probing questions, and actively sought my assistance in class. This was certainly not the case in my new teaching environment. I discovered that before I could be an effective teacher with my Japanese students, I had to learn what they thought an effective teacher was. After I learned more about their previous academic experiences and what they expected from a teacher and themselves, I was able to adjust my teaching style slightly to help motivate them in a manner to which they were more accustomed. At the same time, I was attempting to help them adjust to a more Westernized approach to teaching and learning. At the completion of my first semester, my students and I were able to engage in short, but productive class discussions. We had learned from each other by adjusting our expectations and behaviors.

As an instructional communication scholar, what I learned about different teaching and learning styles while in Japan was fascinating. Because I am interested in the influences of cultural patterns and expectations on teaching and learning, I am concerned about the lack of research in my discipline that focuses on these variables. As the cultural diversity of classrooms in the United States increases, teachers are faced with myriad instructional challenges. Many teachers in the United States who teach international students (not to mention the culturally diverse citizenship of the U.S.) may not be familiar with the cultural influences present in their classrooms; the kinds of cultural values that inform behaviors, and perceptions of those behaviors. There is no question that teachers are faced with innumerable tasks that limit the time and attention we can afford our students. However, if we desire to be truly effective as teachers, then we have the responsibility to not only assess the needs of our culturally diverse student populations, but to address those needs directly.

Most teachers I know have a strong desire to be effective in their work, are concerned about their students, and want to facilitate a desire for learning. The questions I hear raised most often in regard to motivating students are "How? How can I motivate my students to learn?" and "What can I do or say that will make a difference with my students?" These questions were a driving force behind the conception and development of this study. In general, the research presented in this chapter examines issues of teacher effectiveness. More specifically, how teacher behaviors affect student motivation, and the cultural influences on those behaviors and perceptions of those behaviors, especially in regard to Japanese students.

I was compelled to pursue this line of research based on my teaching experiences both in Japan and at highly diverse universities in the U.S. According to the National Center for Educational Statistics (2000), during the 1998-99 year there were 491,000 international students enrolled in institutions of higher education in the United States. South and East Asia combined make up over 56% of the total number of international students studying at the undergraduate or graduate level, and 10% of those students, the highest number of any individual country in the world, came from Japan.

Due to the increasing population of international students and the high percentage of Asian students choosing to study at campuses across the United States, more research must be undertaken that focuses on these types of diverse student populations. In order to better reflect the growing population of international students at all educational levels in the United States, scholars who wish to examine classroom environments must also attempt to understand how cultural perspectives affect learning experiences within those settings. That was the purpose of this study, with a particular focus on cross-cultural perceptions of teacher behaviors and student motivation in Japan and the U.S. The following section offers a review of relevant literature on cultural patterns of communication, teacher immediacy, and student motivation.

REVIEW OF LITERATURE

To better understand the significant findings of this study, it is important to first understand the disparity that exists between Japan and the United States in terms of communication styles. Those who study the effects of cultural patterns on communication generally depict Asian and Western cultures as having the greatest degree of socio-cultural variation (Barnlund, 1975; Hall, 1977; Hofstede, 1982; Samovar & Porter, 1991). Contrasting cultural patterns, assumptions, and behaviors act as major sources of misunderstanding between communicators from those respective cultures.

One of the most commonly cited theories of cultural patterns, is Edward T. Hall's (1977) high-context, low-context continuum. Low context cultures (e.g. European Americans) are those that value direct speech. Therefore, most verbal and written information is stated explicitly. People within these cultures also stress the importance of individuality, competition or success by surpassing others, as well as equality and low power distance (Gudykunst, 1991; Hall, 1983). On the other end of the continuum, we find high-context cultures like Japan. High-context cultures can be identified by the great deal of attention paid to contextual issues, such as relationship status, environment, and timing. They value group goals over individuality, feel a great deal of responsibility to the group's values and rules, and prefer indirect communication (Lustig & Koester, 1999). DeVito (1998) also reports that high-context cultures value a greater distance between teachers and students, which is contrary to low-context cultures (e.g. United States).

These antithetical perspectives point to the inherent difficulties of cross-cultural communication. Damen (1987) suggests that communicative acts take place within the context of socio-cultural frameworks

> whose boundaries are drawn by the identification of a number of individuals as sharing given cultural assumptions, behaviors, and patterns. The setting is also culturally conditioned, for example, in terms of the uses of communication, manner of speech, or style of communication" (p.93).

Therefore, people from different cultures who might perceive certain settings, like a classroom, in very different ways, face barriers to understanding that go beyond language.

The differences in communication styles outlined here were some of the barriers I experienced while teaching and living in Japan, and the stimuli that motivated this study. If the communication styles of these cultures can be so disparate, wouldn't it follow that the educational system of each culture would emphasize or at least mirror these communicative behaviors? Therefore, educators charged with the instruction of students from diverse cultures should be aware of the impact these differences can have in the classroom. In part, it is these differences I have studied and experienced as a teacher that led me to look more closely at particular teacher behaviors that are perceived as motivating.

Teacher Effectiveness and Immediacy

Teacher effectiveness has been a major focus of instructional research both in the communication and education disciplines. A great deal of research conducted by scholars in the discipline of education indicates that effective teacher behaviors such as frequency and intensity of teacher praise, teacher enthusiasm, and teacher clarity have a positive influence on students achievement and ratings of teacher effectiveness (Bettencourt, Gillet, Gall & Hull, 1983; Brigham, Scruggs, & Mastropieri, 1992; Kasser & Ryan, 1996).

Instructional communication scholars have also produced a substantial body of research that focuses on varying aspects of teaching effectiveness. In the last two decades a great deal of this research has been devoted to the effects of teacher immediacy. The concept of immediacy as introduced by

Mehrabian (1969) and developed by Andersen (1979) focuses on communication behaviors that reduce psychological and physical distance between interactants. Most salient to my research are immediacy behaviors displayed by teachers. Throughout the instructional communication literature immediate teacher behaviors have been consistently operationalized as either verbal or nonverbal.

Verbal messages have the ability to bring interactants closer together, as well as drive them apart. Messages that increase immediacy usually express a willingness to participate in conversation and suggest openness, friendliness and empathy. Verbal messages that are the antitheses of these immediate behaviors can create distance between people and decrease immediacy (Richmond & McCroskey, 1989). Studies that focus on the effects of verbal teacher immediacy have shown increases in student affective, behavioral, and cognitive learning (Gorham & Christophel, 1990; Kelly & Gorham, 1988; Sanders & Wiseman, 1990; Sorensen, 1989).

Nonverbal immediacy refers to the physical distance between people. Behaviors such as smiling, touching, sitting or standing close to someone, frequent eye contact, relaxed body position, and leaning forward are interpreted as immediate nonverbal messages. Non-immediate behaviors include frowning, moving away from someone, tense body posture, and averted gaze (Burgoon, 1989; Richmond, McCroskey & Payne, 1987). Nonverbal teacher immediacy behaviors have also been found to affect student affective, cognitive, and behavioral learning (Andersen & Andersen, 1987; Kelly & Gorham, 1988; Gorham & Christophel, 1990; Richmond et al., 1987; Sanders & Wiseman, 1990).

Teacher Immediacy and the Influence of Culture

Because research on teacher immediacy suggests that learning can be influenced by a multitude of variables, one might reason that cultural expectations about teaching and learning may be among those influential variables. Yet, very little communication research to date has focused on the influences of culture in the classroom. The few communication scholars, who have attempted to move the research on teacher effectiveness beyond the Anglo-American mainstream perspective, have found similar results. Their findings point to strong positive relationships between teacher immediacy and variables such as: affective, cognitive, and behavioral learning, teacher clarity on instructional outcomes for culturally diverse students, teacher effectiveness and course utility, and teacher evaluation (Collier & Powell, 1990; McCroskey et al., 1995 & 1996; Neuliep, 1995; Powell & Harville, 1990; Sanders & Wiseman, 1990).

Motivation

Motivation is assumed to be one of the most important elements that contribute to learning (Blumenfeld, 1992; Brophy, 1987; Pintrich & Schunk, 1996). Brophy (1987) suggests that motivation is inherently linked to the predisposition of students derived from previous experiences and conditioning, as well as by modeling and "direct instruction or socialization by significant others, such as parents or teachers" (p. 40).

The literature on motivation has produced a wide variety of teaching strategies to promote student motivation. Among those strategies, two appear consistently throughout the literature: getting students' attention and teacher enthusiasm. As Frymier (1993) notes, "getting students' attention is often considered the first step in motivating students to do a particular task" (p. 456). While this idea may seem simplistic, anyone who has been in charge of a classroom knows that getting students to pay attention is not always an easy task.

A teacher's enthusiasm for teaching and learning is often so clearly visible that it is not surprising that it is positively linked with student motivation. Brophy (1987), Butler, (1994) Patrick, Hisley and Kempler (2000), all contend that teaching is a modeling behavior and that teachers who lack enthusiasm for the subject or course being taught can have negative effects on their students' motivation to learn that subject. On the whole, the literature indicates that teachers who show high levels of energy, and an interest and enjoyment of the subject matter are more likely to instill interest, enjoyment, and ultimately motivation in their students.

Teacher Immediacy and Student Motivation

In an effort to extend previous research on immediacy and learning, several communication scholars have turned their focus to the effects of immediacy on students' motivation to learn (Christophel & Gorham, 1995; Frymier, 1993; Gorham & Millette, 1997). Results from these studies indicate a strong positive relationship between teacher immediacy, student learning and state motivation.

While this line of research indicates that teacher immediacy behaviors may indeed positively influence student motivation, Gorham and Christophel (1992) point out that teacher "misbehaviors" may have an even greater negative impact on student motivation. They also found that students perceived a lack of motivation as a "teacher-owned problem" (p. 250). Through this line of research it has become increasingly clear that perhaps more important than building a student's motivation is not to *reduce* it.

While immediacy behaviors such as humor, direct eye contact, smiling, self-disclosure, and enthusiasm, have been found to be important variables in motivating students in the classroom, the salience of these variables is almost certainly dependent on a culture's perspective toward these behaviors, especially in specific contexts, like education. The idea that teachers perform a modeling role for students is not new and certainly not unique to the United States. What may be unique, however, are the types of behaviors teachers model. One of the basic theories of communication, known as the Sapir-Whorf hypothesis, claims that interpretations of communication behaviors are intrinsically linked with cultural perspectives and therefore might be expected to differ from culture to culture. Therefore, it stands to reason that any attempt to fully understand the impact of teacher immediacy behaviors, needs to examine the cultural context in which those behaviors occur. It was my goal to address these issues through my study.

In an educational system, like Japan's, that places such a high value on the holistic development of the ningen (human being), one might assume that immediate teacher behaviors, as defined in the extant research, would be present in the Japanese classroom. Yet, in light of the overarching differences in communication styles between the Japanese and U. S. Americans, by whom most of the existing research on teacher immediacy behaviors has been conducted, one cannot make the aforementioned assumption. In fact, perhaps the reverse could be expected. Due to the hierarchical nature inherent in the culture and educational system of Japan, it would be more logical to deduce that teachers would be less immediate than their U.S. counterparts. And, those Japanese students being accustomed to that relationship would neither expect nor feel comfortable with teachers who exhibit immediate behaviors in the classroom. No research has been found which addresses this subject. So, while it may seem reasonable to assume that immediate teacher behaviors exist in Japanese classrooms, there is as of yet, no empirical evidence. In order to address this void in the extant research, it was one of the goals of this study to observe the instructional behaviors of both Japanese and Non-Japanese teachers, within the Japanese educational system, to determine the types of teacher behaviors the teachers and students perceive as affecting student motivation.

THE STUDY

The particular theoretical and pedagogical goals of this study were:

a. to examine the generalizability of teacher immediacy behaviors cross-culturally,

b. to add to a cross-cultural understanding of what influences students' motivation to learn, and
c. to examine the relationship between teachers' immediacy behaviors and students' motivation to learn.

To meet these goals the following research questions were addressed.

RQ 1 What factors do Japanese students and teachers, and non Japanese teachers perceive as sources of student motivation and demotivation in the classroom?
RQ 2. Are there significant differences between student perceptions of Japanese and non-Japanese teacher immediacy behaviors?

Research Design/Methods

In order to answer these questions, I utilized both qualitative and quantitative methods of data collection and analysis. This approach allowed me to combine the objectivity of validated measures of motivation and immediacy with the rich description born of case studies involving observation and interviews. Methodological triangulation was obtained through the use of multiple measures and analyses. For example, open-ended questionnaires were used to collect information that was then used to aid in the observation of teacher behavior frequencies, which in turn was corroborated with data from interviews and field notes. Verbal and nonverbal immediacy scores were used to comp are student perceptions of teacher behaviors, which were then triangulated with data collected through teacher and student interviews and field notes. The combined methodology implemented in this study was aimed at supplying detailed understanding and interpretations of the subjective world of the participants, in an attempt to understand the processes by which they construct meaning.

The study took place in two high school English classes in a large metropolitan city in Japan. In order to examine the cultural influences of teacher behaviors, I chose classes that were team-taught by both Japanese and non-Japanese teachers. The 80 students who participated were third year students, the equivalent of 11th graders in the U.S. After conducting a pilot study, I spent six months conducting full classroom observations.

To solicit descriptive information from the teachers and students about general factors of student motivation versus specific teacher behaviors I distributed two open-ended questionnaires during the fifth week of classes. The questionnaires were modeled after those developed by Gorham and Christophel (1992, 1995). The first focused on general motivational factors, which were defined as any attitude, behavior, and/or circumstance that might be perceived as motivating or demotivating to the students within the context of high school. The second questionnaire required the participants to focus specifically on teacher behaviors they perceived as motivating or demotivating. This procedure allowed for the separation of freely generated teacher behaviors found in the first questionnaire, from those generated by the second.

To provide a cross-cultural examination of perceived teacher immediacy behaviors and their relationship to student motivation, the students were asked to complete a modified version of the Verbal Immediacy Scale (Gorham, 1988) and the Nonverbal Immediacy Scale (Richmond et al., 1987). This was done seven weeks into the semester, so as to allow the students time to become familiar with their teachers' behaviors. Both scales have been used in previous research on immediacy and are considered to be valid measures of immediacy behaviors (Christophel, 1990; Gorham & Zakahi, 1990; Sanders & Wiseman, 1990). Christophel (1990) reports the measures as having produced high reliability levels of .94 and .86 to .98 respectively.

While these scales have been found reliable within previously studied populations (predominately Euro-Americans), it became clear through the pilot study and subsequent class observations that the instruments would have to be adjusted slightly to accurately reflect the population in this study. Three items were eliminated from the Verbal Immediacy Scale (Gorham, 1988) because they were not applicable to the context or the similarity of items made it difficult to translate. For instance, the item from the original scale, "calls on students to answer questions even if they have not indicated that they want to talk" was eliminated because it is common practice in Japanese classes for teachers to call on students. It is a very rare occasion in which a student will offer an unsolicited opinion. One item from the Nonverbal Immediacy Scale (Richmond et al., 1987) was eliminated because it did not fit the context "Sits behind a desk while teaching." This item was eliminated because there were no desks for the teachers to sit behind. Two additional items concerning touch were changed to meet the goals of the research. McCroskey et al. (1995) claimed that touch "should not be considered a variable which is commonly employed by teachers...to enhance their immediacy" (p. 289), because it is rarely used at the high school or college level. Touch is used as a variable in this study, however, because it was observed as a frequent behavior in the classes studied. Teachers were often observed touching students' shoulders or arms during close conversation, or tapping students' heads with pencils or books to get attention or discipline. Therefore, one item about touch on the original scale was translated into two items for this study reflecting positive and negative types of touch. The modified instrument produced an alpha rating of .86. Content analysis, as well as descriptive and inferential statistics was used to examine and categorize the data.

The main focus of the observations was frequency counts of verbal and nonverbal interactions between teachers and students. The behaviors were chosen from teacher and students responses to the questionnaires, extant research, and through initial classroom observations during the pilot study. In conjunction with the frequency counts of teacher behaviors, I took field notes on student/teacher, student/student, and teacher/ teacher interactions. The field notes contained details about setting, context, participants, timing, and interactions, as well as my own thoughts and reflections about these contextual features. They mainly served to record the interactions between participants and the general classroom environment in order to identify the context from which the teacher behaviors and student motivation arose.

Finally, interviews were used to access information that could not be directly observed. They were conducted at the beginning and end of the observation period, and were extremely useful in providing in-depth information from the participants regarding their perspectives of teacher behaviors and student motivation.

DISCUSSION AND INTERPRETATION OF RESULTS

While the original manuscript of this study is ripe with statistical results, I have chosen not to include them in this chapter, but rather focus more on the major outcomes of the research. The following sections include the synthesized results for research questions one and two.

Sources of Motivation and Demotivation (RQ1)

Table 1 illustrates the categories that emerged from the content analysis of the questionnaires and the distribution of responses by the teachers and students.

On the whole, the results indicate that teachers and students basically agree on a set of factors central to student motivation to do well in school. Both teachers and students mentioned ten of the 14 motivator and demotivator categories generated by the first questionnaire. However, the frequency with which the categories were reported revealed a gaping difference between teacher and student perceptions of the sources of student motivation. The students perceived context factors, such as parental pressure and the need for good grades, as central to their motivation to do well in school. In contrast, the four teachers perceived their own behaviors to be the most influential factors for both motivating and demotivating the students in their classes. Furthermore, they reported that negative teacher behaviors contributed most to their demotivation in school. This finding is consistent with previous research that indicates students tend to perceive

TABLE 1
Categories for Coding Student and Teacher Responses

CONTEXT	
C1	Internal Motivators; personal growth, likes school/subject (N = 57; S/55, T/2)
C2	Internal Demotivators; personal laziness, physical tiredness, dislike of school/subject (N = 67; S/64, T/3)
C3	External Motivators; want good grades, please parents, pass exams, friends, club activities (N = 170; S/166, T/4)
C4	External Demotivators; parental/societal pressure, qualifying exams, club activities, time of day (N = 33; S/28, T/5)

STRUCTURE/FORMAT	
S1	Comprehension; ability to understand/follow the teacher and/or course (N = 17)
S2	Lack of Comprehension; not able to understand/follow the teacher and/or course material (N = 51)
S3	Class Atmosphere-positive; fun, interesting, active (N = 36)
S4	Class Atmosphere-negative; boring, not fun or active (N = 61)
S5	Organization of Class/Materials-positive; use of audio/visual aids, student participation, speaking English, group work, use a variety of teaching methods, being well prepared (N = 63; S/47, T/16)
S6	Organization of Class/Materials-negative; no student participation poor text, only learn to pass test, too many notes, lecture same as book, lack of preparation, uncompleted tasks, pointless activities (N = 57; S/32, T/25)

TEACHER BEHAVIORS	
T1	Caring/Approachable; good personality, approachable, caring, interested in students, cheerful, nice, reward effort, pay attention to and meet student needs (N = 150; S/127, T/23)
T2	Uncaring/Unapproachable; strict, critical, ignores students, sarcastic, berating students in class, conflict with students or other teachers. lack of patience (N = 134; S/123, T/11)
T3	Presentation of Material-positive; enthusiastic, use of appropriate self disclosure, answers questions clearly, teacher student interaction (N = 126; S/113, T/13)
T4	Presentation of Material-negative; not enthusiastic, poor writing skills, too much self disclosure, bad jokes, confusion (N = 55, S/50, T/5)
T5*	Immediate Nonverbal; smile, funny movements, gentle touch, move around the room, gestures (N = 25; S/22, T/3)
T6*	Non-immediate Nonverbal; touch, frown, no eye contact, distracting gestures, looking angry (N = 54; S/52, T/2)
T7*	Verbal-positive; speaks clearly, good pronunciation, vocal variety (N = 48; S/46, T/2)

(continued)

TABLE 1 (Continued)

T8*	Verbal-negative; poor pronunciation, nags, scolds, speaks too softly. too much Japanese spoken (N = 87; S/85, T/2)
T9*	Competent/Knowledgeable; (N = 8)
T10*	Not Competent/Low Credibility; (N = 28)
T11*	Humor-positive; (N = 3)
T12*	Humor-negative; (N = 2)

Notes: N = number of descriptions
S = student responses
T = teacher responses
* = these categories were produced only from the 2nd questionnaire
Note: Categories only reporting one N (N = 28) are student responses.

motivation as a "student-owned" concept and demotivation as a "teacher-owned" problem (Christophel and Gorham, 1995).

These findings are significant because they indicate an imbalance between teacher and student perceptions concerning student motivation. Therefore, if we who teach want to motivate our students to learn, one step we should take is to find out what behaviors our students perceive as motivating and demotivating. The next step then would be to reflect on our own perceptions of our behavior in order to find the areas of agreement and imbalance. This idea may seem simplistic, but as the next section shows, it is often not as easy as it sounds.

In order to answer the research question two, a second open-ended questionnaire was used to focus the study on teacher behaviors. The participants were asked to describe specific teacher behaviors that they perceived as either motivating or demotivating in their classes. The goal was to discover 1) what behaviors the teachers thought they exhibited that motivated their students and 2) what differences (if any) the students perceived between their Japanese and non-Japanese teachers' behaviors.

Teacher Perceptions and Observations of Immediacy Behaviors

Overall, the teachers reported a desire to motivate their students and discussed strategies for achieving that goal. The Japanese teachers felt that the organization of course materials and the classroom environment were essential to student motivation, while the non-Japanese teachers spoke more about displaying caring and enthusiastic behaviors in order to motivate their students. Although the results indicate that the teachers believed they influenced their students' motivation, and perceived themselves as exhibiting motivating behaviors, the observations of their in-class behaviors did not always reflect that. Both student report and classroom observation data often contradicted the teachers' perceptions of their own behaviors. For instance, one teacher who perceived himself as motivating his students through encouragement, rarely praised or offered critiques of student work or participation in class. On the whole, the teachers seemed unaware of the negative impact their non-immediate or "mis" behaviors had on their students, and placed more emphasis on their personal abilities to motivate their students. These findings are consistent with earlier results found by Gorham (1985) that indicate teachers are not always aware of their behaviors.

Teacher Immediacy Behaviors

As a way of situating the next set of findings, I want to revisit the two opposing assumptions presented earlier about possible cultural influences on the perception of immediacy behaviors. The first assumption stemmed from the holistic Japanese approach to education. Because the professed educational goal is to successfully nurture the intellectual, emotional, spiritual, and physical growth of students, I made the assumption that immediate teacher behaviors, as defined in the extant research, would be present in Japanese classrooms. And, that students would expect and desire their teachers to display immediate behaviors. The opposing assumption was made in light of the overarching differences in communication styles between Japanese and North Americans. So, due to the hierarchical nature inherent in the culture and educational system of Japan, it seemed perhaps more logical to deduce that teachers would be less immediate than their U.S. counterparts, and that Japanese students, being accustomed to that relationship, would neither expect nor feel comfortable with teachers who exhibit immediacy behaviors in the classroom.

Analysis of the data provided mixed results that both support and reject the aforementioned assumptions. First, the findings indicate that the students perceived their Japanese teachers as less immediate than their non-Japanese counterparts. The students reported that their Japanese teachers were too strict and formal, and did not seem to care as much about the individual needs or progress of students as they did about completing lesson plans. This perception is supported by the reports from the Japanese teachers who indicated they believed that a well-organized and executed lesson plan was one of the top sources of motivation for their students. This finding supports the assumption that students want immediate behaviors, but also seems to reject the assumption that those behaviors exist in the Japanese classroom. However, it should not be seen as completely rejecting the first assumption (that immediacy behaviors would be employed by Japanese teachers), because it is not known how the students may have perceived their Japanese teachers' behaviors before being introduced to the non-Japanese teachers' behaviors. The introduction of the foreign teachers into the educational environment may have biased student perceptions of their Japanese teachers' immediacy behaviors.

Overall however, results indicate that the Japanese students did prefer the more immediate behaviors exhibited by the non-Japanese teachers. Several students indicated, during the interviews, that they felt the non-Japanese teachers cared more about them as individuals. Observations also showed that they were more likely to praise students, use direct eye contact, and smile at the class and individuals than the Japanese teachers. This finding rejects the second assumption, which indicated a positive correlation between cultural expectations about status positions and preferences for behaviors that met those expectations. While both of these findings support established theories of immediacy behaviors (Mehrabian, 1969, 1971; Andersen, 1979), they also raise questions about the stability of cultural patterns in the classroom, in light of seemingly "foreign" immediacy behaviors that may be perceived as more caring or student-centered.

CONCLUSION

Five years after my initial encounter with those 30 Japanese students, I stepped from that classroom environment for the last time. Over the years my students and I learned a great deal from our intercultural encounters. And through this study I discovered that my teacher's intuition was right; caring, student centered, personable behaviors both in and out of the classroom can and do have a positive effect on student motivation.

The significance of the findings from this study are that they lend cross-cultural support to basic theories of immediacy behavior; that we are drawn to people who we like and feel close to and move away from those we dislike (Mehrabian, 1971). Of importance also, are the types of teacher behaviors the students claimed to be most motivational. The top ranked motivating factors identified by the students were caring and approachable behaviors, and a positive, thoughtful and enthusiastic presentation of course content. This is consistent with research on motivational factors in the classroom (Butler, 1994; Patrick, Hisley and Kempler, 2000). It is no surprise then that the students reported uncaring and/or unapproachable teacher behaviors as the highest-ranking demotivational factors in their learning experiences. The second ranked factor dealt with the structure of the class atmosphere. Students were demotivated by what they perceived as a static, boring classroom atmosphere that was "not fun or interesting."

What the results of this study indicate, that others have not, is that the students showed preference for teacher behaviors that were not typically found within that cultural context. It may be that in environments like classrooms, the need for acceptance and closeness outweigh other cultural expectations for behavior. Therefore, in an effort to contribute greater understanding of the affects of culture in the classroom, more research needs to be conducted which focuses on diverse cultural groups, both in and outside of the United States. It is my hope that educators, particularly those who teach in multicultural settings, will strive to further understand the impact of immediacy behaviors on student motivation. As teachers learn the types of factors students perceive as motivating and demotivating, they will be better able to develop classroom environments that increase motivation.

While I and the other researches cited here have described behaviors that are deemed immediate, I will not offer you a prescriptive list. Rather, the underlying point seems to be, that teachers need to be reflective about their behavior in ways that account for cultural differences between themselves and their students. Thereby discovering the best ways to motivate, or more importantly to *not demotivate* their students.

REFERENCES

Andersen, J. F. (1979). Teacher immediacy as a predictor of teaching effectiveness. In D. Nimmo (Ed.). *Communication yearbook 3* (pp. 543-449). New Brunswick, NJ: Transaction Books.

Andersen, J. F., Andersen, P. A., & Jensen, A. D. (1979). The measurement of nonverbal immediacy. Journal of *Applied Communication, 7,* 153-180.

Barnlund, D. C. (1975) Communication styles in two cultures: Japan and the United States. In A. Kendone, R. M. Harris, & M. R. Key (Eds.).*Organization of behavior in face-to-face interactions.* Hague, Netherlands: Mouton.

Bettencourt, E. Gillet, M. Gall, M. & Hull, R. (1983). Effects of teacher enthusiasm training on student on-task behavior and achievement.*American Educational Research Journal, 20,* 435-450.

Blumenfeld, P.C. (1992). Classroom learning and motivation: Clarifying and expanding goal theory.*Journal of Educational Psychology, 84(3),* 272-281.

Brigham, F.J., Scruggs, T.E., & Mastropieri, M.A. (1992). Teacher enthusiasm in learning disabilities classrooms: Effects on learning and behavior.*Learning Disabilities Research and Practice, 7,* 68-73.

Brophy, J. (1981). Teacher praise: A functional analysis. *Review of Educational Research, 51,* 5-32.

Brophy, J. E. (1987). On motivating students. In D. C. Berliner & B. V. Rosenshine (Eds.). *Talks to teachers* (pp. 201-245). New York, NY: Random House.

Butler, R. (1994). Teacher communications and student interpretations: Effects of teacher responses to failing students on attributional inferences in two age groups. *British Journal of Educational Psychology, 64, 277-294.*

Christophel, D. M. (1990). The relationship among teacher immediacy behaviors, student motivation, and learning. *Communication Education, 39,* 323-340.

Christophel, D. M. & Gorham, J. (1995). A test-retest analysis of student motivation, teacher immediacy, and perceived sources of motivation and demotivation in college classes. *Communication Education, 44,* 292-306.

Collier, M. J. & Powell, R. (1990). Ethnicity, instructional communication and classroom systems. *Communication Quarterly, 38,* 334-349.

Damen, L. (1987). *Culture learning: The fifth dimension in the language classroom.* Reading, MA: Addison-Wesley.

DeVito, J. A. (1991). *The interpersonal communication book.* New York, NY: Random House

Frymier, A. B. (1993). The impact of teacher immediacy on students' motivation: Is it the same for all students? *Communication Quarterly, 41,* 454-464.

Gorham, J. (1988). The relationship between verbal teacher immediacy behaviors and student learning. *Communication Education, 37,* 40-53.

Gorham, J., & Christophel, D. M. (1990). The relationship of teachers' use of humor in the classroom to immediacy and student learning, *Communication Education, 39,* 46-62.

Gorham, J., & Christophel, D. M. (1992). Students' perceptions of teacher behaviors as motivating and demotivating factors in college classes. *Communication Quarterly, 40,* 239-252.

Gorham, J. & Millette, D. M. (1997). A comparative analysis of teacher and student perceptions of sources of motivation and demotivation in college classes. *Communication Education, 46,* 245-261.

Gudykundst, W.B. (1991). Bridging differences: Effective intergroup communication. Thousand Oaks, CA: Sage.

Hall, E. T. (1977). *Beyond Culture.* Garden City, NY: Anchor.

Hofstede, G. (1982). *Culture's consequences* (abridged ed.). Newbury Park, CA: Sage.

Kasser, T. & Ryan, R.M. (1996). Further examining the American dream: Differential correlates of intrinsic and extrinsic goals. *Personality and Social Psychology Bulletin, 22, 280-287.*

Kelley, D. H., & Gorham, J. (1988). Effects of immediacy on recall of information. *Communication Education, 37,*198-207.

Lustig, M.W. & Koester, J. (1999). Intercultural competence: Interpersonal communication across cultures (3rd ed.). New York, NY: Longman.

McCroskey, J. C., Richmond, V. P., Sallinen, A., Fayer, J. M. & Barraclough, R. A. (1995). A cross-cultural and multi-behavioral analysis of the relationship between nonverbal immediacy and teacher evaluation. *Communication Education, 44,* 281-291

McCroskey, J. C., Sallinen, A., Fayer, J. M., Richmond, V. P. & Barraclough, R. A. (1996). Nonverbal immediacy and cognitive learning: A cross-cultural investigation. *Communication Education, 45,* 200-211.

Mehrabian, A. (1969). Some referents and measures of nonverbal behavior. *Behavior Research Methods and Instrumentation, 1, 203-207.*

Mehrabian, A. (1971). *Silent messages.* Belmont, CA: Wadsworth.

Moore, A., Masterson, J. T., Christophel, D. M. & Shea, K. A. (1996). College teachers' immediacy and student ratings of instruction. *Communication Education, 45,* 29-39.

National Center for Educational Statistics (2000). Online document nces.edu.gov/pubs2001/digest/dt413.html.

Neuliep, J. W. (1995). A comparison of teacher immediacy in African-American and Euro-American college classrooms. *Communication Education, 44,* 266-277.

Patrick, B. C., Hisley, J. & Kempler, T. (2000). 'What's everybody so excited about?': The effects of teacher enthusiasm on student intrinsic motivation and vitality. *Journal of Experiential Education, 68,* 217-237.

Pintrinch, P. R. & Schunk, D. H. (1996). *Motivation in education: Theory, research, and applications.* Englewood Cliffs, NJ: Merrill-Prentice Hall.

Powell, R. G. & Harville, B. (1990). The effects of teacher immediacy and clarity on instructional outcomes: An intercultural assessment. *Communication Education, 39,* 367-379.

Richmond, V. P., Gorham, J., & McCroskey, J. C. (1987). The relationship between selected immediacy behaviors and cognitive learning. In M. McLaughlin (Ed.). *Communication yearbook 10* (pp. 574-590). Beverly Hills, CA: Sage.

Richmond, V. P., McCroskey, J. C., & Payne, S. K. (1987). *Nonverbal behavior in interpersonal relationships.* Englewood Cliffs, NJ: Prentice-Hall

Samovar, L. A. & Porter, R. E. (1995). *Communications between cultures* (2nd ed.). Belmont, CA: Wadsworth.

Sanders, J. A. & Wiseman, R. L. (1990). The effects of verbal and nonverbal teacher immediacy on perceived cognitive, affective, and behavioral learning in the multicultural classroom. *Communication Education, 39,* 341-353.

Sorensen, G. (1989). The relationships among teachers' self-disclosive statements, students' perceptions, and affective learning. *Communication Education, 38,* 259-276.

Thweatt, K.S., & McCroskey, J.C. (1998). The impact of teacher immediacy and misbehaviors on teacher credibility. *Communication Education, 47, 348-357.*

CHAPTER 9

THE SOCIAL MEDIATION OF METACOGNITION

Gregory P. Thomas

INTRODUCTION

I came to a teaching career relatively late in life, at age 28. Prior to teaching high school science I had many jobs. These included insurance clerk, customs officer, sporting goods salesperson, professional sports coach, and semi-professional musician. Engaging in such a range of occupations, if nothing else taught me the value of effective learning. While at university my interest in learning theory and practice and the concept of metacognition was further fueled through contact with people like John Edwards, then at James Cook University, and Dick White at Monash University who were passionate about its study. Such people fired a strong desire in me to teach students how to learn as well as what to learn. Consequently, as a teacher I was always interested in my students' learning, how they learnt, and how to improve their learning. However, much to my surprise this interest was not shared by many staff and students in the schools I taught at. Indeed, the response to my suggestions that students' learning processes and metacognition could and should be improved as an important goal of schooling often met with significant uncertainty and resistance from both groups. This resistance was evident even among some students and teachers who acknowledged the potential value of initiating classroom and curriculum change to improve students' learning strategies and metacognition. I asked myself, "Why was this? What might be the source/s of such uncertainty and resistance?" Surely, if such ideas could improve students' learning then they would be embraced. I thought this should be the case because predictions that enormous premiums would be placed on people's learning efficiency in times of information expansion and social change (e.g., Toffler, 1970) seemed to be being realized. This chapter is an exploration of sociocultural influences of such student resistance and uncertainty. In particular I suggest that students' socially situated and influenced conceptions of teaching and learning, elements of their metacognitive knowledge, substantially influence students' willingness to engage in changing their learning processes and enhancing their metacognition.

METACOGNITION: IMPLICATIONS OF THE IMPORTANCE OF STUDENTS' CONCEPTIONS OF TEACHING AND LEARNING

The importance of metacognition in learning is widely acknowledged (e.g., Hacker, 1998; Sternberg, 1998). Adey and Shayer (1994, p. 67) suggest that metacognition is a "feature of the development of higher-order thinking which seems to carry almost universal support from cognitive psychologists." Studies spanning curriculum areas and student ages have consistently found that enhancing students' metacognition can result in improved learning and that students who are metacognitive seem to achieve better learning outcomes (e.g., Baird, 1986; Biggs, 1986; Garner, 1987; Paris & Winograd, 1990). Not surprisingly therefore, recent years have seen an increase in interest and research related to metacognition. This upsurge is congruent with an increasing educational focus on developing students as life-long learners who possess cognitive and metacognitive strategies that enable them to understand and use information from an ever-increasing range of sources.

While the importance of metacognition is widely accepted, synthesis of a precise and universally accepted definition of metacognition is an ongoing issue (e.g., Hacker, 1998; Kirby, 1984; White, 1988, 1998). Early definitions of metacognition, (e.g., Flavell, 1979; Garner and Alexander, 1989) defined metacognition as a student's knowledge, control and awareness of his or her learning processes. However, more recent considerations of what constitutes metacognition (for a review, see Hacker, 1998) delineate three components that are similar to those in the earlier definitions: Metacognitive Knowledge; Metacognitive Monitoring; and Metacognitive Regulation. Irrespective of which definition is preferred, both earlier and more recent conceptualizations acknowledge metacognitive knowledge as a fundamental constituent of metacognition. Flavell defined metacognitive knowledge as an individual's knowledge and beliefs about the factors influencing the course and consequences of his/her cognitive enterprises. According to Ertmer and Newby (1996, p. 6) metacognitive knowledge provides learners with, "the personal insights needed to regulate their learning processes in relation to changing task demands." The metacognitive knowledge of students' may include their knowledge of, for example, theirs and others' learning strategies, motivations, beliefs, opinions, theories and attitudes. Students' conceptions of learning and teaching can also be considered as integral, important elements of students' metacognitive knowledge. These conceptions together with the sociocultural factors that influence them are a focus of this chapter. Indeed, Gunstone (1992), Marton (1988), and Schmeck (1988) have suggested that it is possible to understand students' learning as, at least, the partial consequence of such conceptions. Further, McRobbie and I (Thomas & McRobbie, 1999) found that students' conceptions of themselves as learners were congruent with the learning processes they employed. These conceptions are often tacit and characterized by images of student passivity and teacher transmission of information (see, e.g., Tasker, 1981; Baird & Mitchell, 1987; Berry & Sahlberg, 1996). Therefore they conflict with the images of students as metacognitive learners that are often promoted within contemporary education discourse. Such learners would actively participate in classroom life and consciously construct and critique knowledge on the basis of their learning experiences and prior knowledge.

While research on students' conceptions of learning is substantial, less is known about the individual development of such conceptions or why and how they change (Tynjälä, 1997). Little is also known about what sustains these conceptions or, if a student reports knowledge and awareness of more than one conception, what factors influence the enactment of a particular conception or conceptions. While it is valuable to consider all elements of metacognitive knowledge in developing a complete understanding metacognition, my aim in this chapter is to be selective. I seek to highlight the significance of, and the need to consider, socio-cultural factors as important influences on students' conceptions of learning and teaching and therefore on their metacognition. To do so involves selecting an appropriate sociological lens for trying to understand the social worlds that students perceive they inhabit and the influence of such worlds on their conceptions of learning and teaching. Investigating how students individually experience their social worlds and how such experiences influence their metacognition has the potential to add a further dimension to conceptualizing metacognition. Therefore, firstly, I consider relevant perspectives on learning and teaching which acknowledge the social and situated nature of students' learning. This is to provide a conceptual lens through which students' intimations regarding their conceptions and the origins of these conceptions can be viewed and interpreted. I then draw on data from research conducted while I was a classroom teacher and propose a model and a set of principles for understanding metacognition as socially mediated. Finally, I propose implications of such a position for future research into metacognition.

LEARNING AS SOCIALLY MEDIATED AND SITUATED

Considering socio-cultural factors in relation to students' conceptions of learning and teaching, and therefore their metacognition, is prudent given that assumptions regarding the value of separating the individual from his/her environment are increasingly called into question (Roth, 2000). For example, Nuthall (1999) has suggested that students' learning processes are "deeply embedded in, or are, in fact, part of the sociocultural processes and structures of the classroom" (p. 244). His assertion is congruent with those of situated learning theorists such as Lave (1990), Lave & Wenger (1991) and Rogoff (1990) who have made a significant contribution to understanding the socially situated nature of learning.

Much early research into metacognition was concerned with investigating interventions aimed at enhancing metacognition. However, rarely, if ever, did such research seek to understand deeply the reasons for the success or otherwise of such interventions from students' perspectives. Metacognition was often conceptualized, with some exceptions (e.g., Day, French & Hall, 1985), as a psychological construct that was uninfluenced by students' social situatedness. However, consideration of social and situational influences in relation to cognition and metacognition and, in some cases, exploration and interpretation of students' perceptions and opinions is increasingly prominent in more recent educational literature (e.g., McInerney, Hinkley, Dowson, & Van Etten, 1998; Pressley, Van Etten, Yokoi, Freebern, & Van Meter, 1998; Ryan, 2000; Schunk & Zimmerman, 1996; Thomas, 1999b; Vosniadou, 1996). Such research and scholarship has either explicitly or implicitly addressed the situationally-variable and multiply-determined nature of cognition and metacognition.While there has been an increase in research that acknowledges the socially situated nature of metacognition, such studies have not explicitly employed a sociological lens for interpreting students' intimations regarding their conceptions of learning and teaching and the influences on such conceptions. I have found the perspectives of critical theorists, for example, Bordieau (1977, 1984, 1989) and McLaren (1986, 1994) of particular interest and value for such purposes. This is not to suggest that other frameworks may not also be useful for such a purpose. My interest in critical theorists stems from their concern about how students learn as well as what they learn, and their casting of doubt on traditional models of teaching (Herideen, 1998). However, my aim is not to attend to the issues of class relationships and culture power relations that are often the focus of critical theorists. Instead my interest is in utilizing their concepts of hegemony and *habitus* for the purposes of understanding students' conceptions of learning and teaching.

Hegemony can be used to describe the system of cultural or ideological domination of one group by another. McLaren (1986) suggests that hegemony "creates an ideology pervasive and potent enough to penetrate the level of common sense through taken-for-granted rules of discourse" (p. 82). This hegemony might be considered as both an element and product of the *habitus* (Bordieau, 1977, 1984, 1989) that is, embodied culture in the form of internalized dispositions and values that guide individuals' behaviors and are internalized by them. While noting that it conjures notions of habit, Bordieau (1984) suggests the *habitus* is something that is acquired from early socialization experiences in which eternal structures become incorporated in the individual as permanent dispositions to the extent that it appears innate. Therefore it has its origins in individuals' histories. He insists that *habitus* is generative and that while it is a product of conditionings, it reproduces the objective logic of those conditionings so that the social conditions of our own production are reproduced.

Support for the influence of the *habitus* in schooling is found in the discourse and metaphors used to describe and, some would argue, direct the processes of schooling. Metaphors pervade individuals' everyday lives in discourse, thought and action and underpin social cognition (Lakoff & Johnson, 1980; Lakoff, 1993). I have noted (Thomas, 1999a; Thomas and McRobbie, 1999) that a dominant metaphor for schools is 'school as workplace.' This metaphor, championed by Doyle (1983, 1986), is pervasive and generally unquestioned in social discourse despite its lack of emphasis on student autonomy and knowledge construction. Accordingly, students often perceive the purpose of attending school to work rather than to learn. The enactment of such metaphors, for example, 'school as a workplace' and 'learning as work' often results in the passive subordination of students and the assumption that learning is predominantly characterized by the transfer of knowledge between teachers and students occurring mainly via a verbal conduit.

In the case studies that follow I highlight evidence for the existence of a pedagogical hegemony within one of my past schools as well as evidence for the existence of the *habitus*. However, my goal is to highlight the sociocultural mediation of students' conceptions of learning and teaching. Therefore, I argue that the pedagogical hegemony within that school, itself a product of the *habitus*, was a key factor influencing students' conceptions of learning and teaching and therefore their metacognition.

School and Classroom Research Contexts

The data interpreted below come from an eighteen-week interpretive study in which I sought to enhance the metacognition of 24 students' in a past Year 11 Chemistry classroom. An interpretive research approach was seen as ideal because interpretive research is concerned with "human social actions and opinions that are locally distinct and situationally contingent"(Erickson, 1998, p. 1155). However, the selection of this research approach means that readers should identify contextual factors that they perceive as similar between the context of this classroom and school and those classrooms and schools they are familiar with in order to draw generalizations.

I was the students' normal chemistry teacher and in addition to my normal teaching responsibilities I took on the role of a participant observer. Because the appropriateness of enhancing students' metacognition as part of typical classroom instruction rather than as part of laboratory studies has been highlighted (e.g., White, 1992; Petersen & Swing, 1983; Duffy & Roehler, 1989), the intervention occurred within students' regular academic instruction. This strengthened the research's ecological validity (Bronfenbrenner, 1979). While such naturalistic enquiry is not without critics (Cohen & Manion, 1994), this research adopted the widely used and accepted trustworthiness criteria of Guba and Lincoln (1989, 1997) to ensure that the research was credible, dependable and confirmable. Further, I had an ethical responsibility for ensuring that the research was compatible with the students' education and well being and that I privileged their learning ahead of my research agenda. This meant that informed consent for the research was obtained from the school, the students and their parents/guardians, and that any member of the class could withdraw from the research or any research related activities at any time.

The school was an independent (private) secondary college operated by a mainline Protestant denomination in Queensland, Australia. I was employed as the Head of the Science Department to teach the senior level subjects chemistry, biology and multi-strand science. My students were mainly from families of middle-class, small business backgrounds that enjoyed above average incomes. The school was well respected for its academic standards.

In the school year in which the research was undertaken, and prior to the research itself, I initiated changes to the chemistry classroom learning environment to make it more constructivist oriented, more student centered and increasingly student controlled. Students were given a wider range of learning opportunities and more freedom to flexibly plan their learning paths. I saw this as important because if we truly want to enhance students' knowledge, monitoring and regulation of their learning processes, then their learning environments should be those in which they have opportunities to take control, regulate their learning strategies, and negotiate responsibility for their learning (Zimmerman, 1994; Thomas, 2001). Such psychosocial dimensions are characteristics of metacognitively oriented learning environments. Students perceived the learning environment in their chemistry classroom to be very different to that of their previous science classrooms. For example, they reported noticeable differences, measured using the Constructivist Learning Environment Survey (CLES)(Taylor, Fraser, and White, 1994), between the learning environ-

TABLE 1
Class Mean Scores Of Students' Perceptions of Their Year 10 Science
Classroom and Their Year 11 Chemistry Classroom*

		Critical Voice	*Shared Control*	*Student Negotiation*
Year 10 Classroom	Mean	18.57	11.11	17.52
	S.D.	5.52	4.54	4.21
Year 11 Classroom	Mean	22.83	19.33	25.12
	S.D.	3.92	4.23	3.37

Notes: NB: Maximum possible score on each scale = 30
　　　　*(n=24)

ments of their Year 10 Science classrooms and their Year 11 Chemistry classroom. The differences were expressed in relation to the degree of (a) Critical voice; the extent to which students feel it is legitimate and beneficial to question the teachers' pedagogical plans and methods (b) Shared control; the extent to which students are invited to share control with the teacher of the learning environment, and (c) Student negotiation; the extent to which opportunities are available for students to explain and justify their evolving ideas (Table 1). These sub-scales within the CLES have internal reliabilities (using Cronbach alpha as a convenient index) of 0.85, 0.91, & 0.89 respectively (Fraser, 1998). The intervention to enhance the students' metacognition took place within such a classroom environment.

LEARNING IS CONSTRUCTING: AN INTERVENTION CENTERED ON METAPHOR

The intervention centered around the metaphor "learning is constructing." I used the metaphor to stimulate the students to seek mappings (Gentner, 1989, 1990) between the concepts of learning and constructing. I was trying to promote ideas like the importance of prior knowledge and the need to construct new understanding on basis of such prior knowledge by providing a metacognitive experience for students, that is, a conscious cognitive experience that was related to their learning (Flavell, 1979). Because metaphor is central to communication I chose to use it to facilitate the development of a shared language of learning and a conception of learning that might be understood and usable by all classroom participants. Developing such a language is necessary because, while the language of learning mediates learning (Shayer & Adey, 1993) and metacognition is enhanced by a rich language of thinking (Perkins, Jay, & Tishman, 1995; Tishman & Perkins, 1997), students have been found to lack a language to discuss the cognitive aspects of their learning processes (Macdonald, 1990). I gave students opportunities to interpret and consider the metaphor in relation to their current conceptions and practices of learning. This was to encourage them to (a) become more aware of their tacit metacognitive knowledge and their learning strategies, (b) modify their conceptions of learning and their learning strategies, and (c) take control of their new or modified learning strategies as they saw appropriate. In doing so they were also engaged in considering their conceptions of the teacher's role in their learning.

The results of the intervention specifically relating to changes in students' metacognition have been previously reported (Thomas, 1999a, 1999b; Thomas & McRobbie, 2001). The intervention succeeded in communicating a conception of learning that was, for most students, contrary to their existing, predominantly tacit conceptions. Twelve students reported changes to their enacted conceptions of learning and teaching as reflected in, for example, their

a.   engagement of a deep approach to learning,
b.   thinking processes for constructing understanding, and
c.   approaches to problem solving. These changes were interpreted as evidence of enhanced metacognition and learning processes.

Most of these students reported that these changes resulted in improved learning outcomes in relation to their formal assessment outcomes or their levels of understanding of course material. Debbie and Tim (all names are pseudonyms) are representative of these students. The remaining students reported that their enacted conceptions of learning and teaching were essentially unaltered. This was despite them reporting that the conception of learning and the learning strategies that they derived from interpreting the metaphor were intelligible, plausible, and fruitful for them. Max is a representative of these students.

The following case studies for Debbie, Tim and Max reflect the data, analyses, and findings from across all the students. The cases are used to enable readers to share in the students' lived experiences and situatedness as they came to consider their conceptions of learning and their learning processes, whether or not to change such conceptions and enact such changes, and the socio-cultural factors that influenced their considerations.

Debbie

Prior to the intervention, Debbie defined learning as

accepting that you don't know something and the teacher does, that you want to know it and learn it, and studying, practicing or extending on something to improve or acquire a skill.

She claimed that performing the available classroom activities was in itself sufficient to learn, but acknowledged the tenuous nature of her views. "I think that by just doing the different classroom activities that learning will take place...I know that's not right but that's what I think." Her enactment of such conceptions resulted in her being a passive learner.

> I'm more one who just sits there. That's just what I'm used to. I've got into the habit over three years of just remembering things for a test and then just forgetting about it. I do that for all my other subjects but especially for science because that's all I used to do in science and that's all I found it used to be. Due to habit and familiarity I find it easier to receive precise information from teachers and store it for later recall. We'd be having a lesson and I'd just write down everything that teachers wrote up on the board. I got so used to that. I just did it. I didn't even think.

The origins of Debbie's conceptions and learning strategies could be traced to her past classroom learning environments including her past teachers. She had relied on her past teachers to the extent that she preferred a transmissionist teacher pedagogy and she sought to cast responsibility for monitoring her learning to me.

> I've found it a bit difficult [in the chemistry class] because sometimes I'm not really sure what I should do. I went from relying on the teacher in every classroom to tell me what to do and to tell me to have something done, like, "Do this for homework and have it done by the next lesson." When I came here it was such a big change and I found it really hard. Last year the teacher would have said, "Do this" and I'd do it...I got very used to teachers telling me what to do and I just got used to just doing it.

Debbie was dissatisfied with her learning quality, which she assessed primarily with reference to her examination results. For example, commenting on the results of an examination taken immediately prior to the research's commencement she noted, "I was happy to pass, but I wasn't too pleased with it. I wasn't expecting any better because I knew I didn't understand or know the work." Not surprisingly therefore, Debbie was willing to make changes to improve her grades and suggested, "I'd have a go at changing it [the way I learn] if I knew an effective way to do it."

Following the intervention there were noticeable changes in her conception of learning. She was able to compare her new perspective with that of her past:

> I thought that just by doing things the learning would happen, which is a physical thing...I think I focussed on the physical aspect more than the men-

tal aspect. But I realize that it's not like that. It [learning] is something that happens mentally. I could write and listen all I wanted, but until I started processing information in my mind, I couldn't learn. When I say processing I mean finding where it fits into the 'construction' already in my mind—finding the links and extending my construction, at the same time developing my understanding.

Debbie was one who persisted with enacting the conception of learning from her interpretation of the metaphor and could describe her new learning strategies. For example, in relation to dealing with new information, she stated:

I try to relate it to what I already know to use it better...I ask myself more questions like "Where does this fit in my mind? What does x tell me about y? Asking these questions makes me start linking and relating concepts.

Despite the benefits of enacting her new conceptions of learning, Debbie found it "very hard" to engage in personal change. She saw the pressures of school, differences in emphases between teachers, and conflict between other teachers' entreaties to simply work harder as barriers to her implementing the changes she recognized as beneficial. The intervention's timing also brought with it its own set of concerns.

There is pressure on us for our tests to get good marks, because we know they count for our Overall Position (university entry score)...we tend to think, "Is it worth changing it now and taking the risk? We're told all through high school and primary school, especially Years 6 and 7, that they're the years you create habits...and then when I get to Year 11 I'm told [by you] that I've got to change the habit that I've got into of how I learn and that contradicts what we've been told before. At the beginning of Year 11 we get the "Work hard! Work hard!" you know? But for those of us who do, people always bringing it up is just extra stress. My learning process obviously was not effective because I was working hard but not getting good results. And they [teachers] keep saying, "Work hard! Work hard!" and we just keep going and working harder and we think that we're not doing enough.

Tim

Prior to the intervention, Tim defined learning as "the input of new knowledge into your mind, whether it be by books, TV or other students." Tim valued only learning that was directly related to his examination outcomes. He claimed, "I don't spend time on learning things that I know won't be asked in the exam...if we don't need to know it for the test then we don't need to know it." Learning for Tim was a submissive process of accepting information from teacher or text at face value and not consciously integrating this information with prior knowledge. He asserted that a key aspect of his learning processes was "To do work." By "work" he meant, "Just this topic's work...learning all about the topic we're set to be doing this term." This conception of learning as work meant that effort and routine were central considerations in relation to his learning processes. His typical classroom engagement, like that of Debbie, focused on acts of doing rather than mental processes.

> Mostly I just work from the textbook in class...just reading through, and then reading through again and taking notes...reread and re-note...I read the textbook and then I have to just believe what the textbook is saying.

Tim's conceptions and learning processes were derived from his past classrooms. In those classrooms it was not necessary to understand why he learned as he did and foci on low level learning tasks and using prescribed methods for completing such tasks was the norm. Consistent with his view, at the start of Year 11 he had expected to be "just taking notes and reading the textbook" and found the chemistry classroom learning environment threatening. Tim's conceptions had negative consequences for him in the context of the chemistry classroom and he preferred to retain this past conception of learning and the corresponding teaching practices.

> The classroom's not like I thought it would be. I thought it would be a lot like Year 9 and Year 10 where the teacher stood up the front of the class and just said to us, "Read pages this, and then note down this," and we'd just do what the teacher always expected us to do. In the past I copied down off the board and learnt definitions off by heart...we've always been shown how to do it in the correct way." At the start [of Year 11 chemistry] I didn't really like the idea because I didn't think that we'd learn enough just by ourselves. I have a difficulty with the way we're doing it now probably because I've never done it before and it's new for most of us this year. I think a lot of people find it hard learning, or trying to learn, new ways. They've been shown for the past ten years how to learn. It would be easier if we were shown a certain way to do it and then just all done it the same way...In other subjects where we're shown exactly what to do and how to apply it...in every subject I know we do it that way. People like me; I'm not that intelligent to work it out by myself. I basically need a little kick along...that's what happened in the past."

Tim was supportive of the conception of learning proposed by the metaphor stating "I believe that the metaphor is like a construction site...you need the ground floor before you can build the first floor. This is like learning." However, he was guarded about adopting ideas from this interpretation for developing his learning processes, suggesting,

> Yes. It would be good. However, I believe that we should have started this a long time ago, in Grade 8. If we had started earlier I believe that this metaphor would benefit each and every one of us.

Despite acknowledging the potential benefits of enacting such a conception of learning Tim reported no changes to his enacted conception of learning immediately following the intervention and was reluctant to change his learning processes. The metaphor of 'learning is work' was prominent in Tim's defense of his reluctance to change.

> I understand what you're doing but I just can't understand how I can do it if I've been doing this for the last 11 years and suddenly just change   I just feel like I've got to keep on going this way or I'm not going to get anything done and I won't learn anything...I'd rather just get all the work done...I think it [enacting the alternative conception of learning] would work but I don't think it is work.

Tim, however, eventually came to enact, at least partially, the conception of learning he had interpreted from the metaphor. A discussion with his peers was a key element in his about-face. A week after reporting no changes to his enacted conception of learning, Tim stated that he had talked with chemistry classmates on the school bus. All the classmates in the discussion were more academically successful than he was. The discussion had been about, as he put it, "how they got on with what you'd been teaching us [about learning] and if it helps them, and what they actually do to go about learning." During this talk these successful peers told him, "that's how they learnt." These students' views were important for Tim and, consequently, he had consciously decided to enact aspects of the conception he interpreted from the metaphor.

> It [the discussion] was important, because I can see the results that they'd achieved by doing what they'd been doing, and I could see that it's going to get the results...so to help me with my work I decided to take it up.

Following this decision Tim summarized his past learning processes as follows. "I would just read through it, take notes and then just hope to learn it off-by-heart...It was really rote learning." This description was in marked contrast with his new processes and his assessment of their effectiveness. In Tim's intimations we see that, despite the difficulties involved in him addressing his previous view of learning, he exhibits enhanced metacognition. He has new knowledge of learning processes and is able to monitor and regulate the use of such processes.

> As I've been going through my work I've been saying to myself mentally, "Where have I seen this in the past? How does it fit in to what I've done in the past?" It's a lot easier to remember things if you think of learning as constructing because it makes it easier to understand I think. I'm finding out that I'm understanding the whole range of where it [new information] fits in and what it has to do with...I saw that it was much faster and easier to learn and I could understand a lot quicker.

Max

Max had a broader, more constructivist oriented conception of learning than Tim and Debbie. Prior to the intervention, he defined learning as "experimenting, reading, or listening in order to remember facts and information." He suggested, "the activities that are the most important are the ones that help my specific learning style…I prefer reading the information and doing the problems the most." However, he added that he valued tasks that could be used "not just for tests" such as those that assisted "learning how things fit together." He further claimed that performing classroom activities needed to be associated with mental processes.

> There's a step after doing. You've got to do it, think about it, link it. When you read something you link it with what you already know or what you know about it. You've got to keep building on it or you're not going to learn.

Despite Max reporting knowledge and conscious use of such learning processes, analysis of videotape of classroom life suggested that he spent considerable time 'off-task' and disengaged from learning. He did not deny this, estimating that he focussed on his learning "about 15 percent" of the time. Max believed that he had learned "fairly well" in his previous science classes. Like Debbie and Tim, he suggested he had "mainly relied on the teacher" in those classes. He acknowledged the benefits of the chemistry classroom environment suggesting, "You can learn how you want to learn in this particular classroom," but conceded that he had difficulty in adjusting to that environment and its expectations, citing a lack of self-discipline as his key concern. "I was a bit unsure about the change…a bit scared…I wasn't sure I could keep myself on track all of the time." Max put his inappropriate use of class time down to his lack of self-discipline and suggested, in keeping with his past experience, that the responsibility for overcoming this problem lay with the teacher and that there should be, "times in class when we're all working quietly. No talk." He added, "I would like it if there was a bit more guidance, just teaching type of stuff…just a bit more up the front…cos that's what I'm used to."

During the intervention Max noted significant congruence between the view of learning he interpreted from the metaphor and his prior, privately held view.

> I am very comfortable with this metaphor because I think it explains learning in a nutshell; always starting with a good foundation and then building on that as you learn more and more…I've always thought of learning as building. When I learn I think of adding on to the other parts of my knowledge, and I think that's a form of construction.

During the intervention, Max intimated that he had found enacting aspects of his interpretation of the metaphor valuable suggesting, "…it was literally helping me to link my thoughts. It makes me think of the whole picture rather than just little activities on their own." After the two-week intervention he further stated, "I can see progress after these initial two weeks."

However, despite Max's claims of the value of engaging such processes, his metacognition did not undergo any revision that persisted past the intervention stage. He stated that the conception of learning he interpreted from the metaphor was not appropriate for his learning and he made a conscious decision not to enact the conception so that it was more influential. Despite the congruence between his pre-intervention conception of learning and the conception of learning that he interpreted from the metaphor he defensively asserted, "I just prefer doing it my own way. I like using my own systems." He emphatically described his own system as, "Do work when I have the time. That's it!" and added, "I didn't see it [the intervention] could help me immediately or long term. I don't believe it can help me or others. We've all learned one way and that's all. No new systems have ever been imposed upon us...the original system has, but that's all."

In defending his position Max suggested that the teachers he had in Years 8, 9 and 10 did "not at all" have a focus on the way students learned. He was not happy about this. Despite the lack of such a focus in his past schooling he strongly asserted that it was unreasonable for me to expect to try to influence his views and practices of learning.

> I believe that, in Year 8, if we'd done what you showed us it wouldn't have been any problem for Years 8, 9, 10, 11 or 12. It's just that to change at the end of your schooling is not appropriate...it's really hard to adapt. By Year 11 it's too hard to change learning styles that have been hammered in for ten years. During my whole life in schools they just tell you something and you do it or you get into trouble. You're being drilled for life. I don't think we were trained for the discipline or the motivation to work like that. Just the way we were taught, with the chalk and the board and someone being out the front and telling us things and making us write things down. You don't have to think for yourself. If someone tells you to do something you do it.

UNDERSTANDING METACOGNITION AS SOCIALLY MEDIATED

To improve their metacognition and learning processes individual students need opportunities to allow them to manage their learning and teacher support as they attempt to change (Baird, 1992). However, these case studies suggest that factors other than opportunity and support are influential should be accounted for. Debbie, Tim and Max were located within a classroom learning environment that was appropriate for developing and enhancing metacognition yet they still identified restraints to enacting what they agreed were intelligible, plausible and fruitful conceptions of learning. Sociocultural influences within and beyond the classroom were prominent in relation to their acceptance of opportunities to revise their conceptions of learning and teaching and to enact any revisions. In the discussion that follows the sociological concepts of hegemony and habitus previously described are employed to help understand students' conceptions of learning and teaching, elements of students' metacognitive knowledge and therefore their metacognition, as reflections and products of sociocultural influences. I have argued previously that conceptualizing students' metacognitive knowledge, consisting in part of their conceptions of learning, enables metacognition to be understood as at least the partial consequence of those conceptions. Such conceptions, as evidenced in these students' intimations, are constructions derived from their interpretations of past and current school experiences, as well as events outside school. Further they are reflections of the conceptions of learning and teaching and associated practices promoted both explicitly and implicitly within and by their school culture. As Max eloquently noted, these conceptions and associated practices are "hammered in" to students during their schooling. Such conceptions were not inert in relation to these students' learning processes. Although the conceptions were possibly tacit initially, the students invoked them in defense of their existing learning processes or in relation to their decisions regarding revision/s of those processes. It is evident that students can possess knowledge and awareness of more than one conception of learning and that they can make conscious choices regarding which conception to enact. Where the students identified alternatives to their existing conceptions of learning they questioned the legitimacy of those alternatives by assessing their credibility and value against the sociocultural norms of their contexts and, to varying extents, denied them legitimacy.

Within this middle class school there were certain expectations of both students and teachers that reflected their values and dispositions. These expectations included that teachers would tell students what they needed to know to pass exams, provide algorithmic frameworks for learning, control students, and be personally responsible for monitoring students' progress. Debbie, Tim and Max cited examples from classes where such expectations where fulfilled. They reported what I term a 'pedagogical hegemony,' that is, a dominant system of lived meanings in relation to teaching and learning. This pedagogical hegemony influenced their thinking, including their metacognition, and promoted substantial conformity in relation to their conceptions of learning and teaching, the learning processes they usually employed, and the type of teaching they expected. The constraints they reported are expressions of the *habitus* and reflect values and norms promoted by and existing within the broad community of practice of which they were members. These norms included notions that assessment is of primary importance and school is a workplace where students are directed to focus on their assessment by working hard. Interest-ingly, Bourdieu (1989) also suggested that the grande écoles of France are characterized by a pedagogy that constitutes a regimented intellectual *habi-tus*. He suggested that the characteristics of the educational environments of such schools, such as competitive examinations, problem sets and a focus on algorithmic 'skill and drill' activities create a pragmatic, utilitarian and narrow learning orientation. These characteristics bear similarity to those Debbie, Tim and Max described as evident in their school. In such environments students' efforts and interests become oriented in terms of what will help them succeed on examinations rather than what will develop a critical and creative orientation. Exam-oriented learning exerts a power-ful influence on students' conceptions of learning, what is valued, how stu-dents seek to achieve what is valued, and how they conceptualize learning. Assessment procedures, including exams, are tuned to social agendas, reflect social ideologies and help determine relationships between stu-dents and their classroom environments. Debbie and Tim's equating learn-ing success with examination grades is not new (see, e.g., Baird & Mitchell, 1987; McRobbie, Roth, & Lucas, 1997; Roth & McGinn, 1998). Such assess-ment orientation can be increasingly related to the strong trend in Austra-lia, as elsewhere, of increased employment opportunities for those with higher levels of education and decreasing opportunities and income levels for less skilled individuals. However, if students' attainment of their assess-ment goals requires only low level cognitive effort, as reported by these stu-dents as being the case in their previous classrooms, then they will form conceptions of teaching and learning that are not always easy to modify, and that make it difficult to engage them in what might be considered more metacognitive higher-order learning processes. As Sternberg (1998, p. 129) has pointed out,

> When students have become used to and have been rewarded over the years
> for passive and rather mindless learning, they will not jump at the chance to
> take a more thoughtful approach to what they are doing.

Interestingly however, despite the questionable quality of some of their conceptions of learning and learning strategies prior to, and in some cases after, the intervention, Debbie, Tim and Max could still be considered metacognitive in relation to their learning prior to entering year 11. They had all passed Year 10 and had gained entry into the science strand that attracted the most successful students at the school. Therefore their con-ceptions of learning and the strategies they employed were viable for them in past science learning environments. However, their metacognition that, by their own admission, involved minimal deep processing and reliance on and high level of acceptance of teacher control of their learning strategies, could be considered by some as unsatisfactory. Yet, I contend that these students were at least in partial control of the regulation of the learning processes and the thinking they employed, irrespective of the quality of such thinking and strategies. Further, they variously monitored and were aware of the consequences of these strategies, even if their awareness of the benefits or lack of benefits of their use varied and was also variously questionable. Their decisions to revise or not to revise their conceptions of learning and learning strategies can be seen to be clearly related to their purposes of schooling and consequent learning goals; reflections of the *habitus*. Debbie, Tim, and Max's pragmatic purposes and learning strategies reflected what was valued and privileged within the broad culture they were members of rather than what might be considered as educationally ideal, i.e., a thorough understanding of the subject material and a profound intrinsic disposition to learn for such understanding. Accordingly, we might consider these students' lack of metacognition as a consequence of the conceptions and practices, both implicit and explicit, of the culture within which they learnt to reason.

Figure 1 locates an individual's metacognition within the social environment of that individual and draws attention to the significance of a range of factors on students' metacognition. The factors emerge as credible in

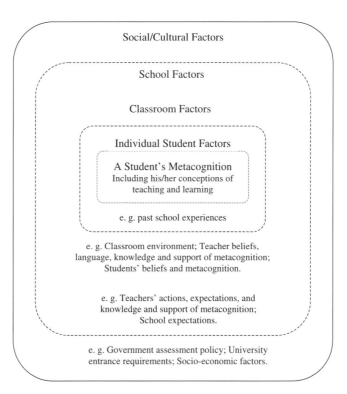

FIGURE 1
Metacognition as Socially Embedded

relation to the case studies presented. A teacher's action in relation to the development of metacognition and a culture of thinking in the classroom for developing and enhancing metacognition can be understood with reference to many factors. Multiple, fuzzy-boundaried social contexts are at play in influencing students' metacognition and whether or not students' conceptions and learning strategies are problematic depends on the social contexts within which such conceptions find life in students' learning strategies

INFORMING THEORY AND FUTURE RESEARCH AND PRACTICE

On the basis of the cases presented, it seems reasonable to consider extending the conception of metacognition from its current predominant niche in cognitive psychology to encompass considerations regarding its social situatedness and the mediating influence of society on students' conceptions of learning. Accordingly, I propose the following principles related to metacognition.

1. Metacognition involves a personal mental construction of metacognitive knowledge by individuals.
2. Learners subscribe to their metacognitive conceptual structures because they are viable for the individual, not because they are absolute.
3. The construction of metacognitive knowledge is mediated by social and cultural processes and language plays an important role in this process.

I contend that the three principles and the representation in Figure 1 have transferability across cultures, and social and educational contexts. The implication of such transferability is that to understand and appreciate individuals' metacognition we must firstly appreciate and understand their cultures and various contexts. Further, if we are to develop interventions to develop and enhance metacognition we should be aware of and sensitive to the cultures and contexts within which we seek to intervene rather than expect that one intervention will be equally effective in all situations.

CONCLUDING REMARKS

A key factor in enhancing students' metacognition in schools relates to challenging students' possibly problematic conceptions of teaching and learning. However, schools are not ideologically neutral learning environments. Asking students to critique their conceptions of learning and teaching might require that they question the dominant and hegemonic beliefs in relation to education held by the society of which they themselves are members and within which they may be implicitly encouraged to conform. Attempts to provide opportunities for students to become more metacognitive need to account for and promote such student critique, even though this may be difficult for them.

Students may disappoint us in our quest for developing their metacognition and learning processes, not because our goals are not justified or our interventions are poorly conceived, but because they are not congruent with what they perceive as the real purposes of schooling and education. As Gunstone (1992, p. 137) noted, "changed approaches to learning need to be considered in the context of what is real and relevant learning." Accordingly, we need to understand the sociocultural nature of students' learning environments before we can suggest whether or not their behaviors, cognition and metacognition are adaptive for those environments. Enhancing students' metacognition, therefore, is not just dependent on developing appropriate classroom learning environments and effective interventions. It requires an understanding and appreciation of education and learning at many levels so that the types of learning processes we seek to have students know about, understand and implement can be seen by more students to have real and relevant value for them in their cultural and social contexts.

REFERENCES

Adey, P., & Shayer, M. (1994). *Really raising standards: Cognitive intervention and academic achievement.* London: Routledge.

Baird, J. R. (1986). Improving learning through enhanced metacognition: A classroom study. *European Journal of Science Education, 8*(3), 263-282.

Baird, J. R. (1992). The individual student. In J. R. Baird & J. R. Northfield (Eds.), *Learning from the PEEL experience* (pp. 37-60). Melbourne, Australia: Monash University.

Baird, J. R., & Mitchell, I. J. (1987). *Improving the quality of teaching and learning: An Australian case study—The PEEL project.* Melbourne, Australia: Monash University.

Berry, J., & Sahlberg, P. (1996). Investigating pupils' ideas of learning. *Learning and Cognition, 6*(1), 19-36.

Biggs, J. B. (1986). Enhancing learning skills: The role of metacognition. In J. A. Bowen (Ed.), *Student learning: Research into practice* (pp.131-148). Melbourne, Australia: Melbourne University Press.

Bourdieu, P. (1977). Symbolic Power. In D. Gleeson (Ed.), *Identity and structure: Issues in the sociology of education.* Nafferton, UK: Driffield.

Bourdieu, P. (1984). *Questions de sociologie*. Paris: Les Editions de Minuit.

Bourdieu, P. (1989). *La noblesse d'Etat: Grand corps et grandes écoles*. Paris: Editions de Minuit.

Bronfenbrenner, U. (1979). *The ecology of human development*. Cambridge, MA: Harvard University Press.

Cohen, L., & Manion, L. (1994). *Research methods in education* (4th edition). New York, NY: Routledge.

Day, J. D., French, L. A., & Hall, L. K. (1985). Social influences on cognitive development. In D. Forrest-Pressley, G. E. McKinnon & G. T. Waller, (Eds.), *Metacognition, cognition, and human performance* (pp. 33-56). Orlando, FL: Academic Press.

Doyle, W. (1983). Academic work. *Review of Educational Research, 53,* 159-200.

Doyle, W. (1986). Classroom organisation and management. In M. C. Wittrock (Ed.), *Handbook of research on teaching* (3rd ed.), (pp. 392-433). New York, NY: Macmillan.

Duffy, G. G., & Roehler, L. R. (1989). Why strategy instruction is so difficult and what we need to do about it. In C. B. McCormick, G. Miller & M. Pressley (Eds.), *Cognitive strategy instruction: From basic concepts to educational applications* (pp. 133-154). New York, NY: Springer-Verlag.

Erickson, F. (1998). Qualitative research methods for science education. In B. J. Fraser & K. G. Tobin (Eds.), *International handbook of science education* (pp. 1155-1173). Dordrecht, Netherlands: Kluwer.

Ertmer, P. A., & Newby, T. J. (1996). The expert learner: Strategic, self-regulated, and reflective. *Instructional Science, 24,* 1-24.

Flavell, J. H. (1979). Metacognition and cognitive monitoring; A new area of cognitive-developmental inquiry. *American Psychologist, 34,* 906-911.

Fraser, B. J. (1998). Science learning environments: Assessment, effects and determinants. In B. J. Fraser & K. G. Tobin (Eds.), *International handbook of science education* (pp. 527-564). Dordrecht, Netherlands: Kluwer.

Garner, R. (1987). *Metacognition and reading comprehension*. Norwood, NJ: Ablex Publishing.

Garner, R. & Alexander, P. A. (1989). Metacognition: Answered and unanswered questions. *Educational Psychologist, 24*(2), 143-158.

Gentner, D. (1989). The mechanisms of analogical learning. In S. Vosniadou & A. Ortony (Eds.), *Similarity and analogical reasoning* (pp. 199-241). New York, NY: Cambridge University Press.

Gentner, D. (1990). *Metaphor as structure mapping: The relational shift*. University of Illinois at Urbana-Champaign: Technical Report No. 488.

Guba, E. G., & Lincoln, Y. S. (1989). *Fourth generation evaluation*. Beverly Hills, CA: Sage.

Guba, E. G., & Lincoln, Y. S. (1997). Naturalistic and rationalistic inquiry. In J. P. Keeves (Ed.), *Educational research, methodology, and measurement: An international handbook* (pp. 86-91). Oxford, UK: Pergamon.

Gunstone, R. F. (1992). Constructivism and metacognition: Theoretical issues and classroom studies. In R. Duit, F. Goldberg, & H. Niedderer (Eds.), *Research in physics learning; Theoretical issues and empirical studies* (pp. 129-140). Kiel: Institut fur die Pedagogik der Naturwissenschaften an der Universitat Kiel.

Hacker, D. J. (1998). Definitions and empirical foundations. In D. J. Hacker, J. Donlosky and A. C. Graesser (Eds.), Metacognition in educational theory and practice (pp. 1-26). Mahwah, NJ: Erlbaum.

Herideen, P. E. (1998). *Policy, pedagogy, and social inequality: Community college student realities in post-industrial America.* Westport, CT: Bergin & Garvey.

Kirby, J. R. (1984). Educational roles of cognitive plans and strategies. In J. R. Kirby (Ed.), *Cognitive strategies and educational performance* (pp. 51-88). Orlando, FL: Academic Press.

Lakoff, G. (1993). The contemporary theory of metaphor. In A. Ortony (Ed.), *Metaphor and thought* (2nd ed., pp. 202-251). New York, NY: Cambridge University Press.

Lakoff, G., & Johnson, M. (1980). *Metaphors we live by.* Chicago, IL: University of Chicago Press.

Lave, J. (1990). The culture of acquisition and the practice of understanding. In J. W. Steigler, R. A. Schweder, & G. Herdt (Eds), *Cultural psychology* (pp. 259-286). Cambridge, UK: Cambridge University Press.

Lave, J., & Wenger, E. (1991). *Situated learning—legitimate peripheral participation.* Cambridge, UK: Cambridge University Press.

Macdonald, I. (1990). *Student awareness of learning.* Unpublished master's thesis, Monash University, Melbourne, Australia.

McInerney, D. M., Hinkly, J., Dowson, M., & Van Etten, S. (1998). Aboriginal, Anglo Australian, and immigrant Australian students' motivational beliefs about personal academic success: Are there cultural differences? *Journal of Educational Psychology, 90*(4), 621-629.

McLaren, P. (1986). *Schooling as ritual performance.* London: Routledge.

McLaren, P. (1994). *Life in schools* (2nd ed.). New York, NY: Longman.

McRobbie, C. J., Roth, W-M., & Lucas, K. B. (1997). Multiple learning environments in the physics classroom. *International Journal of Science Education, 19*(2), 193-208.

Marton, F. (1988). Describing and improving learning. In R. R. Schmeck (Ed.), *Learning strategies and learning styles* (pp. 53-82). New York, NY: Plenum Press.

Nuthall, G. (1999). Learning how to learn: The evolution of students' minds through social processes and culture of the classroom. *International Journal of Educational Research, 31,* 139-140.

Paris, S. G., & Winograd, P. (1990). How metacognition can promote academic learning and instruction. In B. F. Jones and L. Idol (Eds.), *Dimensions of thinking and cognitive instruction* (pp. 15-52). Hillsdale, NJ: Erlbaum.

Perkins, D., Jay, E., & Tishman, S. (1995). *The thinking classroom.* Boston, MA: Allyn and Bacon.

Petersen, P. L., & Swing, S. R. (1983). Problems in classroom implementation of cognitive strategy instruction. In M. Pressley & J. R. Levin (Eds.), *Cognitive strategy research: Educational implications* (pp. 267-287). New York, NY: Springer-Verlag.

Pressley, M., Van Etten, S., Yakoi, L., Freebern, G., & Van Meter, P. (1998). The metacognition of college studentship: A grounded theory approach. In D. J. Hacker, J. Donlosky and A. C. Graesser (Eds.), Metacognition in educational theory and practice (pp. 347-363). Mahwah, NJ: Erlbaum.

Rogoff, B. (1990). *Apprenticeship in thinking: Cognitive development in social context.* New York, NY: Oxford University Press.

Roth, W-M. (2000). Learning environments research, lifeworld analysis, and solidarity in practice. *Learning Environments Research, 2*(3),225-247.

Roth, W-M., & McGinn, M. K. (1998). Science education: /lives/work/voices. *Journal of Research in Science Teaching, 35*(4), 399-421.

Ryan, A. M. (2000). Peer groups as context for the socialisation of adolescents' motivation, engagement, and achievement in school. *Educational Psychologist, 35*(2), 101-111.

Schmeck, R. R. (1988). Strategies and styles of learning: An integration of varied perspectives. In R. R. Schmeck (Ed.), *Learning strategies and learning styles* (pp. 317-347). New York, NY: Plenum Press.

Schunk, D. H., & Zimmerman, B. J. (1996). Modelling and self-efficacy influences on children's development of self-regulation. In K. Wentzel & J. Juvonen (Eds.), *Social motivation: Understanding children's school adjustment* (pp. 154-180). New York, NY: Cambridge University Press.

Shayer, M., & Adey, P. (1993). An exploration of long term far-transfer effects following an extended intervention programme in the high school science curriculum. *Cognition and Instruction, 11*(1), 1-30.

Sternberg, R. J. (1998). Metacognition, abilities, and developing expertise: What makes an expert student? *Instructional Science, 26,* 127-140.

Tasker, R. (1981). Children's views and classroom experiences. *Australian Science Teachers' Journal, 27,*(3), 33-37.

Taylor. P. C. S., Fraser, B. J., & White, L. R. (1994, April). *CLES: An instrument for monitoring the development of constructivist learning environments.* Paper presented at the annual meeting of the American Educational Research association, New Orleans, LA.

Thomas, G. P. (1999a). Developing metacognition and cognitive strategies through the use of metaphor in a year 11 chemistry classroom. Unpublished doctoral dissertation, Queensland University of Technology, Brisbane, Australia.

Thomas, G. P. (1999b). Student restraints to reform: Conceptual change issues in enhancing students' learning processes. *Research in Science Education, 29*(1), 89-109.

Thomas, G. P. (2001, June). *Conceptualising metacognitively oriented learning environments: Insights from research.* Paper presented at the second annual Thinking Qualities Initiate Conference, Hong Kong.

Thomas, G. P. & McRobbie, C. J. (1999). Using metaphor to probe students' conceptions of chemistry learning. *International Journal of Science Education, 21*(6), 667-685.

Thomas, G. P. & McRobbie, C. J. (2001). Using a metaphor for learning to improve students' metacognition in the chemistry classroom. *Journal of Research in Science Teaching, 38*(2) 222-259.

Tishman, S., & Perkins, D. N. (1997). The language of thinking. *Phi Delta Kappan, 78*(5), 368-374.

Toffler, A. (1970). *Future shock.* London: Pan Books.

Tynjälä, P. (1997). Developing education students' conceptions of learning process in different learning environments. *Learning and Instruction, 7*(3), 277-292.

Vosniadou, S. (1996). Towards a revised cognitive psychology for new advances in learning and instruction. *Learning and Instruction, 6*(2), 95-109.

White, R. T. (1988). Metacognition. In J. P. Keeves (Ed.), *Educational research, methodology, and measurement* (pp. 70-75). Sydney Australia: Pergamon Press.

White, R. T. (1992). Implications of recent research on learning for curriculum and assessment. *Journal of Curriculum Studies, 24*(2), 153-164.

White, R. T. (1998). Decisions and problems in research on metacognition. In B. J. Fraser & K. G. Tobin (Eds.), *International handbook of science education* (pp. 1207-1212). Dordrecht, Netherlands: Kluwer.

Zimmerman, B. J. (1994). Dimensions of academic self-regulation: A conceptual framework for education. In D. H. Schunk & B. J. Zimmerman (Eds.), *Self-regulation of learning and performance: Issues and educational applications* (pp. 3-21). Hillsdale, NJ: Erlbaum.

CHAPTER 10

MOTIVATION AND AFRICAN-AMERICAN YOUTH
Exploring Assumptions of Some Contemporary Motivation Theories

**Tamera B. Murdock, Megan Brooks Bolch,
George Dent, and Natalie Hale Wilcox**

INTRODUCTION

School children in the United States are surrounded by messages of both self-sufficiency and equal opportunity. Our contemporary media and history texts are replete with stories such as Horatio Alger, a poor immigrant who, through hard work and determination, was able to "pull himself up by his bootstraps," as well as those of Bill Clinton and Clarence Thomas, two men, Caucasian and African-American, born into modest homes, who rose to the highest ranks of the United States Government. Stories such as these suggest that one's failure to thrive is a direct result of having little personal motivation to achieve. However, while these stories represent a piece of the shared context in which US students grow, learn, and develop, there are wide variations in the educational and economic opportunities afforded to our children, variations which are often a function of what Bronfenbrenner (1979) calls "macro-contexts" that include geography, social class, race/ethnicity, and gender. It is not hard to imagine how macro contextual factors such as poverty and racism, as well as micro-contextual factors such as teaching quality and curriculum, effect the extent to which students are in fact exposed to equal opportunity, or to benefits of hard work. Yet, as with many psychological theories, theories of motivation sometimes presume that the *internal* mechanisms governing people's behavior develop and operate in a shared or neutral context, or limit the study of context effects to classrooms and schools. It is therefore perhaps not surprising that motivation theories have had limited success in addressing one of our nation's most persistent educational crises: the disproportionately high rates of school "drop out," and comparative academic underachievement of African-American youth living in our nation's cities (Pungello, Kupersmidt, Burchinal, & Patterson, 1996; Ramey & Ramey, 1992; Walker, Greenwood, Hart, & Carter, 1994). In this chapter, we introduce some recent work that has attempted to incorporate some elements of cultural context into motivation theories in order to better understand the motivation and achievement patterns of African-American youth. The discussion focuses on the role of self-esteem and values in the development of motivated behavior.

SELF-ESTEEM AND VALUES IN THE DEVELOPMENT OF MOTIVATED BEHAVIOR

Self-Esteem

Self-esteem has been defined as people's subjective appraisals of their satisfaction with themselves. Accordingly, self-esteem is based on people's objective descriptions of themselves (i.e., self-concept), as well as the personal values and standards they use to evaluate those self-descriptions (DuBois, Felner, Brand, Phillips, & Lease, 1996). As such, it is possible for someone to report that they do not have a lot of skills in a particular area, such as school, and also have high self-esteem related to school because their performance is in line with their personal principles. Educators have often assumed that high self-esteem is important for school motivation, because of its links to school achievement (Keltikangas-Jarervinen, 1992; Osborne, 1995). Indeed, increases in self-esteem are seen as both a motivational antecedent and consequence of higher school achievement: feeling better about oneself leads to increased efforts, which in turn increases success, and subsequently self-esteem. However, although African-American students usually have lower achievement than their Caucasian peers, their general and school-related self-esteem is as high or higher than Caucasian students (Bolch, Murdock, & Wilcox, 2001; Graham, 1994; Murdock, 1996; Richman, Clarke, & Brown, 1985).

Numerous studies have been conducted to try to understand the seeming paradox between self-esteem and achievement of African-American youth. In this chapter, we review some recent work that is grounded in two perspectives that attempt to resolve this paradox: disidentification and devaluing. Both of these approaches seek to understand the apparent self-esteem-achievement discrepancies by incorporating some contextual factors associated with the lived experiences of many African-American students (i.e., historical and contemporary stereotypes of African-Americans as having low intellectual abilities).

Disidentification and Self-Esteem

Disidentification refers to the process of reorganizing one's self-concept such that some domain, in this case academic achievement, has little importance to one's overall sense of self. Social psychologist Claude Steele suggests that African-American students disidentify with school because they are members of a group that has been historically and continuously stereotyped as "unintelligent" (Steele, 1992, 1997). By psychologically distancing themselves from academics, where they are expected to fail, Steele maintains that negative intellectual feedback causes limited damage to the self-esteem of African-American youth. Similarly, others suggest that African-American youth, particularly males, invest their energies and thus their self-esteem in other arenas where they are more likely to achieve success (Fordham & Ogbu, 1986; Graham, Taylor, & Hudely, 1998).

Findings from several studies support the idea of disidentification. Major, Spencer, Schmader, Wolfe, & Crocker, J. (1998) documented ethnic differences in college students' scores on a measure of disengagement, with African-American students more likely than Caucasian students to endorse items such as "how I do intellectually has little to do with who I am." Osborne (1995, 1997) has tested the disidentification hypothesis using self-esteem and achievement data from the National Education Longitudinal Study at three points in time: Grade 8, 10, and 12. Specifically, he argued that if disidentification was indeed occurring, then the relations between grades and self-esteem should decrease over time. He analyzed the data separately for different racial (African-American and Caucasian) and gender subgroups, while controlling for family SES. His results indicate that the relations between school success and self-esteem were weakest among African-American males as compared to the other three groups at all points in time. In addition, for African-American males, the association between school achievement and global self-esteem became much weaker across grades 8-12, supporting the hypothesis that African-American males disidentify with academics. However, as Osborne (1997) himself noted, these studies did not directly examine the central tenet of disidentification: that the structure of self-esteem is different across ethnic groups.

We recently completed an additional test of the disidentification hypothesis by examining the structure of self-esteem in a sample of 495 middle-school students, of whom approximately 45 percent were African-American (see Bolch et al., 2001). Students completed a multi-dimensional measure of self-esteem that included both a measure of overall self-esteem and a measure of self-esteem relative to school, family, friends, athletic, and appearance (Dubois et al., 1996). We found that school self-esteem added more to the prediction of the overall self-esteem of Caucasian versus African-American youth, suggesting that school self-esteem is less central to the overall self-worth of African-American versus Caucasian youth in our sample. However, correlational analyses showed that school-self-esteem was significantly and positively related to the global self-esteem of all youth across racial and gender groups.

The presumed motivation behind disidentification is a repeated exposure to stereotypes of African-Americans as being low in intellectual ability. Indeed, in previous research, we found that teachers rated the "ability" of African-American students as lower than Caucasian students with similar achievement test scores (Murdock, 1996). These findings were particularly strong for African-American males. Similar beliefs appear to be held by students themselves: When Graham et al. (1998) asked low-income middle-school students to nominate the students who were low in effort, African-American males were the primary nominees.

Although the withdrawal of self-esteem from school success appears to be a reasonable, and self-protective strategy in an environment where negative stereotypes may prevail, there are several reasons to be concerned about the strategy of disidentification. First, given that self-esteem is presumed to be both a consequence of past behavior as well as a determiner of future behavior, it may be that the withdrawal of self-esteem from school leads to lower academic motivation. Future studies might investigate the relations between school self-esteem (i.e., level of satisfaction with school performance), general self-esteem (i.e., level of satisfaction with oneself generally), effort expenditure (i.e., "how hard a student tries), and achievement over time. In addition, there are some data to suggest that disidentification is more than a passive process of school withdrawal, and that disenfranchised students create identities that are in opposition to school norms, and that are reinforced by peer culture (Fordham & Ogbu, 1986). For example, the low-income African-American males in Graham et al.'s study (1998) who were seen as low in effort, and noncompliant were also the same students who were nominated as being "admired" and "respected" by peers.

Discounting and Self Esteem

A second and similar explanation for the relatively high self-esteem of African-American youth is the discounting hypothesis. Discounting refers to the process of dismissing or delegitimizing feedback as irrelevant or inaccurate. Crocker and Major (1989) argue that members of stigmatized groups may dismiss feedback from the non-stigmatized or majority group as a means of self-esteem protection. Given the years of institutional and personal discrimination against African-American people in our country, it may be that African-American youth are more likely to doubt that the feedback given to them by teachers is a reflection of their true abilities or achievements.

Several studies have been conducted to examine the discounting hypothesis. For example, in an experiment using undergraduate college students, bogus feedback was provided on an intelligence test by an experimenter who either has seen the participant (and therefore knew his or her race), or did not see them (Crocker, Voelkl, Testa, & Major, 1991). When the African-American participants believed a White experimenter had seen them, they were more likely to say the feedback was biased, and it had less of an effect on their ratings of self-esteem than when they had not been seen. In our own data, we also found that teacher feedback in the forms of both grades and perceived teacher expectations were less related to the school-self esteem (e.g., "I am as good of a student as I would like to be," Dubois et al., 1996) of African-American as compared to Caucasian youth (See Bolch et al., 2001). In other words, these data are also consistent with the theory that African-American youth may be more apt to challenge the accuracy of their teacher's feedback.

The discounting hypothesis is grounded in the assumption that African-American youth may feel as though they are not likely to get a fair evaluation from their teachers. Indeed, as noted earlier, there is some evidence to suggest that teachers may more harshly evaluate the abilities of African-American than Caucasian students. Perhaps more important, however, is the growing body of research suggesting that many low achieving African-American youth are apt to report having poor relationships with their teachers, and to feeling devalued and disrespected in the classroom (Farrell, 1990, 1994; Murdock, 1999; Nieto, 2000). In order to more directly examine the extent to which the discounting of feedback is more or less likely depending on students' perceived quality of their relationship with teachers, we reanalyzed the self-esteem and achievement data of the African-American students in the study described earlier (Bolch et al., 2001). In this analysis we included the two forms of feedback, grades and perceived expectations held by teachers, as well as scores from a measure of perceived teacher respect (described in Murdock & Dent, 2000). We hypothesized that grades and perceived teacher expectations would be more strongly associated with school self-esteem among students who per-ceived higher versus lower levels of respect from their teachers.

We used a median split to divide students into higher and lower per-ceived respect groups. Chi-square analysis confirmed that girls and boys were both proportionately represented in the higher and lower respect groups. Consistent with our hypotheses, among students who perceived higher levels of respect from teachers the correlation of school-self esteem with grades was .51, and the correlation of school self-esteem with per-ceived teacher expectations of .58. In contrast, among the low perceived respect group, these correlations were .31 and .36. Moreover, regression analyses showed that grades and perceived teacher expectations account for 41 percent of the variance in the school self-esteem among students who perceive high amounts of respect from their teacher, but only explain 15 percent of the variance in the lower-respect group. In other words, it seems as if students assign more weight to grades and teacher feedback when they perceive their teachers as respectful of them.

Summary and Future Directions

A body of research in the area of African-Americans' self-esteem attempts to explain why it is that despite having lower academic achievement than Caucasians, their self-evaluations are at least equal to those of their White peers. These studies remind us that the context of schooling for many Afri-can-American youth is qualitatively different from the school context of racial majority youth. Specifically, there is some evidence that they face ste-reotypes of their group members as unintelligent, receive feedback that is more biased than Caucasian students, and report less respectful relation-ships with their teachers than do students of the majority culture. In this context, it seems both reasonable and adaptive that the self-esteem of Afri-can-American youth would be "protected" from feedback about intellectual abilities that are received in schools. Although this strategy is adaptive in that it protects against feelings of inadequacy, some people worry that it also potentially feeds a cycle of African-American students' disengagement from school: Students expend their energies in arenas that are potentially rein-forcing to their self-esteem (Graham et al., 1998; Osborne, 1995, 1997). Thus, concerns of disidentification are based on the assumption that because African-American students disidentify with school to protect their self-esteem, then school achievement becomes less motivating.

Perhaps, however, the relatively high measured general and school self-esteem particularly of African American male youth is not an outgrowth of disidentification per se, but rather an outgrowth of living in larger cultural context in which low self-esteem is equated with weakness, and therefore with vulnerability. Anderson (1999) notes that many African-Americans youth live in urban areas that are characterized by poverty and violence, and where norms of "decency" do not prevail. The code of these communities is one in which young men seek respect first and foremost from others, and where lives are lost over perceived disrespect. According to Anderson, most young men in this environment even those who are decent, hardworking and law abiding, adopt a posture towards the world that exudes confidence, and says "don't mess with me." Perhaps, this posturing extends to self-esteem measures as well. Future research might focus on the meaning of self-esteem within various groups, and examine the reciprocal relations between school specific expectancies, global self-esteem, effort, and achievement over time.

Values

According to an expectancy-value motivation paradigm, students' motivation to succeed in school is a joint function of one's expectancies for school success and the value one attributes to education (e.g., Eccles et al., 1983; Eccles & Wigfield, 1992; Feather, 1988) different motivational theories explain variation in students' engagement in ways that reflect an underlying expectancy-value model. For example, research on self-efficacy (e.g., Bandura, 1997; Schunk, 1990) emphasizes students' beliefs that they are capable of completing academic tasks, while self-concept and self-esteem models (e.g., Harter, 1991; Stipek & McIver, 1989) focus on students' generalized sense of competence.

In contrast to the plethora of research on expectancies, the role of values in achievement motivation has been quite neglected (see Graham et al., 1998; Murdock, 1999). Moreover, the literature on values has been dominated by a model that focuses on individual's domain-specific beliefs, such as how much they enjoy a particular subject, how useful they think it will be, or how much they have to give up in order to succeed in that area (e.g., Eccles et al., 1983; Eccles & Wigfield, 1992). Many people have suggested that a broader conception of values might be important for understanding the achievement motivation of African-American youth (Fordham & Ogbu, 1986; Graham et al., 1998; Mickelson, 1990; Murdock, 1999). These perspectives attend to students' *general* school-related attitudes rather than their subject specific beliefs, and call attention to the ways in which race and social class affect the context in which these values develop. In this chapter, we focus on economic values and personal values as possible influences on motivation.

Economic Values

Fordham & Ogbu (1986) argue that African-American youth devalue schooling because they perceive that racism will limit their economic opportunities, regardless of their educational accomplishments. Students in their ethnographic study reported that African-American children, particularly those from low-income urban settings, are not only more likely to doubt the economic value of education than Caucasian students, but also that doubts about the value of education predict a lack of compliance with school norms, low achievement, and school leaving.

The first large-scale study to demonstrate racial differences in the perceived economic value of education was conducted by Mickelson (1990). In her large-scale study of high school students, African-American and low-income Caucasian students reported more exposure to contexts that undermined the links between education economic prosperity than did higher income Caucasian students. More important, however was that increased doubts about the economic value of education predicted lower school performance. Since that time, several studies have found that African-American students tend to have more doubts about the economic value of education than do Caucasian adolescents, and other studies illustrate the negative academic consequences of this devaluing across all students (Ford, 1992a, 1992b, Murdock, 1999; Roeser, Midgley, & Urdan, 1996). In our own research, we have found ethnic differences in the perceived economic value of education among students as young as 7th grade, with African-American students reporting more doubts about the economic pay-offs of education than Caucasian students (Murdock, 1999). The greater the doubts expressed about the economic value of education, the more likely they were to be noncompliant with school norms, and the less likely they were to be engaged in effortful achievement. When these students were followed up in 9th grade, their 7th grade economic doubts continued to predict low academic motivation, and also predicted low future educational aspirations (Murdock, Anderman, & Hodge, 2000).

Personal Values

A second although less examined aspect of Fordham & Ogbu's (1986) theory also has implications for the role of values in the motivation of African-American youth. Specifically, they assert that many African-American children develop identities based on values that are oppositional to the mainstream cultural values of effortful achievement, and that these oppositional values are strongly enforced by the peer culture. This hypothesis is intriguing as students' school successes are clearly affected by the degree to which they internalize the terminal values promoted by the school (Battistich, Solomon, Watson, & Schaps, 1997). In other words, it may not be enough for a student to see school as useful or interesting, he or she must also value the behaviors that are rewarded by schools, including being effortful, prosocial, and compliant. A now classic study by Weiner & Kukla

(1970) found that teachers prefer to reward students who they perceive as more rather than less effortful. Moreover, research by Wentzel (1993) has demonstrated that students' pursuit of prosocial and compliance goals predicts achievement above and beyond other indicators of achievement motivation.

Recent work by Graham and her colleagues (Graham, Taylor, & Hudley, 1998) provides support for the notion that the academic failure of some African-American youth, particularly males, may be due to the adoption of values that are incongruent with those supported in school. They asked low-income African-American students to nominate those classmates who they most admired, respected and wanted to be like. They also nominated students who were effortful, compliant, and disruptive. The authors presumed that the attributes of students who were nominated as those they most respected, admired, and wanted to be like were indirect measures of students' values. Being effortful in school and compliant with school rules was inversely related to received respect from African-American boys. A second study using an ethnically diverse sample (African-American, Caucasian, Hispanic) confirmed these findings: African-American males were the most likely to be nominated as low achieving and highly disruptive. Moreover, these same students were nominated as those that peers most wanted to be like, respected, and admired. These results suggest that African-American males may devalue those students whose attitudes and dispositions are congruent with the values that support school success. One limitation of these studies, however, is that we only gain information about those students who receive the "most" nominations in one category or another.

In this study, we sought to extend the findings of Graham's work by using a continuous scale to assess values, with items asking about the degree to which they admire the qualities of effort, prosocial behavior, and compliance in other students. We were interested in ascertaining the degree to which admiration of those values predicts variation in students' own effort, as assessed both by self-report as well as teacher report. Finally, we examined the values and behaviors of our students within the context of their relationships with teachers as well as peers (see also Murdock & Dent, 2000).

Our data come from a sample of 222 African-American youth (115 female), who attended middle school in a school district immediately adjacent to an urban district. The school was 50 percent African-American, with approximately the same percentage of students receiving free or reduced priced lunch. We created a series of questions to assess valuing of pro-social, compliant, and effortful behavior using the stem "How much do you admire people who..." followed by three items each for prosocial, compliant, and effortful behavior. The prosocial and compliance items were adapted from Wentzel's (1993) measures of compliance and prosocial goals. A principal components factor analysis of our value items revealed that all of the prosocial, compliance, and effort items loaded on one factor

TABLE 1
Scales, Sample Items, and Internal Consistency (a) Coefficients.

Scale Name	Sample Item	a (n = 222)
Positive School Values	I admire my classmates who follow the rules.	
	I admire my classmates who work hard in school.	
	I admire my classmates who do just enough to get by. (Reversed)	.84
Intrinsic Value of Education	I like what we are learning in school.	
	I think what we are learning in school is interesting.	.75
Economic Value of Education	School is not that important for future success.	
	I can make good money someday without an education.	.65
Academic Self Efficacy	I can do even the hardest work if I try.	
	I am certain I can master the skills taught in school this year.	.74
Self Rated Effort	I do the work that my teacher assigns me.	
	I try my best on my school assignments.	.78
Peers' Aspirations and Support	Most of my friends will get a high school diploma.	
	My friends don't really care about school.	.70
Teacher Respect and Commitment	Teachers here respect me.	
	Teachers here keep their promises.	
	I learn a lot from my teacher.	.79

that accounted for 68 percent of the variance; thus we created a score of *Positive School Values* (χ = .78). We also included a traditional measure of *Intrinsic Value of Education* (Pintrich & De Groot, 1990), a measure of *Economic Value of Education* (Murdock, 1999) and a measure of *Academic Efficacy* (Midgley et al., 2000) as an indicator of academic expectancies. Sample items and internal consistency reliability scores for all scales are presented in Table 1.

Economic Value of Education items were developed by Murdock (Murdock, 1994, 1999) based on the work of Mickelson (1990). Items assess the extent to which students have doubts about the relationship between getting an education and being economically successful. The total score reflects an average score on all items, with the items coded such that higher values indicate stronger beliefs in the economic value of education. Previous research (Murdock, 1994, 1999) has demonstrated that these items form a stable factor, and that scores have logical correlations with criterion variables, including school effort and school behavior. The Intrinsic Value of Education assesses these students' assessments of the interest and usefulness of their school work. Items on this scale are congruent with traditional conceptions of valuing within motivational research, and the scale has demonstrated adequate psychometric properties (Pintrich & DeGroot, 1990).

Academic Self-Efficacy was assessed using the 5-item scale from the *Patterns of Adaptive Learning Survey* (Midgley et al., 2000). These items assess the extent to which students believe that, with effort, they can master the material they are learning in school. In previous studies, the scales have demonstrated adequate internal consistency and show logical correlations with relevant criterion variables.

We hypothesized that all of these constructs would be positively related to *School Effort* and that values would predict effort above and beyond expectancies. School effort was assessed in two ways: teacher-ratings and self-ratings. For each student, two of their major subject area teachers (math, English, science, social studies) were asked to rate the student on his/her level of effort and persistence (among other variables) using a 1-5 scale with anchors "never" and "most of the time." Factor analysis of the teacher ratings indicated that the two teacher ratings of effort and persistence load on the same factor, and the four scores have an internal consistency of .88. Thus, these scores were averaged to form a scale of teacher-rated effort. In addition, students responded to seven items pertaining to their own level of effort which were averaged to form a total score ($\chi = .78$)

Interrcorrelations between all variables are presented in Table 2, broken down by gender. Whereas boys' self-rated effort was positively related to academic self-efficacy as well as to all three indices of values (economic value, intrinsic value, and positive school values), among girls, neither intrinsic value nor economic value was related to effort. Similarly, teacher-rated effort was associated with academic self-efficacy, intrinsic values, and positive school values among boys, but was not associated with intrinsic value among girls. Value variables were more intercorrelated with one another among boys than girls. Note also that teacher-rated effort and self-rated effort were moderately correlated with one another, as were self-rated effort and GPA. Teacher-rated effort was strongly correlated with GPA, a finding that is not surprising given that teachers assign student grades.

TABLE 2
Inter-Correlations Among Expectancy, Value, Effort, and Achievement
Variables by Gender

Variable	1	2	3	4	5	6	7
1. Teacher Rated Academic Effort	—	.438**	.077	.010	.283**	.268**	.729**
2. Self Rated Academic Effort	.515**		.026	.095	.514**	.212*	.476**
3. Economic Value of Education	.111	.332**	—	.216*	.164	.214*	-.077
4. Intrinsic Value of Education	.238*	.377**	.349**	—	.322**	.496**	-.056
5. Positive School Values	.254*	.440**	.281**	.480**	—	.252**	.248**
6. Academic Self-Efficacy	.292**	.464**	.318**	.601**	.422**	—	.156
7. GPA	.750**	.522**	.069	.155	.144	.231*	—

Notes: * p < .05; ** p < .01. Females are above the diagonal and males are below it.

Do Values Matter?

To determine the incremental contribution of values above and beyond self-efficacy, a hierarchical regression was conducted in which academic efficacy was entered on step 1, followed by the three values variables on step 2: economic value, intrinsic value, and positive school values. Because of the gender differences noted among the correlations, we also wanted to determine if gender moderated these relations among expectancies, values, and effort. As such, we entered gender on step 3, followed by the interaction terms of gender and all of the predictor variables on step 4. Predictor variables were centered around the mean prior to computing the interaction terms (Aiken & West, 1991).

When teacher-rated effort was used as the criterion variables, academic self-efficacy accounted for 6.7 percent of the variance. Consistent with our hypothesis that value variables would add to the prediction of effort above and beyond self-efficacy, that percentage increased to 10.2 percent (ΔR^2 = 3.5 percent) with the addition of the three values variables. Academic self-efficacy and positive school values were the only significant independent predictors. On step 3, we added gender to the equation and the amount of variance accounted for increased to 15.2 percent (ΔR^2 = 5.0 percent). The statistically significant negative beta weight associated with gender suggests that after controlling for the effects of values and self-efficacy, being male has a negative relation to one's academic effort (as rated by teachers). Once again, in this model increased self-efficacy and positive school values were independent predictors of increased teacher-rated effort. Including the interaction terms of gender with the other predictor variables on step 4 did not improve the amount of variance accounted for in teacher rated effort ($\diagdown R^2$ = -1.2 percent).

The results using self-rated effort as the criterion variable also confirmed the importance of values. Whereas academic-self-efficacy alone accounted for 10.2 percent of the variance, efficacy and values combined explained 25.0 percent ($\diagdown R^2$ = 15 percent) of the variation in reported effort. As with teacher-rated effort, academic self-efficacy and positive school values were the independent predictors. No significant increases in R^2 were observed with the addition of gender (R^2 = 25.0 percent; $\diagdown R^2$ = 0 percent) or the interaction terms (R^2 = 26.5 percent ; $\diagdown R^2$ = 1.5 percent). Consistent with motivation theory, academic efficacy was indeed predictive of students' effort as related by both teachers and students themselves. However, students' values were also significantly related to effort, independently of self-efficacy, with positive school values showing the strongest association. Together these results add support for the importance of the internalization of those values that are consistent with the values structure of schools.

TABLE 3
Hierarchical Regression Analyses:
Value and Expectancy Variables as Predictors of Teacher-Rated Effort

	Step 1	Step 2	Step 3
Variables	β	β	β
Academic Self-Efficacy	.267**	.245**	.256**
Positive School Values		.250**	.216**
Economic Value of Education		.016	.014
Intrinsic Value of Education		-.120	-.107
Gender			-.227**
R^2	6.7%	10.7%	15.5%
β R^2	6.7%	4.0%	4.8%

Notes: * p < .05; **p < .01

TABLE 4
Hierarchical Regression Analyses: Value and Expectancy
Variables as Predictors of Self-Rated Effort

	Step 1	Step 2
Variables	β	β
Academic Self-Efficacy	.326**	.215**
Positive School Values		.426**
Economic Value of Education		.043
Intrinsic Value of Education		-.075
Gender		
R^2	10.2%	25.0%
β R^2	10.2%	14.8%

Notes: * p <.05; **p < .01

Socialization of Values: The Role of Peers and Teachers

A second purpose of the study described above was to examine some of socialization experiences that may underlie the development of students' school values. Our premise was that (a) students' values develop through their interactions with others, and (b) that they are more likely to internalize the values of people with whom they have a mutually respectful and caring relationship (Connell & Wellborn, 1991). Two sets of relationships were examined: those with peers and teachers.

Relationships with peers are central in the lives of adolescents (Dornsbusch, 1989) and a plethora of research suggests that there is a strong congruence between individuals' academic orientation and the behavior of their peer group (e.g., Berndt & Keefe, 1992). Accordingly, it seems reasonable to assume that the values and behaviors of their peer group would affect the values of adolescents. Recall Fordham and Obgu's hypothesis that many African-American youth face groups that endorse anti-academic school values. Indeed, Farrell's (1990, 1994) successful urban high school students spoke of disengaging from their peers who tried to pull them into behaviors that would undermine their academic success. In contrast, the almost dropouts hung out with peers who created arenas of success outside of school.

In this study, we examined the relations between students' own school-related values, and the values and behaviors of their friends. Specifically, we sought to determine the extent to which peers' values and behaviors predicted students' own positive school values (i.e., valuing of effort, compliance, and prosocial behavior). We selected *positive school values* as the criterion variable because of its stronger relationships with students' own effort than either students' intrinsic valuing or economic valuing of education. Peer values were assessed in two ways: based on students' perceptions of their peer values, and the peers' own reported values. Perceived peer values were assessed measures of *peers' academic aspirations* and another of *peer academic support*. Items on the peer academic aspiration scales examine students' perceptions of their friends' interest and commitment to graduating from high school and furthering their education, versus leaving school. Peer academic support items focus on the extent to which students report that their peers engage in supportive (e.g., helping with homework) and unsupportive (e.g., teasing kids for studying) academic behaviors. Factor analysis indicates that the variance in these items could be explained by one factor ($\chi = .69$), thus, items were averaged to form one scale, *perceived peer aspirations and support*. This measure has been used in previous studies conducted by the first author (Murdock, 1999; Murdock et al., 2000) in which their validity has been demonstrated though factor analysis and logical correlations with other variables. (See Table 1 for sample items, and internal consistency coefficients in this sample). The second assessment of peer context was based on the self-reports of peers and ratings made by teachers. Each student in the study nominated five students on their academic team who they perceived to be their closest friends. We then examined the self-reported *positive school values* score (i.e. valuing of effort, compliance, prosocial behavior) of those five peers, and averaged those five scores to form a measure *of peers' self-reported positive school values*. Similarly, the scores of these five nominated peers' on *self-rated effort* and *teacher-rated effort* (both described above) were averaged to create scores of *peers' self-reported effort* and *peers' teacher-reported effort*. In sum, there were four variables (*perceived peer aspirations and support, peers' self-reported positive school values, peers' self-reported effort* and *peers' teacher-reported effort*) that were used as indicators of peer context in which to predict *self-rated positive school values*.

Students' reports of several dimensions of the quality of relationships they have with teachers were also hypothesized to be a potential socializing influence on students' school values. Teachers, as formal representatives of schooling, are apt to communicate values such as being effortful and prosocial. However, many students may not internalize these values because of the lack of caring and respect they feel in their school (Battistich, Solomon, Watson, & Schaps, 1997). In a recent study, we found that African-American students may be "at-risk" for developing poor relationships with their teachers as compared to Caucasian students (Murdock, 1999). Moreover, various studies suggest that negative relationships with teachers are a good predictor of school failure, whereas encouraging and supportive relationships have been linked to success (Farrell, 1990, 1994;

Goodenow, 1993; Murdock et al., 2000; Murdock, Hale, & Weber, 2001; Roeser, Midgley, & Urdan, 1996; Wehlage & Rutter, 1986; Wentzel, 1997; 1998). Finally, recent data suggests that teacher-student relationship variables predict changes in students' motivation over the course of two years, after controlling for both prior motivation and achievement (Murdock & Miller, manuscript in preparation).

In this study, we assessed quality of teacher relationship using a 12-item scale of teacher commitment and respect that was developed by the authors based on the previous work of Roberts, Hom, and Battistich (1995). The scale had demonstrated adequate internal consistency in similar samples, and logical correlations with criterion variables (e.g., Murdock, Hale, & Weber, 2000). We hypothesized that teacher commitment and respect would contribute to predicting variance in students' positive school values, above and beyond the variance accounted for by the peer variables. Gender was also included as moderating variables so that we could seek to determine if any of these variables might help to elucidate the source of achievement differences between African-American male and female students.

Table 5 presents the simple correlations between students' own positive school values, and the peer and teacher variables presumed to influence the development of those values. The results are presented separately for males and females. Note that across both gender groups, students' own self-reported values are most strongly correlated with the values they perceive their peers to have, rather than with the values reported by peers themselves or with the peers' self and teacher reported behaviors. Values as reported by peers are significantly, although modestly, correlated with

TABLE 5
Inter-Correlations Positive School Values and Context Variables
Separately for Girls and Boys

Variable	1	2	3	4	5	6
1. Positive School Values	—	.191*	.082	.149	.195*	.284**
2. Peers' Self- Reported Positive School Values	.072	—	.268**	.595**	.134	.073
3. Peers' Teacher-Rated Effort	.099	.261*	—	.414**	.010	.106
4. Peers' Self-Rated Effort	.029	.404**	.191	—	.160	.022
5. Teacher Support and Respect	.358**	.322**	.079	.112	—	.145
6. Perceived Peer Aspirations and Support	.429**	.121	.153	.009	.351	—

Notes: Correlations above the diagonal are for girls, below the diagonal are for boys;
         * p < .05; ** p < .01

TABLE 6
Regression Analysis of Positive School Values on Potential Peer and
Teacher Influences

Variable	Beta	R^2
Friends' Positive School Values	.924	
Friends' Teacher –Rated Effort	.282	
Friends' Self-Rated Effort	.618	
Perceived Teacher Commitment and Respect	2.69**	
Perceived Friends' Aspirations and Support	4.16***	
Total		14.2%

Notes: Models with gender, and the gender by predictor interaction terms did not improve the amount of variance accounted for;
    * $p < .05$; ** $p < .01$

peers' own values among girls but not boys. Similarly, students' perceptions of the support and respect they have received from their teachers were positively associated with their self-reported positive school values among both girls and boys. Although these findings are somewhat consistent with the idea that students who feel more respected in an environment are more likely to internalize the norms and values of that environment, the discrepancy between values that peers report to hold, and those that are perceived to hold suggests another interpretation. That is, it becomes difficult to discern whether the values and behaviors of others actually influence students' own values and behaviors, or, if they in fact, simply form personal view of the world in which they see their values as reinforced and perhaps even justified by the values and behaviors of those around them.

To examine the joint predictive value of peer and teacher socialization variables, we conducted a multiple regression analysis using positive school values as the criterion variable. Predictor variables included *perceived peer support and aspirations, perceived teacher commitment and respect, friends' teacher-rated effort, friends' self-reported effort,* and *friends' self-reported positive school values.* In order to test for the moderating effects of gender, the gender variable, as well as the centered interaction terms were also entered. Variables were entered in three steps: on step one, we entered the predictor variables, on step 2, gender was added to the equation, and on step 3, we added the interaction terms. Neither the gender variable, nor the gender interactions terms increased the amount of variance accounted for. Thus, results in Table 6 are for step 1 only. Together, the teacher and peer socialization variables accounted for 14 percent of the variance in positive school values, with two independent predictors: teacher commitment and respect, and perceived peer aspirations and support.

IMPLICATIONS AND FUTURE DIRECTION

Data from this study support the need to continue to expand our concep-tualization of the role that values play in supporting and directing stu-dents' motivated behavior in school. For the African-American students in this study, it was their positive school values (e.g., compliance, effort) that were most closely associated with their level of academic effort. The strength of the relations between students' self-reported values and their self-reported effort suggests at a minimum, that students are interested in portraying themselves in ways they admire: those who report holding posi-tive school values also report they work hard (see also Juvonen & Murdock, 1993; 1995). However, positive school values were also predictive of teacher-rated effort, suggesting perhaps that while values may determine behavior, teachers may prefer students who hold values that are consistent with their own.

In regression analyses, students' reports of their intrinsic valuing of edu-cation were largely unrelated to their self- or teacher-rated effort. These findings echo previous research in which African-American students, even those doing poorly, reported that schoolwork is important (Goodenow & Grady, 1993; Steinberg, Dornsbusch, & Brown, 1992). However, it should be noted that when simple correlations are examined, intrinsic valuing of school is associated with effort. It seems likely that it was not a predictor in the regression due to its moderate correlations with positive school values, and with academic self-efficacy, particularly among boys. Consistent with the devaluing hypothesis discussed earlier, those students who felt more capable also found school more intrinsically interesting. It also maybe, however, that intrinsic values did not emerge as an independent predictor because it was a psychometrically weaker variable. Although the scale had reasonable reliability on this sample, unlike the measures of positive school values, students were directly asked their opinions about school, rather than the behaviors "they admire." Previous research on values suggests that this direct form of questioning may pull for socially desirable answers, hence, our use of the "admire" stem in the development of the positive val-ues scale (Scott, 1991). Students' doubts about the economic value of edu-cation were only minimally related to self-reported effort, and were also not unique predictors of student behavior. These results are surprising given the many previous studies that have documented the predictive power of this construct for a host of school outcomes (Mickelson, 1990; Murdock, 1999, Murdock et al., 2000; Steinberg et al., 1992). Moreover, although the reliability of this scale was somewhat low, similar internal con-sistencies have been reported in these previous studies. Clearly, motivation theories would benefit from time spent on psychometric research aimed at improving our ability to measure students' values.

African-American boys in this study had self-views that were more dispar-ate from other views than did girls. Boys had lower grades and lower teacher-ratings of effort than girls yet their views of themselves, and their professed values about school, were no different than those of the girls. However, boys' positive views did not extend to their perceived peer group. Recall that there were no gender differences in self-reported effort or values of friends, but that boys did perceive their peers as less supportive of academic achievement than did the girls. Similar peer devaluing of school by African-American boys has been documented in several ethnographic studies of African-American youth. Graham and her colleagues (Graham et al., 1998) have suggested that this trend is more prevalent among boys than girls because African-American boys are more subject to negative stereotypes, and therefore are more defensive than girls. It also seems possible, however, that boys have more to "protect" than girls, given our society's gender-role stereotypes that presume boys will be the primary wage earners. In other words, it may be that academic failure, particularly the economic costs associated with that failure are more devastating for boys, resulting in more protective self images. Clearly, however, the discrepancy between self-views and other views suggests that researchers who are interested in understanding motivation need to consider multiple sources of data.

Students in this study who were most apt to have positive school values were those students who perceived their relationships with teachers as characterized by mutual caring and respect. These results support the important role that "pedagogical caring" plays in students' achievement behavior (Wentzel, 1998) and suggest that caring may be a mechanism that promotes the internalization of positive school values (Grusec & Goodnow, 1994). However, because these data are cross-sectional, we do not know how perceived caring, values, and behaviors develop over time. It may be that students' who hold positive school values perceive their teacher as "more caring" primarily because the groups have similar sets of expectations. In all likelihood, teacher and students mutually influence each others attitudes and behaviors such that students who come into a classroom with more socially acceptable school behaviors, get treated better, thereby reinforcing the behavior pattern they have. Future research should focus on the relationships between values, teacher behavior, and students' behavior over time. It also will be important to conduct observational studies of classrooms so that we can clarify the teacher behaviors that are perceived by students as more and less respectful and supportive.

Although the impetus to broaden our conceptualization of values stemmed from a desire to better understand the motivation of African-American youth, it may well be that our understanding of achievement motivation generally would benefit from a focus on broader study of values. As noted earlier, motivational psychologists have typically used measures of task-specific values to try to explain either subject specific motivation or subject-level differences in students' performance. However, the relative under-achievement of African-American students across subject areas, reminds us that there are usually high correlations among subject area grades, and more variation between students than between subject areas. By thinking more broadly about "motivation for school," we can begin to ask a series of questions about the factors that promote adaptation to a school environment.

REFERENCES

Aiken, L. S., & West, S. G. (1991). *Multiple regression: Testing and interpreting interactions.* Newbury Park, CA, Sage.

Anderson, E. (1999). *Code of the street: Decency, violence, and the moral life of the inner city.* New York, NY : Norton.

Bandura, A. (1997). *Self-efficacy: The exercise of control.* New York, NY: W. H. Freeman.

Battistich, V., Solomon, D., Watson, M., & Schaps, E. (1997). Caring school communities. *Educational Psychologist, 32,* 137-151.

Berndt, T. J. & Keefe, K. (1992). Friends' influence on adolescents' perceptions of themselves at school. In D. Schunk & J. L. Meece (Eds.), *Student perceptions in the classroom* (pp. 51-73). Hillsdale, NJ: Erlbaum.

Bolch, M.B. Murdock, T.B., & Wilcox, N.H. (2001). *Relations of academic performance to school self-esteem among African-American and Caucasian adolescents: Disidentification or devaluing.* Unpublished manuscript.

Bronfenbrenner, U. (1979). *The ecology of human development: Experiments by nature and design.* Cambridge, MA: Harvard University Press.

Connell, J. P; & Wellborn, J. G. (1991). Competence, autonomy, and relatedness: A motivational analysis of self-system processes. In M. R. Gunnar & A. L. Sroufe, Eds. (1991). *Self processes and development. The Minnesota symposia on child psychology, Vol. 23.* (pp. 43-77). Hillsdale, NJ: Erlbaum.

Crocker, J., & Major, B. (1989). Social stigma and self-esteem: The self-protective properties of stigma. *Psychological Review, 96,* 608-630.

Crocker, J., Voelkl, K., Testa, M., & Major, B. (1991). Social stigma: The affective consequences of attributional ambiguity. *Journal of Personality and Social Psychology, 60,* 218-228.

Dornsbusch, S. M. (1989). The sociology of adolescence. *Annual Review of Sociology, 15,* 233-259.

Dubois, D.L., Felner, R.D., Brand, S., Phillips, R.S.C., & Lease, A.M. (1996). Early adolescent self-esteem: A developmental-ecological framework and assessment strategy. *Journal of Research on Adolescence, 6,* 543-579.

Eccles (Parsons), J., Adler, Y., Futterman, R., Goff, S. B., Kaczala, C. M., & Midgley, C. (1983). Expectancies, values and academic behaviors. In J. T. Spence (Ed.), *Achievement and achievement motives: Psychological and sociological approaches* (pp. 75-149). San Francisco, CA: W. H. Freeman.

Eccles, J. S., & Wigfield, A. (1992). The development of achievement task values: A theoretical analysis. *Developmental Review, 12,* 265-310.

Farrell, E. W. (1990). *Hanging in and dropping out: Voices of at-risk high school students.* New York, NY: Teachers College Press.

Farrell, E. W. (1994). *Self and school success: Voices and lore of inner-city students.* Albany, NY: State University of New York Press.

Feather, N. T. (1988). Values, valences, and course enrollment: Testing the role of personal values within an expectancy-valence framework. *Journal of Educational Psychology, 80,* 381-391.

Ford, D.Y. (1992a). The American achievement ideology as perceived by urban African-American students: Explorations by gender and academic program. *Urban Education, 27,* 196-211.

Ford, D.Y. (1992b). Self-perceptions of under achievement and support for the achievement ideology among early adolescent African-Americans. *Journal of Early Adolescence, 12,* 228-252.

Fordham, S., & Ogbu, J. (1986). Black students' school success: Coping with the burden of "acting white." *Urban Review, 18,* 176-205.

Goodenow, C., & Grady, K. E. (1993). The relationship of school belonging and friends' values to academic motivation among urban adolescent students. *Journal of Experimental Education, 62,* 60-71.

Goodlad (1984). *A place called school: Prospects for the future.* New York, NY: Mc-Graw-Hill.

Graham, S. (1994). Motivation in African-Americans *Review of Educational Research, 64,* 55-117.

Graham, S., Taylor, A. Z., & Hudley, C. (1998). Exploring achievement values among ethnic minority early adolescents. *Journal of Educational Psychology, 90,* 606-620.

Grusec, J.E, & Goodnow, J. J. (1994). Impact of parental discipline methods on the child's internalization of values: A reconceptualization of current points of view. *Developmental Psychology, 30,* 4-19.

Harter, S. (1991). The perceived competence scale for children. *Child Development, 53,* 87-97.

Juvonen, J., & Murdock, T. B. (1993). How to promote social approval: The effect of outcome and audience on publicly communicated attributions. *Journal of Educational Psychology, 85,* 365-376.

Juvonen, J., & Murdock, T. B. (1995). Perceived social consequences of effort and ability attributions: Implications for developmental changes in self-presentation tactics. *Child Development, 66,* 1694-1705.

Keltikangas-Jarervinen, L. (1992). Self-esteem as a predictor of future school achievement. *European Journal of Psychology of Education, 7,* 123-130.

Major, B., Spencer, S., Schmader, T., Wolfe, C., & Crocker, J. (1998). Coping with negative stereotypes about intellectual performance: The role of psychological disengagement. *Personality and Social Psychological Bulletin, 24,* 34-50.

Mickelson, R. A. (1990). The attitude-achievement paradox among black adolescents. *Sociology of Education, 63,* 44-61.

Midgley, C., Maehr, M.L., Hruda, L.Z., Anderman., E., Anderman, L., Freeman, K.E., Gheen, M., Kaplan, A., Kumar, R., Middleton, M.J., Nelson, J., Roeser, R., & Urdan, T. (2000). *Manuals for the Patterns of Adaptive Learning Scales.* Ann Arbor, Michigan: University of Michigan.

Murdock, T. B. (1994). *Understanding alienation: Towards ecological perspectives on student motivation.* Unpublished doctoral dissertation, University of Delaware, Newark.

Murdock, T.B. (1996). *Expectations, achievement, and academic self-concept: The continuing significance of race.* Paper presented at the annual meeting of the American Educational Research Association, New York, NY.

Murdock, T. B. (1999). The social context of risk: Predictors of alienation in middle school. *Journal of Educational Psychology, 91*, 62-75.

Murdock, T. B., Anderman, L. H., & Hodge, S. A. (2000). Middle grades predictors of high -school motivation and behavior. *Journal of Adolescent Research, 15, 327-351.*

Murdock, T.B., & Dent, G. (2000). *Expectancies and values as predictors of effort and achievement among African-American adolescents.* Paper presented at the annual meeting of the American Educational Research Association, New Orleans, LA.

Murdock, T.B., Hale, N. & Weber, M. J. (2001). Predictors of cheating among early adolescents: Academic and social motivations. *Contemporary Educational Psychology, 26*, 96-115.

Murdock, T.B. & Miller, A. (2001). *Teacher-student relationships as predictors of changes in motivation over time.* (Unpublished manuscript).

Nieto, S. (2000). *Affirming diversity: The sociopolitical context of multicultural education* (3rd edition). White Plains, NY: Longman.

Noddings, N. (1992). *The challenge to care in schools: An alternative approach to education.* New York, NY: Teachers College Press.

Osborne, J. W. (1995). Academics, self-esteem, and race: A look at the underlying assumptions of the disidentification hypothesis. *Personality and Social Psychology Bulletin, 21*, 449-455.

Osborne, J.W. (1997). Race and academic disidentification. *Journal of Educational Psychology, 89*, 728-735.

Pintrich, P. R., & De Groot, E. V. (1990). Motivational and self-regulated learning components of classroom academic performance. *Journal of Educational Psychology, 82*, 33-40.

Pungello, E. P, Kupersmidt, J. B, Burchinal, M. R, & Patterson, C. J.(1996). Environmental risk factors and children's achievement from middle childhood to early adolescence. *Developmental Psychology, 32*, 755-767.

Ramey, S. L., & Ramey, C. T. (1992). Early educational intervention with disadvantaged children: To what effect? *Applied & Preventive Psychology*, 1, 131-140.

Richman, C.L., Clark, M. L., & Brown, K. P. (1985). General and specific self-esteem in late adolescent students: Race x gender x ses effects. *Adolescence, 20*, 555-566.

Roberts, W., Hom, A., & Battistich, V. (1995). *Assessing students' and teachers' sense of the school as a caring community.* Paper presented at the annual meeting of the American Educational Research Association, San Francisco, CA.

Roeser, R.W., Midgley, C., & Urdan, T.C. (1996). Perceptions of the school psychological climate and early adolescents' psychological and behavioral functioning in school: The mediating roles of goals and belonging. *Journal of Educational Psychology, 88*, 408-422.

Scott, W. A. (1991). Personal value scale, 1965. In J. P. Robinson, P. R Shaver, & T.S. Wrightsman (Eds.), *Measures of personality and social psychological attitudes,* (Vol. 1). New York, NY: Academic Press.

Schunk, D. H. (1990). Self efficacy and academic motivation. *Educational Psychologist, 26*, 207-231.

Steinberg, L., Dornsbusch, S. N., & Brown, B.B. (1992). Ethnic differences in adolescent achievement: An ethological perspective. *American Psychologist, 47*, 723-729.

Steele, C. (1992, April). Race and the schooling of Black Americans. *The Atlantic Monthly, 269 (4),* 68-78.

Steele, C.M. (1997). A threat in the air: How intellectual stereotypes shape intellectual identity and performance. *American Psychologist, 52,* 613-629.

Stipek, D. J., MacIver, D. (1989). Developmental changes in children's assessment of intellectual competence. *Child Development, 60,* 521-538.

Walker, D., Greenwood, C. R.,Hart, B., & Carta, J. (1994). Prediction of school outcomes based on early language production and socioeconomic factors *Child Development, 65,* 606-621.

Wehlage, G. G., & Rutter, R. A. (1986). Dropping out: How much do schools contribute to the problem? *Teachers College Record, 87,* 374-392.

Weiner, B. & Kukla, A. (1970). An attributional analysis of achievement motivation. *Journal of Personality and Social Psychology, 15,* 1-20.

Wentzel, K. R. (1998). Social relationships and motivation in middle school: The role of parents, teachers, and peers. *Journal of Educational Psychology, 90,* 202-209.

Wentzel, K. (1997). Student motivation in middle school: The role of perceived pedagogical caring. *Journal of Educational Psychology, 89,* 411-417.

Wentzel, K. (1993). Does being good make the grade? Social behavior and academic competence in middle-school. *Journal of Educational Psychology, 89,* 411-419.

CHAPTER 11

COMMUNITIES SHARING RESEARCH
An American Indian Case Study

Dawn Iwamoto and Henry Radda

INTRODUCTION

Across a range of reports, American Indian drop-out rates appear considerably in excess of the national norms. For example, a 1989 Report from the National Center for Educational Statistics indicated that American Indians and Alaskan Native students have a dropout rate of 35.5 percent per year. This rate represents the highest dropout rate of any United States ethnic or racial group studied (as cited in Reyhner, 1992). Platero, Brandt, Witherspoon and Wong (1986) conducted a Navajo student dropout study. An analysis of roster data provided an estimate of student dropout rates for the Navajo group studied. The dropout rate at the secondary level was 35.4 percent during the 1984-1985 school year and 24.5 percent for the 1985-1986 school year. Swisher, Hoisch, and Pavel (1991) summarized recent dropout rates of American Indian and Alaskan Native students in grades 9-12 as compiled and reported by the state of Arizona. American Indian and Alaskan Native dropout rates in Arizona appear to be approximately three to five times higher than the dropout rates reported for White, middle income level students nationally.

In summary, there is legitimate concern for the lower rate of retention in high school for American Indian students. American Indian students drop out of high school at a far greater rate than most other students. Historically, the experiences in school for American Indian students have been more negative than positive which may influence achievement motivation. The focus of this study was to investigate the possible influences on student motivation in school. Some research has been conducted to examine the obstacles presented in this chapter. Very little research has led to systemic change within schools to strengthen opportunities for American Indian youth (McInerney & Swisher, 1995). Therefore, this practical research was designed to influence current practices in the education of these students.

Socio-cultural Factors Influencing Students

A 1992 report from the U.S. Department of Education outlines the various reasons students in grades 10 through 12 drop out of high school. The number one reason reported (42.9 percent) was a dislike for school, while 38.7 percent reported that they dropped out of school because they were failing (McMillen, 1994). A 1985 report from the Arizona State Department of Education indicated that American Indian students, without exception, demonstrated the lowest scores on reading, language, and mathematics of all racial and ethnic groups at every grade level (Red Horse, 1986).

Wilson (1991) asserted that when teachers do not believe American Indian students are capable of success, the students believe the best thing to do is to drop out of school. The U.S. Department of Education reported that far too many American Indian students are found in low-ability, remedial track programs and represent the highest population of school dropouts in the nation (as cited in McCarty, 1993). Reyhner (1992) postulates that tracked classes with low expectations and boredom may be contributing to American Indian students dropping out of school. He believes that these students are often tracked into remedial or vocational education classes, which have negative effects on self-esteem and the desire to succeed.

According to Reyhner (1989), a noted author on American Indian education, at least eight ethnocultural factors are potentially responsible for the poor academic achievement of Indian students:

- disparity between native culture and dominant culture
- native culture is not understood among school staff
- students' and teachers' values are not the same

- native students' learning styles are different from the dominant culture
- poor motivation of Indian students
- language differences between students and teachers
- students' home and community difficulties and
- inappropriate use of tests with Indian students

McInerney & Swisher (1995) and Reyhner (1992) suggest that the cultural differences that exist between home and school may contribute to American Indian students dropping out of school. They believe factors such as home environment, geographical isolation, inappropriate school curriculum, negative teacher expectations, and socio-economic factors may be contributors to failure as well.

Swisher and Deyhle (1989) suggest that the differences between the contexts of American Indian students' home learning methods and those experienced in the school environment may result in poor academic performance. They believe that American Indian children may be exposed to a particular learning style in the home that contrasts with the learning opportunities they are exposed to in the school environment. Through their studies, they have come to believe that some American Indian children, for example, are taught by their families to be observers. In these families, the children are expected to observe a task several times before attempting the task in public. In most schools, according to these researchers, teachers encourage students to use the method of trial and error to practice a new concept. This teaching method and the American Indian student's learning styles are not compatible; therefore, these students are often viewed as unmotivated or uncooperative. Swisher and Deyhle conclude that teachers need to become more fully aware of the cultural differences stemming from the home environment that affect learning in the classroom. These children bring with them many gifts and talents that can be utilized as effective learning tools in the classroom. They propose that if we were to create a connection between the cultures in the home and the school, American Indian students would make better academic and emotional growth.

Cross-cultural Influences on Educational Practice

Some researchers believe a lack of cultural understanding on the part of school personnel can contribute to American Indian student failure (Reyhner, 1992; Wilson, 1991). Reyhner (1992) states that teachers may become frustrated with American Indian students, because they may not be sure how to teach them effectively. Some teachers may not understand that these children learn differently from non-native students. Reyhner believes teacher training programs do not typically address cultural issues and learning styles of American Indian students. He concludes that comprehensive teacher education programs can help facilitate skills that are designed to assist diverse learners in the classroom. Staff development programs should focus on topics such as cultural diversity and learning styles (Reyhner, 1992).

Swisher and Deyhle (1989) recommend that teachers who have been frustrated with the low academic achievement of American Indian students need to take the initiative to educate themselves to be particularly aware of the cultural differences that exist in classrooms. According to O'Hair (1995), we need to build a connection between the schools and teacher education programs. "If American public schools are to become centers of excellence, then their most important human resource (e.g. teachers) must be effectively developed" (Sternberg & Horvath, 1995, p. 9).

Effective teaching depends on a teacher's ability to choose appropriate materials, objectives and activities and recognize the diverse needs of learners in a classroom. It is inappropriate to think teachers can take principles and techniques and make them applicable in all situations with all children (House & Lapan, 1988). Swisher and Deyhle (1989) state that teaching styles and classroom contexts can have a significant effect on the academic failure or success of American Indian students. They found that in many classrooms, new concepts are introduced orally which is in direct opposition to the visual learning style of the majority of American Indian students. The use of multisensory techniques can prove beneficial for students who need alternate methods of instruction (House & Lapan, 1988; McLaughlin & Talbert, 1990; Swisher & Deyhle, 1989).

Educational practices and opportunities for American Indian youth have progressed during the twentieth century. The dynamics of tribes and schools vary significantly. Working toward cooperative efforts that include tribal councils and education committees, school district administrators and teachers, parents, and students can help students achieve.

The Fort McDowell Yavapai Nation

It is important to understand the characteristics of the Fort McDowell Yavapai Nation since the factors influencing students within school systems may be different for individual tribes. Khera (1995) reports that only a hundred years ago, thousands of Yavapai occupied much of the land expanding from Flagstaff to Kingman and as far south as Yuma. They lived in the mountains north of the Gila and Salt Rivers and as far north as the Mogollon Rim. According to Schneider (1995), the Yavapai tribe, numbering over 6,000 lived on some ten million acres of land throughout Arizona.

The Fort McDowell Indian Reservation is only a small parcel of land once considered ancestral territory of the Yavapai Indians. This reservation is located within Maricopa County, approximately 23 miles northeast of the Phoenix metropolitan area. The 24,680-acre reservation sits at an elevation of 1,350 feet (Chaudhuri, 1995). Currently, the Fort McDowell Yavapai Tribe consists of 887 tribal members although approximately 450 of these members live on this reservation.

Within American Indian communities, socio-cultural issues underlie the perspective, orientation and action of its members. Cultural practices and perspectives, the concept of sovereignty and resistance to being assimilated by the majority are at the forefront of many discussions, interactions with other communities and decisions regarding American Indian educational practices. The Tribe only recently had to fight for their sovereignty and land. Fifteen years earlier they stood their ground against the government, who had plans to turn a significant part of the reservation into a lake. The new town being developed next door was to have lake front property. As divisive as this process was there was recognition from people on both sides of the cattleguard that the plan was unacceptable. The cattleguard is symbolic and real in that the reservation is split from the local town by cattleguards at its entrances. A number a church groups and the Audobon society stood with the Tribe in forestalling and ending the Orme Dam project that would have flooded the reservation.

The Tribe currently owns and operates a casino, farm, sand and gravel operation, gas station, convenience store and western adventure facility. The Fort McDowell Gaming Center is a significant source of revenue and along with the other enterprises provides employment opportunities for tribal members. In the early nineties the people of Fort McDowell halted the State and the FBI from confiscating their gaming machines. They negotiated the first gaming compact with the State of Arizona.

The community offers a range of facilities including a center for the elderly, recreation center, sports fields, and a library. A medical clinic, behavioral health center and social service agency are all operated by the Tribe. Furthermore, the police department and new fire station has started to serve the community.

The tribe established a Department of Indian Education to oversee the educational programs for reservation students. The H'man Shawa Day School, located on the reservation, provides an option for parents who chose to educate children in a reservation school for preschool through second grade. The Indian Education Committee works with the bordering school districts in planning educational opportunities for American Indian students (Chaudhuri, 1995). The Fountain Hills School District has a tribal representative from this committee on the school board as a non-voting member. Site councils at individual schools within the school district reserve spaces for parents from Fort McDowell to serve as active members.

Records maintained by the Fort McDowell Indian Education Department indicate that approximately 80 percent of the students living on Fort McDowell Indian Reservation attend school in the Fountain Hills School District. Twenty-six percent of the American Indian students in this school district qualify for special education services. Table 1 illustrates the concern of the community and school district over the number of American Indian students who graduate from high school. Only one American Indian student graduated from the Fountain Hills High School between the 1992-93 and the 1995-96 school years. As shown in this table, attrition has consistently occurred as American Indian students made the transition from the elementary level to junior high and continued to occur throughout high school.

It should be noted that the collaborative efforts between the school district and the tribal community began in 1996. Although improvement may be noted in the retention rates between the onset of the study in 1996 and the present, the specific causes of this warrant further investigation.

Two Communities Find Common Cause

This study highlights the collaborative effort of two communities in establishing the parameters of a study with a vision that the results would be relevant and practical so that policy and practice would be influenced.

Early in 1996 representatives of the Fort McDowell Yavapai Nation approached administrators from the Fountain Hills School District to ask for their cooperation in conducting a study that would help both entities gain a better understanding of the American Indian children who were educated within this dominant culture school system. The administration was responsive and joined Fort McDowell in their search for information and a process of collaborative problem solving.

The Working Committee was then formed, comprising representatives from Fort McDowell, Fountain Hills Unified School District, and Arizona State University - Center for Indian Education. This Working Committee reported to the Fountain Hills School Board, the Fort McDowell Indian Education Committee and the Fort McDowell Tribal Council. Ultimately, the School Board and the Tribal Council control the extent of change.

This committee's goal was to study factors contributing to school achievement, motivation, and retention in school for American Indian and non-Indian students. In working collaboratively, it was felt that a motivational study of the whole school district would yield data that would assist in examining programming, policies, and teaching methods for any number of subgroups. The group wanted to be able to help all children by understanding the complexity of motivation.

TABLE 1
Fcuntain Hills Unified School District Enrollment of American Indian Students in Grades 5-12

Grade	92-93	93-94	94-95	95-96	96-97	97-98	98-99	99-00	00-01
12th	0	0	0	1	3	3	6	6	14
11th	1	3	3	6	5	6	6	6	16
10th	2	2	7	7	11	9	5	18	20
9th	5	8	10	11	9	11	17	29	21
8th	5	9	11	9	20	16	13	14	20
7th	10	8	12	11	16	16	16	16	8
6th	11	12	18	25	21	19	21	8	21
5th	12	15	24	22	23	32	10	29	22

It is often reiterated that the time lag between research and implementation of that research is about seven years. The Working Committee had no intention of waiting seven years to offer information to policy makers. The overall structure of this study was created to ensure timely, relevant research that could guide policy decisions and create a model feedback loop that would serve this research as well as future issues.

When studying a phenomenon the old quandary of missing the forest for the trees is relevant. As humans we want to live competently - understanding our world and living in a meaningful way (Kegan, 1985). We strive for perspectives that inform us in making decisions. We realize that our perspective of the world, at any one time, highlights certain meanings and understandings and yet, precludes us from seeing, feeling and understanding other things. This quandary was addressed by developing a research methodology that would be quantitative in phase one and qualitative in phase two.

Quantitative studies yield wonderful numbers and charts that can be displayed, analyzed, re-analyzed, added, multiplied and most importantly, generalized. This type of study is helpful in understanding the forest and even for understanding groups of trees. The answers are quite powerful because they are based on numbers, statistics and are reproducible. The strength of this method is that it gives definition to the big picture.

Qualitative studies, on the other hand, are not as clear. They deal with the depth of an individual's feelings, understandings and perspectives of the world. The world from this perspective is rich. Practitioners tend to enjoy this model because it seems more relevant and accessible.

In cross cultural research it is important to understand phenomena from an overall view which allows consideration of general factors that may vary in importance, and yet be common to all groups. It is important to be able to analyze those factors that are more specifically relevant to the group one wishes to study. The researchers wanted information that at once is generally relevant to all the children in school and yet specifically relevant to Fort McDowell children.

The goal was to study all students with three quantifiable instruments. This information provided a broad view of motivational factors and influences on school achievement and retention in high school. After completing the quantitative phase, the general results were presented to the educational boards, tribal council, and administrators. The information was presented with the intent to create dialogue about the issues rather than expert answers. From the discussions of the preliminary results of the quantitative study, the Working Committee developed preliminary recommendations for the Tribal Community and School District to implement. Further questions from boards, administrators, teachers and staff were gathered during presentations of phase one results. These questions guided the refinement of the qualitative study and resulted in action plans to implement recommendations. These will be discussed later. The committee wanted the research to stay close to the marrow and wanted to know the perspectives, language and understandings from groups that would benefit from this knowledge. The information had to be communicated to teachers and staff so that they could make a difference and be involved in the implementation of recommendations.

In the fall of 1997, Dennis McInerney, initiated the qualitative study, and will continue until 2003 when the cohort group graduates from high school. The qualitative research is reported in McInerney & McInerney (2000).

Questions resulting from the committee for the initial study were summarized as follows: 1) What motivational factors influence achievement and retention in school? 2) What facilitating conditions influence achievement and intent to complete high school? 3) How are these factors similar and different for American Indian and non-Indian students? 4) What recommendations can we make to educators, parents and community members to maximize success in school for our students?

COLLABORATIVE CASE STUDY

The Design

The Fountain Hills School District comprises 2350 students ranging from preschool through twelfth grade. The American Indian student population in the district is approximately 10 percent. The overall graduation rate for the district is 96 percent, which is above the state and national average.

All students attending Fountain Hills Unified School District in grades five through twelve were surveyed in an effort to understand motivational factors for all students. For the purposes here, the data obtained from the American Indian population were used to focus on this particular group of students. This age range was chosen because American Indian students tend to drop out of school in the highest numbers in the eighth and ninth grades as indicated in records maintained by the Fort McDowell Indian Education Department. It was important to cover a wide enough span of ages to gain as much information from as many American Indian students as possible.

Participants

A total of 1171 students were administered three surveys across these grade levels. Surveys were administered to 375 elementary students (fifth and sixth grade), 326 junior high students (seventh and eighth grade), and

470 high school students (ninth through twelfth grade). A total of 81 American Indian students were included in this study from the original group of 1171 students. Forty of the elementary group, 21 of the junior high group, and 20 of the high school group were American Indian students. Most of the American Indian students in this district live within the Fort McDowell Yavapai Nation. Approximately 80 percent of the school age children from this community attend school within the Fountain Hills School District.

Instruments

Three survey instruments were used in this study. The Inventory of School Motivation (McInerney & Swisher, 1995), McInerney & Sinclair (1991,1992), McInerney, Roche, McInerney, & Marsh (1997) was designed to measure goals, values, and sense of self components of motivation in cross cultural settings. The ISM was designed with sixty-three items assigned to ten scales (task-effort, competition, power, affiliation, social concern, recognition, token, sense of purpose, sense of competence, and self esteem) based on confirmatory factor analysis of the items. In this study, Cronbach's alphas were calculated to test the internal consistency of the scales. The calculation results were indicative of a highly reliable instrument (Iwamoto, 1998).

The Facilitating Conditions Questionnaire [McInerney, 1989, 1992, 1995) Keats, Munro & Mann (Eds.)] deals with environmental pressures on motivation in the school setting, such as family, peer, and teacher influences. The FCQ has shown relevance in cross-cultural settings (McInerney, 1989, 1992). The FCQ was designed with forty-one items randomly assigned throughout the instrument and assigned to four scales (peer influences, teacher support, personal relevance and parental support) The appropriateness of the scales was demonstrated by confirmatory factor analysis of the items (Radda, Iwamoto & Patrick, 1998).

The third instrument, the Behavioral Intentions Questionnaire (McInerney, 1991) measures perceived consequences, norms, values, affect, and how these influence educational motivation. These factors were viewed through the student's perspective of making parents proud, teachers proud, friends proud, families proud and employability.

Analyses

As well as a range of descriptive analyses used to examine the salient predictors for the participants, separate multiple regression analyses were also conducted to determine whether the scales on the ISM, FCQ and BIQ were predictors of grade point average and intention to complete high school. Grade point average was entered as a numerical value. Intention to complete high school was entered as a value comprised of a formula combining the variables (Iwamoto, 1998). All data were analyzed using the Statistical Program for the Social Sciences (SPSS). The instruments contained responses from 1, strongly agree to 5, strongly disagree. Therefore, lower mean scores indicated more positive responses. These analyses are reported in detail in Iwamoto (1998). In the sections below we briefly describe the general findings in order to focus on the implications for intervention.

RESULTS AND DISCUSSION

Demographic Characteristics of the Population

The initial part of each survey was designed to elicit demographic information in order to describe the characteristics of this population of American Indian students. Forty-six percent of the respondents indicated that they live with their mother and father. Thirty-two percent reported living with a mother only, 1 percent with father only, and 18 percent with other relatives. Twenty-six percent of the students described their fathers as semi-skilled workers (jobs requiring minimal training), 12 percent as unemployed, and 13 percent as working in professional positions. Forty-six percent of the students indicated that their fathers graduated from high school, and 45 percent of the students reported not knowing how much schooling their fathers had. Twenty-three percent of the students stated that their mothers worked in a clerical/sales position, 20 percent in semi-skilled positions, and 21 percent as homemakers. Fifty-nine percent of the students reported that their mothers graduated from high school, and 30 percent indicated that they did not know. Over 80 percent of the participants reported having at least one brother or sister. Forty-two percent of the students indicated that they were the oldest child in the family. The composition of families ranged from one to nine children.

The American Indian students in this school district reported that they had been retained at a rate three times higher than reported by non-Indian students. Thirteen percent of the dominant population of students and more than 33 percent of the American Indian students indicated that they had been involved in special education. The American Indian students in this study experience lower achievement than their non-Indian peers.

The Inventory of School Motivation indicated similarities for both groups (Iwamoto, 1998; Radda, Iwamoto, & Patrick, 1998). Achievement and retention in school were most closely related to the students' self-esteem for both the American Indian and non-Indian groups. For both groups, sense of purpose in learning was an important predictor for success in school. These results are notable for educators. Since these variables are most significant for all students, educators need to explore the value of promoting self-esteem in the classroom. Parents and peers should be cognizant of the importance of self worth and recognize how their actions may affect children. Furthermore, too often, students ask "why" the learning objectives are essential in their lives. It is the responsibility of educators to help students make connections, to understand the purpose of learning. It is when students are able to comprehend the logical relevance of learning to their lives, that they are most successful. Planning and goal setting must become important for students as they relate directly to envisioning a sense of purpose in education. In a comprehensive study conducted by Cleary and Peacock (1998), teachers of American Indian students were interviewed in an effort to gain a better understanding of these students in an educational setting. They found,

> When students learned from being involved in projects that had real audiences and real purposes, they understood how to read their world, how to collect information, and how to act of their world (p. 218).

Both groups responded negatively to valuing competition (such as beating others in tests) and power (such as leading a group) in order to enhance their school achievement (Iwamoto, 1998; Radda, Iwamoto, & Patrick, 1998). This is also an important point as many authors believe there is a difference between American Indians and non-Indian groups in the valuing of competitiveness and power seeking, and that this influences achievement differentially for the two groups. However, our data suggest that the two groups are more similar than different on these two dimensions. It appears that competition and power seeking is perceived negatively by both groups within the academic setting. Hence, schools need to reconsider any programs that highlight competition and power seeking as a means of gaining and measuring success, as these programs may set up dysfunctional motivational systems for students in general. However, this negative attitude towards competition and power is related to academic situations specifically, rather than to extra-curricular activities such as sports, in which many American Indian and non-Indian students are intensely competitive and from which they derive considerable status and power within the school setting through their role as athletes.

In contrast, students from both groups valued learning in collaborative groups designed to promote individual achievement. American Indian students also valued helping one another at school. This value was not as apparent in the analysis for non-Indian students. Cultural differences may account for the American Indian students' emphasis on the importance of working together and helping one another in the community.

The two groups reported significant differences in valuing achievement recognition in school (Iwamoto, 1998; Radda, Iwamoto, & Patrick, 1998). The non-Indian students responded positively to recognition of their efforts, while the American Indian students responded more negatively. These findings are consistent with the literature, which suggests the American Indian students do not seek or appreciate public recognition. Cleary and Peacock (1998) asked teachers to respond to questions regarding recognising American Indian student achievement. An American Indian teacher responded,

> You don't withhold praise, but make sure that you do it discreetly … Growing up here and being here as an adult, I can see that if one person gets too much recognition, then other people have a hard time dealing with that and you set up that one person to become almost an object of scorn (p. 205).

Non-Indian students indicated that task-effort was not essential for success, while American Indian students valued putting forth effort in order to achieve tasks. For the American Indian students task-effort was related to achievement outcomes. This could indicate that learning does not come easily for the American Indian students in this context; therefore, effort is essential for success. On the other hand, it might also mean that, traditionally, effort is valued for its own sake within this American Indian community (Iwamoto, 1998; Radda, Iwamoto, & Patrick, 1998). High achieving non-Indian students do not value the importance of effort to the same extent. This is consistent with attribution theory findings that for Western adolescents, ability is perceived to be less in an individual that has to apply effort in order to achieve. The American Indian students may have a better perception of the value of effort for a variety of reasons. Despite this, there are many students from the full sample who do not value effort and it may be that many students have to undergo attribution retraining in order to learn to value the relationship between effort and achievement.

Differences were also apparent for the motivational importance of token rewards (Iwamoto, 1998). While non-Indian students did not value token rewards for their achievement the American Indian students did. Many of these students value token rewards because the practice of giving token rewards is common within the Tribe. Consequently token rewards take on an extra significance for this group. The American Indian students in this study receive monetary rewards and community recognition for achievement. A significant monetary reward is given to those students within the Fort McDowell community who graduate from high school. These students openly express their anticipation of receiving this reward on completion of High School, and for many it is a major motivator. However, the reward is contingent on completion of schooling rather than the quality of the work done, so in a sense it may act as a de-motivator of excellent work. In contrast, the non-Indian students did not value token rewards, and token rewards were not related to achievement outcomes for this group. It is important for the tribe to reconsider the application of token rewards in this manner as it might be counterproductive to excellent performance for American Indian students.

Both groups indicated on the Facilating Conditions Questionnaire that parental support for 5th and 6th graders correlates with achievement, and teacher support in grades 7th through 12th correlates with achievement (Radda, Iwamoto & Patrick, 1998). This suggests that programming focusing on parental support for the younger grades is essential. Likewise, the involvement of teachers on a more intense level with older students should improve student retention by helping them feel a connection to school.

Although both groups reported high levels of interest in completing high school, almost four times more American Indian students indicated that they were not confident about their ability to do so (Radda, Iwamoto & Patrick, 1998). The results of the Behavioral Intentions Questionnaire suggest that in forming the intention to complete high school American Indian and non-Indian students are strongly influenced by their parents. Those students who intended to complete high school and who had strong academic achievement indicated that they had strong parental support. Conversely, students performing poorly and who had a less strong intention of completing school indicated that they did not have strong parental support.

Students differed in their perception of employability. The American Indian students intent to complete high school was uncorrelated to employability, while it was significantly correlated for non-Indian students.

RECOMMENDATIONS TO IMPROVE
EDUCATIONAL OUTCOMES

Teacher training opportunities should be offered to address the needs of students as reflected on the motivation scales and in the facilitating conditions. One phase of staff development in schools needs to be designed to help teachers understand how to promote and build academic self-esteem in students. Hardeman (1985) discusses the importance of role models, "some outstanding scientists and engineers have reported initially low self-esteem, but stressed the influence of a role model who provided encouragement." The focus should be on maintaining high expectations for students, helping them set academic goals, and designing instruction to help promote student success. Students should naturally assess their own achievement and receive intrinsic rewards for success. In promoting self-esteem, it is important to provide honest, constructive feedback to students. Although these students need some type of praise to encourage effort, it is crucial that teachers are sensitive to the discomfort some students may feel about open praise.

School incentive programs need to be designed to promote improvement as well as success. It is imperative that the improvement component is emphasized. In order for American Indian students to benefit from an incentive plan, GPA cannot be the only criterion for achievement. Teachers should recognize students for improvement and provide opportunities to improve, as this is an important motivational factor for these students.

Schools need to prepare staff to help students understand the purpose of learning. Clearly, students did not connect to future benefits of completing school such as further education and employability. Staff members need to help students plan, set goals and understand what is needed to be successful in accomplishing such goals. Student Mentoring Programs should be initiated to encourage students to explore the possibilities of higher education and vocational programs designed to stimulate interest and involvement in the educational process.

Cleary and Peacock (1998) found in their research that the curriculum is often disconnected from the relevance of life, particularly as children progress into junior and senior high school. Our research also indicated this. Therefore, daily instruction should be designed with a sense of purpose. Teachers need to understand how to use instructional strategies that clearly demonstrate a purpose and applied valued of the material and skills learned.

The students in our study indicated a strong concern for peers and a desire to help others succeed at school. This positive desire should be used to benefit children in collaborative learning environments intended to promote skills such as group problem solving and teamwork. Schools need therefore, to facilitate collaborative learning activities designed to benefit groups as opposed to competitive activities intended to promote individuals. Teachers need to respect the preference of American Indian students to work in groups with peers.

Our research shows that families play a crucial role in promoting values and attitudes such as self-esteem and a sense of purpose for education. They are crucial in students forming an intention to complete schooling. Family support with such things as homework, special projects, and school attendance has a significant influence on achievement. Families should be further helped to understand the significance of helping their children set goals for the future and participate in planning each step with their children. American Indian communities, in collaboration with the school districts, should therefore, sponsor parent workshops designed to teach families how to promote and support education.

Reyhner (1992) suggests that we need to get parents actively involved in real decisions about what and how their children learn in schools. Schools need to encourage more parent and community involvement by allowing them to have some control in the schools. Swisher and Deyhle (1989), suggest that teachers get out into the community in an effort to understand the culture and the needs of the American Indian people. As indicated in the findings on the Facilitating Conditions Questionnaire, teachers need to increase involvement with students as they progress into high school. Their involvement needs to reach beyond the classroom walls. The Fort McDowell Yavapai Nation has several agencies in place to work with children and families. The staff members from the Education Department and Family and Community Services can use the findings of this study to develop programs to benefit students. They can continue encouraging students to explore opportunities and interests in higher education and vocational education. Role models need to be identified within this community to encourage students to succeed. Community education opportunities can be designed to educate parents and community members about the education of their children. By understanding the specific influences on student achievement and retention in school, parents and community members can help facilitate successful experiences for children. Fort McDowell and Fountain Hills both realize that the children are the future leaders of their respective communities.

The Fort McDowell Yavapai Nation should develop summer work programs for youth. In these positions they can learn the necessity of academic achievement to take on leadership and technical roles in these departments. It was recommended that a formally developed internship program and mentoring program be developed within Fort McDowell. Collaboration between the school district and the tribe could create structured internships where students would get academic credit for learning new skills on the job. These programs would help nurture the personal relevance of work and school to the individual. By establishing a mentoring program, tribal members that are already employed at Fort McDowell could take students under their wings. Radda (1992) describes the benefit of the mentoring relationship. Mentors would offer the students role models, hope, vision and a connection to the mission of the Fort McDowell Community.

The Strength of Collaborative Community Research

One of the significant accomplishments of this research is the development of relationship between the communities. This study provides a framework for encouraging tribal and dominant communities to collaborate and work cooperatively with one another. Through this process, the members of the communities that work together gained a better understanding of one another and their perspective on the issues. The time spent working on common interests through problem solving and group discussions began to bridge the gap between these communities.

Metz (1990) says that policy makers need to understand the diversity that exists in schools and base policy changes on the unique needs of schools within their own contexts. Self-study within communities can help educators develop a better understanding of how to meet the needs of American Indian students within particular contexts. In educational policy and practice, we must recognize the importance of social and community values (Louis, 1990). American Indians should not be assimilated together as though they all have the same attributes. Various tribes and communities exist as unique populations with diverse characteristics. It was important, therefore, to have research questions that were relevant to community members. It was the role of the researchers to facilitate this process and encourage direct involvement of both communities. As each group had its own concerns, problems and successes, it was imperative that the research began with individual differences in mind. The process orientation of discussing the issues, doing research, feedback to the stakeholders, further refinement of the issues occurs in a continued process loop.

Furthermore, without the establishment and nurturing of the relationship between the communities it would be difficult, at best, to implement changes based on the research. Because stakeholders were willing to be involved and learn from each other real changes could be made for the benefit of the children.

The collaborative partners involved in the research from the Tribe and the school district implemented a number of solutions suggested by the initial research (Radda, Iwamoto & Patrick, 1998). Since the onset of the study, the school district has formally placed better relations and networking with Fort McDowell on their list of priorities. For the 1998 school year they dedicated in-service training to the research group to discuss results of the quantitative study and recommendations to all teachers in the school district. Sharing results of the survey and specific recommendations for the teachers insures timely feedback of relevant information.

Prior to the training, teachers indicated that they thought the study would result in significant differences between the Indian and non-Indian students. They also indicated that they found educating American Indian students to be more challenging than their non-Indian counterparts. Teachers were concerned about lack of motivation, attendance issues, and lack of parental support. They were surprised at the similarities and reported feeling positive about approaching the education of all students in a new way. They recognized the importance of promoting self-esteem in the classroom with renewed enthusiasm. Many teachers said they realized that communicating the purpose of learning, providing relevance to students, was important. They were, however, astounded at how many students expressed the lack of relevance they reported feeling in the educational process.

After the training, teachers were given a book entitled, *Collected Wisdom: American Indian Education.* They were also invited to attend a meeting at Fort McDowell Indian Community to participate in a meeting with the Indian Education Committee and the Fountain Hills Board of Education. The teachers reported positive feelings about the support and connectedness they experienced through these efforts.

The Fort McDowell Indian Community re-organized their educational services into one department in order to focus effort. This reorganization allowed for concerted education efforts from pre-school to graduate education. For the first time priorities were established with coordination from the Tribal Council, the Education Committee, and Directors of other Fort McDowell Departments. Fort McDowell made education a priority and supported the innovative restructuring suggestions as a result of the study.

These efforts included the Human Resource Department development of a comprehensive summer internship program for Tribal Youth. This program exposed students to the varieties of employment open to them and the educational training and experience necessary to fulfill those positions. This program exposed children in a structured and consistent way to the other Tribal members who achieved leadership positions in Tribal employment.

In the reorganization and with the coordination of other Fort McDowell Departments attendance in school became a priority. The message from the Council and other adults in the community to the children and through a number of departments was that attendance and success in school were important and would be supported by policy and action.

A mentorship program was started with 6th graders. After the first year it would be expanded to older grades. Adult Tribal members were mentoring children while in the school environment. The students reported encouragement in seeing adults from their community involved with them on the campus at Fountain Hills. This had the added benefit of teachers working collaboratively with adult tribal members for the benefit of the children. The teachers invited elders into their classrooms benefiting not only the American Indian students; but also expanding the world-view of the other children in the classroom.

The Tribal Council, the tribal education and social service departments, and the Fountain Hills School District decided to continue the qualitative study that started. They believed that through further study they would develop a greater understanding of students in school and how to bridge issues that might be effected by socio-cultural influences.

Such collaborative initiatives are often difficult to maintain over time with the changes in personnel and administration. This partnership offered significant results in terms of improved relationships between agencies and may have had a positive effect on retention of students. As can be viewed in Table I, there has been an increased number of students retained and completing school. Although, causation cannot be conclusively determined from present data, there are suggestions that the collaborative work of practical research resulted in the implementation of new initiatives and the formulation of constructive attitudes. It is because of the perceived success of this collaborative work that the efforts have continued.

CONCLUSION

In the study of school motivation we needed to understand the socio-cultural perspectives that influence children from Fort McDowell, their parents and their interactions in the neighboring schools. We needed to go beyond the theoretical and look at how the socio-cultural underpinnings effect the school motivation of students from Fort McDowell. Having the support and the involvement of the local school district was important. It was this kind of collaboration that would assist the communities to work together for the benefit of all students as well as giving the researchers the ability to provide practical and real solutions. What methods of teaching, what peer interactions, what school policies were relevant to all children in the school district and which ones appear to effect students' motivation differently based on socio-cultural factors? The goal of the working committee was to be able to study school motivation through the lens of socio-cultural issues with the outcome of practical and down to earth solutions that could be implemented to increase retention and completion of high school. Through the on-going qualitative research and collaborative process further success appears imminent.

REFERENCES

Chaudhuri, J. O. (1995). Tribal development. In J. O. Chaudhuri (Ed.), *The Yavapai of Fort McDowell* (pp.90-97), Mesa, AZ: Mead Publishing.

Cleary, L. M. & Peacock, T. D. (1998). *Collected wisdom: American Indian education.* Boston, MA: Allyn and Bacon.

Hardeman, C. H. (1985, October) *The quest for excellence/pupil self esteem.* In invited paper: Elementary/secondary education date redesign project.

House, E. & Lapan, S. (1988). The driver of the classroom: The teacher and school improvement. In R. Haskins & D. Macrae (Eds.). (1988). *Policies for public schools: Teachers, equity and indicators.* (pp. 70-86). Greenwich, CT: Ablex Publishing.

Iwamoto, D. (1998). *Motivational factors influencing Native American student achievement and retention in high school.* Unpublished doctoral dissertation, Northern Arizona University.

Kegan, R. (1982). The evolving self: Problem and process in human development. Cambridge, MA: Harvard University Press.

Khera, S. (1995). The Yavapai: Who they are and from where they come. In J. O. Chaudhuri (Ed.), *The Yavapai of Fort McDowell* (pp.8-25), Mesa, AZ: Mead Publishing.

Louis, K. S. (1990). Social and community values and the quality of teachers' work life. In M.W. McLaughlin, J. E. Talbert, & N. Bascia (Eds.), *The contexts of teaching in secondary schools: Teachers' realities (pp 17-39)* New York, NY: Teachers College Press.

McCarty, T. L. (1993). Language, literacy, and the image of the child in American Indian classrooms. *Language Arts, 70* (3) 182-192.

McInerney, D. M. (1989). A cross-cultural analysis of student motivation. In D. M. Keats, D. Munro & L. Mann (Eds.). *Heterogeneity in Cross-cultural Psychology.* Lisse: Zwets & Zeitlinger.

McInerney, D. M. (1991). The behavioural intentions questionnaire. An examination of construct and etic validity in an educational setting. *Journal of Cross-Cultural Psychology, 22,* 293-306.

McInerney, D. M. (1992). Cross-cultural insights into school motivation and decision making. *Journal of Intercultural Studies, 13,* 53-74.

McInerney, D. M. (1995). Achievement motivation research and indigenous minorities: Can research be psychometric? *Cross-Cultural Research, 29,* 211-239.

McInerney, D. M., & Sinclair, K. E. (1991). Cross-cultural model testing: Inventory of school motivation. *Educational and Psychological Measurement, 51,* 123-133.

McInerney, D. M. & Sinclair, K. E. (1992). Dimensions of school motivation: A cross-cultural validation study. *Journal of Cross-Cultural Psychology, 23,* 389-406.

McInerney, D. & Swisher, K. (1995). Exploring Navajo motivation in school settings. *Journal of American Indian Education, 33,* 28-51.

McInerney, D. M., & McInerney, V. (2000). A longitudinal qualitative study of school motivation and achievement. Paper presented at the annual meeting of the American Educational Research Association, New Orleans, LA.

McInerney, D. M., Roche, L., McInerney, V., & Marsh, H. W. (1997). Cultural perspectives on school motivation: The relevance and application of goal theory. *American Educational Research Journal 34,* 207-236.

McLaughlin, M. W. & Talbert, J. E. (1990). The contexts in question: The secondary school workplace. In M. W. McLaughlin, J. E. Talbert, & N. Bascia (Eds.), *The contexts of teaching in secondary schools: Teachers' realities* (pp. 40-107). New York, NY: Teachers College Press.

McMillen, M. (1994). *Dropout rates in the United States: 1993.* (Report No. NCES-94-669). Washington, DC: National Center for Education Statistics.

Metz, M. H. (1990). How social class differences shape teachers' work: In M. W. McLaughlin, J. E. Talbert, & N. Bascia (Eds.), *The contexts of teaching in secondary schools: Teachers' realities (pp. 40-170).* New York, NY: Teachers College Press.

O'Hair, M. J. (1995). Uniting theory, research, and practice: Purpose, beliefs and change revisited. *Action in Teacher Education, XVII* (1) 89-91.

Platero, P. R., Brandt, E. A., Witherspoon, G., & Wong, P. (1986). *Navajo students at risk. Final report for the Navajo area student dropout study.* Window Rock, AZ: Navajo Nation.

Radda, H. (1992). Therapeutic mentoring: Beyond teaching and therapy. In L. Crosier (Ed.), *Healthy choices, healthy schools* (pp. 131-138). Washington, DC: Avocus Publishing Inc.

Radda H., Iwamoto, D., Patrick, C. (1998). Collaboration, research and change: Motivational influences on American Indian students. *Journal of American Indian Education, 37 (2) 2-20.*

Red Horse, J. (1986). Editorial commentary: Education reform. *Journal of American Indian Education, 36* (2) 40-44.

Reyhner, J. (1989). *Changes in American Indian education: A historical retrospective for educators in the United States* (Report No. EDO-RC-89-1). Washington, DC: Office of Educational Research and Improvement. (ERIC Document Reproduction Service No. ED 314 228)

Reyhner, J. (1992). American Indians out of school: A review of school-based causes and solutions. *Journal of American Indian Education,* 37-56.

Schneider, G. (1995). Historical documents of the Fort McDowell Reservation. In J. O. Chaudhuri (Ed.), *The Yavapai of Fort McDowell* (pp.26-29), Mesa, AZ: Mead Publishing.

Sternberg, R. & Horvath, J. (1995). A prototype view of expert teaching. *Educational Researcher, 24* (6) 9-17.

Swisher, K. & Deyhle, D. (1989). The styles of learning are different, but the teaching is just the same: Suggestions for teachers of American Indian youth. *Journal of American Indian Education,* 1-14.

Swisher, K., Hoisch, M. & Pavel, D. (1991). *American Indian Alaskan Native dropout study.* Washington, DC: National Education Association.

Wilson, P. (1991). Trauma of Sioux Indian high school students. *Anthropology and Education Quarterly, 22* (4).

PART III

FOCUS ON METHODS

CROSS-CULTURAL DIFFERENCES IN AFFECTIVE MEANING OF ACHIEVEMENT
A Semantic Differential Study

Farideh Salili and Rumjahn Hoosain

INTRODUCTION

The study reported in this chapter is part of a program of research exploring differences between the achievement orientation of Chinese students and their Western counterparts. The focus of the present study will be on cross-cultural differences in the meaning of achievement. In the following sections, we will first present a brief historical background that provided the impetus and the rationale for our research. We will then present a review of relevant literature on Chinese culture and context of achievement as a backdrop for the study that follows.

Historical Background

The construct of achievement motivation first appeared in Western scientific literature in the writings of William James in his discussions of achievement striving and self-evaluation (1890, pp. 309-311). Murray (1938), however, was the first to formalize the construct of achievement motive as a psychological disposition in his taxonomy of psychological needs. He developed and advocated the use of projective and self-report techniques to measure the need for achievement (Elliot, 1997). Murray's work provided a foundation for the seminal cross-cultural research of David McClelland and his associates (McClelland, Atkinson, Clark, & Lowell, 1953). McClelland et al.'s research and theories are credited for highlighting the importance of achievement motivation, by linking it to economic development and the rise and fall of nations.

In their book *The Achievement Motive*, McClelland et al. defined achievement motivation as a learned personality disposition to compete against a standard of excellence in achievement situations where performance is evaluated in terms of success and failure. Achievement motivated individuals were characterized by their mastery, initiative, independence, desire for challenging tasks, and persistence in the face of difficulties. These motivated individuals always strive to do better and tend to choose entrepreneurial occupations.

McClelland's definition has been used widely in Western research and literature. However, in the past few decades the emphasis has shifted from motivation as a general disposition to a more situationally determined, process-oriented variable (Elliot, 1997). Cognitive factors such as meanings, goals and perceived causes of success and failure are assumed to play important roles in determining motivation to achieve (see Ames, 1984b; Dweck, 1975; Maehr & Braskamp, 1986).

The nineteen seventies and early 80's were marked by challenges to McClelland's theory of achievement, and the birth of new theoretical models of achievement motivation, such as the goal theory (see Dweck & Leggett, 1988; Nicholls, 1984). McClelland's theory was criticized for being ethnocentric, biased towards individualistic cultures, and for not placing enough emphasis on sociocultural, situational and contextual variables (Maehr & Braskamp, 1986). The role of situational and contextual variables in mediating achievement behavior was demonstrated in many studies. As an example, in an earlier study we (Salili, Maehr & Sorenson, and Fyans, 1976) manipulated feedback on students' performance in a language related task and found an increase or decrease in continuing motivation (intrinsic motivation) depending on the type of feedback students received. These findings suggested that classroom context and in particular, teachers' feedback can be crucial for students' intrinsic motivation. Similar findings have been reported by other researchers (see Ames and Archer, 1988; Maehr & Stallings, 1972).

The context of achievement also varies according to differences in cultural beliefs, values, societal expectations, and norms of behavior that are prevalent in a particular society (Feather, 1986). Cross-cultural studies provide evidence that the psychological dynamics underlying achievement behavior may vary in different cultures. The factors that motivate individuals to do productive work in one culture may be different in other cultures. Japan, for example, is one of the most economically developed nations. Japanese, however, are known for being affiliatively oriented with strong family loyalties, and their achievement is apparently invoked by group and social membership (Spence, 1985).

De Vos (1973) found that in Japan striving to achieve was motivated more by concern for the reactions of others rather than pursuit of individual satisfaction. Galimore, Boggs, and Jordan (1974) reported that need for affiliation, rather than need for achievement predicted academic performance of native Hawaiians, Fillipinos, and Japanese Hawaiian-Americans. Similarly, Ramirez and Price-Williams (1976) found that Mexican and African-Americans were motivated by 'family achievement' more than White Anglo-Americans who were motivated by individualistic need to achieve. Other researchers also reported similar findings in studies of delay of gratification (see for example, Mitschel, 1974). Gallimore (1981), concluded that there were considerable variations in antecedent of achievement.

Similarly, cross-cultural studies among the Chinese indicate that the traditional personality theory of motivation has limitations when applied to socially oriented cultures such as the Chinese. Individualistically oriented definitions of achievement motivation emphasize the self as the primary source of responsibility for achievement behavior and its outcome evaluation. In collectivistic cultures, on the other hand, the social group and social role are the primary sources of motivation to succeed (Salili, 1995; Yu & Yang, 1987). Socially oriented people, however, appear just as achievement motivated as their individualistic counterparts.

If different cultures have different values for achievement, how is this reflected in their development of achievement judgment? We tried to explore this question by replicating Weiner and Peters' (1973) study on the development of achievement and moral judgments among students in Iran, also known as being socially oriented. We found interesting differences in the developmental patterns of achievement judgment of Iranian and American students in line with their respective cultural beliefs (Salili, Maehr, & Gilmore, 1976). Similar to the development of moral judgment, young American children based their achievement judgment on the outcome of achievement. By age 8 to 9, however, effort became the most important factor on which their judgement was based. Effort continued to be important for the next few years, but for students 14 and above, the outcome of achievement gained prominence once again (Weiner and Peters, 1973). Weiner and Peters attributed this reversal to the production-oriented American cultural values. For Americans, it is not enough to make an effort, one must also achieve a successful outcome. The pattern of achievement judgment for young Iranian students was similar to their American counterparts. However, for older children no reversal was found.

Effort continued to be the most important factor in their judgment. We attributed this finding to differences between cultural values of the two groups with regards to achievement. In Iran it is enough to make an effort even if one does not succeed, as indicated in Iranian folklore and children's stories.

Our findings demonstrated that achievement judgment is not only influenced by developmental factors, but also by sociocultural values. This suggested that different cultures may hold different meanings for achievement. We thus attempted to explore cultural differences in the meaning of achievement in our next study (see–Fyans, Salili, Maehr & Desai, 1983). Charles Osgood and his associates' (Osgood, May & Miron, 1975) Semantic Differential (SD) research provided us with easy access to cross-cultural data. During the 1960's, Osgood and his associates selected 620 concepts for their Atlas of Affective Meanings following a painstaking "pruning and translation-checking of a large number of culture-common nominal" (Osgood & Tzeng, 1990, p.15). The concepts were selected to sample wide areas of life including activities, relationships and other achievement related concepts. These concepts were then rated by 600 teenage males in some 22 different language cultures including Hong Kong. From this available data, we selected for analysis, 100 concepts judged by a panel of seven specialist scholars to be related to different aspects of achievement motivation.

A good deal of similarities across these cultures were found.

> There appears to be something like achievement ethic that is universally recognized as an identifiable behavioral category which stresses work, knowledge and freedom while downgrading the importance of family, tradition and interpersonal relations" (Fyans, Salili, Maehr & Desai, 1983, p. 1010).

Hence, our analysis determined the existence of "an arguably valid cross-cultural standard of achievement meaning, and cultures scoring high and low in this regard could be identified. (Fyans et al., 1983, p. 1006)

There were many interesting differences between cultures that scored low and those which scored high. For example, the high scoring cultures tended to perceive success as associated with self, initiative, freedom, education, work, and masculinity. In low scoring cultures, the meaning of success took on a different, almost contrasting, form. For example we found success to be associated with femininity in these language groups (for more detail, see Fyans, Salili, Maehr, & Desai, 1983).

Osgood's data however, were collected in the 1960's and from 16-year-old boys attending high schools. No data existed on girls or adults. Hence, our findings may have been specific only to these particular male subjects living in the 1960s. No other systematic data existed to confirm our initial findings due to the difficulties involved in conducting cross-cultural studies. Readers are advised to read Osgood et al.'s (Osgood, May & Miron,

1975) book on *Cross-Cultural Universals of Affective Meaning* for a detailed analysis of problems involved in conducting cross-cultural research of this nature. The purpose of the present study was to explore cross-cultural differences in the affective meaning of achievement among male and female British and Chinese students of all ages and in the present time. The focus of this chapter is on high-school students.

Culture and Context of Achievement

Hong Kong a former British colony, has a sizable British expatriate community. Although British and Chinese communities live in harmony together, they seldom mix in social situations. Influenced by modern technology and electronic media, younger generations in Hong Kong are adapting to some Western values (see for example, Wu, 1996; Lau, 1988, 1992, 1996; Lau & Wong, 1992). However, many of the traditional collectivistic values such as close family ties and social orientation still persist and are passed on to the new generation through child rearing practices. Family and social ties may also be strong among the Westerners, however, there are important differences in the way these ties influence individual's life goals and behaviors as our studies showed (see Salili, 1994; Salili, Chiu & Lai, 2001 discussed below). Child rearing in Western societies encourages independence and individualism. Children are often allowed to take initiative independently in their daily activities with minimum interference from parents. As a result, they grow up to feel autonomous and act independently in making important life decisions. It is well known, for example, that young Western youths often strive to assert their independence and individualism by rebelling against parental authority. In Asian cultures, however, the individual's decisions are often influenced by their families' approval and circumstances even in present times. Under the influence of Confucian philosophy, Chinese people place great importance on family relationships. Filial piety is the cornerstone of Chinese cultural values and much attention is paid to the child's behavior and discipline to prepare him/her for filial obligations in adulthood. Research (Zhang, 2000) suggests that the child-rearing patterns of parents in Hong Kong is authoritarian and controlling. Parents have strict and well established rules of behavior for their children and "believe that criticism, scolding, and even physical punishment may be helpful for their development" (p. 64).

According to McClelland et al., achievement motivation traits are developed through child rearing processes that emphasize independence, mastery, and competitiveness. Such behaviors are, however, not encouraged by Chinese parents who are very concerned about filial training and impulse control. Indeed Chinese parents tend to discourage independence and exploratory activities because of the risk of physical injuries to the child (Tseng & Hsu, 1970). In a study Ho and Kang (1984) found that

> filial piety was correlated with proper behavior, strict discipline and less emphasis on the child's expression of opinion, independence, creativity, self–mastery and all-round personal development (cited in Salili, 1995, p. 78).

Education is highly valued in Chinese culture and considered not only necessary for getting a good job, but also for building one's character. Parents and teachers set a very high standard of achievement for children and encourage them to work hard and achieve academic excellence. Ho and Kang (1984) reported that competence and achievement were characteristics most expected of children by Chinese parents. Parents spend a considerable amount of time supervising their children's academic work and providing help when they have difficulties with homework (Stevenson & Lee, 1990). Excelling in academic work would make the family proud and is considered one of the duties of a filially pious son or daughter (Salili, 1995).

The Education system in Asian countries in general is very competitive and described as "Exam Hell" (see Wu, 1996). The situation is described by Rohlen (1983 cited in Wu, 1996) as one in which "students are not going to be examined on expressive or critical skills, but on diligence in mastery of facts (p. 30)". According to Chen, Stevenson, Hayward and Burgess (1995), in ancient China scholars who could pass competitive administrative examinations were given prominent positions in the Government. They believe that the existing competitive system of education in China as well as other East Asian countries is a continuation of this ancient tradition. Under Western influence in recent years, new ideas are being introduced and attempts are being made to re-structure the education system in order to make it more child-centered and less competitive.

Until very recently, the Hong Kong education system was very competitive and examination oriented with authoritarian teachers. Students were given a high volume of homework assignments, constant tests, and examinations. The standard of education is still extremely high and geared towards bright and highly motivated students. Parents and teachers exert great pressure on students to do well in school. A consequence of this harsh learning environment and family pressures has been student suicide. There have been more than a dozen student suicides in each of the last few academic years. While there are many reasons for student suicide, a common cause is a sense of despair for letting one's parents down after failing to meet their expectations in academic achievement.

In a recent cross-cultural study comparing Hong Kong and Canadian students, we (Salili, Chiu, & Lai, 2001) found that Hong Kong students spent significantly more time studying than Canadian students, but felt less competent, more anxious and received lower grades from their teachers than their Canadian counterparts. This suggests that the standard of evaluation was set so high that no matter how hard students tried, they could not obtain good grades, thus affecting their psychological well being. It is well known in Hong Kong that when students who are not doing well in Chinese schools are transferred to expatriate or international schools they tend to outperform their new classmates.

Our study also showed that Chinese students in Hong Kong and in Canada scored significantly higher on goals of pleasing their families, teachers and friends than European Canadian students. Previous research among the Chinese has also reported that children with higher perceived parental expectations tend to perform better in academic work than children with lower parental expectations (Au & Harackiewicz, 1986). Such findings suggest that family, teachers, and friends may have strong motivating effect on Chinese students.

Achievement orientation of Chinese students

As our earlier studies above showed, many studies in recent years also suggest that Western models of achievement may not always apply to other cultural contexts (see Salili, 1995 for a review). Western studies generally show a positive correlation between authoritative parenting and academic performance for Western children but not for Chinese (Weiss & Schwarz, 1996). In Western cultures such as the USA, adolescents raised by authoritative parents were reported to have superior performance compared with peers from non-authoritative families. However, authoritarian parenting is reported to have a negative effect on children's sense of competence and achievement (Lamborn, Mounts, Steinberg & Dornbusch, 1991). Such a relationship, does not seem to hold for Chinese students who are usually raised in authoritarian homes, as they perform better academically than their American counterparts (Stevenson & Lee, 1990). Steinberg, Dornbusch, and Brown (1992) reported that regardless of child-rearing practices, Asian students had higher grades in school than American students. They argued that the reason for this superior performance was the Chinese belief that good education leads to career success. Since academic performance has an impact on the entire family, it is the fear of negative consequences that motivates Asian students to work harder and perform well. (Steinberg et al., 1992)

Having been socialized to value education, hard work and effort as well as impulse control and training for filial duties, in time children internalize these values as their own. Thus Chinese students have a higher level of achievement motivation which is more socially based than their Western counterparts (Salili, 1995, Yu & Yang, 1987). They attribute the causes of their success and failure predominantly to effort and study skills, both internal and controllable causes (Hau & Salili, 1990). Chinese students tend to believe that with effort and diligence one can accomplish even the most difficult task. As the Chinese proverb suggests, with diligence, one can grind an iron bar into a needle. Hence, a lot of time is spent on studying at the expense of social life. The diligence of Chinese students is well-known in U.S. universities. It is sometimes reported that students avoid registering in courses with too many Chinese students, as it is difficult to match their hard work in order to get good grades

Meaning of Achievement

Although there is considerable interest in the role of meanings in mediating achievement behavior, systematic studies on this topic are very limited. Triandis (1972), in a cross-cultural study of "subjective culture" used a sentence completion format and asked participants to provide antecedents and consequences of 20 concepts, including 'success' as well as other achievement related concepts. He found that the Indian group differed from the other three cultures in that they emphasized social factors as important antecedents of success

In a study using the Semantic Differential technique we found that for the Chinese in Hong Kong success was clustered with family relationship and friendship (Salili & Mak, 1988). In another cross-cultural study (Salili, 1994), we used the Repertory Grid technique to elicit situations of success and their constructs (i.e., characteristics) from British and Chinese high-school students. We found two major areas of achievement: individualistic and affiliative success. While these two areas were equally relevant for both groups, they were differentially salient for each. Within affiliative success, the British placed more importance on love and romance, personal relationship and marriage, while for the Chinese, being good daughters or good sons and family relationships in general were more important. Within individualistic achievement, career was more important for the British, while academic achievement was more important for the Chinese. For the British, there was no relationship between affiliative and individualistic success, whereas for the Chinese these two areas were highly correlated. The results also showed three distinct dimensions of achievement: outcome of achievement, causal attributions for achievement, and instrumental activities. These dimensions were the same for both groups.

These studies suggested that the meaning of achievement may be different for Chinese and Westerners. However, there are not enough systematic and well conducted cross-cultural studies to lend support to our findings. The reason for this is the difficulty in devising methods that are equivalent in different cultural contexts. Our study above has not been replicated. Researchers often search for easier methods of data collection. Methods such as the Repertory Grid technique are not easily understood and while it is a suitable tool for cross-cultural research, it is extremely time consuming and difficult to administer, requiring a lot of effort and patience.

THE PRESENT STUDY

An important tool that has been used to measure affective meaning is the Semantic Differential technique (SD) developed by Osgood and his associates (Osgood, May and Miron, 1975). The present study used the SD technique to further explore differences in affective meanings of achievement between the British and Chinese high-school students who participated in our previous Repertory Grid study.

Measurement of Affective Meaning: The Semantic Differential Technique

The term "affective meaning" was used by Charles E. Osgood in his comparative study of cultures (Osgood, Suci & Tannenbaum, 1957). He constructed the SD technique to circumvent the language barrier in measuring affective or connotative aspects of language, that is the "subjective culture" in diverse societies.

In a SD task the participant is asked to judge a series of concepts related to the topic of interest against a set of 12 bipolar adjectives, representing the three independent dimensions of meaning: Evaluation (E), Potency (P), and Activity (A) each represented by four 7-point scales defined by verbal opposites (e.g., good-bad, important-unimportant, active-passive for E, P, and A respectively) with the concept provided at the top of the page. The data thus generated can be analyzed in various ways depending on the purpose of the study (e.g. correlation among the scales or across the subjects to explore "cultural meaning, or cluster /factor analysis to examine the dimensions of meaning"). Osgood reported that over the years, studies conducted using the SD have all shown the same three underlying dimensions.

This does not, however, mean that the concepts judged have similar meaning for all people, but rather it indicates that the

> semantic framework within which these affective judgements are made is constant....Indeed, it is only by virtue of this common frame of reference that differences between people for the same concept and between concepts for the same people can be specified. (Osgood & Tzang, 1990, p., 306)

It is these features of the SD technique that have made it a very useful cross-cultural tool in measuring affective meaning of achievement. The common framework that is used in SD provides equivalence of measurement while enabling the researcher to make meaningful comparisons across cultures. The Semantic Differential technique also enables the researcher to look at all three important dimensions of meaning rather than only one dimension—evaluation which is commonly looked at in many studies. Hence, '*femininity*' for example, could be judged as good or pretty in the evaluation dimension, but also perceived as weak in the potency dimension.

METHOD

Participants

Participants were a total of 1952 male and female students aged 13-19 from local British and Chinese high schools. There were 692 (M = 480 and F = 210) European students, predominantly British and 1260 Chinese students (M = 640 and F = 620).

Chinese high-school students were selected from grades 9 to 13 of four Anglo-Chinese schools in Hong Kong. The schools were selected randomly from among more prestigious schools in Hong Kong. Anglo-Chinese schools formed the majority of schools in Hong Kong up until last year. The only feature that distinguished these schools from other types of schools (i.e., the "Chinese" schools and "British" schools—see below) is use of the English language in these schools as the medium of instruction from grade 7 onwards. This group of students will be referred to as "Chinese." An approximately equal number of students were selected from different streams. The students were all from predominantly middle class background and the schools used a standard curriculum. English students were selected from the three British schools catering to English speaking expatriates. At the time of data collection, the majority of these students were British, hence, they will be referred to as "British." The socioeconomic background of the British participants were similar to those of the Chinese, all from the middle class professional families. There are some south Asian students in these schools as well. We excluded the data collected from these students from the analyses so as to provide a contrast between the Western and Chinese students.

Material
Two sets of instruments were administered to the participants:

1. A questionnaire with items regarding the demographic information of the participants. These included, age, gender, grade and educational background of the participants, as well as questions concerning their socioeconomic backgrounds.
2. A questionnaire with 104 selected achievement-related concepts, each presented on top of a page followed by the SD scales (see Appendix I for the English version).

In our previous study we had already identified 100 achievement-related concepts from Osgood's Atlas (see Fyans, Salili, Maehr, & Desai 1983). In the present study we added four more concepts deemed important.

As we can see in Table 1 the concepts selected for this purpose represented different aspects of achievement. These included the role of self in achievement (i.e., *'I myself'*), the characteristics of people in achievement situations, the style of achievement (e.g., *'Capable'*), the traditional/modernism beliefs (e.g., *'Tradition'*), achievement situations or goals (e.g., *'Top of the Class'*), gender roles (e.g., *'Femininity'* and *'Masculinity'*), and the outcome of achievement (i.e., affective, e.g., *'Pride'*, concrete, e.g., *'Leader'*, and abstract, e.g., *Freedom'*). These concepts were judged to be relevant to achievement in the literature and by colleagues in this field. Both the Cantonese Chinese and English versions were used respectively for the Chinese and the British students. The translation and back translation methods were used to ensure the accuracy of Chinese translation and preliminary trials confirmed the equivalence of the concepts in the two languages with regard to their meanings.

Data Analysis

The differences in the meaning of achievement were measured by the affective structure of the achievement related concepts. This included dimension scores, conceptual organization of the concepts, and the inter-concept distances in semantic space (not reported in this chapter). Dimension scores are the algebraic summation of the scores for Evaluation, Potency, and Activity scales for each concept. The mean score of each dimension across each group was taken as the group score.

Using Ward's Minimum Variance method of clustering (see Romesburg, 1984 for more information), several cluster analyses were performed separately for the two cultures and the two genders within each culture. Concepts and clusters are listed according to the natural order in which they join together. The clusters were labeled based on their composition and on our judgement of underlying commonality between the concepts that formed each cluster. Several colleagues in the field of psychology were then asked to judge our accuracy of labeling and a final decision was made after these comments were taken into consideration.

RESULTS AND DISCUSSION

Taking all the dimensions together we conducted cluster analyses separately for each group. Tables 1 and 2 present the results of these analyses for Chinese and British students respectively. For the sake of clarity, we will only discuss some of the key findings. First, it is interesting to note that the Clusters formed portray different achievement situations, or aspects of achievement behavior presented by different theoretical perspectives. For example, cluster 1 for both British and Chinese students grouped together concepts that are related to self-efficacy and independent achievement situations as described by Bandura (1997). Clusters 2 and 3 for the Chinese (see Table 1) represent individualistic notions of achievement as proposed by McClelland et al. (1953). Cluster 3 for the Chinese (in Table 1) and Cluster 4 for the British (in Table 2) represent self-concept and ideal-self. Some of the characteristics of individualistic achievement are also in Cluster 1 for the British, making the Cluster much larger for this group. Clusters 5 and 6 for the Chinese students and Clusters 6 and 8 for the British represent meanings attached to feminine and masculine achievement (see Tables 1 and 2 respectively). Again, these Clusters confirm much of what has been shown by previous research on sex-role stereotypes in achievement (see for example, Bem 1974). There are also clusters of concepts that are related to androgynous achievement orientation for both groups (see Table 1, Cluster 4 and Table 2, Cluster 7 for both Chinese and British students respectively) as well as socially oriented clusters of achievement-related concepts (see Table 1, Cluster 7, and Table 2, Cluster 2 for Chinese and British students respectively). Finally, there are clusters that are related to negative outcome of achievement, '*failure*', '*punishment*', and '*defeat*'. These are again grouped together with other negatively loaded concepts for both groups (see Table 1, Cluster 9 for the Chinese and Table 2, Clusters 14 and 15 for the British students). In many of these clusters there is one or more identifiable achievement goals or situations, instrumental activities and personal characteristics perceived to be appropriate for reaching the goal/s as well as the outcome (e.g., Cluster 2 in Table 1).

As we can see there are considerable agreements between the groups, but also some interesting differences. Tables 1 and 2 show 12 distinct clusters of concepts for the Chinese and 15 for the British respectively. Cluster 1 (*Self-efficacy/Self-competence*) for both cultures, group together concepts that represent self-efficacy (i.e., '*being capable*') and individualistic achievement goals and characteristics. Many of the concepts representing achievement characteristics were similar for both cultures (e.g., '*being capable*', '*efficient*', '*intelligent*', '*clear thinking*', '*free will*', '*independent*'). These concepts describe characteristics that are typically attributed to individuals high in self-efficacy or self-competence (see Bandura, 1997). However, the two groups differed in terms of the achievement goals they associated with

TABLE 1
Clusters Formed with All Three Dimensions Together for Chinese
Participants

Concept No.	1. Self-efficacy/ Self-competence	Concept No.	2. Success	Concept No.	3. Ideal-Self/ Individualistic Ach.
1	Capable	11	Effort	3	Foresight
88	Ability	82	Success	68	Individuality
34	Freedom	55	Devotion	14	Questioning things
41	Efficient				
52	Intelligent	77	Top of class	103	I myself
37	Courage	39	Determination	72	Performing arts
47	Health	31	Knowledge	81	Play
4	Clear thinking	58	Lone	104	Taking initiatives
50	Self-insight				
8	Free will				
15	Independent				
35	Progressive				
40	Self-reliant				
44	Alert				

Concept No.	4. Future Success/ Androgynous Ach.	Concept No.	5. Power/ Masculinity	Concept No.	6. Affiliative Ach./ Femininity
6	Purpose	30	Power	9	Luck
32	Wealth	59	Leader	74	Social relationship
21	Future	95	Forceful	46	Femininity
102	Scientific work	43	Ambition	33	Easy going
38	Planful	45	Masculinity	57	Sympathy
66	Personal growth	62	Competition	63	Romance
93	Progress			19	Being stable
101	Being oneself			49	Religious
25	Family			64	Community service
78	School			92	Cautious
36	Mature			70	Having children
51	Work				
42	Thorough				
94	Organized				
69	Personal relationship				
83	Reward				

(continued)

TABLE 1
(Continued)

Concept No.	7. Filial Piety/ Collectivistic Ach.	Concept No.	8. Follower	Concept No.	9.Failure/Negative Outcome
12	Industrious	2	Shallow	10	Fatalism
13	Education	60	Follower	23	Compliant before authority
48	Family relation-ship			98	Shame
99	Filial piety			29	Fear
65	Marriage			87	Stubborn
67	Scholarship			97	Punishment
100	Self-control			84	Failure
16	Responsible			85	Insecure
56	Respect			90	Inhibited
17	Sincere			86	Pessimistic
76	Charity				
54	Cooperation				
73	Friendship				

Concept No.	10. Choice/ Present	Concept No.	11. Traditionalism/ Conventional	Concept No.	12. Examination
5	A choice	7	Accepting things as they are	27	Pride
22	Present	26	Conforming	28	Defeat
24	Past	53	Lotteries	80	Examination
18	Persistence	20	Tradition	89	Demanding
71	Mission	75	Conventional	61	Aggressive
79	Business	91	Big family		
96	Dominant				

these characteristics. The Chinese group associated with abstract goals of '*freedom*', '*health*', and '*self-insight*', showing the Chinese emphasis on keeping one's body fit so as not to inflict pain on one's parents (i.e., in Chinese traditional belief, one's body parts belong to one's parents and injury or disease to any part of the body is like inflicting pain or injury on one's parents). Similarly, '*self-insight*' and '*freedom*' are among highly valued and important long term goals in the Chinese culture. For the British group, the goals were more concrete (i.e., '*wealth*', '*personal growth*', and '*respect*'). In addition, concepts such as '*individuality*', '*self-control*', '*determination*' and '*ambition*' are also clustered with the above concepts, suggesting that they associated more individualistic characteristics with self-efficacy.

TABLE 2
Clusters of Concepts Formed with All Three Dimensions Together for
British Participants

Concept No.	1. Self-efficacy/ Independent Achievement	Concept No.	2. Success/ Personal Relationship	Concept No.	3. Family/ Affiliative Achievement
1	Capable	34	Freedom	37	Family
41	Efficient	48	Family relation-ship	47	Health
52	Intelligent	67	Scholarship	58	Lone
101	Being oneself	63	Romance	73	Friendship
15	Independent	69	Personal relation-ship		
16	Responsible	82	Success		
32	Wealth	88	Capable		
6	Purpose	54	Cooperation		
66	Personal growth	83	Reward		
8	Free will	76	Charity		
11	Effort				
68	Individuality				
39	Determination				
43	Ambition				
4	Clear thinking				
31	Knowledge				
55	Devotion				
36	Mature				
100	Self-control				
56	Respect				

Concept No.	4. Ideal-self	Concept No.	5. Play	Concept No.	6. Power/ Masculinity
25	Family	81	Play	30	Power
77	Top of class			45	Masculinity
93	Progress			59	Leader
103	I myself			62	Competition
35	Progressive			79	Business
104	Taking initiative				
44	Alert				
70	Having children				

(continued)

TABLE 2
(Continued)

Concept No.	7. Androgynous Achievement	Concept No.	8. Femininity	Concept No.	9. Filial Piety/ Conventional
3	Foresight	9	Luck	7	Accepting things as they are
27	Pride	46	Femininity	26	Conforming
71	Mission	33	Easy going	75	Conventional
13	Education	12	Industrious	92	Cautious
40	Self-reliant	78	School	99	Filial piety
50	Self-insight	91	Big family	60	Follower
65	Marriage	22	Present		
5	A Choice	24	Past		
94	Organized	51	Work		
19	Being stable	102	Scientific work		
14	Questioning things				
72	Performing arts				
74	Social relationship				
17	Sincere				
64	Community service				
20	Tradition				
38	Planful				
49	Religious				
42	Thorough				
57	Sympathy				

Concept No.	10. Reliant on others and luck	Concept No.	11. Examination	Concept No.	12. Aggressive/ Futuristic
23	Compliant before authority				
53	Lotteries			21	Future
				95	Forceful
				96	Dominance
				61	Aggressive
				89	Demanding

Concept No.	13. Shallow	Concept No.	14. Failure/ Negative Outcome	Concept No.	15. Defeat/ Punishment
2	Shallow	84	Failure	10	Fatalism
		85	Insecure	28	Defeat
		86	Pessimistic	97	Punishment
		98	Shame	29	Fear
		90	Inhibiting	87	Stubborn

Similar to our previous findings (Salili, 1994) that suggest Chinese students are highly motivated to achieve academically, in this study we also found '*success*' for the Chinese to be associated with concepts '*top of the class*', '*effort*', '*devotion*', '*determination*', '*knowledge*', and '*lone*' (see Table 1, Cluster 2, *Success*). *Success* for the British, on the other hand, was associated with '*freedom*', '*family relationship*', '*scholarship*', '*personal relationship*', '*capable*, '*cooperation*', '*reward*', and '*charity*' (*see Table 2, Cluster 2, Success/Personal Relationship*). This finding suggests that '*success*' for the British has a broader meaning and applies to different areas of life. It is also possible that for the teenagers in the British group, there are more choices at this stage of their lives and success may not necessarily be tied to '*being on top of the class*'. Being on '*top of the class*', however, was also important for the British and was associated with '*family*', '*progress*', '*I myself*', '*progressive*', '*taking initiative*', '*alert*' and '*having children*'—a mixture of individualistic and socially oriented achievement related concepts (see Table 2, Cluster 4, *Ideal-self/Androgynous Achievement*). There could also be a distinction between '*success*' and '*being on top of the class*' for the British students. Although scholarship is valued, it is as important to succeed in '*personal relationship*', '*romance*', '*feeling of freedom*', and '*family relationship*' (see Cluster 2, Table 2). In this connection, the British response appears to be more in line with what is expected in typical adolescent stage of development described in Western literature. On the one hand, they associated '*I myself*' with '*top of the class*' showing that being on '*top of the class*' is important to them, on the other hand, being accepted by '*friends*', having '*romance*' and good '*family relationship*' are also very important. The Chinese students, however, have more restricted lives than the British. They are also more concerned about getting good grades and achieving academic excellence. The concept '*lone*' in this cluster suggests that Chinese students consider being '*on top of the class*' an individualistic endeavor. As discussed above, Chinese parents exert more pressure on their children to do well in school and they also have more authority over their teenage children than those in Western cultures. Hence, school work occupies most of out of school time for the Chinese students, leaving little or no time for socializing or engaging in romantic relationships.

The concept '*I myself*' for the Chinese is grouped together with individualistically oriented achievement-related characteristics such as '*foresight*', '*individuality*', '*questioning things*', '*performing arts*', '*play*', and '*taking initiative*', all highly rated on E, P, and A dimensions (see Table 1, Cluster 3, *Ideal-self/Individualistic Achievement*). This suggests that the collectivistic Chinese teenagers view themselves ideally to be more individualistic (see Table 1, Cluster 3). Whereas, the individualistic British, view 'self' ideally all rounded with both social and individual goals (see Table 2, Cluster 3).

It is interesting to note that '*romance*' for the British is clustered with '*success*' (see Table 2, Cluster 2), whereas for the Chinese '*romance*' is grouped together with 'femininity' (see Table 1, Cluster 6). In a previous study (Salili, 1994), we also found that British students considered '*romance*' an important success goal, whereas for the Chinese students '*being a good son*' or '*good daughter*' was more important.

Another interesting difference between the two groups is related to '*filial piety*', a highly valued characteristic for the Chinese. As we can see in Table 1 (Cluster 7, *Filial Piety/Collectivistic Achievement Orientation*), '*filial piety*' is grouped together with a number of concepts rated highly on E, P, and A, which include '*family relationship*', '*education*', '*marriage*', '*self control*', '*responsible*' '*scholarship*', '*sincere*', '*cooperation*', and '*friendship*'. These concepts represent typical qualities required of a dutiful son or daughter in Chinese culture and are also characteristics of collectivistic achievement orientation. '*Filial piety*' for the British students is grouped together with concepts that are rated low on E, P, and A, such as '*accepting things as they are*', '*conforming before authority*', '*conventional*', '*cautious*', and '*follower*' (see Table 2, Cluster 9, *Filial Piety/Conventional*). These differences quite clearly reflect differences in the cultural beliefs of the two groups of students.

Clusters 5 and 6, (*Power/ Masculinity* and *Affiliative Achievement/ Femininity* clusters respectively in Table 1, for the Chinese) and 6 and 8 (*Power/ Masculinity and Femininity* clusters respectively in Table 2 for the British) show groups of concepts associated with '*femininity*' and '*masculinity*'. '*Femininity*' for the Chinese students was clustered with concepts traditionally associated with female sex-role stereotypes, including: '*luck*', '*social relationship*', '*easy going*', '*sympathy*', '*romance*', '*having children*' and other similar concepts. For the British students, however, '*femininity*' was not only associated with traditional female role concepts such as '*luck*', '*easy going*', and '*big family*' but also with concepts such as '*school*', '*work*', and '*scientific work*' representing the dual role of many modern females, one related to home and the other to career. There was more consensus however on '*masculinity*' which was associated with '*power*', '*leader*', '*competition*' for both groups and additionally with '*being forceful*' and '*having ambition*' for the Chinese group and with '*business*' for the British group. All these characteristics are related to the stereotype of masculine sex-roles. The meaning associated with 'femininity' and 'masculinity' will be explored in further analyses presented in the following section.

The meaning associated with '*failure*' was similar for both cultural groups (see Table 1, Cluster 9, *Failure/Negative Outcome* for the Chinese students and Table 2, Clusters 14, and 15, *Failure/Negative Outcome and Punishment respectively* for the British students). Concepts of '*failure*', and '*punishment*' are both clustered with '*fatalism*', '*compliant before authority*', '*shame*', '*fear*', '*stubborn*', '*insecure*', '*inhibited*', and '*pessimism*'. They are all rated low and negatively on E, P, and A dimensions. However, *failure*' and '*punishment*', for the British, were in two different clusters. Not surprisingly, this finding shows that in both cultures '*failure*' is associated with negative affect and negative outcome. The concept '*examination*' for the British students was a single concept cluster and rated neutrally on E (M = 3.7) and on A (M = 3.6), but high on P (M = 5.2) (see Table 2, Cluster 11, *Examination*). For the Chinese students, the concept was also rated neutrally on E (M = 3.8), and on A (M = 4), and as important on P (M = 4.9). However, for the Chinese '*examination*' was also associated with both '*pride*' and '*defeat*' as well as with '*demanding*' and '*aggressive*' (see Table 1, Cluster *12, Examination*). This suggests that for the Chinese examinations are very demanding and could either result in pride or defeat, both of which are rated marginally potent (M = 4.5 for '*pride*', and 4.7 for '*defeat*'). Clearly the affective

TABLE 3
Evaluation Dimension: Perception of Sex Role by Chinese Male and Female Students

Males			
Femininity		*Masculinity*	
Concept	*Avg. Rating*	*Concept*	*Avg. Rating*
Scientific work	5.6	Masculinity	6.1
Wealth	5.6	Self-insight	6.1
Progressive	5.6	Respect	6.1
Femininity	5.6	Sympathy	6.0
Purpose	5.6	Charity	6.1
Alert	5.5		

Females			
Femininity		*Masculinity*	
Concept	*Avg. Rating*	*Concept*	*Avg. Rating*
Clear thinking	5.9	Luck	5.0
Self-insight	5.9	Scientific work	5.0
Cautious	5.9	Having children	5.0
Self-control	5.9	Power	5.0
Individuality	5.9	Present	4.9
Personal growth	5.8	Masculinity	5.0
Progress	5.9	Social relationship	5.1
Femininity	5.8	Foresight	5.1
Independent	5.9	Business	5.0
Romance	5.8	Competition	4.9
Capable	5.9	Mature	5.1
Sympathy	5.8	Dominant	4.8
Free will	6.0	Past	4.7
Community service	6.0	Ambition	4.7
Family relationship	6.0	Conforming	4.7

meaning associated with examination seems to be different for the two groups. This finding is not surprising and is probably related to the school experience of the Chinese students.

Culture and Gender Differences in Perceptions of 'Masculinity' and 'Femininity'

In order to further examine the gender differences in clusters of concepts associated with '*femininity*' and '*masculinity*', separate cluster analyses were conducted for each of the three dimensions (i.e., E, P, & A) for male and female British and Chinese students. The results are presented in Tables (3 to 10). The tables show students rated these concepts differently in different dimensions. Generally, on evaluation dimension (see Tables 3 and 4), which represents students' attitudes, clusters of concepts related to '*femininity*' and '*masculinity*', were rated highly by both boys and girls, showing a positive attitude towards both gender roles. However, boys rated the *Masculinity* cluster higher than *Femininity* and the reverse was true of the girls. This self-serving bias was present for both cultures and both sexes.

On the potency dimension which represents students' views on how important, strong, or potent '*femininity*' and '*masculinity*' are, we found a very different picture. Generally, '*femininity*' was clustered with socially undesirable and negatively or neutrally rated concepts, whereas, '*masculinity*' was clustered with highly rated, socially desirable concepts. Interestingly, even the females associated '*femininity*' with such negative concepts, while having a very positive view on '*masculinity*'. Again a similar pattern of findings emerged for both cultures (see Tables 5 to 8).

On the activity dimension, there were clear sex and cultural differences on *Masculinity* and *Femininity* clusters (see Tables 9 and 10). First, Chinese students rated *Masculinity* cluster more active than their British counterparts. Second, the composition of the clusters were also different for the Chinese and contained more individualistically-related concepts such as '*wealth*', '*scientific work*' and '*top of the class*' for the female students and '*planful*', '*mature*', '*power*', '*work*', '*purpose*', and '*individuality*' for the male students. All groups rated the *Femininity* cluster as significantly less active than the *Masculinity*. The *Femininity* cluster for both male and female British students painted a stereotypical picture of female roles such as '*conforming before authority*', '*conventional*', '*devotion*' and '*being stable*' for males, and '*easy going*', '*lotteries*', '*self-insight*', '*mission*', and '*marriage*' for females (see Table 10). On the other hand, for both male and female students, the *Masculinity* cluster contained highly desirable and active characteristics such as '*responsible*', '*self-reliant*' and '*capable*'.

TABLE 4
Evaluation Dimension: Perception of Sex Role by British Male and
Female Students

Males			
Femininity		*Masculinity*	
Concept	*Avg. Rating*	*Concept*	*Avg. Rating*
Questioning things	4.9	Taking initiatives	5.2
Individuality	4.9	Marriage	5.1
Planful	4.9	Foresight	5.2
Tradition	4.9	Masculinity	5.1
Follower	4.8	Luck	5.2
Femininity	4.9	Competition	5.2
Scientific work	4.8	Alert	5.2
Mission	4.8		
Filial Piety	4.8		
Cautious	4.8		
Education	5.0		

Females			
Femininity		*Masculinity*	
Concept	*Avg. Rating*	*Concept*	*Avg. Rating*
Personal growth	5.6	A choice	5.1
Efficient	5.4	Masculinity	5.1
Top of class	5.6	Self-reliant	5.1
Individuality	5.6	Progressive	5.1
Femininity	5.6	Power	5.0
Sympathy	5.6	Easy going	5.1
		Business	5.1
		Tradition	5.0
		Industrious	4.9
		Present	5.0
		Having children	4.9
		Big family	5.0
		Past	4.9
		Mission	4.8
		School	4.8

TABLE 5
Potency Dimension: Perception of Sex Role by
Chinese Male Students

Femininity		Masculinity	
Concept	Avg. Rating	Concept	Avg. Rating
Femininity	4.3	Responsible	5.5
Tradition	4.3	Self-reliant	5.4
Stubborn	4.3	Capable	5.5
Community service	4.3	Effort	5.5
Romance	4.3	Self-insight	5.5
Performing arts	4.4	Intelligent	5.5
Punishment	4.3	Progressive	5.4
Having children	4.4	Scientific work	5.4
Easy going	4.3	Mature	5.5
		Ambition	5.4
		Filial piety	5.4
		Alert	5.4
		Knowledge	5.5
		Industrious	5.4
		Power	5.6
		Planful	5.7
		Devotion	5.6
		Lone	5.6
		Wealth	5.7
		Success	5.8
		Determination	5.9
		Courage	6.0
		Masculinity	6.0

TABLE 6
Potency Dimension: Perception of Sex Role by Chinese Females

Femininity		Masculinity	
Concept	Avg. Rating	Concept	Avg. Rating
Social relationship	4.3	Planful	5.3
Romance	4.3	Personal growth	5.3
Femininity	4.3	Devotion	5.3
Luck	4.3	School	5.3
Fear	4.3	Alert	5.3
Conventional	4.3	Self-reliant	5.3
Inhibited	4.3	Effort	5.3
Punishment	4.4	Respect	5.3
Insecure	4.2	Friendship	5.4
Failure	4.2	Masculinity	5.4
Past	4.1	Being oneself	5.4
Conforming	4.0	Examination	5.3
Accepting things as they are	4.1		
Pessimistic	4.0		
Follower	3.2		
Fatalism	3.8		
Compliant before authority	3.6		
Lotteries	3.4		
Shallow	3.3		

TABLE 7
Potency Dimension: Perception of Sex Role by British Male Students

Femininity		Masculinity	
Concept	Avg. Rating	Concept	Avg. Rating
Femininity	3.5	Leader	5.7
Failure	3.6	Success	5.7
Inhibited	3.6	Health	5.7
Shame	3.7	Business	5.7
Insecure	3.0	Self-insight	5.6
Shallow	2.9	Determination	5.7
		Wealth	5.6
		Persistence	5.6
		Mature	5.6
		Devotion	5.6
		Scholarship	5.6
		Being oneself	5.6
		Knowledge	5.8
		Lone	5.8
		Self-control	5.8
		Having children	5.8
		Capable	5.9
		Friendship	6.0
		Masculinity	6.1
		Power	6.2

TABLE 8
Potency Dimension: Perception of Sex Role by British Females

Femininity		Masculinity	
Concept	Avg. Rating	Concept	Avg. Rating
Future	4.8	Independent	5.8
Fear	4.7	Devotion	5.8
Femininity	4.7	Family relationship	5.8
Stubborn	4.7	Personal relationship	5.8
Present	4.8	Ambition	5.8
Compliant before authority	4.7	Responsible	5.7
Fatalism	4.8	Romance	5.8
Conforming	4.6	Success	5.8
		Effort	5.9
		Determination	6.0
		Masculinity	5.9
		Courage	6.0
		Power	6.1
		Lone	6.3
		Friendship	6.4

TABLE 9
Activity Dimension: Perception of Sex Role by Male and Female Chinese Students

Males			
Femininity		Masculinity	
Concept	Avg. Rating	Concept	Avg. Rating
Planful	4.6	Capable	5.1
Defeat	4.6	Devotion	5.1
Femininity	4.6	Clear thinking	5.1
Mature	4.6	Masculinity	5.1
Power	4.6	Foresight	5.2
Work	4.6	Free will	5.1
Purpose	4.6	Taking initiative	5.2
Individuality	4.7	Progressive	5.2
		Efficient	5.2
		Play	5.2
		Health	5.3
		Courage	5.3
		Freedom	5.4
		Intelligent	5.6
		Alert	5.6

(continued)

TABLE 9
(Continued)

Females

Femininity		*Masculinity*	
Concept	*Avg. Rating*	*Concept*	*Avg. Rating*
Wealth	4.6	Cooperation	4.9
Charity	4.7	Masculinity	4.9
Performing arts	4.7	Lone	4.9
Femininity	4.6	Progress	4.9
Scientific work	4.6	Planful	4.8
Top of class	4.6	Devotion	5.0

TABLE 10
Activity Dimension: Perception of Sex Role by
British Male and Female Students

Males

Femininity		*Masculinity*	
Concept	*Avg. Rating*	*Concept*	*Avg. Rating*
Performing arts	4.1	Leader	5.0
Conventional	4.1	Business	5.0
Conforming	4.1	Courage	5.0
Being stable	4.1	Competition	5.0
Devotion	4.1	I myself	5.1
Thorough	4.2	Having children	5.0
Femininity	4.2	Masculinity	5.1
		Future	5.1
		Health	5.2
		Power	5.3

Females

Femininity		*Masculinity*	
Concept	*Avg. Rating*	*Concept*	*Avg. Rating*
Easy going	4.3	Masculinity	5.1
Femininity	4.3	Present	5.1
Lotteries	4.3	Competition	5.1
Self-insight	4.3	Business	5.0
Mission	4.3	I myself	5.0
Reward	4.4	Health	5.2
Marriage	4.4	Aggressive	5.2
Scholarship	4.4	Big family	5.3
Luck	4.3	Play	5.4
A choice	4.3		

GENERAL DISCUSSION AND CONCLUSIONS

Most theoretical models and research on achievement motivation origi-
nated in the West and are biased towards the individualistic notion of
achievement. Our previous cross-cultural studies suggested that Western
models of achievement might not apply to Asian cultures. Under the influence of mass media and technological development, Asian people are
becoming more like their individualistic counterparts in the West. Our
recent studies, however showed that traditional Chinese cultural values
continue to influence achievement orientation of Chinese students and
that Chinese students may have a different meaning for achievement to
that of their Western counterparts (Salili, 1994).

The purpose of the study reported here was to confirm our previous
findings as well as further exploring similarities and differences in affective
meaning of achievement between British and Chinese students using the
SD technique. When the SD ratings of the two groups were subjected to
separated cluster analyses, we were able to explore composition of the clusters for each group. Clusters represented aspects of achievement already
described in the literature on achievement motivation. Several interesting
patterns emerged: clusters that were formed for each culture were roughly
similar, although they sometimes appeared in different order. This suggests that the dimensions of achievement may be the same for both cultures, thus supporting our previous findings (see Salili, 1994). There were
also some differences in the composition of the clusters for the two cultures. For example, for both cultures *'failure'* was rated low on all three
dimensions and associated with such negative characteristics as *'follower'*,
'insecure', *'pessimism'* and *'shame'*. However, for the Chinese failure was also
associated with *'fear'* and *'punishment'*, showing the gravity of one's failure
in the Chinese culture and the pervasive fear associated with it, driving
some victims to suicide.

Similarly the positive outcome of achievement, *'success'* was rated highly
by both groups on all three dimensions and associated with positively
loaded concepts, but the composition of the cluster was different for the
two groups. Typically, for the Chinese students, 'success' was associated
with *'effort'*, *'devotion'*, *'top of the class'*, *'determination'*, *'knowledge'* and *'lone'*,
showing the serious nature of academic work in Hong Kong. The inclusion
of the concept *'lone'* may suggest that Chinese students perceive that *'success'* in being *'on top of the class'* is an individualistic activity, accompanied by
loneliness, and not rewarding. *'Success'* for the British students, however,
had a different meaning and was associated with a wider area of life including both individualistic and affiliative achievements (see Tables, 1 & 2) and
results in *'reward'*.

The results also showed the two cultures hold common stereotypes for
sex roles (see Tables 1 and 2), although the British had a more modern

view of '*femininity*' by also associating it with such concepts as '*industrious*', '*school*', *and* '*scientific work*'.

Analyses directed at gender differences in sex-role concepts showed '*masculinity*' and '*femininity*' were perceived differently in different dimensions of meaning (see Tables 3-10). The findings suggested that even though females are perceived to be sweet and nice (in evaluation dimension), they are considered weak and powerless in the potency dimension. Even females themselves hold a negative stereotype of their own sex-role suggesting that we have a long way to go before achieving real equality between the sexes. This view of females from students of today's modern age is not surprising, as males still occupy the positions of power and leadership and females are often discriminated against. Both sexes attached a very positive meaning to masculinity in all dimensions and both male and female British students associated '*I myself*' with '*masculinity*'.

An important cluster (see cluster 1, Tables 1 and 2) for both cultures represented *Self-efficacy/Self-competence*. This cluster was rated high on all three dimensions and contained many similar concepts for both groups, but, not surprisingly, for the British students the cluster also contained concepts representing more individualistically oriented achievement characteristics. In line with their cultural values the two groups also associated different achievement goals with self-efficacy. For the British, the goals were more worldly and concrete (e.g., '*wealth*'), whereas for the Chinese they were somewhat abstract (e.g., '*freedom*').

Our results also showed an interesting pattern of self-serving bias in ratings and in composition of the cluster that related to '*I myself*' (see clusters 3 and 2 in Tables 1 and 2 respectively for Chinese and British students). The concepts clustered with '*I myself*' were all desirable in nature and were highly rated in all three dimensions, showing that both cultural groups enjoyed a high level of self-esteem/ideal-self. Interestingly, Chinese students saw their ideal-self as more individualistic than is usually expected. Whereas, the ideal-self for the British was a balance of both individualistic and socially related achievement concepts. This finding may reflect the influence of westernization and Western media on Chinese students in Hong Kong. Similarly, the British students living in Hong Kong may have been influenced by the Chinese culture. We speculate that Hong Kong, a cosmopolitan Chinese city with a mix of Western and Chinese cultures, could act as a melting pot, where each culture is influenced by the other.

One of the most striking differences between the two cultures were related to the meaning attached to '*filial piety*', which is the cornerstone of the Chinese collectivistic cultural value. '*Filial piety*' for the Chinese was associated with '*being industrious*', '*family relationship*', '*marriage, scholarship, respect*'. etc... (see Table 1) and was rated highly by the Chinese group. However, '*filial piety*' for the British represented conformity and being conventional and clustered with concepts associated with low achievement motivation. This shows clearly, that some aspects of the traditional Chinese cultural value such as filial piety is very resistant to westernization influences.

The findings of this study have both theoretical and practical implications. On the theoretical level our results clearly show that there are both commonalties and differences in affective meaning of achievement. Many clusters supported the Western formulated aspects of achievement. There were many similarities between the two cultures in these clusters, with the same themes and many overlapping concepts. The similarities were often based on shared hedonistic principles of human nature (e.g., the concept success and failure had positive and negative connotations respectively for both groups. Similarly groups had very positive meaning for 'I myself'), and others were based on the shared cultural values (e.g., self-efficacy), societal expectations and common experiences (e.g., the meanings attached to '*femininity*' and '*masculinity*').

The composition of the clusters were not, however, exactly the same and some of them were entirely different. These differences appeared to reflect the unique cultural values and different learning experiences of the two groups (e.g., meaning attached to the concepts, '*filial piety*' and '*success*') that can be easily identified by people who are familiar with these cultures. Our findings showed that the two cultures generally agreed on dimensions of achievement, but they sometimes differed in the type of goals they associated with each dimension, the characteristics or instrumental activities they considered important in achieving the goal/s and their consequences (see for example, Table 1 and 2, Cluster 2 'Success').

On a practical level, this study provided important clues for the educators and counselors about students' affective meaning of achievement so that they could have a better understanding of students' difficulties, if any and design appropriate approaches to intervention. This is particularly important in multicultural educational settings where teachers need to understand values and meanings that students from different cultures attach to achievement. In the case of Chinese students in particular, the composition of the 'Success' cluster (see Table 1, Cluster 2) reflects the culture of the school and the pressure that parents and teachers exert on students for academic excellence. This is of course at the expense of students' social development and mental health, driving some to commit suicide for fear of shame and punishment that failure can cause (see Table 1, Cluster 9 'Failure').

Findings concerning gender differences also revealed that we need to work harder so as to eliminate gender inequality for both cultures. In order to effect change in that direction, we need to address the issue not only through appropriate legislation, but also through education in order to change the stereotype of sex-roles at the individual level.

Our study shows that the Semantic Differential technique is a very useful tool in investigating cross-cultural differences in affective meaning of achievement. The SD technique enables us to look into all three dimensions of meaning rather that only one—the evaluation dimension. One problem with the SD technique, however, is that concepts are not elicited from the participants, but provided by the researcher. The concepts are also presented individually and out of context, although in the present study, the instruction given asked the participants to relate the concepts to their own experiences when making their judgements. Future studies combining the phenomenological approach with semantic differential are needed to confirm our findings.

APPENDIX 1. ENGLISH SEMANTIC DIFFERENTIAL SCALES

	-3	-2	-1	0	+1	+2	+3	
Awful								Nice
Strong								Weak
Sour								Sweet
Big								Little
Fast								Slow
Noisy								Quiet
Shallow								Deep
Powerful								Powerless
Helpful								Unhelpful
Unfamiliar								Familiar
Good								Bad
Dead								Alive
Young								Old

REFERENCES

Ames, C. (1984b). Achievement attributions and self-instructions in competitive and individualistic goal structures. *Journal of Educational Psychology*, 76, 478-487.

Ames, C. & Archer, J. (1988). Achievement goals in the classroom: Students' learning strategies and motivation processes. *Journal of Educational Psychology*, 80 (3), 260- 267.

Au, T.K.F. & Harackiewicz, J.M. (1986). The effects of perceived parental expectations on Chinese children's mathematics performance. *Merrill-Palmer Quarterly*, 32 (4): 383-392.

Bandura, A, (1997). *Self-efficacy: The experience of control.* New York, NY: Freeman.

Bem, S. (1974). The measurement of psychological androgyny. *Journal of Consulting and Clinical Psychology*, 42, 155-162.

Chen, C., Stevenson, H.W., Hayward, C. & Burgess, S. (1995). Culture and academic achievement: Ethnic and cross-national differences. In M.L. Maehr &

P.R. Pintrich, *Advances in motivation and achievement: Culture, motivation and achievement*, vol. 9, pp. 119-152. Greenwich, CT: JAI Press.

De Vos, G.A. (1973). *Socialization for achievement: Essays on the cultural psychology of the Japanese.* Berkeley, CA: University of California Press.

Dweck, C.S. (1975). The role of expectations and attributions in the alleviation of learned helplessness. *Journal of Personality and Social Psychology, 31*, 674-685.

Dweck, C. & Leggett, E.L. (1988). A social-cognitive approach to motivation and personality. *Psychological Review, 95*, 256-273.

Elliot, A.J., (1997). Integrating the "classic" and "contemporary" approaches to achievement motivation: A hierarchical model of approach and avoidance achievement motivation. In M.L. Maehr & P.R. Pintrich, *Advances in motivation and achievement Motivation* (vol. 10, pp. 143-180). Greenwich, CT: JAI Press.

Feather, N.T. (1986). Value systems across cultures: Australia and China. *International Journal of Psychology, 21*, 697-715.

Fyans, L.J., Jr., Salili, F., Maehr, M.L. & Desai, K.A. (1983) A cross-cultural exploration into meaning of achievement. *Journal of Personality and Social Psychology, 44*, 1000-1013.

Gallimore, R. (1981). Affiliation, social context, industriousness, and achievement. In R.L. Munroe, R.H. Munroe & B. Whiting (Eds.), *Handbook of cross-cultural human development.* New York, NY: Garland.

Gallimore, R., Boggs, J.W. & Jordan, C. (1974). *Culture, behavior, and education: A study of Hawaiian-Americans.* Beverly Hills, CA: Sage.

Hau, K.T. & Salili, F. (1990). Examination results attribution, expectancy and achievement goals among Chinese students in Hong Kong. *Educational Studies, 16* (1), 17-31.

Ho, D.Y.F. & Kang, T.K. (1984). Intergenerational comparisons of child-rearing attitudes and practices in Hong Kong. *Developmental Psychology, 20*(6), 1004-1016.

Lamborn, S.D., Mounts, N.S., Steinberg, L. & Dornbusch, S.M. (1991). Patterns of competence and adjustment among adolescents from authoritative, authoritarian, indulgent, and neglectful families. *Child Development, 62*, 1049-1065.

Lau, S. (1988). The value orientations of Chinese university students in Hong Kong. *International Journal of Psychology, 23*, 583-596.

Lau, S. (1992). Collectivism's individualism: value preference, personal control and the desire for freedom among Chinese in Mainland China, Hong Kong and Singapore. *Personality and Individual Difference, 13* (3): 361-366.

Lau, S. (Ed.) (1996). *Growing up the Chinese way.* Hong Kong: The Chinese University Press.

Lau, S. & Wong, A.K. (1992). Value and sex-role orientation of Chinese adolescents. *International Journal of Psychology, 27*(1), 3-17.

Maehr, M.L. & Stallings, W.M. (1972). Freedom from evaluation. *Child Development, 43*, 177-185.

Maehr, M.L. & Braskam, L.A. (1986). *The motivation factor: A theory of personal investment.* Lexington, MA: Lexington Books.

McClelland, D.C., Atkinson, J., Clark, R. & Lowell, E. (1953). *The achievement motive.* New York, NY: Appleton-Century-Crofts.

Mitschel, W. (1974). Processes in delay of gratification. In L. Berkowitz (Ed.) *Advances in experimental social psychology* (Vol.7, pp. 249-292). New York, NY: Academic Press.

Murray, H.A. (1938). *Explorations in personality.* New York, NY: Oxford University Press.

Nicholls, J.G. (1984). Achievement motivation: Conception of ability, subjective experience, task choice, and performance. *Psychological Review, 91,* 328-346.

Osgood, C.E. & Tzeng, O.C.S. (1990). *Language, meaning, and culture: The selected papers of C.E. Osgood.* Centennial Psychology Series. New York, NY: Praeger.

Osgood, C.E., May, W.H. & Miron, M.S. (1975). *Cross-cultural universals of affective meaning.* Urbana, IL: University of Illinois Press.

Osgood, C.E.,, G.J., Suci, P. H., Tannenbaum (1957). *The measurement of meaning.* Urbana, IL: University of Illinois Press.

Ramirez, M. III, & Price-Williams, D.L. (1976). Achievement motivation in children of three ethnic groups in United States. *Journal of Cross-Cultural Psychology, 7,* 49-60.

Rohlen, T.P. (1983). The facts just the facts. *Winds,* 26-36.

Romesburg, C.H. (1984). Cluster analysis for researchers. Belmont, CA: Lifetime Learning Publishers.

Salili, F. (1994). Age, sex, and cultural differences in the meaning and dimensions of achievement. *Personality and Social Psychology Bulletin, 20* (6), 635-648.

Salili, F. (1995). Explaining Chinese students' motivation and achievement: A socio-cultural analysis. In M.L., Maehr & P. R., Pintrich, *Advances in motivation and achievement,* (vol. 9, pp. 73-118).

Salili F., Maehr M.L. & Gilmore, G. (1976). Achievement and morality: A cross-cultural analysis of causal attribution and evaluation. *Journal of Personality and Social Psychology, 33*(3), 327-337.

Salili, F. & Mak, P.H.T. (1988).Subjective meaning of success in high and low achievers. *International Journal of Intercultural Relations, 12,* 125-138.

Salili F., Maehr, M.L. Sorenson, R. & Fyans L.J., (1976). A further consideration of the effects of evaluation on motivation. *American Educational Research Journal, 13* (2), 85-102.

Salili, F., Chiu, C-Y. & Lai, S. (2001). The influence of culture and context of learning on student's motivational orientation and performance. In F. Salili., C-Y. Chiu, & Y-Y. Hong, *Student motivation: The culture and context of learning.* New York, NY: Plenum.

Spence, J.T. (1985). Achievement American style: The rewards and costs of individualism. *American Psychologist, 40,* 1285-1295.

Steinberg, L., Dorbusch, S.M. & Brown, B.B. (1992). Ethnic differences in adolescent achievement: An ecological perspective. *American Psychologist, 47,* 723-729.

Stevenson, H.W. & Lee, S. (1990). Context of achievement, *Monographs of the Society for Research on Child Development,* Serial No, 222,Vol. 55, Nos 1-2.

Triandis, H.C. (1972). *The analysis of subjective culture.* New York: Wiley.

Tseng, W.S. & Hsu, J. (1969-70). Chinese culture, personality formation and mental illness. *International Journal of Social Psychiatry, 16,* 5-14.

Weiner, B. & Peter, N. (1973). A cognitive developmental analysis of achievement and moral judgements. *Developmental Psychology, 9,* 290-309.

Weiss, L.H. & Schwarz, J.C. (1996). The relationship between parenting types and older adolescents' personality, academic achievement, adjustment, and substance use. *Child Development, 67,* 2101-2114.

Wu, D.Y.H. (1996). Parental control: Psychocultural interpretations of Chinese patterns of Socialization. In S. Lau (Ed.), *Growing up the Chinese way*. Hong Kong: The Chinese University Press.

Yu, A.B. & Yang, K.S. (1987). Social- and individual-oriented achievement motivation: A conceptual and empirical analysis. *Bulletin of the Institute of Ethnology*, Academica Sinica (Taipei, Taiwan), *64*, 51-98. (in Chinese).

Zhang, L-F. (2000). Abilities, academic performance, learning approaches, and thinking styles: A three-culture investigation. *Journal of Psychology in Chinese Societies 1* (2), 123-149.

CHAPTER 13

MOTIVATION AND LEARNING STRATEGIES
A Cross-Cultural Perspective

**David Watkins, Dennis McInerney, Clement Lee,
Adebowale Akande, and Murari Regmi**

INTRODUCTION

The quality of learning in schools and universities is a major concern for developing countries because there is a clear link between economic development and educational progress (Altbach & Selvaratnam, 1989). Research has made clear that the strategies a student adopts for learning an academic task influence the quality of the learning outcomes they achieve in both Western (Biggs, 1987; Schmeck, 1988) and non-Western cultures (Watkins, 2000) even if this quality is not always rewarded in the grades they obtain. Thus an understanding of factors which influence the adoption of such strategies may help us devise ways of improving such outcomes.

Deep learning strategies which tend to lead to higher quality outcomes involve the intention to understand typically by means of trying to interrelate ideas, reading widely, and thinking independently and critically. They have been shown to be associated in many different cultures with personal characteristics of the learner such as high intelligence and self-esteem and aspects of the learning context such as a stimulating learning environment and appropriate assessment (Biggs, 1987; Entwistle & Ramsden, 1983; Schmeck, 1988; Watkins, 2000). Superficial learning strategies, on the other hand, tend to be associated with fear of failure and an external locus of control and a context characterized by boredom or fear and assessment methods, such as multiple choice items, perceived as rewarding low quality learning. The third commonly found strategy is achieving where the students tend to work hard and be well organized and use whatever specific strategy they feel will maximize their chances of high marks be it gaining mastery of what is to be learnt or, in extreme cases, cheating. Adoption of this strategy is thought to be dependent on both the students need for success and their perception of the assessment task.

Theorists from both the Approaches to Learning (Entwistle & Ramsden, 1983; Marton & Saljo, 1976) and the Self-Regulation (Pintrich & Garcia, 1991; Zimmerman, 1990) traditions, dominant in Europe and North America respectively, have proposed that the motive(s) with which a student approaches a learning task is likely to influence the way they tackle that task. However, both these theoretical approaches are based on conceptualizations of achievement motivation which may be inappropriate for non-Western students. This chapter uses a recently developed instrument based on a less individualistic view of motivation to investigate the relationship between learning motivation and strategies for secondary school students in a range of African and Asian countries.

Approaches to Learning Tradition

In this tradition this link is clearest in the motive/strategy model of learning processes advocated by Biggs (1987). In this model external, intrinsic, and achievement motivation are linked to the adoption of surface, deep, and achieving learning strategies, respectively. Biggs operationalized his theory in two well-known questionnaires, the Learning Process Questionnaire (LPQ) and the Study Process Questionnaire (SPQ), which have three pairs of motive/strategy scales. According to Biggs congruence between the motive and strategy a student adopts (e.g. surface motive and surface strategy) is a sign of metacognition and is likely to lead to better learning outcomes. He and other researchers have supported empirically the underlying model or similar models in Western and non-Western cultures (Biggs, 1987; Entwistle & Ramsden, 1983; Watkins & Akande, 1994; Watkins & Biggs, 1996).

Self-Regulation of Learning Tradition

The American approach in this area is primarily based on achievement goal theory (Ames, 1992; Dweck, 1986). According to the latter there are two incompatible types of general goals: performance goals and mastery goals. The former refer to demonstrating one's superiority to others whereas the latter refer to beliefs that individual effort leads to academic success and that learning has intrinsic value.

A recent review of classroom and laboratory studies (Covington, 2000) concluded that there was adequate empirical support for the theoretical propositions that mastery goals are associated with deeper, meaning-oriented learning strategies whereas performance goals tend to be associated with superficial, rote-level processing. Covington warned, however, that the bulk of the research he reviews is based on mainstream American students and there is little evidence that the theory and these findings can be generalized to other cultural groups.

Cross-Cultural Relevance

A weakness of the above theorizing and research is that both traditions are based on views of motivation which may not be appropriate for non-Western students. For example, Watkins and Biggs (1996) reviewed research on Chinese students and concluded that such students tend to espouse multiple even seemingly contradictory motives. Moreover, the Western polarity of intrinsic versus extrinsic motivation collapsed in the Chinese context and also a socially-oriented rather than the Western individually-oriented concept of achievement motivation was more relevant for Asian cultures.

More specifically, those authors argued that most Western students, teachers, and researchers see intrinsic motivation as the only way of defining what is both meaningful and worthwhile to learn and thus a deep learning strategy tends to be associated with deep, intrinsic motivation. However, research indicates that many Chinese students (like Confucius before them) see things more pragmatically and that a deep approach can be triggered by motivational impetus based not only on interest but also on a mix of intense personal ambition, family face, peer support, and/or material reward. Even more fundamental to Confucian-heritage cultures are internal dispositions that encourage a sense of diligence and receptiveness (Hess & Azuma, 1991) which encourage the perception that academic work is worthwhile far more powerfully than the Western concept of intrinsic motivation.

It also needs to be recognized that the Western concept of achievement motivation is largely based on the work of Atkinson (1964) and McClelland (1961) and emphasizes individual competition between those whose need for success exceeds their fear of failure. Winning in 'competitions' such as exams is very ego-enhancing to such persons. But in Asia family pressure for academic success is stronger and a matter of family face. What constitutes success is likely to be decided by significant others such as the family and peer group as well as the individual student. Thus in Asia and probably in other collectivist societies group and affiliation goals are likely to be more salient than is reflected in Western theorizing, at least until recently (Chang, Wong, & Teo, 2000; Yang & Yu, 1988).

But what goals influence the learning strategies students adopt? Ng (2000), in a study of Hong Kong secondary school students, did find support for the hypothesis that mastery and performance goals were related to deep and surface approaches to learning, respectively. Unfortunately this study, by focusing on the relationship between goals and learning approaches (= motives + strategies), confounded the motivation/strategy link. One of the aims of the research reported here is to provide further evidence.

A New Model of Motivation

Goal theory in its earlier formulations has also been criticized for not allowing students to hold both performance and mastery goals and deemphasizing social goals (Blumenfeld, 1992; Urdan & Maehr, 1995). In response to such criticisms McInerney, Yeung, and McInerney (2000, 2001) proposed a hierarchical, multidimensional model of goal orientations designed to reflect a wider range of goals relevant for both Western and non-Western students (see Figure 1). At the base of this model are nine

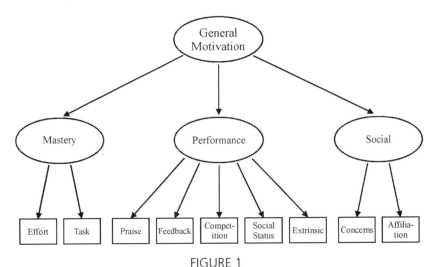

FIGURE 1
The Basic Model of Motivation as Proposed by McInerney et al.

specific goals (task, effort, praise, feedback, competition, social status, extrinsic, social concern, and affiliation) which can be grouped into three more general goals (mastery, performance, and social), and at the apex of the hierarchy is general motivation.

This research utilizes the Inventory of School Motivation Revised (ISMR; McInerney et al., 2000, 2001) which is based on this model to investigate the power of the ISMR scales to predict the extent to which the students reported using surface, deep and achieving learning strategies in a range of cultures. The task and effort goals are collapsed into one scale for this study (see McInerney, Marsh, & Yeung (under review) for a description of the refinement of the theoretical model). It should be noted that intentionally the analyses reported here do not include mean cross-cultural comparisons. Although always of interest the validity of such comparisons must always be in doubt as it is very difficult to justify the equivalence of the metrics involved (see Van de Vijver & Leung, 1997, for an in-depth discussion of this issue).

METHOD

The Participants

The focus of this research were 1657 students from secondary schools in Hong Kong, Malawi, Nepal, South Africa (separate Black and White samples), and Zambia. There were almost equal numbers of males and females and most were aged 13-14 years. As no gender differences were found in the correlations which were the focus of this research combined data are reported here. In each country effort was made to ensure that the schools and pupils sampled were typical of that country.

The Instruments

Utilized in this research were the ISMR and the strategy scales of the Learning Process Questionnaire (LPQ; Biggs, 1987). Both scales were to be responded to on five-point Likert scales from '1 = strongly disagree' to '5 = strongly agree'. In all but Hong Kong the questionnaires were presented in English, the medium of instruction, after checking that the wording was relevant for each school context. In Hong Kong a Chinese version of the ISMR was developed (Watkins, McInerney, & Lee, 2001) and the Chinese version of the LPQ (Biggs, 1992) was utilized.

The ISMR as used in this study is composed of eleven scales relating to the following motivational goals and sense of self values influencing learning:

- *Task-Effort (11 items):* Interest in the task and willingness to expend effort to improve schoolwork. Examples of items representing this dimension are "I like to see that I am improving in my schoolwork" and "I always try hard to understand something new in my school work."
- *Competition (8 items):* Competitiveness in learning. Examples of this dimension are "I like to compete with others at school" and "I am only happy when I am one of the best in the class."
- *Social Status (7 items):* Seeking social status through group leadership. Examples of this dimension are "I like being in charge of a group" and "I work hard at school to have the class notice me."
- *Praise (9 items):* Social recognition for schoolwork. Examples of this dimension are "I work best when I am praised at school" and "I like to be encouraged for my schoolwork."
- *Extrinsic (10 items):* Tangible rewards for schoolwork. Examples of this dimension are "I work best in class when I get rewards" and "Getting good marks is everything for me."
- *Affiliation (8 items):* Belonging to a group when doing schoolwork or positive influence of friends while doing schoolwork. Examples of the dimension are "I can do my best work at school when I work with others" and "I like to work with other students at school rather than work alone."
- *Social Concern (5 items):* Concern for other students and a willingness to help them with their school work. Examples of this dimension are "It is important for students to help each other at school" and "I like helping other students with their school work."
- *Self-reliance (8 items):* Self-regulation within academic settings. Examples of items representing this dimension are "I do not need anyone to tell me to work hard" and "Difficult school work does not bother me if I am working alone."
- *Self-esteem (12 items):* Confidence about general academic ability at school. Examples of items representing this dimension are "I am bright enough to finish high school" and "I can succeed at whatever I do at school."
- *Sense of purpose (6 items):* Valuing school for the future. Examples of items representing this dimension are "It is good for me to plan ahead to complete high school" and "I want to do well at school to have a good future."
- *General mastery (5 items):* Motivation that comes from mastering one's learning. A typical item is "I am most motivated when I see my work improving."

- *General performance (8 items):* Motivation that comes from recognition of doing well and beating others. Typical items are: "I like my teacher to show my work to the rest of the class" and "I am most motivated when I am competing with others."
- *General social (5 items):* Motivation that comes from working with others. A typical item is "I am most motivated when I am in a group."
- *Global motivation (8 items):* Assesses overall motivation. A typical item is "I am motivated at school."

Exploratory factor analysis in each sample supported the model of motivation on which they were claimed to be based. The scales have also been validated by exploratory and confirmatory factor analysis in a number of Western and non-Western cultural groups (McInerney & Swisher, 1995;

TABLE 1

Internal Consistency Coefficient Alpha for Responses to Items of the ISMR Motivation Scales and LPQ Strategy Scales for All Six Samples

	Hong Kong (n = 697)	Malawi (n = 199)	Nepal (n = 208)	South African (Black) (n = 206)	South African (White) (n = 207)	Zambia (n = 140)
Specific Motivation Scales						
Task Effort	.74	.89	.61	.82	.83	.74
Praise	.84	.80	.76	.72	.80	.76
Extrinsic	.75	.83	.69	.71	.75	.72
Competition	.80	.79	.67	.82	.81	.77
Social Status	.80	.77	.79	.82	.80	.75
Affiliation	.72	.50	.34	.59	.69	.69
Social Concern	.68	.72	.38	.55	.58	.45
General Motivation Scales						
Mastery	.74	.77	.59	.68	.71	.64
Performance	.84	.75	.75	.78	.81	.75
Social	.68	.72	.38	.55	.58	.45
Global	.77	.80	.74	.82	.78	.73
Sense of Self Scales						
Self-Reliance	.57	.50	.34	.59	.69	.69
Self-Esteem	.75	.60	.60	.52	.60	.59
Sense of Purpose	.74	.85	.70	.77	.76	.76
LPQ						
Surface Strategy	.54	.65	.36	.55	.43	.59
Deep Strategy	.66	.77	.61	.69	.70	.74
Achieving Strategy	.75	.76	.68	.71	.71	.83

McInerney, Roche, McInerney, & Marsh, 1997; McInerney et al. 2001). The internal consistency reliability estimates, coefficient alphas, for responses of the six samples to items of the ISMR are shown in Table 1. Using the criteria that for group analyses an alpha of .70 and over is very adequate and of over .50 is acceptable for research purposes (Nunnally, 1978) it can be seen that the alphas of the great majority of the ISMR scales were very adequate in each sample. While generally adequate, more scales were less satisfactory for the Nepalese group, and in general, the Social Concern, Affiliation and Social General scales were weaker across the groups.

The LPQ strategy scales consisted of three six-item scales assessing Surface, Deep, and Achieving Strategies (see Biggs, 1987; 1991 for further details). It can also be seen in Table 1 that the alphas obtained for responses to the LPQ scales were very adequate for both Deep and Achieving Strategies but of borderline adequacy for Surface Strategy. However, the figures obtained were similar to those found for the Australian norming sample (Biggs, 1987).

Analysis

A series of Multiple Regression analyses were conducted with the scales of the ISMR as the independent variables and the surface, deep, and achieving strategy scales of the LPQ each as the dependent variables. These analyses were conducted separately for each cultural group and for the specific and general motivation and sense of self scales of the ISM.

RESULTS

Tables 2, 3, and 4 present the Beta weights for each of the six samples from three separate regression analyses with Surface, Deep, and Achieving strategy scales as the dependent variables, respectively, and Specific Motivation, General Motivation, and Sense of Self scales as the independent variables.

It can be seen that across all samples the specific and general motivation and self scales were all able to predict deep and achieving strategies quite well. However, prediction of the use of surface strategies was less successful and some scales contributed much more to these predictions than others. The main trends were as follows:

- *Surface Strategy:* The results for Surface Strategy are not as clear cut for Deep and Achieving Strategies Extrinsic Motivation, Social Status, Performance General, Self-Reliance, and Self Esteem provided the highest Beta weights across most samples.
- *Deep Strategy:* Task-Effort and Sense of Purpose scales were strong predictors across all samples while Mastery General, Global Motivation

and Self-Reliance scales were consistent moderate predictors across most samples. Again, Self-Esteem was a moderate predictor for the Nepalese group.

- *Achieving Strategy:* Across all samples Task-Effort, Global Motivation and Sense of Purpose, scales were strong to moderate predictors while Self-Reliance was a moderate predictor for most groups. Again the Self-Variables were moderate predictors for the Nepalese group.

Consistent moderate to strong predictors for the deep and achieving strategies for all groups were Task-Effort, Sense of Purpose, and Global Motivation. The extrinsic scales Praise, Extrinsic, and Competition, as well

TABLE 2

Beta Weights and Multiple Regression Coefficients for (a) Specific and (b) General Motivation and (c) Self ISMR Scales as Predictors of Surface Strategies for Different Ethnic Groups

	Hong Kong	Malawi	Nepal	South African (Black)	South African (White)	Zambia
Specific Motivation						
Task Effort	-.22**	-.13	-.15	-.04	-.13	-.15
Praise	-.05	.15	.03	.17	-.07	.06
Extrinsic	.29**	-.09	.27**	.06	.21*	.28*
Competition	-.11*	.11	-.08	.20*	-.02	-.27*
Social Status	.09*	.42**	.06	.19*	.26**	.20
Affiliation	.05	-.09	.10	-.08	-.03	.03
Social Concern	-.03	.23**	-.07	.13	.18*	.11
Multiple R	.31**	.57**	.31**	.52**	.37**	.38**
General Motivation						
Mastery General	-.15**	-.06	.02	-.07	-.01	.01
Performance General	.08	.40**	-.01	.31**	.25**	.13
Social General	.09	.12	.05	.19*	-.01	.22*
Global Motivation	-.17**	-.02	-.11	.17*	-.01	-.24*
Multiple R	.21**	.43**	.10	.50**	.24*	.31**
Self-Variables						
Self-Reliance	-.04	.58**	-.04	.34**	.12	.04
Self-Esteem	-.19*	-.36**	-.18*	-.12	-.18*	-.26*
Sense of Purpose	.02	-.06	.06	.10	.07	.07
Multiple R	.21**	.56**	.19	.38**	.18	.24*

Notes: ** $p < .01$

      * $p < .05$

as Performance General showed little relationship to either of these latter learning strategies as did the social scales Social Status, Affiliation, and Social Concern, while Social General was a significant predictor for some of the groups. The models worked less well and consistently for the surface strategies across all groups. However, in these analyses Extrinsic, Competition, Social Status, and Performance General appeared to be the most consistent across the groups.

In summary, it was the mastery oriented scales Task Effort, Mastery General, Global Motivation and Sense of Purpose scales which showed the strongest relation to the use of deep and achieving learning strategies

TABLE 3

Beta Weights and Multiple Regression Coefficients for (a) Specific and (b) General Motivation and (c) Self ISMR Scales as Predictors of Deep Strategies for Different Ethnic Groups

	Hong Kong	Malawi	Nepal	South African (Black)	South African (White)	Zambia
Specific Motivation						
Task Effort	.44**	.53**	.32**	.57**	.35**	.41**
Praise	-.06	.16	.14	.12	.22*	.00
Extrinsic	.02	.16	-.19*	.02	-.05	.15
Competition	.03	.00	.17*	-.03	.23**	.04
Social Status	.17**	.06	-.06	.20**	-.15	.05
Affiliation	-.02	-.10	.12	-.11	-.04	-.21**
Social Concern	.04	-.13	.17*	.11	.11	.14
Multiple R	.53**	.74**	.53**	.75**	.60**	.56**
General Motivation						
Mastery General	.13**	.22**	.12	.30**	.17*	.24**
Performance General	.09	.09	.11	.13*	.12	.13
Social General	.09*	.20**	.17*	.13	.17*	-.01
Global Motivation	.30**	.32**	.12	.29**	.34**	.22*
Multiple R	.49**	.71**	.41**	.68**	.68**	.43**
Self-Variables						
Self-Reliance	.30**	.39**	.06	.43**	.22**	.20**
Self-Esteem	.03	.02	.20**	.09	.04	-.01
Sense of Purpose	.26**	.40**	.23**	.35**	.39**	.35**
Multiple R	.48**	.71**	.37**	.72**	.54**	.47**

Notes: ** $p < .01$

   * $p < .05$

TABLE 4
Beta Weights and Multiple Regression Coefficients for (a) Specific and
(b) General Motivation and (c) Self ISMR Scales as Predictors of
Achieving Strategies for Different Ethnic Groups

	Hong Kong	Malawi	Nepal	South African (Black)	South African (White)	Zambia
Specific Motivation						
Task Effort	.47**	.59**	.38**	.47**	.49**	.45**
Praise	-.14**	.11	.10	-.01	.14	.10
Extrinsic	.12*	.09	-.06	.10	.05	-.08
Competition	-.09	.12	.05	-.02	.07	-.07
Social Status	.19**	-.02	.02	.08	-.09	.13
Affiliation	-.03	-.01	.07	.00	.04	-.15
Social Concern	.10	-.10	.19**	.15*	.07	.11
Multiple R	.54**	.74**	.56**	.62**	.64**	.51**
General Motivation						
Mastery General	.10*	.41**	.12	.08	.17	.24**
Performance General	.05	.00	.09	.03	-.01	-.03
Social General	.09*	.14	.10	.25**	.22**	.04
Global Motivation	.40**	.27**	.27**	.32**	.30**	.27**
Multiple R	.53**	.74**	.46**	.56**	.58**	.45**
Self-Variables						
Self-Reliance	.18**	.29**	.15*	.28**	.15*	.28**
Self-Esteem	.15**	-.06	.24**	.10	.05	.02
Sense of Purpose	.29**	.54**	.21**	.34**	.47**	.31**
Multiple R	.47**	.72**	.42**	.58**	.57**	.51**

Notes: ** $p < .01$

   * $p < .05$

across a range of cultures. It was the performance oriented scales that showed the strongest relation to the use of surface strategies.

DISCUSSION

Despite our expectation that a deep approach to learning might be triggered by motivational impetus based not only on mastery but also on a mix of intense personal ambition, family face, peer support, and/or material reward for various groups in our study, the scales significantly related to deep and surface strategies were remarkably similar across the groups. Considering the diversity of the samples utilized in this study it does seem that motivational variables relate in similar ways to the learning strategies students adopt in a range of cultures. The results are consistent with previous Western research showing that performance goals tend to be associated with superficial learning strategies whereas mastery/task oriented goals tend to encourage deeper, better organized strategies. As the latter are likely to lead both to better academic achievement and higher quality learning outcomes this suggests that discouraging the former but encouraging the latter should be the aim of interventions designed to improve student learning across all cultures.

Despite our expectation that social and affiliation goals were more likely to be salient to collectivist groups, widening the range of motivational variables to include socially oriented ones shows they seem to play no consistent role in the learning strategies students adopt across all the ethnic groups in our study. However, there is some evidence from both South Africa and Malawi that social status and social concern may indeed play such a role in these societies, at least as far as surface and achieving strategies are concerned. Perhaps, future research could probe such a relationship more deeply in both societies. It is also possible that such social goals may need to be reconceptualized separately for each society.

It concerned us that the models worked less well for the Nepalese group typically predicting less variance across each of the analyses than for the other groups. Furthermore, for the Nepalese group the Self-Variables were consistently significant predictors in contrast to the other groups. Further work needs to be conducted to examine the reasons for this. Certainly the adequacy of the scales for this group needs to be considered. Across all groups the alphas were less strong for the Nepalese group. The results may also have something to do with the remoteness of the Nepalese group from mainstream educational experiences.

It was also of concern that the analyses demonstrated a poorer relationship between the various scales and surface strategies across all ethnic groups. One possibility is that the Surface Strategy scale is a weaker scale across all groups (see Table 1). Perhaps a different measure of surface learning needs to be utilized to further examine the relationship of motivational and sense of self scales to this form of learning.

Implications

Two sorts of interventions have been tried with some success in Western societies to encourage students to adopt less superficial strategies. At the individual level motivational training (Purdie & Hattie, 1995) and attributional retraining (van Overwalle & De Metsenaere, 1990) have both produced promising results. However, Purdie and Hattie found that such individual programs work best with high academic performers. Moreover, Hattie, Biggs, and Purdie (1996) found interventions which target the development of such strategies in a specific educational context tend to be more successful with lower performing students.

The second approach takes context as the starting point. A number of studies have shown that many students choose to adopt different goals in different classes and that the choice of specific instructional practices is related to specific instructional strategies. A review of such research by Anderman and Maehr (1994) points particularly to ability grouping, external recognition, evaluation methods, and the nature of the learning tasks set, in this regard. Teachers who emphasize the importance of doing best (for example by displaying the top projects in the classroom) have been shown to encourage performance goals (Anderman & Young, 1993).

The overall philosophy of the school can be salient here. A school culture which displays honor rolls and rewards the top students at prize givings is likely to foster performance goals that can even undermine classroom teachers attempts to foster intrinsic motivation (Anderman & Young, 1993). These latter authors go on to describe how goal theory has been used in US schools to guide school change. It seems that encouraging task goals rather than minimizing performance goals may be the best approach. Moreover, reforms of specific aspects of schooling such as abandoning ability grouping, team teaching, and changes in the honors roll and reward program should be incorporated in an overall conceptual scheme before real progress can be achieved. Whether these Western interventions would be effective in non-Western schools to foster task goals and deep level learning strategies remains to be seen. But this research which has demonstrated considerable cross-cultural consistency in the link between learning motivation and strategy suggests they may well be worth trying.

Furthermore, the strong link between Self-Reliance and Sense of Purpose for schooling and Deep Strategies suggests that it is universally important for students to understand why they are at school and what they can get out of it. School programs should address this need and thereby enhance the adoption of deep strategies in their learners.

NOTES

An earlier version of this paper was presented at 9th Conference of the European Association for Research on Learning and Instruction, Fribourg, Switzerland, August 28-September 1, 2001. This research was fully supported by a grant to the first author by the Research Grants Council of the Hong Kong Administrative Region, China.

REFERENCES

Altbach, P.G., & Selvaratnam, V. (Eds.) (1989). *From dependence to autonomy: The development of Asian universities.* Dordrecht, Netherlands: Kluwer.

Ames, C. (1992). Classrooms: goals, structure, and classroom structure. *Journal of Educational Psychology, 84,* 261-271.

Anderman, E.M., & Maehr, M.L. (1994). Motivation and schooling in the middle grades. *Review of Educational Research, 64,* 287-309.

Anderman, E.M., & Young, A.J. (1993). *A multilevel model of adolescents' motivation and strategy use in academic domains.* Paper presented at the Annual Meeting of the American Educational Research Association, Atlanta, GA.

Atkinson, J.W. (1964). *An introduction to motivation.* New York, NY: Van Nostrand.

Biggs, J.B. (1987). *Student approaches to learning and studying.* Melbourne, Australia: Australian Council for Educational Research.

Biggs, J.B. (1992). *Why and how do Hong Kong students learn? Using the Learning and Study Process questionnaires.* Education Paper No.14, Faculty of Education, University of Hong Kong.

Blumenfeld, P.C. (1992). Classroom learning and motivation: clarifying and expanding goal theory. *Journal of Educational Psychology, 84,* 272-281.

Chang, W.C., Wong, W.K., & Teo, G. (2000). The socially oriented and individually oriented achievement motivation of Singaporean Chinese students. *Journal of Psychology in Chinese Societies, 1,* 39-63.

Covington, M.V. (2000). Goal theory, motivation, and school achievement: An integrative review. *Annual Review of Psychology, 51,* 171-200.

Dweck, C.S. (1986). Motivational processes affecting learning. *American Psychology, 41,* 1040-1048.

Entwistle, N.J., & Ramsden, P. (1983). *Understanding student learning.* London: Croom Helm.

Hattie, J.A., Biggs, J.B., & Purdie, N. (1996). Effects of learning skill interventions on student learning: A meta-analysis. *Review of Educational Research, 66,* 99-136.

Hess, R.D., & Azuma, M. (1991). Cultural support for schooling: contrasts between Japan and the United States. *Educational Researcher, 20*(9), 2-8.

Marton, F., & Säljö, R. (1976). On qualitative differences in learning I: Outcome and process. *British Journal of Educational Psychology, 46,* 4-11.

McInerney, D.M., & Swisher, K. (1995). Exploring Navajo motivation in school settings. *Journal of American Indian Education, 33,* 28-51.

McInerney, D.M., Roche, L., McInerney, V., & Marsh, H.W. (1997). Cultural perspectives on school motivation: The relevance and application of goal theory. *American Educational Research Journal, 34,* 207-236.

McInerney, D.M., Yeung, S.Y., & McInerney, V. (2000). *The meaning of school motivation. Multidimensional and hierarchical perspectives and impacts on schooling.* Paper presented at the annual meeting of the American Educational Research Association, New Orleans, LA.

McInerney, D.M., Yeung, S.Y., & McInerney, V. (2001). Cross-cultural validation of the Inventory of School Motivation (ISM). *Journal of Applied Measurement, 2,* 134-152.

McInerney, D.M., Marsh, H.W., & Yeung, A. S. (under review). Toward a hierarchical model of school motivation. *Educational measurement: Issues and practices.*

McClelland, D.C. (1961). *The achieving society.* Princeton, NJ: Van Norstrand.

Ng, C.H. (2000). A path analysis of self-schema, goal orientations, learning approaches and performance. *Journal of Psychology in Chinese Societies, 1,* 93-121.

Nunnally, J.O. (1978). *Psychometric theory.* New York, NY: McGraw-Hill.

Pintrich, P.R., & Garcia, T. (1991). Student goal orientation and self-regulation in the college classroom. In M.L. Maehr & P.R. Pintrich (Eds.), *Advances in motivation and achievement: Goals and self-regulatory processes* (Vol. 7, pp.371-402). Greenwich, CT: JAI Press.

Purdie, N., & Hattie, J. (1995). The effects of motivation training on approaches to learning and self-concept. *British Journal of Educational Psychology, 65,* 227-236.

Schmeck, R. (Ed.) (1988). *Learning strategies and learning styles.* New York, NY: Plenum.

Urdan, T.C., & Maehr, M.L. (1995). Beyond a two-goal theory of motivation and achievement: A case study for social goals. *Review of Educational Research, 65,* 213-243.

Van de Vijver, F., & Leung, K. (1997). *Methods and data analysis for cross-cultural research.* London: Sage.

Van Overvalle, F., & de Metsenaere, M. (1990). The effects of attribution-based intervention and study strategy training on academic achievement in college freshmen. *British Journal of Educational Psychology, 60,* 299-311.

Watkins, D. (2000). Correlates of approaches to learning: A cross-cultural meta-analysis (pp.165-196). In R. Sternberg, & L.F. Zhang (Eds.), *Perspectives on thinking, learning, and cognitive styles.* Mahwah, NJ: Erlbaum.

Watkins, D., & Akande, A. (1994). Approaches to learning of Nigerian secondary school students: emic and etic perspectives. *International Journal of Psychology, 29,* 165-182.

Watkins, D., & Biggs, J. (Eds.) (1996). *The Chinese Learner: cultural, psychological, and contextual influences.* Hong Kong/Melbourne: Comparative Education Research Centre/Australian Council for Educational Research.

Watkins, D., McInerney, D., & Lee, C. (2001). *Assessing the academic motivation of Hong Kong Chinese students.* Manuscript submitted for publication.

Yang, K.S., & Yu, A.B. (1988). *Social- and individual-oriented achievement motives: Conceptualisation and measurement.* Paper presented at the symposium on Chinese Personality and Social Psychology, International Congress of Psychology, Sydney, Australia.

Zimmerman, B.J. (1990). Self-regulated learning and academic achievement: An overview. *Educational Psychology, 25,* 3-17.

CHAPTER 14

TRANSLATION ISSUES IN CROSS-CULTURAL RESEARCH
Review and Recommendations

Teresa García Duncan

INTRODUCTION

One of the greatest challenges to cross-cultural research is designing instruments that are equivalent. Translating instruments so that items are comparable and meaningful across cultures is no small feat; without well-designed, conceptually equivalent measures, comparisons of learning and achievement across cultures lack validity.

The purpose of this chapter is twofold. First, to synthesize the literature from current perspectives on instrument translation and adaptation. There is a tremendous amount of research that is published as technical reports or as bulletins, but is unknown to, or difficult to access by many outside of the field of large-scale assessment. The incorporation of publications from entities such as the International Test Commission and from the U.S. National Center of Education Statistics is a key component of the literature review (e.g., Abedi, Lord & Plummer, 1997; Hambleton & Bollwark, 1991; Hambleton, 1996). For example, the Third International Mathematics and Science Study was a multinational (45 countries) program that addressed students', teachers', and principals' attitudes, experiences and practices: this work is not cited outside of assessment circles, but its methodology merits greater attention, for it has a great deal to offer to the cross-cultural researcher (International Association for the Evaluation of Educational Achievement, 1996). Although this body of work focuses on testing, the adaptation issues directly bear on translating other forms of instruments, such as surveys and questionnaires.

The second purpose of this chapter is to offer the reader a concrete set of research-based guidelines to use in adapting instruments. This pragmatic focus is critical, in order to assist those planning to conduct cross-cultural research as much as possible. By performing a review of the literature and by offering a concrete set of guidelines to the reader, I hope this chapter will be useful to a broad audience of researchers and consumers.

REVIEW OF THE LITERATURE

Despite the existence of rigorous test-equating methodologies, it is only relatively recently that attention has been paid to addressing the equivalence of tests across languages. The general assumption seems to have been that translations into other languages simply involved a mechanical transformation of source language vocabulary to target language vocabulary, and that test properties such as validity and level of difficulty were a function of test content, which somehow transcended any specific language. However, the rise of high-stakes, cross-national research in recent years has resulted in a keener awareness of the naivete of this assumption of simple conversion from one language to another (Hambleton, 1996).

A set of professionally developed and validated guidelines for translating instruments was therefore called for. This project was undertaken by the International Test Commission (ITC), a council composed of representatives of several prestigious international organizations: European Association of Psychological Assessment; European Test Publishers Group; International Association for Cross-Cultural Psychology; International Association for Applied Psychology; International Association for the Evaluation of Educational Achievement; International Language Testing Association; and International Union of Psychological Science (Hambleton, 1996). Their three-year effort resulted in a set of 22 guidelines for adapting educational and psychological tests and forms the foundation of this review of the literature. These guidelines fall into four categories: context, instrument development and adaptation, administration, and documentation/score interpretations (see Table 1).

Context

The context category addresses construct equivalence across the language groups being examined. This is perhaps the most challenging area

TABLE 1
Guidelines for Adapting Educational and Psychological Tests (from
Hambleton, 1996)

Context

1. Effects of cultural differences which are not relevant or important to the main purposes of the study should be minimized to the extent possible.

2. The amount of overlap in the constructs in the populations of interest should be assessed.

Instrument Development and Adaptation

1. Instrument developers/publishers should insure that the adaptation process takes full account of linguistic and cultural differences among the populations for whom adapted versions of the instrument are intended.

2. Instrument developers/publishers should provide evidence that the language use in the directions, rubrics, and items themselves as well as in the handbook are appropriate for all cultural and language populations for whom the instrument is intended.

3. Instrument developers/publishers should provide evidence that the choice of testing techniques, item formats, test conventions, and procedures are familiar to all intended populations.

4. Instrument developers/publishers should provide evidence that item content and stimulus materials are familiar to all intended populations.

5. Instrument developers/publishers should implement systematic judgmental evidence, both linguistic and psychological, to improve the accuracy of the adaptation process and compile evidence on the equivalence of all language versions.

6. Instrument developers/publishers should ensure that the data collection design permits the use of appropriate statistical techniques to establish item equivalence between the different language versions of the instrument.

7. Instrument developers/publishers should apply appropriate statistical techniques to (1) establish the equivalence of the different versions of the instrument, and (2) identify problematic components or aspects of the instrument which may be inadequate to one or more of the intended populations.

8. Instrument developers/publishers should provide information on the evaluation of validity in all target populations for whom the adapted versions are intended.

9. Instrument developers/publishers should provide statistical evidence of the equivalence of questions for all intended populations.

10. Non-equivalent questions between versions intended for different populations should not be used in preparing a common scale or in comparing these populations. However, they may be useful in enhancing content validity of scores reported for each population separately.

(continued)

TABLE 1
(Continued)

Administration

1. Instrument developers and administrators should try to anticipate the types of problems that can be expected, and take appropriate actions to remedy these problems through the preparation of appropriate materials and instructions.

2. Instrument administrators should be sensitive to a number of factors related to the stimulus materials, administration procedures, and response modes that can moderate the validity of inferences drawn from the scores.

3. Those aspects of the environment that influence the administration of an instrument should be made as similar as possible across populations for whom the instrument is intended.

4. Instrument administration instructions should be in the source and target languages to minimize the influence of unwanted sources of variation across populations.

5. The instrument manual should specify all aspects of the instrument and its administration that require scrutiny in the application of the instrument in a new cultural context.

6. The administrator should be unobtrusive and the administrator-examinee interaction should be minimized. Explicit rules that are described in the manual for the instrument should be followed.

Documentation/Score Interpretations

1. When an instrument is adapted for use in another population, documentation of the changes should be provided, along with evidence of the equivalence.

2. Score differences among samples of populations administered the instrument should not be taken at face value. The researcher has the responsibility to substantiate the differences with other empirical evidence.

3. Comparisons across populations can only be made at the level of invariance that has been established for the scale on which scores are reported.

4. The instrument developer should provide specific information on the ways in which the socio-cultural and ecological contexts of the populations might affect performance on the instrument, and should suggest procedures to account for these effects in the interpretation of results.

to address, because it calls for an understanding of the differences in norms, values, traditions, and worldviews between cultures. A construct may have a different connotation, or it may not even be meaningful in a particular culture. It is perhaps unsurprising to see that contextual factors lead the list of ITC guidelines.

The importance of context was highlighted in the results found in studies based on a Spanish-language translation of the Comprehensive Tests of Basic Skills (CTBS). Early elementary school aged children enrolled in bilingual education programs were given either the English CTBS or Spanish CTBS. A small number of children were given both versions because teachers were unable to determine which language the children should be tested in; the data on the students tested twice revealed surprising results.

The translation of the CTBS from English was done rigorously, developed and supervised by measurement and language arts specialists. According to McArthur (1981), the CTBS

> was subjected to a 4-step editorial procedure designed to reduce bias: included were studies of content validity, application of editorial guidelines in item construction, reviews for bias and separate ethnic group studies." (p.5)

Despite these precautions and the resultant "rather faithful translation of the English original," bilingual students' performance on the Spanish version was markedly lower than their performance on the English version (Cabello, 1981; McArthur, 1981). Cabello's (1981) discussion of these anomalous findings focuses on contextual factors. She notes that differences in performance may be due to the match between the test and the instruction and curricula offered in these bilingual classrooms, the knowledge elicited, the values implied, and the assumptions about the intended audience that are represented in the content of the questions.

Instrument Development and Adaptation

The second category of guidelines focuses upon instrument development and adaptation. This subset is the longest series of the four categories, which reflects the complex task of translating a test from one language to another (see Table 1).

Translation from the Source to the Target Language

Fundamentally, good translations ensure that the source and target versions of the instrument are comparable in level of word difficulty, readability, grammar use, writing style, and punctuation (Hambleton, 1996). It is interesting to note, however, that literal, word-for-word translations are rarely done. Professional translators typically use "de-centering," a process that involves modification of words or phrases during the translation in order to achieve equivalence between the original and translated items (Hambleton & Bollwark, 1991). For example, the English phrase "like father, like son" could be translated literally to Chinese, but would sound strange and stilted to a Chinese listener. De-centering this phrase to "tigers do not breed dogs" results in the semantic equivalence that is desired. Although semantic equivalence is the product, Hambleton and his colleagues (e.g., Hambleton, 1996; Hambleton & Bollwark, 1991; Hambleton & Kanjee, 1993) caution that psychometric non-equivalence may also result. That is, de-centering during the forward and back translations may cause the items to be centered in neither the original nor the target language. To avoid such a situation, these authors suggest that test developers avoid use of culturally specific words and phrases in the initial creation of the test, which would then allow for easier translation. De-centering also appears to be most effective if done after back translation is performed, when divergence from the original connotation would be more visible. The degree of de-centering that was necessary should be reported, along with illustrations of what was done.

Finding equivalent words or phrases is a challenge because meaning must be checked not only across the languages, but also across the sub-cultures that form a language group. That is, identifying the target language is simple; ensuring a translation that spans the array of dialects existing in the target language is quite another matter. Cabello (1981) offers this powerful analogy:

> creating a Spanish language test which is equally comprehensible, useful and fair to Mexicans, Puerto Ricans and other Hispanic students of varying educational and social backgrounds, is as difficult as creating a test in English to serve American, British, Australian, and other English-speaking students around the world equally well. (p.1)

To illustrate: "boot" and "bonnet" in American English refer to apparel and never to sections of an automobile, as they might in U.K. English. In Spanish, the common item butter may be called "mantequilla" or "manteca" depending on the Spanish-speaking country; to complicate things further, for those who use the word "mantequilla" for butter, the word "manteca" specifically connotes lard, a substantially different food product.

A fine example of how one might properly address intra-language diversity is the set of procedures used to create the Spanish translation of the Woodcock-Johnson Psycho-Educational Battery (as cited in Hambleton, 1993). The original translation was first done by several Spanish-speaking professionals. The test was checked independently by several reviewers and then the reviewers met with the translators to discuss problems in the translation and attempted to achieve a consensus about the necessary revisions (it should be noted that this first step is standard operating procedure in commercial translation companies). Next, a translation review team made up of representatives from different regions of the Spanish-speaking world met to check the Spanish version of the test prepared at Step 1. Finally, at the field test stage, test administrators compiled lists of translation and scoring problems that arose.

It is clear that careful selection of translators is paramount. Successful translations are done by persons who have knowledge of the subject matter, as well as cultural familiarity—not just fluency—in both the target and source languages. Knowledge of the subject matter being translated is necessary to avoid any odd word usage, for example, translating the psychometrician's term "item pools" into "item oceans" (Hambleton, 1993). Having experience in both languages and cultures provides the required sensitivity to the subtleties of both languages and helps to ensure that word selection is not awkward or changes the purpose of the question. It also appears that translations are better when the languages are more similar in structure (e.g., English and Spanish versus English and Chinese) and when translators are given practice and feedback before they begin the task. Finally, the ideal case would exist if test translators also had general knowledge of test or questionnaire development. This sort of background can prevent common translation problems such as unusually long correct answers, response options that have the same meaning, awkward item stems, and so forth (Hambleton, 1993).

Assessing the Quality of the Translation

Evaluating the adequacy and accuracy of the translation is the next step. Two types of assessment methods are used to establish translation equivalence and to identify biased items: judgmental methods and statistical methods (Hambleton, 1996; Hambleton & Bollwark, 1991). Judgmental methods are more subjective, involving the use of experts or judges who evaluate the quality of the translation. Forward (source to target language) and back (target to source language) translations provide preliminary evidence for the quality of the translation. Of course, judges familiar with the languages and cultures involved are necessary for addressing contextual factors and for determining a general conceptual equivalence across versions. But research suggests that judges are not very accurate in identifying problematic items. For example, use of the same translation rules could result in high comparability between the original version and the back-translated version of the instrument, even if the forward translation was poor. Studies that utilize quasi-experimental designs and that then analyze data using statistical methods such as item response theory (IRT) or structural equation modeling are more precise gauges of differential item functioning (DIF) or differences in factor structures (Hambleton & Bollwark, 1991).

Hambleton & Bollwark's (1991) comprehensive review of methods for establishing the quality of a translation is particularly useful. No single format is without its drawbacks, but the least problematic mode of assessing translation equivalence is the case in which source language monolinguals take the source version and target language monolinguals take the target version (see Table 2). If characteristics such as prior knowledge and socioeconomic status are factored in, this approach offers the clearest perspective on the equivalency of the source and target versions of an instrument.

TABLE 2

Problems Associated with Various Methods of Establishing Translation Equivalence (from Hambleton & Bollwark)

Methods for Establishing Equivalence of Translated Test Items	Problems Associated with the Methods of Establishing Translation Equivalence					
	Improper to generalize results to the items of interest	Improper to generalize results to the populations of interest	Differences in judges' or examinees' ability	Use of back translations	Sensitivity to examiner/ prober– examinee interactions	Labor intensive
Judgmental Methods						
Judgmental single-translation methods						
Post-translation probes					X	X
Bilingual judges check errors	X	X^1	X			
Performance criteria – perform a task using translated instructions					X	X

Judgmental back-translation method

Source language monolinguals check for errors	X	X	
Statistical Methods			
Statistical single-translation methods			
Bilinguals take source and target versions	X^1	X^2	X^3
Source language monolinguals take source version; target language monolinguals take target version		X^2	X^3
Statistical back-translation method			
Source language monolinguals take source and back-translated versions	X	X	X^3

Notes: An X indicates the problem is associated with the method.
1 Most likely less of a problem than using only source language monolinguals.
2 Less of a problem if conditional statistical techniques are used.
3 Most likely less of a problem than with using probes or performance criteria.

Administration

The third set of ITC guidelines is directed toward administration procedures. We must not neglect the fact that a key element of the development process is the selection and training of administrators. Test administrators (or survey interviewers) and developers must maintain a sensitivity to the adequacy of item formats (even pictorial stimuli are subject to bias, according to Hambleton & Kanjee, 1993) and in the instructions conveyed to the respondents, for these factors can attenuate the validity of the inferences drawn from scores. As is stated in virtually all measurement textbooks, administrators influence the reliability and validity of a test. Clear, unambiguous, unbiased communication and adherence to instructions and time limitations comprise the ideal administration setting. Accordingly, administrators should be drawn from the target communities; be familiar with the culture, language, and dialects; and have adequate administration skills and experience (Briggs, 1986; Hambleton, 1996).

Documentation/Score Interpretations

The final set of guidelines articulated by the ITC addresses the documentation and the use of the scores obtained from the translated instruments. Documentation of equivalency procedures is crucial for establishing validity. The Commission closes the series of guidelines with cautions regarding the interpretation of scores. Socioeconomic and political factors, availability of resources and quality of instruction are all factors that affect performance (Hambleton, 1993; 1996), and differences in test scores that are uncovered may stem from these socioeconomic and political factors rather than from scholastic ability. The same caveat applies to survey items, where differences in responses may, for instance, be a function of context. For example, Bischoping and Schuman (1992) suggest that the discrepancy between many Nicaraguan pre-election polls in the 1990 election and the actual results had to do with suspicion of the pollster and the intent of the survey. These researchers speculate that voters may have suspected that pre-election polls were partisan, and therefore were less than candid in expressing their voting intentions. Accordingly, pre-election polls predicted a Sandinista landslide, but the actual polls resulted in an opposition victory.

Research on Test Instruments Adapted from English

There exist only a few validity studies that address the comparability of tests across languages. For brevity's sake, I will focus on the Third International Math and Science Study (TIMSS, 1997) and the language background and National Assessment of Educational Progress (NAEP) mathematics performance studies conducted by the Center for the Study of Evaluation (Abedi, Lord & Plummer, 1997; Abedi, Lord & Hofstetter, 1998). The procedures used in these studies and their results are presented in this section of the chapter. For ease of presentation, I address factors that these researchers raised in their discussions and interpretations of their results in the section that follows this one.

Third International Mathematics and Science Study

The Third International Mathematics and Science Study (TIMSS, International Association for the Evaluation of Educational Achievement, 1996) required an extensive translation effort because a total of 31 different languages were represented across the 45 countries that participated in the study. To ensure the valid translation of the items, TIMSS established procedures and translation guidelines for the participating countries. The procedures and guidelines were then distributed to the National Research Coordinators (NRCs) who were responsible for translating the items from English to their country's language. The guidelines included the following procedures:

- Identify and minimize cultural differences.
- Find equivalent words and phrases.
- Ensure that the reading level is the same in the target language as in the original English version.
- Make sure that the essential meaning does not change.
- Make sure that the difficulty level of achievement items does not change.
- Be aware of changes in layout that result from translation.

The guidelines also identified characteristics the NRCs should look for when selecting translators:

- Good knowledge of English.
- Excellent knowledge of the target language.
- Experience in both languages and cultures.
- Experience with students of the target population.
- Skills in test development.

According to the TIMSS technical manual (1997), multiple-forward translation was the recommended translation technique. With this technique, an item is translated by more than one translator. The translations are then compared to determine the equivalency of the translations. When the translations differ, the differences are discussed, changes are made if necessary, and then the best translation is selected. Examples are provided below to describe how TIMSS handled certain item translations.

Some translations changed the meaning of an item but not its original intention. Items with references to the seasons are an example of this type of translation. A specific example provided in the TIMSS technical manual was the adaptation of an item that showed a graph representing winter clothes sales (e.g., sweaters and coats) on a monthly basis. The graph indicated increased sweater and coat sales in November and December and decreasing sweater and coat sales in July and August, which are seasonal changes common in the Northern Hemisphere. To translate the item to one that better reflected a country's clothing sales in relation to its seasons, some countries changed the clothing from sweater and coats to shorts and some countries changed the months to reflect the months of increased sweater sales in their country.

Some of the translations required two steps, first a translation and then a reality check of the translation. For example, some items required examinees to use currency to purchase something (e.g., a train ticket). These items were translated by first replacing the U.S. dollar symbol with the country's currency symbol. The NRC translator then reviewed the item to ensure that the currency amount was realistic given the item that was purchased. If the value was unrealistic, the reference to the item being purchased was changed to reflect the currency value. This type of translation always maintained the currency value but changed the context and currency symbol to reflect the culture of the particular country.

If the NRC translators were uncertain about how to change an item, they could either refer to the translation guidelines or they could ask content specialists at the International Study Center (ISC) for recommendations. Furthermore, the translators kept records to document the translation of every item. The records were sent to content specialists at the ISC to determine whether the translations seemed appropriate from a content perspective. Their evaluations and comments were returned to the NRCs so that necessary corrections could be made to the items.

The TIMSS project used two and sometimes three procedures to verify the translation of the items. Translators not involved in the original translations were employed to verify the translations. Multiple-forward translation was used as the first step to ensure the valid translation of items. The second procedure entailed the use of a translation review by bilingual judges. This procedure focused on the appropriateness of both the target language and the original language. The bilingual judges also reviewed the appropriateness of the cultural changes made to the items (e.g., change dollar to local currency) and compared the consistency of the reading levels between the original and translated items. The third procedure was a statistical review. Item statistics from both the pilot and field tests were delivered to the NRCs for their respective tested populations. Items with different item statistics were re-checked by NRC's translators to determine whether a translation problem existed or whether the statistical anomalies resulted from some other error (e.g., printing error).

The translation and verification procedures were judged by TIMSS to be very effective. The guidelines and procedures verified, in some instances, that the NRCs produced accurate and appropriate translations. In other instances, the guidelines and procedures allowed the translators to flag the items with questionable translations so that the items could be changed prior to being administered to the examinees.

Language Background and NAEP Mathematics Performance

I have included this study here because it highlights the importance of language simplification in constructing items that are clear and more amenable to accurate translations across cultures. The purpose of this study was to examine the impact of student English language proficiency and background characteristics on performance on the NAEP mathematics assessment. Nearly 1,400 8th grade students (limited English proficient (LEP) and non-LEP) from ethnically diverse schools in southern California were administered one of three test booklets: Spanish, English, or modified English. The Spanish test booklet was comprised of the Spanish language items from the 1996 NAEP Grade 8 bilingual mathematics booklet, and the English test booklet was comprised of the English language items of the bilingual mathematics test booklet.

The linguistically modified English test booklet differed from the English language test booklet in its use of simpler grammar and vocabulary, but the test booklets contained the same items. Citing research that showed language minority students tend to score lower than language majority students on standardized mathematics achievement tests at all grade levels, Abedi, Lord & Hofstetter (1998) sought to examine to what extent this differential performance was due to differences in English language proficiency. Students who are less than fully bilingual are likely to encounter difficulties with efficient language processing (regardless of the language in which the test is administered) and therefore demonstrate poorer test performance. For example, students who may be bilingual speakers but not bilingual readers may be handicapped on speed tests that involve reading.

Accordingly, the modified English test booklet was constructed by first identifying linguistic complexity features, and by next analyzing NAEP math items to determine which features were present for each item. Those items with potentially difficult language were rewritten to remove or reduce linguistic complexity. Only linguistic structures and non-technical vocabulary were modified; mathematics vocabulary and math content were preserved. A mathematics education expert reviewed the modified items to ensure that the modifications did not change the mathematical concepts or the problem to be solved. Linguistic features considered to be potential causes of difficulty were these:

- Word frequency or familiarity
- Word length
- Sentence length
- Length of item
- Passive voice constructions
- Long noun phrases
- Long question phrases
- Comparative structures
- Prepositional phrases
- Sentence and discourse structure
- Clause types
- Conditional clauses
- Relative clauses
- Concrete versus abstract or impersonal presentations

For example, an original item reads as follows: "If X represents the number of newspapers that Lee delivers each day, which of the following represents the total number of newspapers that Lee delivers in 5 days?" The modified version reads, "Lee delivers X newspapers each day. How many newspapers does he deliver in 5 days?" The modified version represents the following changes (Abedi et al., 1998):

- Conditional clause changed to separate sentence
- Two relative clauses removed and recast
- Long nominals shortened
- Question phrase changed from "which of the following represents" to "how many"
- Item length changed from 26 to 13 words
- Average sentence length changed from 26 to 6.5 words
- Number of clauses changed from 4 to 2
- Average number of clauses per sentence changed from 4 to 1

Abedi and his colleagues (1997) reviewed research that suggests that word problems given to schoolchildren are often ambiguous because of presuppositions in the text. Experienced problem solvers have developed semantic schemas that compensate for omissions and ambiguities in the problem statement. For example, 17 percent of nursery school children and 64 percent of 1st graders answered the following word problem correctly: "There are 5 birds and 3 worms. How many more birds are there than worms?" In contrast, 83 percent of nursery school children and 100 percent of 1st graders answered the question correctly when the last line was changed to: "Suppose the birds all race over and each one tries to get a worm! How many birds won't get a worm?" If a child did not possess the conceptual knowledge to solve a problem, then performance should not improve as a result of minor linguistic modifications.

Limited English proficient (LEP) students were identified using NAEP inclusion criteria and schools' local evaluations; on the basis of these criteria, 62 percent of the sample was classified as LEP. LEP students were randomly administered one of the three test booklets (English, modified English or Spanish). Non-LEP students were randomly administered one of the two English test booklets. Randomization was done with intact math classrooms. A NAEP reading proficiency test and a 45-item student background questionnaire were also administered.

Results showed that performance was highest among LEP students who were administered the modified English test booklet, followed by those who took the English test booklet and then by those who took the Spanish test booklet. Non-LEP students performed consistently better than LEP students, regardless of the test booklet administered. These two factors (booklet type and LEP status) interacted significantly; LEP students administered the English or modified English test booklets scored significantly higher than those who used the Spanish test booklet. The two main effects and interaction held even after controlling for reading proficiency.

The authors concluded that linguistic modification benefited non-LEP students most, and that the modified English test booklet only marginally benefited LEP students, relative to the English-only test booklet (i.e., within chance levels). Interestingly, LEP students in either of the two English booklet conditions did not significantly differ in performance from one another, but did perform significantly higher than LEP students who were administered the Spanish test booklet. Abedi et al. interpret this result as suggesting that LEP students perform best on math tests where the language in which they are tested matches the language in which they are instructed. Follow-up analyses of sub-samples of students who were given math instruction in Spanish showed that these students performed best when given the Spanish test booklet (followed by the modified English and English test booklets).

These issues parallel the recommendations that survey methodologists make with regard to writing questionnaire items. The principle of simplicity underlies survey-writing guidelines: for example, using higher-frequency words (e.g., clear, vs. intelligible; main vs. principal), shorter questions, avoiding double-barreled questions and dangling alternatives (Converse & Presser, 1986; Sudman & Bradburn, 1982; Sudman, Bradburn & Schwarz, 1996). Simply- and directly-written survey items optimize the likelihood of establishing common concepts and maintaining the consistency of each item's purpose and intent across diverse respondents, thereby achieving the standardization that is desired.

Factors Affecting Student Performance on Dual Language Tests and on Tests Adapted from English

Quality of the Translation

A high-quality translation is certainly critical. As the studies cited above show, and as the guidelines from the International Test Commission indicate, test adaptation from one language to another is no easy feat. Test items cannot be simply translated by a single staff person familiar with the target language; the nuances of language require input from multiple sources. Ideally, a translator should

- be familiar with the culture or cultures represented by the source and target languages;
- be familiar with the dialects that exist in the source and target languages;
- have a substantive background in the content area of the test; and
- understand the basic principles of item writing.

Standard operating procedure for professional translators is for a pair of translators to work together. One person does the initial translation, then the other reviews it for accuracy. Next, the two meet to reconcile any discrepancies and deliver the final product to the client. A manager may perform a quality control check before turning the translated materials to the client. Good translation companies have on staff individuals who represent a wide array of substantive expertise (e.g., advertising, research, education) and who come from or are at least familiar with different cultures. The backgrounds and expertise of staff persons chosen to perform a translation are matched with the client's needs.

The research reviewed here suggests that perhaps professional translators supervised by bilingual test or survey developers would offer a good combination of linguistic, technical, and content area expertise. Both forward (source to target language) and back (target language to source) translations should be done, and by separate teams of translators, as a quality control check. The forward translation should be presented to a group of panelists representing diverse subcultures and dialects of the target language. Ideally, content area specialists would be represented in the panel reviewing the translated items. In this manner, grammar, vocabulary, culture and subject area content could be reviewed and difficulties resolved before data collection (Geisinger, 1994; Olson & Goldstein, 1997; Sandoval & Duran, 1999). The back translation should then be carefully compared with the original version of the test in the source language. And as was done in the research on language simplification (Abedi et al., 1997; 1998), content area specialists should be the ones performing this examination of the adapted items, to identify any lack of fidelity between the original and the back translated versions. Items that are found to be discrepant should first be examined to see whether the divergence in content occurred in the forward or in the back translation. Ideally, the panel that reviews the forward translation should have caught any changes in the item during its deliberations. If the problem was indeed at the forward translation, then the item must be re-translated to make the content more faithful to the original. If the problem was at the back translation, the forward and back translation teams, along with the test developers, should consult with one another to reach agreement on the item wording and content.

As was noted previously, despite rigorous and careful translation procedures, items may still prove to be weak in discriminatory power, show poor item statistics, or be found to have problematic translations or flawed word choices. As test developers and survey researchers know, despite the fact that items are carefully written and screened for bias, not all survive during pilot and field testing. It is only when empirical data are available that flawed items can be removed from the item pool. The same is true for translated items: data must be gathered so that the quality of the translation may be gauged.

An option might be to build a test from the ground up, as what was attempted with the Spanish language version of the SAT, the Prueba de Aptitud Academica (PAA). Measuring the same constructs in different languages is a challenging and far more costly endeavor, requiring native language speakers with content area expertise to write test items and raising the difficult question of finding appropriately fully bilingual samples on which to calibrate the tests. Nor does building a test from the ground up guarantee better measurement. For example, Angoff & Cook (1988) compared the SAT and the PAA using IRT methods and found a number of examples of differential item functioning (DIF), especially with items involving analogies and antonyms. There was less DIF on items that included more context, such as sentence completion and reading comprehension tasks. Angoff & Cook (1988) concluded that context-heavy items were more likely to retain their meaning after translation into a different language. This assumes, of course, that the translation was carefully done.

Given the paucity of research on test adaptations and the cost of creating native language versions of tests from the ground up, it seems reasonable to pursue the translation route for a while longer. The research reviewed in the previous sections has largely relied on traditional quantitative analyses to examine the quality of translations. Although more research in this vein is certainly called for, qualitative methodologies such as focus group interviews and cognitive interview studies would help shed light on how individuals use adapted instruments (Ericsson & Simon, 1984; Morgan, 1988). For example, cognitive interview studies where students think aloud as they respond to questions would provide researchers a better understanding of students' thought processes and interpretation of items, instead of relying on the opinion of translators or instrument developers (Ericsson & Simon, 1984). The information gathered from qualitative methodologies can also provide information to help interpret results from quantitative analyses. There is still quite a bit more work that needs to be done to attain a full understanding of the best methods for adapting tests.

Item Content and Wording

Having noted the difficulties of translation, and keeping in mind that the content of test items reflects not only content knowledge but also implied values and assumptions of the respondents or test-takers. I believe that the work on language simplification by Abedi et al. (1997; 1998) appears to be promising for instrument adapters. Simplified language makes for a more straightforward translation task, thus decreasing the likelihood of errors in translation. Although item length and vocabulary are sometimes deliberately used to alter the difficulty of an item, it does appear possible to write a linguistically simplified item while preserving the difficulty of the content being tested. Abedi et al. (1997) cite Shuard & Rothery (1984), who explicitly made the following rather succinct set of recommendations regarding the writing of mathematics test items:

- Use short sentences.
- Use simple words.
- Remove unnecessary expository material.
- Keep to the present tense and particularly avoid the conditional mode. For instance, "Given that butter costs 47p a block, what would be the cost of 5 such blocks?" can be replaced by "Butter costs 47p a block. How much do 5 blocks cost?"
- Avoid starting with sentence clauses. For example, "Draw a circle of radius 4.2 cm." is more readable than "Using a radius of 4.2 cm., draw a circle."

RECOMMENDATIONS

Instrument adaptation is a challenging task that requires instrument development skills as well as linguistic and cultural sensitivity. The research reviewed in this paper has amply demonstrated how formidable an assignment adapting a test, assessment, or survey from one language to another truly is. I would like to close by offering the reader a brief set of recommendations:

- A translation *team* should take the responsibility for the adaptation, not just one or two bilingual developers. Language carries many subtleties and nuances. Instrument adaptation requires input from content area specialists, psychometricians/survey developers, and language experts who are familiar with dialects and cultures of the target language. Ideally, the translation team would have at least one member who represents an intersection between two or all three of these areas of expertise.

- The translated instrument should undergo both forward and back translations, to serve as an initial check on the quality of the adaptation (data obtained from the administration of the instrument will serve as the final check of the quality of the translation). A content area expert should carefully review the back translation to the original to target any discrepancies.

- Quantitative and qualitative methodologies provide complementary data that allow a fuller evaluation of the quality of a translation. Focus groups and cognitive laboratory studies can help illuminate differential item functioning, classical test statistics, and IRT results. In any case, data should be collected to assess the quality of the translation. Hambleton and his colleagues (Muñiz, Hambleton & Xing, unpublished manuscript) have conducted computer simulations of small sample (n's of 50-100) differential item functioning to detect flawed translations. This preliminary work suggests that even with restricted sample sizes, it is possible to identify problematic items. The message here is to conduct as much pre-testing and "front-end" work as possible, to obtain a final data set that is as clean and accurate as possible.

- Modifying the original instrument in English by simplifying the vocabulary and syntax used should be seriously considered. Shorter, more direct sentence constructions that use more familiar words ease the linguistic burden. This would make the translation task simpler.

- Contextual factors should also be considered when interpreting student performance on a dual language or adapted test. We should not lose sight of the impact of the quality of instruction, availability of resources, and match between the curriculum and what was tested in student performance on achievement tests.

REFERENCES

Abedi, J., Lord, C., & Hofstetter, C. (1998). *Impact of selected background variables on students' NAEP math performance* (Report No. CSE-478). Los Angeles, CA: Center for the Study of Evaluation.

Abedi, J., Lord, C., & Plummer, J.R. (1997). *Final report of language background as a variable in NAEP mathematics performance* (Report No. CSE-429). Los Angeles, CA: Center for the Study of Evaluation.

Angoff, W.H. & Cook, L.L. (1988). *Equating the scores of the Prueba de Aptitud Académica and the Scholastic Aptitude Test* (Report No. 88-2). New York, NY: College Entrance Examination Board.

Bischoping, K., & Schumann, H. (1992). Pens and polls in Nicaragua: An analysis of the 1990 pre-election surveys. *American Journal of Political Science, 36*, 331-50.

Briggs, C.L. (1986). *Learning how to ask: A sociolinguistic appraisal of the role of the interview in social science research.* New York, NY: Cambridge University Press.

Calvello, D. (1981). *Potential sources of bias in dual language achievement tests* (Report No. CSE-R-178). Los Angeles, CA: Center for the Study of Evaluation. (ERIC Document Reproduction Service No. ED 218 320)

Converse, J.M. & Presser, S. (1986). *Survey questions: Handcrafting the standardized questionnaire.* Newbury Park, CA: Sage.

Ericsson, K.A. & Simon, H.A. (1984). *Protocol analysis: Verbal reports as data.* Cambridge, MA: MIT Press.

Geisinger, K.F. (1994). Cross-cultural normative assessment: Translation and adaptation issues influencing the normative interpretation of assessment instruments. *Psychological Assessment, 6*(4), 304-312.

Hambleton, R.K. (1993). *Translating achievement tests for use in cross-national studies.* Washington, DC: National Center for Education Statistics. (ERIC Document Reproduction Service No. ED 358 128)

Hambleton, R.K. (1996). *Guidelines for adapting educational and psychological tests.* Paper presented at the joint annual meetings of the American Educational Research Association and the National Council on Measurement in Education, New York, NY. (ERIC Document Reproduction Service No. ED 399 291)

Hambleton, R.K. & Bollwark, J. (1991). Adapting tests for use in different cultures: Technical issues and methods. *Bulletin of the International Test Commission, 18*, 3-32. (ERIC Document Reproduction Service No. ED 337 481)

Hambleton, R.K. & Kanjee, A. (1993, April). *Enhancing the validity of cross-cultural studies: Improvements in instrument translation methods.* Paper presented at the joint annual meetings of the American Educational Research Association and the National Council on Measurement in Education, Atlanta, GA. (ERIC Document Reproduction Service No. ED 362 537)

International Association for the Evaluation of Educational Achievement (1996). *Third International Mathematics and Science Study (TIMMS): Technical Report, Volume 1.* Boston College, MA: Center for the Study of Testing, Evaluation and Educational Policy.

McArthur, D.L. (1981). *Performance patterns of bilingual children tested in both languages.* (Report No. CSE-R-164). Los Angeles, CA: Center for the Study of Evaluation. (ERIC Document Reproduction Service No. ED 218 321)

Morgan, D.L. (1988). *Focus groups as qualitative research.* Newbury Park, CA: Sage.

Muniz, J., Hambleton, R.K., & Xing, D. (unpublished manuscript). *Small sample studies to detect flaws in item translations.*

Olson, J.F., & Goldstein, A.A. (1997). *The inclusion of students with disabilities and limited English proficient students in large-scale assessments: A summary of recent progress* (Report No. NCES 97-482). Washington, DC: National Center for Education Statistics.

Sandoval, J. & Duran, R.P. (1999). Language. In J. Sandoval, C.L. Frisby, K.F. Geisinger, J.D.Scheuneman, & J.R. Grenier (Eds.), *Test interpretation and diversity:*

Achieving equity in assessment (pp. 181-211). Washington, DC: American Psychological Association.

Sudman, S. & Bradburn, N.M. (1982). *Asking questions: A practical guide to questionnaire design.* San Francisco, CA: Jossey-Bass.

Sudman, S., Bradburn, N.M. & Schwarz, N. (1996). *Thinking about answers: The application of cognitive processes to survey methodology.* San Francisco, CA: Jossey-Bass.

AUTHOR BIOGRAPHIES

The aim of this section is to provide a little background information on the authors, information that covers education, affiliation, and/or research interests. The order of authors is alphabetical.

Adebowale Akande is Chair Professor in the Department of Psychology at the University of Potchefstroom, South Africa. He has taught in universities in his native Nigeria and Zimbabwe and has published widely in areas such as health, management, and educational psychology.

Eric M. Anderman is an Associate Professor and the Director of Graduate Studies in the Department of Educational & Counseling Psychology, at the University of Kentucky. His major research interest is motivation in adolescent populations. He teaches courses in Motivation, Educational Psychology, and Statistics. His work has been published in numerous journals, including the Journal of Educational Psychology, Contemporary Educational Psychology, the Journal of Early Adolescence, Review of Educational Research, and the Journal of Learning Disabilities.

Megan B. Bolch, B.A., is a doctoral student in the counseling psychology program at the University of Missouri-Kansas City. Her research focuses on gender and ethnic differences in self-esteem. Currently, she is completing a dissertation on the self-presentation value of high self-esteem among urban youth. Ms. Bolch is a student affiliate of the American Psychological Association, and a member of APA's the Division 17 student affiliate group.

David Yun Dai is an Assistant Professor in the Department of Educational & Counseling Psychology at the University at Albany, SUNY.

George Dent, M.A., is a doctoral student in the counseling psychology program at the University of Missouri-Kansas City. He is interested in understanding the family and school context variables that contribute to the development of pro-social and aggressive behaviors in early adolescents. Mr. Dent is a student affiliate of the American Psychological Association, and a member of APA's Division 17 student affiliate group.

Teresa García Duncan is currently a Senior Research Analyst at the American Institutes for Research (AIR). Prior to joining AIR, she was an Assistant Professor at the University of Texas at Austin from 1993 to 1999, holding a joint appointment between the Quantitative Methods and the Learning, Cognition, and Instruction domains in the Department of Educational Psychology. She also taught at the Summer Institute for Survey Research Techniques at the University of Michigan at Ann Arbor from 1996-1998. Dr. García is the author or co-author of publications appearing in journals such as Educational and Psychological Measurement, Journal of Personality and Social Psychology, and Contemporary Educational Psychology. She currently serves on the editorial boards of Learning and Individual Differences, Contemporary Educational Psychology, and Journal of Experimental Education.

Gerard Fogarty is Professor of Psychology at the University of Southern Queensland, Australia. His research interests include the role of individual differences on career decision-making, educational achievement, and student attrition at high school and university.

William L. Greene is an educational psychologist and an associate professor in the Education Department at Southern Oregon University. His research interests include teacher cognition, self-efficacy, and the influence of ethnicity and culture on learning. Dr. Greene recently co-authored an article on community values and education published in the Pacific Educational Research Journal and is currently completing a study on self-efficacy and ethnic identity. He has taught in California, Hawaii, Oregon, and American Samoa and at various levels including elementary, secondary, and higher education.

Diana L. Haleman is an assistant professor in Elementary, Reading and Special Education at Morehead State University (Kentucky) where she teaches courses in early childhood education and social policy. Her research interests include single mothering, socioeconomic issues that affect educational attainment, and welfare reform in Eastern Kentucky.

Rumjahn Hoosain is a Professor in the Department of Psychology, the University of Hong Kong. His research interests are in cognition and multicultural education.

Dawn Iwamoto is currently the Director of Education, Health and Human Services for the University of Phoenix. She supervises, supports, and develops degree programs in the areas of education, counseling, nursing, human services and criminal justice. Dr. Iwamoto teaches graduate courses for the University of Phoenix and Northern Arizona University. Formerly, she held the position of Director of Special Programs in the Fountain Hills School District in Arizona. In this position, she was responsible for the oversight of eighteen special programs including American Indian Education, Special Education, and English as a Second Language, among others. Her interest and expertise in multicultural education and motivation developed with the formation of a collaborative long-term study with the Fort McDowell Indian Community.

Jane Jensen holds a Ph.D. in cultural anthropology and higher education from Indiana University in Bloomington. A Fulbright Scholar, Dr. Jensen conducted ethnographic research Canada where she investigated community values for post-secondary education in an economically marginalized coaltown. Currently, Dr. Jensen is an assistant professor of education at the University of Kentucky in Lexington where she teaches courses in qualitative field methods, college student success, theories of student development, and the socio-cultural study of post-compulsory education. Her current research interests involve the relationship between community development and post-compulsory education in rural areas. In addition, Dr. Jensen is co-author of a textbook on college student academic success published by Prentice Hall.

Clement Lee is a post-graduate research student at the University of Hong Kong and his thesis is on academic motivation in a Chinese culture. He is a former teacher in Hong Kong secondary schools.

Dennis M. McInerney was awarded the first Personal Chair in Educational Psychology at the University of Western Sydney. Dennis's major research interests are motivation and learning in cross-cultural contexts, and multicultural education. Dennis has had a longstanding interest in indigenous education and works extensively with Aboriginal Australians, Navajo and Yavapai Native Americans, as well as with many minority groups in Australia. Dennis has published extensively and his textbook Educational Psychology: Constructing Learning (3rd Ed., 2002, Prentice Hall Australia, co-authored with Associate Professor Valentina McInerney) is the best selling educational psychology text in Australia and New Zealand.

Tamera B. Murdock is an associate professor of educational psychology at the University of Missouri-Kansas City. Her research interests are in the area of motivation, with a particular emphasis on using motivational theories to explain alienation among youth. Professor Murdock is a member of the

American Educational Research Association, the American Psychological Association, and the Society of Research on Adolescence. Some of her previous publications have appeared in the Journal of Educational Psychology, Contemporary Educational Psychology, and the Journal of Adolescent Research.

Chi-hung Ng is an Assistant Professor at Open University, Hong Kong. His interest in sociocultural influences on motivation and learning is related to his studying and working experiences in various culturally different countries. His current research focuses on self-schemas, achievement goals, and sociocultural influences.

Pedro R. Portes is a professor of educational psychology and counseling at the University of Louisville. His research focuses on adolescent identity development, sociocultural theory, and cognitive growth. He was born in Havana, Cuba and emigrated with his family to the United States in 1961. He is a Fulbright Scholar (Peru, 1988; Columbia, 1996), University Scholar (1998), and contributor to the Handbook of Educational Psychology (Macmillan, 1996).

Nanette Potee is an Assistant Professor of Communication at Northeastern Illinois University. She received her doctoral degree in instructional communication from Southern Illinois University in 1998. Her research interests include cultural and intercultural communication competence in relationships and instructional environments. She is currently involved in a US Department of Education grant to better prepare pre-service teachers for careers in urban settings.

Kimberley Pressick-Kilborn began her career as a primary teacher in 1995, having graduated from the University of Sydney with a Bachelor of Education (Hons. 1) in 1994. Her research interests include sociocultural approaches to understanding motivation and the use of qualitative methods of data collection and analysis in educational psychology. She has also collaborated in research projects focused on science education and learning beyond the classroom, specifically in museum settings. Kimberley is currently a recipient of an Australian Postgraduate Award and is a Doctor of Philosophy candidate at the University of Sydney. She is also a part-time lecturer in the Faculty of Education at the University of Technology, Sydney.

Henry T. Radda currently serves as the Behavioral Health and Substance Abuse Administrator for Arizona's Division of Children, Youth and Families. In his previous position, as director of Family and Community Services for the Fort McDowell Yavapai Nation he took special interest in cultural relevance and academic performance. He developed a collaborative relationship between the Tribe and neighboring school district in the creation of a study of cross cultural issues and school motivation. In 1985 Dr. Radda co-founded the John Dewey Academy, a residential therapeutic school in New York. He received his Masters in Community School -Psychology from the College of New Rochelle and his Doctorate in Clinical Psychology from the Union Institute. He enjoys working across systems and communities in the development of effective programs and initiatives.

Murari Regmi is Professor and Head of the Department of Psychology at Tribhuvan University in Kathmandu, Nepal. His many publications range from research into the personality and learning strategies of the Nepalese and people from other cultures to literary criticism.

Peter D. Renshaw is a Professor of Education at Griffith University, Australia. He has contributed to sociocultural research on peer interaction and collaboration, to parent-child interaction during problem-solving tasks and reading episodes, to the study of mathematics learning in primary and secondary schools, and to the analysis of language learning in primary grades.

Farideh Salili is a Professor in the Department of Community Medicine and the Unit of Behavioral Science, the University of Hong Kong. Her research interest is in cross-cultural differences in student motivation.

Gregory P. Thomas is an Assistant Professor in the Faculty of Education at The University of Hong Kong. He lectures in the areas of science education, curriculum studies, and the study of learning environments. His particular research interests lie in cultural aspects of learning and cognition, metacognition, learning environments and the use of computers in science teaching and learning. Prior to teaching in universities he taught elementary and high-school general science, physics, chemistry and biology in Australian schools for almost ten years and completed the majority of his post-graduate studies while teaching full-time. He maintains a strong interest in working with teachers and students from all disciplines across a broad spectrum of socio-cultural settings.

Jennifer A. Vadeboncoeur is an assistant professor of educational psychology and foundations at Montana State University. Her expertise lies primarily in sociocultural and critical theory, with applications in identity development, and more specifically, the social construction of "at risk" identities for young people. She was recently a Visiting Scholar at the University of Queensland, concluding work in sociolinguistic analyses.

Shawn Van Etten is the Director of Institutional Research at SUNY Herkimer County Community College. Shawn is responsible for designing and implementing research/evaluation projects aimed at enhancing and applying our extant knowledge about curricular, faculty, student, social, and cultural development. Shawn regularly reviews educational texts/manuscripts for top-shelf publishers and journals, he is well published, he is engaged in a programmatic research effort to better understand a range of educational processes from the phenomenological perspective of student, he teaches/advises/mentors graduate and undergraduate students, and he often serves as a research/evaluation consultant.

Richard Walker teaches in educational psychology at undergraduate and postgraduate levels in the Faculty of Education at the University of Sydney. While his longstanding research interests have centred on student learning and academic achievement (with a particular emphasis on interrelationships amongst cognition, metacognition and motivation) more recent interests are in socio-cultural-historical approaches to learning and motivation. This more recent interest has led to his involvement in the creation of collaborative electronic learning environments designed to support the activities of tertiary students in educational psychology classes.

David Watkins is a professor in the Department of Education at the University of Hong Kong. His main research interests are in student learning, approaches to teaching, and self-concept from a cross-cultural perspective. He is a former executive committee member of both the International Association of Applied Psychology and the International Association of Cross-Cultural Psychology.

Colin White worked for eight years as the Support Officer in Kumbari Ngurpai Lag, the Indigenous Study Centre at the University of Southern Queensland, and completed a PhD on the role of values in academic achievement. Colin currently works for a government agency that provides educational support to rural doctors. Between them, the authors have published a number of papers on the experiences of Indigenous Australians at University.

Natalie H. Wilcox, M.A., is a doctoral student in the counseling psychology program at the University of Missouri-Kansas City. Her research focuses on family relationships among adolescents. For her dissertation, she is examining the moderating role of ethnicity in the attachment-adjustment relationship of middle school students. Ms. Wilcox is a student affiliate of the American Psychological Association, and the past co-chair of APA's Division 17 student affiliate group.